Violence: A Philosophical Anthology

Also By Vittorio Bufacchi
VIOLENCE AND SOCIAL JUSTICE

Violence: A Philosophical Anthology

Edited by

Vittorio Bufacchi
University College Cork

First published 2009 by
PALGRAVE MACMILLAN

Palgrave Macmillan in the UK is an imprint of Macmillan Publishers Limited,
registered in England, company number 785998, of Houndmills,
Basingstoke, Hampshire RG21 6XS.

Palgrave Macmillan in the US is a division of St Martin's Press LLC,
175 Fifth Avenue, New York, NY 10010.

Palgrave Macmillan is the global academic imprint of the above companies
and has companies and representatives throughout the world.

Palgrave® and Macmillan® are registered trademarks in the United States,
the United Kingdom, Europe and other countries.

ISBN-13: 978-0-230-53770-5   hardback
ISBN-10: 0-230-53770-7   hardback
ISBN-13: 978-0-230-53771-2   paperback
ISBN-10: 0-230-53771-5   paperback

This book is printed on paper suitable for recycling and made from fully
managed and sustained forest sources. Logging, pulping and manufacturing
processes are expected to conform to the environmental regulations of the
country of origin.

A catalogue record for this book is available from the British Library.

A catalog record for this book is available from the Library of Congress.

10 9 8 7 6 5 4 3 2 1
18 17 16 15 14 13 12 11 10 09

Printed and bound in Great Britain by
CPI Antony Rowe, Chippenham and Eastbourne

Contents

Notes on Contributors

Robert Audi is Professor of Philosophy and David E. Gallo Professor of Business Ethics at the University of Notre Dame. His most recent book is *Moral Value and Human Diversity* (Oxford University Press 2007).

Allan Bäck is Professor of Philosophy at Kutztown University of Pennsylvania. He is the author of *Aristotle on Predication* (Brill 2000).

Susan J. Brison is Professor of Philosophy at Dartmouth College, New Hampshire. She is the author of *Speech, Harm, and Conflicts of Rights* (Princeton University Press, forthcoming).

Vittorio Bufacchi is College Lecturer in the Department of Philosophy, University College Cork, Ireland. He is the author of *Violence and Social Justice* (Palgrave Macmillan 2007).

C. A. J. Coady is Professor of Philosophy at the University of Melbourne, Australia. His most recent book is *Messy Morality: The Challenge of Politics* (Oxford University Press 2008), which is based on his 2005 Uehiro Lectures on Practical Ethics at the University of Oxford.

John Dewey (1859–1952), a leading proponent of the American school of thought known as 'pragmatism', was Professor of Philosophy at the universities of Michigan, Chicago and Columbia. All of his published writings can be found in *The Collected Works of John Dewey*, Jo Ann Boydston, ed., 37 volumes (Southern Illinois University Press, 1967–91).

Johan Galtung is a Norwegian sociologist, and founder of the International Peace Research Institute. He has taught at the universities of Santiago (Chile), Geneva (Switzerland), Columbia, Princeton and Hawaii, USA. His most recent book is *Pax Pacifica: Terrorism, the Pacific Hemisphere, Globalization and Peace Studies* (Paradigm 2005).

Newton Garver is Professor Emeritus in the Department of Philosophy at the University of Buffalo, New York. His most recent book is *Limits to Power: Some Friendly Reminders* (2006).

Bernard Gert is Stone Professor of Intellectual and Moral Philosophy at Dartmouth College. His most recent book is *Common Morality: Deciding What to Do* (Oxford University Press 2007).

John Harris is the Sir David Alliance Professor of Bioethics at the University of Manchester, England. His most recent book is *Enhancing Evolution: The Ethical Case for Making Better People* (Princeton University Press 2007).

Robert L. Holmes is Professor of Philosophy at the University of Rochester, New York. He is the co-editor (with Barry Gan) of *Nonviolence in Theory and Practice*, 2nd edn, (Waveland Press 2004).

Frederic C. Lane (1990–1984) was Professor of History at Johns Hopkins University, and from 1951 Assistant Director of the Social Sciences for the Rockefeller Foundation in Europe. He was the author of *Venice: A Maritime Republic* (The Johns Hopkins University Press 1973).

Steven Lee is Professor of Philosophy at Hobart and William Smith College, New York. His most recent book is *What Is the Argument? Critical Thinking in the Real World* (McGraw-Hill 2002).

Robert F. Litke is Professor of Philosophy at Wilfred Laurier University, Waterloo, Canada. He is the co-editor (with Deane Curtin) of *Institutional Violence* (Rodopi 1999).

Kai Nielsen is Professor Emeritus of Philosophy at the University of Calgary. His most recent book is *Atheism and Philosophy* (Prometheus 2005).

Gerald C. MacCallum (1925–1987) was Professor of Philosophy at the University of Wisconsin, Madison. He is the author of *Political Philosophy* (Prentice Hall 1987).

Jamil Salmi is an economist with the World Bank, and deputy director of the World Bank's Education Department. He is the author of *Violence and Democractic Society* (Zed Books 1993).

Sheldon S. Wolin is a political theorist, and Professor Emeritus at Princeton University. He is the author of *Politics and Vision: Continuity and Innovation in Western Political Thought* (Princeton University Press 2004).

Robert Paul Wolff is a political theorist who has taught at Harvard, the University of Chicago, Columbia University, and the University of Massachusetts. He is currently Professor Emeritus in the W. E. B. Du Bois Department of Afro-American Studies, at the University of Massachusetts. He is the author of *In Defense of Anarchism* (University of California Press 1998).

Acknowledgements

It has taken the best part of four years to bring this project to completion. This anthology was made possible thanks to the generosity of the Irish Research Council for the Humanities and Social Sciences (IRCHSS), who awarded me a one-year research fellowship in 2004–05, and the Publication Fund of the College of Arts, Celtic Studies and Social Sciences at University College Cork. I'm very thankful to both institutions for their support.

Both the editor and publisher gratefully acknowledge the following permissions granted to reproduce the copyright material in this volume:

1. John Dewey, 'Force, Violence and Law', and 'Force and Coercion', from *John Dewey: The Middle Works, 1899–1924, Vol. 10: 1916–1917*, ed. Jo Ann Boydston, pp. 211–15 and pp. 244–51. ©1976. Reprinted by permission of Southern Illinois University Press.
2. Frederic C. Lane, 'The Economic Meaning of War and Protection', from *Journal of Social Philosophy and Jurisprudence*, Vol. VII, 1942, pp. 254–70.
3. Sheldon S. Wolin, 'Violence and the Western Political Tradition', from *American Journal of Orthopsychiatry*, Vol. 33, 1963, pp. 15–28. ©1963. Reprinted by permission of the American Orthopsychiatric Association.
4. Robert Paul Wolff, 'On Violence', from *The Journal of Philosophy*, Vol. 66, No. 19, 2 October 1969, pp. 601–16. ©1969. Reprinted by permission of *The Journal of Philosophy*.
5. Bernard Gert, 'Justifying Violence', from *The Journal of Philosophy*, Vol. 66, No. 19, 2 October 1969, pp. 616–28. ©1969. Reprinted by permission of *The Journal of Philosophy*.
6. Johan Galtung, 'Violence, Peace and Peace Research', from *Journal of Peace Research*, Vol. 3, 1969, pp. 167–91. ©1969. Reprinted by permission of Sage Publications Ltd.
7. Gerald MacCallum, 'What is Wrong with Violence', from M. Singer and R. Martin (eds), *Legislative Intent and Other Essays in Law, Politics and Morality*, Madison, WI: Winsconsin University Press, 1993, pp. 235–56. ©1993. Reprinted by permission of The University of Wisconsin Press.
8. Robert Audi, 'On the Meaning and Justification of Violence', from J. A. Shaffer (ed.), *Violence*, New York: David McKay, 1971, pp. 45–99. Reprinted by permission of the author.
9. Newton Garver, 'What Violence Is', from A. K. Bierman and J. Gould (eds), *Philosophy for a New Generation*, 2nd edition, New York: Macmillan, 1973, pp. 256–66. Reprinted by permission of the author.

10. John Harris, 'The Marxist Conception of Violence', from *Philosophy and Public Affairs*, 1974, Vol. 3, pp. 192–221. ©1974. Reprinted by permission of Blackwell Publishing Ltd.
11. Kai Nielsen, 'On Justifying Violence', from *Inquiry*, Vol. 24, March 1981, pp. 21–59. ©1981. Reprinted by permission of Taylor & Francis.
12. C. A. J. Coady, 'The Idea of Violence', from *Journal of Applied Philosophy*, Vol. 3, No. 1, 1986, pp. 3–19. ©1986. Reprinted by permission of Blackwell Publishing Ltd.
13. Robert L. Holmes, 'Violence and the Perspective of Morality', from R. L. Holmes, *On War and Morality*, Princeton, NJ: Princeton University Press, 1989, pp. 19–49. ©1989. Reprinted by permission of Princeton University Press.
14. Robert Litke, 'Violence and Power', from *International Social Science Journal*, May 1992, Vol. 44, Issue 2, pp. 173–83. ©1992. Reprinted by permission of Blackwell Publishing Ltd.
15. Jamil Salmi, 'The Different Categories of Violence', from J. Salmi, *Violence and Democratic Society*, London: Zed Books, 1993, pp. 16–24. ©1993. Reprinted by permission of Zed Books.
16. Steven Lee, 'Poverty and Violence', from *Social Theory and Practice*, Vol. 22, Issue 1, 1996, pp. 67–82. ©1996. Reprinted by permission of Florida State University.
17. Susan J. Brison, 'Outliving Oneself', from S. J. Brison, *Aftermath: Violence and the Remaking of a Self*, Princeton, NJ: Princeton University Press, 2002, pp. 37–66. ©2002. Reprinted by permission of Princeton University Press.
18. Allan Bäck, 'Thinking Clearly about Violence', from *Philosophical Studies*, Vol. 117, Issue 1, 2004, pp. 219–30. ©2004. Reprinted by permission of Springer Publishers.

Every effort has been made to trace copyright holders and to obtain their permission for the use of copyright material. The publisher apologizes for any errors or omissions in the above list and would be grateful if notified of any corrections that should be incorporated in future reprints or editions of this book.

Introduction

Vittorio Bufacchi

The subject of violence is important on many different levels: socially, politically, economically, anthropologically and morally. Not surprisingly research on violence is one of the fastest growth industries in the social sciences, and publications on all aspects of violence abound, with each discipline monopolizing specific areas of violence according to some unwritten but widely accepted rule of partition: wars and related conflict studies are the domain of International Relations; crime is the domain of Criminology; punishment is the domain of Law and Jurisprudence; domestic violence is the domain of Sociology; terrorism and other forms of political violence are the domain of Political Science; and so on. In our concerted efforts to understand one of the most ubiquitous forms of human action, philosophy too can play its part. In fact, philosophy's contribution to this debate is unique, essential and potentially transformative.

This is an anthology of philosophical essays on the nature of violence. These essays explores a range of philosophical issues pertaining to violence, written mostly (but not exclusively) by professional philosophers. Two basic questions are scrutinized by all the essays in this anthology: 'What is violence?' and 'Can violence be justified?'. These two questions are also fundamental to all empirically driven research in the social sciences on every permutation of violence, and yet the contribution of philosophy is too often marginalized.[1]

Take, for example, the question, 'What is violence?' (or to be more precise, 'How do we define the concept of violence?'). All empirical research requires a clear definition of the topic or concept being subjected to quantitative or qualitative investigation, and the study of violence is not an exception.[2] Yet, reading the works on violence coming out of the social sciences, there seems to be much confusion about what violence is. Is violence by definition an intentional act, or can violence also be unintentional? Does violence require an act, or can it be the result of an omission? Should we define violence from the perspective of the perpetrator, or from the point of view of the victim? Is violence essentially an act of excessive force, or is it a violation? And if it is a violation, what exactly is being violated by an act of violence?

In trying to make sense of violence, and searching for an answer to all the above questions, philosophy can make an indispensable contribution. Back in the seventeenth century John Locke famously compared the work of philosophy to that of an under-labourer: 'in an age that produces such masters as the great Huygenius, and the incomparable Mr Newton, with some other of that strain, it is ambition enough to be employed as an under-labourer in clearing the ground a little, and removing some of the rubbish that lies in the way to knowledge'. Locke goes on to explain that the 'rubbish' he refers to is specifically 'vague and insignificant forms of speech, and abuse of language'.

Three centuries later many philosophers still understand their job description as that of providing clarity and precision to the meaning of concepts used in everyday language,[3] even though they rightly hold some reservations concerning Locke's description of philosophy as merely parasitic on other disciplines, particularly the sciences.[4] Philosophers may be experts at clearing up linguistic confusions, but there is much more to philosophy than providing clear definitions of key concepts, and therefore removing ambiguities and misunderstandings that arise from vague forms of speech. After the concept of violence has been defined, we want to know what the moral status of violence is; and when it comes to the question 'Can violence be justified?', it is inevitably to philosophers that we turn. The aim of this anthology is therefore not only to draw attention to the problem of violence in contemporary debates in moral and political philosophy, but also to propel the contribution of philosophy at the forefront of all research in the social sciences on the topic of violence.[5]

This anthology is not exhaustive of every published philosophical analysis of every aspect of violence. In deciding what to include and what to exclude, and with an eye to producing a tome that would be suitably comprehensive but not unduly voluminous, a set of necessary filters were put in place. This anthology reproduces works published in English in the last 100 years.[6] It deals exclusively with the general concept of violence, and not with specific forms of violence. In other words, this is not an anthology on terrorism, revolutions, war, civil war, torture, genocide, the death penalty, street violence, sexual violence, domestic violence, or any other specific form of violence. Also, and for the same reason as just stated, this anthology does not include pieces on the philosophy of non-violence. Of course, all the above forms of violence feature in this anthology, but the focal subject matter for all the pieces reproduced here is the more elusive idea of 'violence' itself. There is a valid reason for focusing on the concept of violence itself, rather than on violence's many configurations: if we have a good understanding of what violence is, and under what conditions it can be justified, we have a good starting point for analysing all other specific forms of violence. Finally, all the authors in this anthology work within the Anglo-American analytical tradition in philosophy; while very influential and eminent in their own right, authors such as Benjamin, Derrida, Levinas, Sartre and Žižek have not been included.

Perhaps the most noticeable absentee from the list of authors who feature in this anthology is Hannah Arendt. In fact, her omission is so conspicuous that it needs to be explained. The decision not to include Arendt is not to be interpreted as a dismissive condemnation of her contribution to philosophy, or her undisputed influence. Furthermore, there is no question regarding the analytical rigour of her work. Arendt's *On Violence* was immensely influential in 1969 when it was first published, and it is still widely read today, and rightly so.[7] Not surprisingly Arendt's work is already widely available to the reader, indeed her essay on violence has been reprinted in many recent anthologies on violence; for that reason, it was felt that it was not necessary to do so again.[8]

The pieces selected are reproduced here in chronological order, based on the date of their first publication. The only exception to this rule is the essay by Gerald MacCallum (Chapter 7), which was written sometime between 1969 and 1970, but only published for the first time posthumously in 1993. There is, I believe, a valid reason for respecting the chronological order in which these pieces were written. Starting from John Dewey's two short articles on violence, first published in 1917, and ending with Allan Bäck's invitation to think clearly about violence 87 years later, the reader can readily see a dynamic progression in the analysis and understanding of the phenomenon of violence. As each generation of scholars builds upon the foundations laid by its previous generation, new dimensions of violence are introduced and debated. It was felt that the only way to portray this conceptual development and theoretical intricacy over many decades was to reproduce the material in the chronological order it first appeared in print.

To facilitate readers in their efforts to navigate the many issues raised in this anthology, a short commentary will follow each of the 18 essays reproduced here. It is hoped that these commentaries will help to establish conceptual bridges between the works of different authors, and to highlight central philosophical issues regarding violence. Thus, it will be shown how Dewey's narrow definition of violence, centred on the use of force, was over the years extended to include all sorts of violations, of the person, rights or integrity, only to be brought back to its original starting point whereby violence is intrinsically related to an act of force, albeit with some reservations. We also see how the perspective on violence has changed over the years, starting from a narrow preoccupation with the intentions of the perpetrator, growing into a broader approach which includes the issue of omitting actions, and, finally, giving priority to the voices of the victims of violence.

The nature of violence is such that it is difficult even to agree on a definition of violence, and virtually impossible to agree on what constitutes a valid justification of violence. The aim of this anthology is not to provide conclusive answers to these questions, but simply to remind the reader of the complexities of these timeless questions, and of the valuable contribution made by philosophers over many generations on these important issues.

Notes

1. An exception to this rule is Richard Mizen, 'A Contribution Towards an Analytic Theory of Violence', *Journal of Analytical Psychology*, Vol. 48, 2003, pp. 285–305.
2. John Locke, 'The Epistle to the Reader', *An Essay Concerning Human Understanding*, Hertfordshire: Wordsworth, 1998, pp. 6–7.
3. This is a well-known joke amongst philosophers: 'Asked at a New York cocktail party what philosophers actually do, one replied: "You clarify a few concepts. You make a few distinctions. It's a living." ' Taken from Adam Swift, *Political Philosophy: A Beginners' Guide for Students and Politicians*, Cambridge: Polity, 2001, p. 4.
4. See Peter Winch, *The Idea of a Social Science and its Relation to Philosophy*, London: Routledge, 1958, Chapter 1.
5. Allan Bäck makes a similar point in the essay reproduced in this anthology, see his 'Thinking Clearly about Violence', Chapter 18 in this volume.
6. For a more historical anthology, in French, featuring many twentieth-century French philosophers, see H. Frappat (ed.), *La Violence*, Paris: Flammarion 2000. See also B. Lawrence and A. Karim (eds), *On Violence: A Reader*, Durham, NC: Duke University Press, 2007.
7. Hannah Arendt, *On Violence*, New York: Harcourt, 1969. On Arendt's analysis of violence, see B. Bar-On, *The Subject of Violence: Arendtean Exercises in Understanding*, Lanham, MD: Rowman & Littlefield, 2002.
8. See, for example, Nancy Scheper-Hughes and Philippe I. Bourgois (eds), *Violence in War and Peace: An Anthology*, Oxford: Blackwell, 2004; Catherine Besteman (ed.), *Violence: A Reader*, Basingstoke: Palgrave Macmillan, 2002; Manfred Steger and Nancy Lind (eds) *Violence and Its Alternatives: An Interdisciplinary Reader*, Basingstoke: Palgrave Macmillan, 1999.

1
Force, Violence and Law *and* Force and Coercion

John Dewey

FORCE AND COERCION

The empirical perplexities which attend the question of the relationship of force and law are many and genuine. The war brings home to us the question not only of the relation of force to international law, but the place of force in the economy of human life and progress. To what extent is organization of force in the multitude of ways required for the successful conduct of modern war a fair test of the work of a social organization? From another angle, the reform of our criminal law and our penal methods compels us to consider the significance of force. Are the Tolstoians right in holding that the state itself sets the great example of violence and furnishes the proof of the evils which result from violence? Or, from the other side, is not the essence of all law coercion? In the industrial domain, direct actionists lead us to inquire whether manifestation of force, threatening and veiled if not overt, is not, after all, the only efficacious method of bringing about any social change which is of serious import. Do not the usual phenomena attending strikes show us that the ordinary legal forms are just a kind of curtain drawn politely over the conflicts of force which alone are decisive? Are our effective legislative enactments anything more than registrations of results of battles previously fought out on the field of human endurance? In many social fields, reformers are now struggling for an extension of governmental activity by way of supervision and regulation. Does not such action always amount to an effort to extend the exercise of force on the part of some section of society, with a corresponding restriction of the forces employed by others? In spite of the fact that the political thinking of the seventeenth and eighteenth centuries is out of date, were not the thinkers of that period clearer headed than we are in acknowledging that all political questions are simply questions of the extension and restriction of exercise of power on the part of specific groups

First published in *International Journal of Ethics* 26 (1916): 359–67.

in the community? Has the recent introduction of an idealistic terminology about moral and common will, about juridical and moral personalities, done anything but muddle our minds about the hard fact that all our social questions at bottom concern the possession and use of force; and the equally hard fact that our political and legal arrangements are but dispositions of force to make more secure the other forms of its daily use?

In taking up the writings of the theorists it is not easy to persuade oneself that they are marked by much consistency. With a few notable exceptions, the doctrine that the state rests upon or is common will seems to turn out but a piece of phraseology to justify the uses actually made of force. Practices of coercion and constraint which would be intolerable if frankly labelled 'Force' seem to become laudable when baptized with the name of 'Will,' although they otherwise remain the same. Or, if this statement is extreme, there seems to be little doubt that the actual capacity of the state to bring force to bear is what has most impressed theorists, and that what they are after is some theoretical principle which will justify the exercise of force; so that in a great many cases such terms as common will, supreme will, supreme moral or juridical personality, are eulogistic phrases resorted to on behalf of such justification. The one thing that clearly stands out is that the use of force is felt to require explanation and sanction. To make force itself the ultimate principle is felt to be all one with proclaiming anarchy and issuing an invitation to men to settle all their difficulties by recourse to fighting it out to see which is the stronger. And yet what every political student is profoundly convinced of, is, I suppose, that at bottom every political struggle is a struggle for control, for power.

Although I have raised large questions, it is not my ambition to answer them. I have but outlined a large stage upon which to move about some quite minor figures. In the first place, something can be done, I think, by clarifying certain of the ideas which enter into the discussion. We may I think profitably discriminate the three conceptions of power or energy, coercive force, and violence. Power or energy is either a neutral or an eulogistic term. It denotes effective means of operation; ability or capacity to execute, to realize ends. Granted an end which is worth while, and power or energy becomes an eulogistic term. It means nothing but the sum of conditions available for bringing the desirable end into existence. Any political or legal theory which will have nothing to do with power on the ground that all power is force and all force brutal and non-moral is obviously condemned to a purely sentimental, dreamy morals. It is force by which we excavate subways and build bridges and travel and manufacture; it is force which is utilized in spoken argument or published book. Not to depend upon and utilize force is simply to be without a foothold in the real world.

Energy becomes violence when it defeats or frustrates purpose instead of executing or realizing it. When the dynamite charge blows up human beings instead of rocks, when its outcome is waste instead of production, destruction instead of construction, we call it not energy or power but violence. Coercive force occupies, we may fairly say, a middle place between power as energy and power as violence. To turn to the right as an incident of locomotion is a case of power: of means deployed on behalf of an end. To run amuck in the street is a case of violence. To use energy to make a man observe the rule of the road is a case of coercive force. Immediately, or with respect to his activities, it is a case of violence; indirectly, when it is exercised to assure the means which are needed for the successful realization of ends, it is a case of constructive use of power. Constraint or coercion, in other words, is an incident of a situation under certain conditions – namely, where the means for the realization of an end are not naturally at hand, so that energy has to be spent in order to make some power into a means for the end in hand.

If we formulate the result, we have something of this kind. Law is a statement of the conditions of the organization of energies which, when unorganized, conflict and result in violence – that is, destruction or waste. We cannot substitute reason for force, but force becomes rational when it is an organized factor in an activity instead of operating in an isolated way or on its own hook. For the sake of brevity, I shall refer to the organization of force hereafter as efficiency, but I beg to remind you that the use of the term always implies an actual or potential conflict and resulting waste in the absence of some scheme for distributing the energies involved.

These generalities are, it will be objected, innocuous and meaningless. So they are in the abstract. Let us take the question of the justification of force in a strike. I do not claim, of course, that what has been said tells us whether the use of force is justified or not. But I hold that it suggests the way of finding out in a given case whether it is justifiable or not. It is, in substance, a question of efficiency (including economy) of means in the accomplishing of ends. If the social ends at stake can be more effectively subserved by the existing legal and economic machinery, resort to physical action of a more direct kind has no standing. If, however, they represent an ineffective organization of means for the ends in question, then recourse to extra-legal means may be indicated; provided it really serves the ends in question – a very large qualification be it noted. A recourse to direct force is a supplementation of existent deficient resources in effective energy under some circumstances.

Such a doctrine is doubtless unwelcome. It is easily interpreted so as to give encouragement to resorting to violence and threats of violence in industrial struggles. But there is a very large 'if' involved – the 'if' of greater relative economy and efficiency. And when so regarded, it at once occurs to mind that experience in the past has shown that it is not usually efficient for parties to be judges in their own cause: that an impartial umpire is an energy saver. It occurs to mind, also, that the existing legal machinery, whatever its defects, represents a contrivance which has been built up at great cost, and that the tendency to ignore its operation upon special provocation would so reduce the efficiency of the machinery in other situations that the local gain would easily be more than offset by widespread losses in energy available for other ends. In the third place, experience shows that there is general presumption on the side of indirect and refined agencies as against coarse and strikingly obvious methods of utilizing power. The fine mechanism which runs a watch is more efficient than the grosser one which heaves a brick. Thus the bias against any doctrine which seems under any circumstances to sanction resort to personal and primitive methods of using force against the more impersonal juridical contrivances of society turns out to be *prima facie* justified on the principle of efficiency in use of means.

Over and above this bare presumption, it must be admitted that our organized contrivances are still so ineffective that it is a delicate matter to tell how far a standing menace to resort to crude methods may be a necessary stimulus to the better working of the more refined methods. There is a general presumption in politics against doing anything till it is clearly necessary; and indication of potential force operates as a sign of necessity. In other words social reorganization is usually a response to a threatened conflict – witness the present 'preparedness' agitation.

This conclusion that violence means recourse to means which are relatively wasteful may be strengthened by considering penal measures. Upon the whole, the opinion seems to be current that in such matters force is hallowed by the mere fact that it is the State which employs it, or by the fact that it is exercised in the interests of 'justice' – retribution in the abstract, or what is politely called 'vindicating the law.' When the justification of force is sought in some kind of abstract consideration of this sort, no questions are to be raised about the efficiency of the force used, for it is not conceived as a specific means to a specific end. It is the sacrosanct character thus attributed to the State's use of force which gives pungency to the Tolstoian charge that the State is the arch-criminal, the person who has recourse to violence on the largest scale. I see no way out except to say that all depends upon the efficient adaptation of means to ends. The serious charge against the State is not that it uses force – nothing was ever accomplished without using force – but that it does not use it wisely or effectively. Our penal measures are still largely upon the level which would convince a man by knocking him down instead of by instructing him.

My treatment is of course very summary. But I hope that it suggests my main point. No ends are accomplished without the use of force. It is consequently no presumption against a measure, political, international, jural, economic, that it involves a use of force. Squeamishness about force is the mark not of idealistic but of moonstruck morals. But antecedent and abstract principles can not be assigned to justify the use of force. The criterion of value lies in the relative efficiency and economy of the expenditure of force as a means to an end. With advance of knowledge, refined, subtle and indirect use of force is always displacing coarse, obvious and direct methods of applying it. This is the explanation to the ordinary feeling against the use of force. What is thought of as brutal, violent, immoral, is a use of physical agencies which are gross, sensational and evident on their own account, in cases where it is possible to employ with greater economy and less waste means which are comparatively imperceptible and refined.

It follows from what has been said that the so-called problem of 'moralizing' force is in reality a problem of *intellectualizing* its use: a problem of employing so to say neural instead of gross muscular force as a means to accomplish ends. An immoral use of force is a stupid use. I sometimes hear apologies for war which proceed by pointing out how largely all social life is a disguised contest of hostile powers. Our economic life, so it is said, is but a struggle for bread where the endurance and even the lives of laborers are pitted against the resources of employers. Only lack of imagination fails to see the economic war, the industrial battlefield with its ammunition trains and human carnage. Let the point be admitted. What still remains true is that the decisive question is the level of efficiency and economy upon which the deploying of forces goes on. Our present economic methods may be so wasteful, so destructive, as compared with others which are humanly possible, as to be barbarous. Yet competitive commercial methods may represent an advance in the utilization of human and natural resources over methods of war. In so far as they involve greater indirection and complexity of means, the presumption is that they are an advance. Take, however, on the other extreme the gospel of non-resistance. Except upon a doctrine of quiescence more thorough-going than any St. Simeon Stylites has ever adopted, the non-resisitance doctrine can mean only that given certain conditions, passive resistance is a more *effective* means of resistance than overt resistance would be. Sarcasm may be more effective than a blow in subduing an adversary; a look more effective than sarcasm. Only upon such a principle of expediency can the doctrine of non-resistance be urged, without committing ourselves to the notion that all exercise of energy is inherently wrong – a sort of oriental absolutism which makes the world intrinsically evil. I can but think that if pacifists in war and in penal matters would change their tune from the intrinsic immorality of the use of coercive force to the comparative inefficiency and stupidity of existing methods of using force, their good intentions would be more fruitful.

As my object is rather to make a point clear than to convince anyone, let me take another example. In the labor struggle we sometimes hear a right of free labor and free choice appealed to as against the movement for a closed shop. Men like President Eliot are sincerely convinced that they are continuing the fight for human freedom. Perhaps they are. I do not pretend to pass upon the merits of the question. But *perhaps* they are only fighting in behalf of the retention of methods of waste against those of efficient organization. There was a time when our ancestors had the personal right of inflicting punishment upon offenders. When the movement set in to restrict this office to a limited number of designated officers and thereby to deprive the mass of their prior right, one wonders whether the spiritual ancestors of President Eliot did not protest against this invasion of sacred personal liberties. It is now clear enough that the surrender of the power was an incident of organization absolutely necessary to secure an efficient utilization of the resources entering into it. It may turn out in the future that the movement for the closed shop is an incident of an organization of labor which is itself in turn an incident in accomplishing a more efficient organizaition of human forces.

In other words, the question of the limits of individual powers, or liberties, or rights, is finally a question of the most efficient use of means for ends. That at a certain period liberty should have been set up as something antecedently sacred *per se* is natural enough. Such liberty represented an important factor which had been overlooked. But it is as an efficiency factor that its value must ultimately be assessed. Experience justifies the contention that liberty forms such a central element in efficiency that, for example, our present methods of capitalistic production are highly inefficient because, as respects the great body of laborers, they are so coercive. Efficiency requires methods which will enlist greater individual interest and attention, greater emotional and intellectual liberty. With respect to such a liberation of energies, older and coarser forms of liberty may be obstructive; efficiency may then require the use of coercive power to abrogate *their* exercise.

The propositions of this paper may then be summed up as follows: First, since the attainment of ends requires the use of means, law is essentially a formulation of the use of force. Secondly, the only question which can be raised about the justification of force is that of comparative efficiency and economy in its use. Thirdly, what is justly objected to as violence or undue coercion is a reliance upon wasteful and destructful means of accomplishing results. Fourthly, there is always a possibility that what passes as a legitimate use of force may be so wasteful as to be really a use of violence; and *per contra* that measures condemned as recourse to mere violence may, under the given circumstances, represent an intelligent utilization of energy. In no case, can antecedent or *a priori* principles be appealed to as more than presumptive: the point at issue is concrete utilization of means for ends.

FORCE, VIOLENCE AND LAW

What is force, and what are we going to do with it? This, I am inclined to think, is the acute question of social philosophy in a world like that of to-day. A generation which has beheld the most stupendous manifestation of force in all history is not going to be content unless it has found some answer to the question this exhibition has stirred into being. Having witnessed the spectacle of continuous wholesale bombing, can we henceforth reprimand the sporadic and private bombing of the anarchist without putting our tongues in our cheeks? Or shall we say that he is right in principle, but wrong just in that his exercise of force is casual and personal, not collective and organized? We are to 'prepare.' How are we to decide whether this willingness to resort to the threat of force is a pledge of the final loyalty to ideals, or an evidence of growing contempt for the precious fruits of human labor, the only things which stand between us and the brutes? Is force the highest kind of laborious industry or is it the negation of industry?

We cannot ask this about war without being led to extend our questioning. Once we have uttered the question, everything in civilization throws it back at us. From the barracks it is but a step to the police court and the jail. Behind the prison rises the smoke of the factory, and from the factory roads lead to the counting-house and the bank. Is our civic life other than a disguised struggle of brute forces? Are the policeman and the jailer the true guardians and representatives of the social order? Is our industrial life other than a continued combat to sift the strong and the weak, a war where only external arms and armor are changed? Is the state itself anything but organized force? In the seventeenth century political theorists talked frankly in terms of force and power. We have invented a more polite terminology. Much is now said of the common will and consciousness; the state figures as a moral personality, or at least as a juridical one. Hasn't our thinking lost in clearness and definiteness as our language has become more sentimentally courteous?

Yet common sense still clings to a *via media* between the Tolstoian, to whom all force is violence and all violence evil, and that glorification of force which is so easy when war arouses turbulent emotion, and so persistent (in disguised forms) whenever competition rules industry. I should be glad to make the voice of common sense more articulate. As an initial aid, I would call to mind the fact that force figures in different roles. Sometimes it is energy; sometimes it is coercion or constraint; sometimes it is violence. Energy is power used with a eulogistic meaning; it is power of doing work, harnessed to accomplishment of ends. But it is force none the less – brute force if you please, and rationalized only by its results. Exactly the same force running wild is called violence. The objection to violence is not that it involves the use

First published in *New Republic* 5 (1916): 295–97.

of force, but that it is a waste of force; that it uses force idly or destructively. And what is called law may always, I suggest, be looked at as describing a method for employing force economically, efficiently, so as to get results with the least waste.

No matter what idealists and optimists say, the energy of the world, the number of forces at disposal, is plural, not unified. There are different centres of force and they go their ways independently. They come into conflict; they clash. Energy which would otherwise be used in effecting something is then used up in friction; it goes to waste. Two men may be equally engaged about their respective businesses, and their businesses may be equally reputable and important, and yet there may be no harmony in their expenditures of energy. They are driving opposite ways on the road and their vehicles collide. The subsequent waste in quarreling is as certain as the immediate waste in a smash-up. The rule that each shall turn to the right is a plan for organizing otherwise independent and potentially conflicting energies into a scheme which avoids waste, a scheme allowing a maximum utilization of energy. Such, if I mistake not, is the true purport of all law.

Either I am mistaken, or those persons who are clamoring for the 'substitution of law for force' have their language, at least, badly mixed. And a continuous use of mixed language is likely to produce a harmful mixture in ideas. Force is the only thing in the world which effects anything, and literally to substitute law for force would be as intelligent as to try to run an engine on the mathematical formula which states its most efficient running. Doubtless those who use the phrase have their hearts in the right place; they mean some method of regulating the expenditure of force which will avoid the wastes incident to present methods. But too often the phrase is bound up with intellectual confusion. There is a genuine emotional animosity to the very idea of force. The 'philosophy of force' is alluded to scornfully or indignantly – which is somewhat as if an engineer should speak deprecatingly of the science of energy.

At various times of my life I have, with other wearied souls, assisted at discussions between those who were Tolstoians and – well, those who weren't. In reply to the agitated protests of the former against war and the police and penal measures, I have listened to the time-honored queries about what you should do when the criminal attacked your friend or child. I have rarely heard it stated that since one cannot even walk the street without using force, the only question which persons can discuss with one another concerns the most effective use of force in gaining ends in specific situations. If one's end is the saving of one's soul immaculate, or maintaining a certain emotion unimpaired, doubtless force should be used to inhibit natural muscular reactions. If the end is something else, a hearty fisticuff may be the means of realizing it. What is intolerable is that men should condemn or eulogize force at large, irrespective of its use as a means of getting results. To be interested in ends and to have contempt for the means which alone secure them is the last stage of intellectual demoralization.

It is hostility to force as force, to force intrinsically, which has rendered the peace movement so largely an anti-movement, with all the weaknesses which appertain to everything that is primarily anti-anything. Unable to conceive the task of organizing the existing forces so they may achieve their greatest efficiency, pacifists have had little recourse save to decry evil emotions and evil-minded men as the causes of war. Belief that war springs from the emotions of hate, pugnacity and greed rather than from the objective causes which call these emotions into play reduces the peace movement to the futile plane of hortatory preaching. The avarice of munition-makers, the love of some newspapers for exciting news, and the depravity of the anonymous human heart doubtless play a part in the generation of war. But they take a hand in bringing on war only because there are specific defects in the organization of the energies of men in society which give them occasion and stimulation.

If law or rule is simply a device for securing such a distribution of forces as keeps them from conflicting with one another, the discovery of a new social arrangement is the first step in substituting law for war. The ordinary pacifist's method is like trying to avoid conflict in the use of the road by telling men to love one another, instead of by instituting a rule of the road. Until pacifism puts its faith in constructive, inventive intelligence instead of in appeal to emotions and in exhortation, the disparate unorganized forces of the world will continue to develop outbreaks of violence.

The principle cuts, however, two ways. I know of no word more often deprived of meaning and reduced to a mere emotional counter than the word 'end,' of which I have made free use. Men appeal to ends to justify their resort to force when they mean by ends only footless desires. An end is something which concerns results rather than aspirations. We jusitify the use of force in the name of justice when dealing with criminals in our infantilely barbaric penal methods. But unless its use is actually an effective and economical means of securing specific results, we are using violence to relieve our immediate impulses and to save ourselves the labor of thought and construction. So men justify war in behalf of words which would be empty were they not charged with emotional force – words like honor, liberty, civilization, divine purpose and destiny – forgetting that a war, like anything else, has specific concrete results on earth. Unless war can be shown to be the most economical method of securing the results which are desirable with a minimum of the undesirable results, it marks waste and loss: it must be adjudged a violence, not a use of force. The terms honor, liberty, future of civilization, justice, become sentimental fantasies of the same order as the catchwords of the professional pacifist. Their emotional force may keep men going, but they throw no light on the goal nor on the way traveled.

I would not wish to cast doubt on anything which aims to perceive facts and to act in their light. The conception of an international league to enforce peace, an international police force, has about it a flavor of reality. Nevertheless force is efficient socially not when imposed upon a scene from without, but when it is an organization of the forces *in* the scene. We do not enjoy common interests and amicable intercourse in this country because our fathers instituted a United States and armed it with executive force. The formation of the United States took place because of the community of interests and the amicable intercourse already existent. Doubtless its formation facilitated and accelerated the various forces which it concentrated, but no amount of force possessed by it could have imposed commerce, travel, unity of tradition and outlook upon the thirteen states. It was their union, their organization. And no league to enforce peace will fare prosperously save as it is the natural accompaniment of a constructive adjustment of the concrete interests which are already at work. Not merely the glorification of either war or peace for their own sakes, but equally the glorification of diplomacy, prestige, national standing and power and international tribunals at large, tends to keep men's thoughts engaged with emotional abstractions, and turns them away from the perception of the particular forces which have to be related. The passage of force under law occurs only when all the cards are on the table, when the objective facts which bring conflicts in their train are acknowledged, and when intelligence is used to devise mechanisms which will afford to the forces at work all the satisfaction that conditions permit.

COMMENTARY ON DEWEY

John Dewey (1859–1952), the American philosopher universally associated with the philosophical school of Pragmatism, is not best known for his political writings.[1] Nevertheless, he was in his prime when the First World War broke out, and like many intellectuals of his time he took a keen interest in the debate between those who were in favour of US military intervention in Europe, and those who opposed the war on pacifist grounds. It is in light of this historical backdrop that his two articles on force and violence ought to be read.

Dewey's two short pieces are philosophically important for at least four reasons. Firstly, because Dewey is offering an embryonic version of the thesis, made famous by Max Weber only two years later, suggesting that the modern state is founded on force, and that the relation between the state and violence is not only an especially intimate one, but one that prompts pressing moral questions. The similarities between Dewey and Weber on this point are revealing. Thus while in 1916 Dewey was asking 'is the state itself anything but organized force?' and contemplating 'the hard fact that all our social questions at bottom concern the possession and use of force; and the equally hard fact that our political and legal arrangements are but dispositions of force to make more secure the other forms of its daily use', in 1918 Weber presented us with arguably the most famous definition of the modern state: 'a state is a human community that (successfully) claims the monopoly of the legitimate use of physical force within a territory.'[2]

Secondly, Dewey makes an effort to distinguish between three closely related but distinct concepts: power (or energy), coercive force (or law) and violence. All three concepts are elaborations on the idea of force, or to put it differently, force can take on different meanings, depending on its role. Dewey tells us that power or energy is a dispositional concept, which denotes the ability or capacity to execute, or to realize ends; but it is force nonetheless. Coercive force or law is a method of employing force economically, efficiently, so as to get results without waste. Violence is the destructive, wasteful use of force. It is interesting to see how Dewey tries to explain the way these three meanings of force are interrelated. Thus, he tells us that coercive force occupies a middle place between power as energy and power as violence.[3]

Thirdly, in approaching the moral dimension of force, Dewey seems to suggest that everything turns on the issue of efficiency or economy: 'the criterion of value lies in the relative efficiency and economy of the expenditure of force as a means to an end.' It follows that, according to Dewey, what makes violence particularly objectionable is its wasteful nature. Also, there is nothing intrinsically evil about the state, notwithstanding its considerable use of force; it is only when the state fails to use its force wisely or effectively that we ought to be concerned: 'The objection to violence is not that it involves the use of force, but that it is a waste of force; that it uses force idly or destructively. And what is called law may always, I suggest, be looked at as describing a method for employing force economically, efficiently, so as to get results with the least waste.'[4]

Finally, in raising questions about the justification of coercive force, Dewey is reminding us that the distinction between the legitimate use of force and violence is at best a blurry one: 'there is always a possibility that what passes as a legitimate use of force may be so wasteful as to be really a use of violence; and *per contra* that measures condemned as recourse to mere violence may, under the given circumstances, represent an intelligent utilization of energy.'

Notes and further reading

1. A notable exception is John Dewey's short history of liberalism, from John Locke to John Stuart Mill, first published in 1935. See his *Liberalism and Social Action*, New York: Prometheus Books, 1999.
2. Max Weber, 'Politics as a Vocation', in H. H. Gerth and C. W. Mills (eds), *From Max Weber*, London: Routledge, 1970, p. 78. For a critique of Weber's definition of the modern state, see Michael Taylor, *Community, Anarchy and Liberty*, Cambridge: Cambridge University Press, 1982.
3. For a more recent analysis of violence and coercion, see T. Pogge 'Coercion and Violence', in J. Brady and N. Garver (eds), *Justice, Law and Violence*, Philadelphia: Temple University Press, 1991.
4. For a critique of Dewey's views on force and violation, see J. Betz, 'Violence: Garver's Definition and a Deweyan Correction', *Ethics*, Vol. 87, No. 4, July 1977.

2
The Economic Meaning of War and Protection

Frederic C. Lane

Because wars reduce national wealth in many ways it is often said that even for the victors wars never pay and never have paid except under quite primitive conditions. On the other hand, one of the ways in which an individual may gain his livelihood is by specializing in the use of force, and history records many groups of men famous mainly for their efficiency in war who gained relatively great wealth. Of course they had to live in a society with others engaged in occupations more commonly called productive. Cannot a nation, living in a relation of give and take with other nations, similarly add to its income by showing superiority over others in its ability to use force? Some of its capital and labor will have to be diverted from other employments, but it may be argued that under some circumstances war is the employment which will be most productive of national income. Although economists have done little to define the conditions under which the use of force may be the most advantageous of occupations, their usual method of theoretical analysis seems applicable to this problem so long as it is admitted that the use of force may be productive of a utility. That utility is protection.

Every economic enterprise needs and pays for protection, protection against the destruction or armed seizure of its capital and the forceful disruption of its labor. In highly organized societies the production of this utility, protection, is one of the functions of a special association or enterprise called government. Indeed, one of the most distinctive characteristics of governments is their attempt to create law and order by using force themselves and by controlling through various means the use of force by others. The more successful a government is in monopolizing all use of force between men within a particular area, the more efficient is its maintenance of law and order. Accordingly, the production of protection is a natural monopoly. The territorial extent of this monopoly is prescribed more or less loosely by military geography and historical circumstances. Breaks in the monopoly occur, as when there is an insurrection or a boom in the rackets of gangsters, but such rival enterprises in the use of force substitute monopolies of their own if successful. The These illegal monopolies may be quite transitory and highly localized, perhaps as fleeting as that of the stick-up man who finishes his robbery before the policeman comes around the corner. When, as in that exteme example, no protection is given against immediate additional seizure by the same bandit or some other user of violence, it is a clear case of plunder. Both the history of nations and the stories of gangsters contain plenty of borderline cases, but clearly force is not only used in plundering but also in preventing plundering, and a government which maintains law and order is rendering a service in return for the payment it collects.

The cost of producing this service varies greatly and affects the size of the real national income since the amount of goods and services other than protection which can be distributed to the nation is reduced when more capital and labor is employed in the production of protection.[1] Sometimes, as in the recent Spanish civil war, internal conflicts prevent any single enterprise from securing general recognition as the only legitimate monopolist of force and so reducing its costs. Sometimes fear of powerful neighbors causes more to be spent on arms. In the United States the amount of our nation's capital and labor now being employed for the production of protection is strikingly larger than the amount so employed a few years ago. Some nations have lower protection costs than others because of their cultural heritage or geographic position. A nation with easily defended frontiers, for example, may have a lower protection cost due to this gift of nature. The United States still devotes to the production of other goods a larger proportion of its productive capacity than does Great Britain, and our geographic position has, so far, enabled us to enjoy more protection while paying less for it.[2]

Thus broadly stated from a national point of view, the importance of protection as a factor in production is easily recognized. But from the point of view of private economic enterprises the relation is frequently obscured. The ordinary economic enterprise operating within the territory of a government which has a monopoly of the use of force pays for protection in the process of paying taxes. Of many an individual entrepreneur it can be said that he does not normally 'vary the *amount* of "law and order," or security, by variations in the taxes he pays.' To him, '. . . law and order is in general a free good, in the sense that any payment which must be made for it will presumably come out of general taxation and will not be counted as specific expense of production at all.'[3] In this way economists generally dismiss protection from their calculations. But even for individual economic enterprises, protection costs are variable and to a significant extent affect the earnings of such enterprises. What they pay in taxes can in some cases be reduced by paying for protection in some other form – by lobbying, by bribes, or even by revolution.[4] To be sure, changes in protection cost are not often effected by an individual entrepreneur acting by and for himself alone. They are generally effected by group decision and group action. The decisions are made by governments in consultation with and for the benefit of a group of enterprises. They involve action in the forum and perhaps on the battlefield as well as in the market place or factory, but in so far as they are attempts to gain a utility at minimum cost they are subject to economic analysis. When an associate of Cecil Rhodes estimated that 'good government' in the Boer states would bring a saving of six shillings per ton on gold ore production costs and an increase in consequence of $12,000,000 a year in dividends, we may say that protection was being included by an entrepreneur among the factors of production and the principle of substitution was about to be applied.[5]

For individual enterprises engaged in international trade protection hardly ever appears a free good. Costs of protection are vital factors in production since their variations frequently determine profits. Competing enterprises are subject to different governments, and pay in taxes and tariffs different costs of protection. Usually they pay at least two governments for protection and not infrequently they hope that the action of one government, which they call their own, will effect a reduction in what they pay to another government. For that purpose they can afford to increase their payments to their own government if their total protection costs, the sum of their payments to both governments, will be reduced.

To isolate the element in business profits which results from minimized protection costs, imagine a case of various enterprises competing in the same market and having the same costs except that they pay different costs of protection. The sale price of their product will be high enough to cover the highest protection cost, namely that of the marginal producer whose offering is needed to satisfy the demand. The profits of the enterprises enjoying lower protection costs will include the difference between their protection costs and that of the marginal competitor. This difference I will call protection rent. Just as differences in the fertility of land result in rents to owners of more fertile fields, so differences in the ease of securing protection result in returns to enterprises which enjoy cheaper protection, returns for which the best name seems to be protection rent.[6]

The simplest illustration of such a protection rent is provided by enterprises competing under a tariff differential. For example, Hawaiian sugar was admitted to the United States free of duty from 1876 to 1890 while to meet the American demand much sugar was being imported from Cuba or Java. These full duty imports were the marginal supply and fixed the price. The Hawaiian producers received a protection rent of two cents a pound.[7] Other examples abound in the history of the wealth of nations and the analysis of a few instances in which protection rents determined major changes in international trade will assist an analysis of the possibilities of increasing national income by the use of force.

The Venetians obtained in 1082 a charter exempting them from all tariffs in the Byzantine Empire and thus secured a differential in their favor even against the Greeks. These privileges were secured by placing the Venetian navy at the service of the Byzantine emperor in his war against the Norman king of Sicily. For more than a hundred years they were renewed or elaborated by continued use of Venetian arms, sometimes against the enemies of Byzantium, sometimes against the Byzantine emperor himself to compel renewal of the charter. The privileges were used in trade between different parts of the Byzantine Empire and between that empire and other markets of the Levant as well as in trade between East and West. The Venetians alone did not satisfy all demands for commercial interchange within so large a field. Although their earlier chief rivals, the Amalfitans, were soon reduced to insignificance, the Venetians continued to have competitors, not only the Greek and Jewish subjects of the Byzantine emperor, but also new groups, the Pisans who paid a tariff of 4 per cent and the Genoese who paid the usual 10 per cent until 1155 and then 4 per cent.[8] Since such merchants found the trade worthwhile they too must have been necessary to meet the demand. Among them were the 'marginal producers.' The Venetians were able to sell wares at prices which must often have been higher by reason of the higher protection costs of less privileged traders. Consequently the profits of the Venetian merchants in that area were swelled by fat protection rents procured for them by their government's use of its naval power.

At a much later date, the trade of the French West Indies at the time of Colbert illustrates how a government could, by changing protection costs, shift a carrying trade from one nation to another. The trade of the French islands was almost entirely in the hands of Dutch enterprises when Colbert became minister, and there is every indication that the Dutch would have had no difficulty holding their own against possible French competitors if there had been no appeal to force. Under Colbert's direction the Dutch trade was declared illegal and a fleet of three naval vessels was sent to seize any Dutch ships visiting the French islands. This caused the Dutch some loss, threatened them with more, and increased the cost of protection of those who continued to trade as smugglers. When Colbert died, some two hundred French ships were receiving passports each year for voyages to the French West Indies. The rise in the protection costs of the Dutch had made the trade profitable for French enterprises by giving them protection rents.[9]

But profits for French enterprises trading to the West Indies, or for Venetian enterprises trading in the Byzantine Empire, did not necessarily mean a profit for France or Venice as a whole – did not necessarily mean any increase in the totals of their national incomes. To consider the effects of these uses of force on national income, a way must be found to balance against the protection rents of the Venetian traders in the Byzantine Empire the cost of the naval action which secured their privileges, to balance against the profits made by French traders to the West Indies such expenses as that of maintaining naval squadrons there. In short we must investigate the *national* protection costs in these cases. And we must first inquire further into what is to be included in these costs and what additions to national income besides protection rents they may produce.

When we adopt this point of view we can hardly avoid stretching the meaning of the word protection to include aggressive action. The cost of using armed force at sea and in lowering foreign tariffs must be counted, although protection on the high seas is not a natural monopoly and international trade, by definition, extends beyond the territory of any single government monopoly. In this connection there are some protection costs which are obviously defensive – such as the cost of convoys to ward off pirates; others – such as the cost of capturing ships of other nations engaged in competing enterprises – might be called offensive protection costs. But it would be useless to try to classify the suppression of smuggling as offensive or defensive action. Whatever the verbal contradiction involved in applying it to aggressive actions, one term is needed to cover both what a government spends to prevent the plundering of its own enterprises and also what it spends in plundering enterprises of other nations; in attempting to create protection rents for its own enterprises, or in extending its monopoly of force so as to levy tribute.

By tribute it means payments received for protection, but payments in excess of the cost of producing the protection. The possibility of tribute arises from the fact that a government, like many another monopoly, does not need to sell its product at the cost of production. Most governments have been so constituted that ruling classes have been able to exploit these monopolies and raise the price of protection for other classes so as to increase their own incomes.[10] The tribute collected by one class from another need not in itself change the total of national income. It may merely move money from one pocket to another within the nation.[11] But tribute may be collected from outside the nation, and the income of a nation is increased by any sums which its ruling class is able to collect as tribute from members of some other nation. The Venetian penetration of the Byzantine Empire, for example, came to a dramatic climax in 1204. Finding a large supply of armed force, the knights of the Fourth Crusade, available for its purposes at bargain prices, Venice employed them to overthrow the Byzantine Empire and seize a portion of it. By that conquest the Venetians not only arranged to collect their protection rents for many more years but they also secured a sensational amount of booty and were enabled to levy tribute in the portion of the empire which passed under Venetian dominion. This tribute was paid by Greek subjects in taxes or in servile services and was received by Venetian nobles as manorial revenues or as salaries of government offices. Since it is readily admitted that plunder and tribute added to national wealth in earlier times, this conquest has been much emphasized. But the tariff privileges of the Venetians had gained them much wealth from the Byzantine Empire before they became strong enough to overthrow it; the growth of wealth in Venice during that period as a whole came less from booty and tribute than from protection rents.

The variety of uses to which may be put the force organized by governments makes the national cost of protection an overhead cost and creates the practical difficulties involved in allotting such costs. When the Venetians were fighting the Norman king of Sicily in 1081–84, they were acting not only to secure privileges in the Byzantine Empire but also to prevent the king from extending his rival monopoly of force over both sides of the Adriatic and Ionian Seas. Had he succeeded he would have been able to take plunder and tribute from the Venetians. The problem of allotting the cost of an army or navy is as difficult a problem in cost accounting as allotting the cost of a dam among its various uses for power production, irrigation, and flood control, but perhaps no more difficult. Defense of the home territory against the devastation of invasion may be compared to the prevention of floods in a populous country. At least such defense may be accepted as a starting point. Additions to national protection costs beyond that point may be judged profitable or unprofitable according to the amount they add to national income in the form of booty, tribute for the ruling class, or protection rents for privileged private enterprises. Colbert created a navy larger than was needed to prevent the plundering of France; its cost was predicated on the desirability of extending France's commercial and colonial empire. The cost of the portion of the navy used in the West Indies may fairly be alloted to whatever France gained by that commerce.

In estimating the cost to the nation of any acquisitions of booty, tribute, or protection rent, it is particularly important, and difficult, to reckon the opportunity costs. Allowance must be made for any violation of the law of comparative advantage involved either in the military effort or in the new enterprises created by the stimulus of the protection rents. For it is evident that all tariffs and forceful restraints involve less income immediately for someone than would have been gained if everyone concerned had acted freely, peacefully, without restraining or being restrained by force, and with a perfect eighteenth century reasonableness. As Adam Smith argued so convincingly in regard to similar cases, West Indian wares could have been sold more cheaply in France, and European wares would have been cheaper in the West Indies, if that trade had been left to the Dutch and if the French capital and labor, which was in fact diverted to the West Indies trade, had been allowed to find employment according to 'the system of natural liberty.' The protection rents of the new French enterprises were being paid for not only in royal expenditure on the naval squadron but also in higher prices paid by consumers both in France and in the French West Indies. On the other hand, the protection rents of Venetian traders in the Byzantine Empire, although dependent on the higher prices produced by the duties levied on their competitors, were not paid for in the main by Venetian consumers since relatively little of the merchandise found its ultimate market in Venice. The cost of the violation of the law of comparative advantage was borne by foreign consumers and was therefore no deduction from Venetian national income.

The only substantial opportunity cost to the Venetians was the opportunity cost of the war fleets by which their privileges were won. If the capital and labor employed in those war fleets had been secured by bidding for them in an open market against competing demands for their use in other activities – such as continuance of the trade without special privilege – then there would be no opportunity cost requiring special investigation. But most war fleets are not secured simply by competitive bidding in a free market and their costs are not therefore fully expressed by figures in a government budget. Although Colbert's navy was partly paid for at market prices and the squadron sent to the West Indies was too small to make the difference of great weight, the Venetian fleets which fought for and against the Byzantine Empire were major mobilizations of the maritime force of the nation. The government decided whether in a given year ships should be allowed to sail as usual or whether certain trades should be suspended and a fleet prepared for war. Roughly put, the choice before the Venetians was whether to withdraw their ships and crews from trade for certain years and use the same capital and labor during those years in fighting. The opportunity cost of a year's war was primarily the loss of the returns on a year's trade. War also risked damage to the ships and the loss of productive labor through casualties, but when successful, the Venetians may have made up for these losses by plundering the enemy.[12] Assuming they were going to have a successful campaign, the Venetian leaders might sometimes have calculated in the following terms: With our privileges, the employ of our merchants and seamen in the Byzantine Empire in trade yields each year 20 per cent more than it would if we had no privileges.[13] Employing those merchants and seamen as fighters for a year will mean a 100 per cent loss of return from them for this year but it will be worthwhile if it secures us our privileges for five years or more. Of course the Venetians did not work out the problem precisely this way and the sources do not permit us to calculate it in exact accord with attested facts. But it illustrates how it was possible for the Venetian use of force in securing tariff differentials to be productive of increase in Venetian national income. During the century after 1082 Venetian national income did increase very substantially. Other developments of that century helped, especially the rise of Western markets for Eastern products. That aided all the seaboard cities of the Mediterranean which were intermediaries in the trade, but Venetian commercial enterprise was then focused particularly on the Byzantine Empire and was very largely devoted to exchange within that empire and to the commerce between it and other markets of the Levant. To be sure, the Venetians acted partly for their own security, as has been explained, and our picture of how Venice grew rich in this general period is complicated by the events of the Fourth Crusade. Yet, everything considered, Venetian policy from 1082 to 1204 appears an unusually successful use of force to increase national income.

Colbert's capture of trade with the West Indies seems, by contrast, to have failed to produce any immediate gain in French national income. When we count all aspects of the national protection cost and the opportunity cost of the new enterprises, a formidable list of losses must be subtracted from the addition to national income embodied in the profits of traders to the West Indies. Besides the big deficit of the French West India Company which pioneered the voyage, there was the direct cost of employing a French naval squadron, and, since the exclusion of the Dutch from the West Indies was one reason for the outbreak of war between France and Holland in 1672, some part of the expense of that war would have to be included. To allow for national opportunity costs, the price of sugar to French consumers would have to be investigated, and if the islanders be considered part of the French nation, their losses in paying for supplies prices two or three times as high as those previously charged by the Dutch must be added. Even in authors highly favorable to Colbert the evidence presented indicates that a loss rather than a gain in national income resulted during Colbert's life-time from the capture of the trade.[14]

A case of attempting to increase national wealth by military power which presents enlightening similarities and contrasts with those just discussed was the temporary capture of the spice trade by the Portuguese. In the second half of the fifteenth century nearly all the spices reaching Europe from the Indian Ocean passed through the Red Sea and the lands of the Soldan of Egypt, paying him well for his protection on the way, before they reached the Venetians and other Europeans. After the Portuguese found the way to India around Africa, the Portuguese king decided to assume a royal monopoly of the most valuable spices. At the same time he attempted by armed force to bar the passage of all spices into the Red Sea. His success was not complete, but the destruction of some ships of Arab traders and the risk of capture for others was sufficient for some decades to raise greatly the protection costs of the Red Sea route. While he kept these costs up, the Portuguese king sold spices in the West at prices above those which the Venetians had charged in the later fifteenth century. So long as he raised the protection cost of the Red Sea route sufficiently, the king, as monopolist of the Cape route, could fix his price so as to secure the protection rent arising from the higher protection costs of his rivals.[15]

But in attempting to extend his government's monopoly of force over the Indian Ocean the Portuguese king assumed a heavy burden of expenditure which can properly be charged as protection cost to his own spice trading enterprise. The overawing of Indian princes, the seizing of trading posts, and the assertion of naval supremacy in the Indian Ocean were the king's means of raising the protection costs of his competitors, and such was the inefficiency of Portuguese methods of trade and government that these offensive protection costs soon proved excessive. The Ottoman Turks lowered tariffs in Egypt after they conquered it, and they challenged the Portuguese control of the Indian Ocean.[16] About 1560 a substantial part of Europe's spice imports again came through the Red Sea,[17] a sign that the protection costs of the Portuguese king were at times higher than those of his rivals on the competing route. Reviewing the economic history of the Portuguese in India and taking into account the military expenses, J. Lucio de Azevedo asserts: 'The truth is that only in the period of conquest did India pay its cost ... ' and, then as he says, only by 'booty, tribute, prizes, and the ransom of Moors.'[18]

Tribute was an extremely important factor in this case and especially so if we shift our point of view to consider not simply the royal enterprise of governing and spice trading but the changes in Portuguese national income as a whole. When Lucio de Azevedo says that the cost of the Indian empire exceeded the receipts, he seems to include under the costs the salaries and pensions with which the Portuguese king rewarded the nobles who conquered and governed the empire. Whatever increase in the income of this ruling class came from charges levied on non-Portuguese subjects constituted an addition to national income. Royal officials in India did increase their revenue illegally also by booty, bribes, and private trade. This sort of corruption was probably the chief factor in undermining the profitableness of the royal monopoly, but it was a positive factor in national income. Although in political or legal theory they were part of the royal enterprise, the corrupt officials were from an economic point of view acting as entrepreneurs on their own. Each sold for his own profit the protection of the force at his disposal. The revival of the Red Sea route was not an interference with their income but a sign that they preferred selling their protection for bribes to Arab traders instead of extending it to the king's monopoly as they were supposed to do. If we count all the increased income of the ruling class, legitimate and illegitimate, booty and tribute as well as protection rent, there seems no doubt that Portuguese national income did increase for a time.

The opportunity cost remains to be considered. With the same geographical discoveries and the same skill in navigation, could Portuguese capital and labor have been used more profitably in another way than that to which it was directed by military action in the Indian Ocean? Although it is hard to see how the Portuguese could have followed 'nature's simple plan' in this case, any more easily than the Venetians could have adopted such a plan in dealing with the Byzantine Empire, some contemporaries did conceive policies requiring less military action. Observers at Venice – ironically enough now that Venice, three hundred years after the conquest of Constantinople, was no longer making wars pay – pointed out that the Portuguese might operate advantageously without attempting a monopoly of force, simply because the Cape route would enable the Portuguese to avoid the high customs levied in Egypt.[19] Instead, the Portuguese decided to seek their protection rents by raising the protection costs of possible rivals rather than by trying themselves to operate with protection costs below the existing level.[20] The consequent increase in the prices to Portuguese consumers of Indian products was of trifling importance since the bulk of these products was sold abroad. But less military action against Arab traders and the employ of more capital and labor in commercial activity might have increased the volume and the value of the Eastern wares which the Portuguese could offer for sale in Europe. Would the returns of such an expanded commerce have increased Portuguese national income more than it was increased by plunder, tribute, and the small trade actually developed?

To frame the question in this way suffices to suggest that a full estimate of opportunity cost involves two considerations which were passed over lightly in the cases discussed earlier. The first concerns the kind of capital and labor there was in Portugal, in other words nothing less than the character of Portuguese society in 1500. The activity in which the Portuguese then displayed superiority over other nations was not shrewd trading but bold adventuring both in navigation and in war. Because of the military and religious traditions of the Portuguese and their class structure, the crusading policy pursued in India may well have stimulated energies which obtained more wealth than the Portuguese could have gained by less bellicose means. A Venetian of 1500 was likely to believe that the Portuguese could gain more by a more peaceful policy because such might have been the case had the Portuguese ruling class been similar in character to the Venetian in 1500. At that date many Venetian nobles had become wedded to peaceful trade or to the management of country estates. They were no longer, as they had been three or four hundred years earlier when bullying Byzantium, equally efficient either as merchants or as sea raiders.

The second consideration is that two different answers are possible – one for the short run and one for the long run. The policy which the Portuguese adopted in India yielded so much tribute and plunder that a greater immediate increase in national income under a more peaceful policy seems improbable. But the king's attempt to conquer an Indian empire, and the closely connected decision to make the chief items in the trade a royal monopoly, diverted Portuguese capital and labor from the commercial development of the voyage and focused the energies of his people on war, plunder, and the taking of bribes and tribute. The large immediate rewards attracted the youth of the nation to these warlike activities which soon yielded diminishing returns. A royal policy which relied less on force and opened more opportunities for those with trading skill would have favored the development of mercantile capacities among the Portuguese. In the long run of a hundred or two hundred years these capacities might well have made Portugal richer. The possibility raises very complex questions since a change in the type of capacity possessed by a nation's labor, both managerial and manual, involves a basic change in social structure, in this case a decline of the military and a rise of the commercial and industrial classes. Because the ensuing centuries were to bring greater wealth to commercial and industrial nations, it is generally held that the conquest of India, although it increased Portuguese national income for a time, caused a decrease later by undermining the productivity of the nation's labor.

On the other hand, Colbert's West Indian policy, although in the short run it decreased French national income, is generally judged successful in the long run. Within a century after his death, the West Indies 'proved the most valuable colonial asset which France possessed and contributed more to her commercial prosperity than any other single branch of trade.'[21] The particular type of labor and capital which Colbert fostered by providing protection rents for West Indian traders became in the long run of a hundred years exceptionally productive. The same can be said of many of his efforts. After describing Colbert's East India Company, Professor Cole concludes: 'The value of navigators who knew the routes to the East, of merchants who could carry on the Indies trade, of agents who had learned oriental ways, were all assets which did not appear on the balance sheet, but which formed a significant contribution from the Company of Colbert to its successors.'[22] By a variety of measures many of which depended on force of arms, Colbert increased the proportion of his nation's capital and labor devoted to oceanic commerce and to manufacturing. He often diverted capital and labor from employments in which they would have produced more national income at the time. But manufacturing and oceanic commerce were to become more and more profitable as they attracted more and more labor and capital. In so far as Colbert drew resources away from conspicuous consumption or from agricultural investments which were subject to the law of diminishing returns and directed them into commercial and industrial activities which were in the future to yield increasing return, his activity as a statesman did contribute to the future wealth of his nation.

This contrast between short-run loss and long-run gain is present in many cases of mercantilism. Against England's immediate losses from enforcing the Navigation Acts, losses from higher freight rates and from naval action, may be put some of the advantage which the size of the British merchant marine later gave many British enterprises. Against the immediate cost to the British of winning and holding colonial outposts may be balanced not only any immediate return in protection rents, but also some of the benefits of the internal economies made possible to British industries in following centuries by the size of Britain's overseas market. The recent continuator of the Smithian tradition, Alfred Marshall, admits that the national income of England in the eighteenth century, and even more in the nineteenth century depended much on 'the action of the law of increasing return with regard to her exports.'[23]

During a long earlier period of history the chief hope of making war pay was tribute. In the Age of Mercantilism the wealth which governing classes took directly for themselves from other nations became relatively small. As economic life became less largely agricultural and more intricately organized through differentiated enterprises, the profits secured by favored economic enterprises came to form a larger part of national income. Tribute became less important than protection rents. The change made immediate success in increasing national income by military action less frequent, for protection rents were secured by violations of the law of comparative advantage which were usually to the detriment of all nations concerned. Yet in the long run military victories added more to national income when used to gain protection rent than when used to gain tribute. Tribute-paying empires yielded diminishing returns as they drew more manpower into the maintenance and extension of such conquests. The protection rents stimulated oceanic commerce and industries which found new markets from wider trade. In another epoch the premiums given commerce and industry might have been thrown away. In that particular period of social and technological change, the period of the expansion of Europe, those fields of enterprise yielded increasing return.

In more recent times the forms in which national income may be increased by military pressure on other nations have been enormously complicated and especially recently by exchange controls and marketing quotas. At the same time the armed forces used by governments have been consolidated into enduring military and naval establishments so that national protection costs are even more largely overhead costs. A part of these costs may be allotted to security against invasion, but another part arises from desire for 'a place in the sun' or for escape from 'economic strangulation.' Even if it were clearly demonstrated that military pressure never gained immediate additions to national income sufficient to justify the added cost, historical perspective emphasizes the extreme difficulty of guessing the results in the long run. The long-run success of present military efforts to increase national income depends on whether these efforts direct the labor of a victorious nation into those types of activities which will prove to be most productive of increasing return during the technological and social revolutions of the future.

Notes

1. Assuming no change in the extent to which the nation's capital and labor is employed in some form of production.
2. This article was written and submitted before December 7, 1941. [Editor of the *Journal*]
3. L. M. Fraser. *Economic Thought and Language* (London, 1937), p. 210 and note.
4. *Ibid.*, note.
5. Parker Thomas Moon, *Imperialism and World Politics* (New York, 1926), p. 174.
6. The term protection rent seems preferable to the term protection profit because this element in income arises so largely from conditions which are beyond the

control of the individual entrepreneur and are unaffected by his ability as a business manager. Admittedly the analogy to land rent is imperfect. Land rent normally refers to what an entrepreneur pays for the use of land, whereas protection rent does not refer to what an entrepreneur pays for protection, for that payment is here called protection cost. In the case outlined in the text, the protection rent is paid by the consumer; it is what he pays to secure the offering of the producer whose offering is marginal by reason of high protection costs.

If we look at protection rent from the point of view of the nation, instead of looking at it as in the text above from the point of view of individual enterprises, we may say that protection rent *for a nation* arises from the geographical or cultural conditions which make the production of protection easier for one nation than for another. These conditions may be called gifts of nature or gifts of history. Whether the protection rent will be collected by the government or will be passed on to private enterprises depends, as is indicated below in note 10, on the form of government.

7. Frank William Taussig, *Some Aspects of the Tariff Question* (Cambridge, Mass., 1915), Chaps. iv and v. The protection rent was, to a certain extent, a result of the strategic geographical position of the islands.

8. H. Kretschmayr, *Geschichte von Venedig* (Gotha, 1905), I, 361–64; Adolf Schaube, *Handelsgeschichte der romanischen Völker des Mittelmeergebiets bit zum Ende der Kreuzzüge* (Munich and Berlin, 1906), pp. 226, 229. For the full story of Venetian-Byzantine relations see Kretschmayr, I, Chaps. vii and viii; Schaube, pp. 19–25, 223–47; Wilhelm von Heyd, *Histoire du commerce du levant au moyen dge* (Leipzig, 1886), I, 116–20, and Richard Heynen, *Zur Entstehung des Kupitalismus in Venedig* (Stuttgart and Berlin, 1905), Chaps. iii–v.

9. Stewart L. Mims, *Colbert's West India Policy* (New Haven, 1912).

10. The possibilities are clarified by considering the two 'ideal types' of states contrasted by A. De Viti de Marco, *Principii di economia finanziaria* (Turin, 1934), pp. 12–19. In the 'ideal' popular state, in which all groups freely compete to arrive at power so that all equally shape the financial decisions of the government in their interests, the costs of protection for private enterprises would be equal to the cost to the government of producing their protection. In the 'ideal' absolute state, or monopolistic state as De Viti there calls it, in which one man or one ruling class determines the financial decisions of the state entirely in their own interest, the government's monopoly of protection would be fully exploited. In the latter case the amount collected is not limited by the shape of the demand curve, since protection is a necessity, but it may be restrained by the danger that too high a tribute will stimulate attempts to break the monopoly, i.e., will attract invaders, stimulate smuggling, or provoke insurrection.

11. If a ruling class collects more tribute and, while thus making its position more enviable, spends its added income on luxuries, it is more likely to be overthrown by invasion or insurrection. It has, in this sense, good reason to spend its increased income on armies or police forces. If it does so, the cost of production of protection in that society is thereby increased. Accordingly, the higher the tribute paid to a ruling class, especially a ruling class of military traditions, the higher is likely to be the cost of producing protection. Escapes from this vicious circle have come through the fact that most states have not been ruled simply by one all-powerful ruling class.

12. This does not allow adequately, I confess, either for the directly received pains of fear, anxiety, or wounds, nor for the directly received pleasures of those who found

satisfactions in killing and glory. Except when soldiers are hired for war in a free labor market, how do these satisfactions or dissatisfactions manifest themselves in action in such a way as to be measurable in prices or wages? Perhaps, even if they were reflected in the price of mercenaries, the pleasure one man may take in killing should not be counted part of the total satisfactions which form national income, but the pain caused by wounds should be counted as diminution of the total satisfactions? The question emphasizes the inability of economic analysis to deal with the relative worth of various satisfactions except in money terms and the resulting limitations of the meaning of national income as commonly used and as used here. Cf. Alfred Marshall, *Principles of Economics* (8th ed.; London, 1936), pp. 14–25, 57–60, 76.

13. Although the tariff differentials were 4 per cent or 10 per cent, many more than one tariff were added to the price of wares sold during a year's trading.
14. Stewart L. Mims, *Colbert's West India Policy;* Charles Wolsey Cole. *Colbert and a Century of French Mercantilism* (New York, 1939).
15. The Portuguese policy and particularly its effect on pepper prices is presented more fully in Chap. 22, above.
16. A. H. Lybyer, 'The Ottoman Turks and the Routes of Oriental Trade,' *English Historical Review*, XXX (1915), 586.
17. See Chapter 2, above.
18. *Epocas de Portugal economico* (Lisbon, 1929), p. 155; also, pp. 118–31.
19. Girolamo Priuli, *I diarii* (Vol. II; Bologna, 1933), in *Rerum Italicarum scriptores*, 2d ed.; II, Tom XXIV, Part III, 156.
20. The motive of the Portuguese king may have been to add a new title to his name as João de Barros implies, *Da Asia* (Lisbon, 1727), Decada I, Part II, Libro VI. Cap. I. pp. 8–9; but this discussion is concerned with results of historic actions not with the motives.
21. Mims, *Colbert's West India Policy*, p. 339.
22. *Colbert and a Century of French Mercantilism*, I, 523.
23. *Principles of Economics*, p. 672.

COMMENTARY ON LANE

Frederic Chapin Lane (1900–1984) was an economic historian, best known for his work on Venice in the fourteenth and fifteenth centuries. The piece reprinted here is one of his very rare forays outside of his discipline, published in 1942 in the *Journal of Social Philosophy and Jurisprudence*.[1]

It is precisely because of Lane's expertise as an economic historian that this piece is particularly interesting, in fact one could say that Lane is putting forward one of the earliest efforts to elaborate an economic analysis of politics, pre-dating the rational choice model elaborated by Anthony Downs in his classic *An Economic Theory of Democracy*.[2]

Lane is interested in the functions performed by the state. He argues that economic history has failed to appreciate the extent to which the use of violence by the state is part of the domain of economics. Lane believes that the use of violence ought to be considered a productive activity, since the use and control of violence by the state is the means by which economic output is generated.

Of course there is nothing new in suggesting that violence is often used as a means to secure an economic benefit. Centuries of wars and plunder are testimony to the economic incentives spurring violence. But what makes Lane's analysis particularly original is the emphasis he places on the state's crucial function of protection, not aggression: 'force is not only used in plundering but also in preventing plundering, and a government which maintains law and order is rendering a service in return for the payment it collects'.

The concept of protection needs closer analysis. From an economic point of view, protection is a means of production: 'every economic enterprise needs and pays for protection, protection against the destruction or armed seizure of its capital and the forceful disruption of its labor'. Protection rent is therefore a fundamental cost of production, to be compared with traditional concepts such as wages, interest and land rent.[3]

Governments deal in protection; 'In highly organized societies the production of this utility, protection, is one of the functions of a special association or enterprise called government.' As Lane explains, protection costs can be either defensive or offensive. National defensive protection costs include what is spent by a nation for the defence of the economic enterprises of its own members, while offensive protection costs include what a nation spends in raising the protection costs of competing enterprises of other nations. Economic prosperity is achieved by a combination of minimizing the costs of protection, or protection rent, to its own members, while increasing the protection rent for its competitors.

Lane's work is important because, by looking at violence through economic lenses, he is able to explain both the reason why nation-states evolved as they did, and their increasing monopoly of the use of violence within a territory. Lane is also keen to remind us that there is a lot more to state violence than waging wars as a way of securing economic resources. As Lane explains, military victories added more to national income when used to gain protection rent than when used to gain booty or extract tribute.[4]

Notes and further reading

1. Two other essays on violence by Frederic Lane worth reading are: 'Economic Consequences of Organized Violence', *The Journal of Economic History*, Vol. XVIII, No. 4, December 1958, and 'National Wealth and Protection Costs', in F. C. Lane, *Venice and History*, Baltimore, MD: The Johns Hopkins University Press, 1966.
2. A. Downs, *An Economic Theory of Democracy*, New York: Harper & Row, 1957.
3. On the concept of protection in the economic analysis of the mafia in Russia, see Federico Varese, *The Russian Mafia*, Oxford: Oxford University Press, 2001.
4. For a more recent economic analysis of violence, by another distinguished economic historian, see Robert H. Bates, *Prosperity and Violence*, New York: W. W. Norton, 2001.

3
Violence and the Western Political Tradition

Sheldon S. Wolin

Western political systems have sought to concentrate, and hence increase, the instruments of violence in the hands of the state and to diminish the means of violence available to private groups. Three basic approaches have been put forward: the 'disguise of violence,' the introduction of a 'mediator' and the creation of a 'science of violence.' One of today's critical problems is that all three approaches have steadily lost their efficacy and appeal.

Man is not unique among the animals in resorting to violence or in organizing groups to enhance his striking power and his ability to inflict pain and injury. Other animals employ force to overcome fear or to slake desire; animals, too, will hunt in packs. Man's unique talent is his capacity for systematically experimenting with violence and for justifying the results. He alone has devised a wide assortment of methods for inflicting violence and a subtle scale for indicating the degrees and shades of violence that time and experience have shown to be most effective for controlling the behavior and attitudes of other men. To man alone belongs the ability to compose elaborate systems of religious values, political ideologies and scientific myths that, by the beauty of their poetry and the cleverness of their reasoning, have succeeded over long periods of time in legitimizing violence and concealing its otherwise ugly profile. At the same time, long experience has taught men how to establish and refine an ingenious maze of political and social practices or institutions which enables collectivities to gain in an indirect and circuitous way the same ends that may be, and often are, attained by the crudities of force and violence.

Centuries of exposure to law and order have bred habits of civility, obviating the need for crude applications of coercion. The very extension of civilization has come to be identified with the progressive abolition of violence, or, more accurately, with the substitution of various forms of authority, such as the law, the political authority of a parliament, or the decision of a judicial tribunal. However, experience teaches that each of these authorities, no matter how benign or democratic, is capable of dropping its stately and measured demeanor when it feels threatened; it will lash out at its critics, enemies or tormentors in an unexpected display of force and violence. The policeman, whom popular folklore may depict as the tolerant, half-amused and kindly friend to the tipsy reveller, suddenly turns on the sexual deviate with fury or, in sexual excitement and hatred, drags the student from a political demonstration and down the steps of a building ironically named the Hall of Justice.

That we speak of 'brute' force or 'naked' violence, however, suggests that Western societies have aimed not so much at eliminating violence as at concealing or softening its exercise and restricting extreme instances of force to a marginal existence. Moreover, the political revolutions of the seventeenth and eighteenth centuries have impressed on the modern world the dogma that the only legitimate authority is one that rests on the consent of the governed. The triumph of this idea has further contributed to disguising the amount of violence directed at society, for it somehow strikes us as incongruous that we should even think of the lawful exercise of power by a democratic authority as an act of violence. In this respect the West has fully absorbed Rousseau's teaching that freedom and authority can be reconciled if the citizens of a political society are persuaded that the power controlling them is their own; since one does not naturally think in terms of self-coercion, the power of a democratic government over its members is, by the wonderful alchemy of political belief, transformed into 'self-government' – an internal directive we give ourselves, rather than the coercion of an outside or alien power.

In the history of Western political philosophy, several writers have taken the view that the state represents nothing but organized force, a theory whereby the history of Western political institutions is but a chronicle of the several ingenious ways that coercion has been disguised by laws, constitutions, judicial guarantees and civil rights. This conception of the state is at least as old as Thrasymacus's assertion of it in Plato's *Republic*. It reappears in Bodin in the sixteenth century, Marx in the nineteenth, and in the works of the greatest sociologist of our century, Max Weber. We cannot pause to criticize this view, but only to point out that force and violence are not always identical, although the two may share certain common attributes. As does force, violence implies the application of power over unwilling objects, but, once this has been stated, the differences between the two begin to crowd in on our attention.

If we examine these, we may better understand the political significance of violence. In the first place, violence denotes an intensification of what we 'normally' expect a particular power to be. Thus it is not unusual for high winds to accompany a gale but, when the winds attain an unexpected intensity beyond what we usually associate with storms, we substitute 'hurricane' or 'tornado' for 'gale,' to convey its violent scale. Similarly, when the debates of a legislative assembly exceed the normal level of controversy, the proceedings are described as violent.

In the second place, violence possesses another characteristic closely related to the unexpected, its eruptive or unpredictable quality. Force and concentrated power are not strangers to human society; society learns to tolerate them by making them familiar. It does not come as a surprise when policemen and soldiers employ coercion or when punishment follows on the violation of legal rules. It does genuinely alarm us, however, when force appears unexpectedly, that is, when our previous expectations or conditioning have not prepared us for what occurs: the teacher suddenly resorting to a box on the ear, the benign father unexpectedly brandishing a club or the army officers of a Western ally torturing natives. In each instance the authority figures are expected to have to employ force at certain times, but we designate their acts as violent because the amount or degree of force does not seem commensurate with the circumstances or with what we have come to accept as the characteristic style of modern teachers, parents and soldiers. Accordingly, the language of politics has described as arbitrary or capricious the authority that uses legitimate powers in an unpredictable, that is, violent, way. This is also why the champions of legality have always distrusted vague delegations of power and ill-defined discretionary authority; they have believed that discretionary authority tempts those in power to depart from normal procedures and to relax ordinary safeguards.

Third, violence implies that an unusual amount of destruction will accompany a designated act. The exercise of authority in enforcing laws or maintaining order may entail some destruction, but we do not habitually specify such acts as violent unless they exceed the requirements of the circumstances. In that case, significantly, we speak, not of 'needless' violence but, with a suggestion of redundancy, 'needless violence'; that is, we differentiate between the application of force or compulsion ordinarily encountered in certain situations and what seems excessive. Further on I shall try to show that a wholesale transformation has occurred in our way of viewing the acceptable limits of destruction.

In the long political history of the West a special relationship has obtained between the state, or political order, and the application of violence. In retrospect it seems an altogether pragmatic occurrence that force has been put at the disposal of political authorities to enable them to protect the members of society from external threats and internal disorders. All utilitarian views of political authority, and this one is no exception, overlook a highly significant aspect of the development that transformed violence into an accepted technique of political rule. To begin with, the use of violence to maim or destroy human lives has always been viewed with abhorrence in the Western tradition. Although the political order has been clothed in authority and sanctified by legality, its defense of order has inevitably compelled it to commit acts traditionally regarded as the height of wrongdoing when committed by private persons.

A brief history of homicide in ancient Greece shows clearly what is involved when the political order assumes the burden of applying violence to wrongdoers, and how the assumption of this burden has resulted in a highly significant change whereby the legacy of guilt and shame has been lifted from private souls and handed over to an impersonal public authority.

Prior to the fourth century B.C. the act of homicide, whether intentional or not, was held to be a matter for the relatives of the victim. They were obliged to bring the accused to trial and, if he were found guilty, to 'wreak their vengeance violently on him.'[i] Homicide was abhorred because of the belief that the act defiled the killer and, through him, polluted the entire community.[ii,iii] 'Punish the murderer and cleanse the city,' runs a line from an ancient writer.[iv] Thus pollution *(miasma)* demanded purification *(katharsis)* and violence was the accepted ritual for achieving it. This belief in the cleansing or purifying quality of violence has remained a persistent strand in Western thought. The seventeenth century Puritan fanatic Richard Sibbes[v] could advocate 'a holy violence' to rid England of a corrupt religious-political order; Saint-Just,[vi] the theoretician of the French revolutionary terror, regarded violence as a means for purifying a political and social order despoiled by the old regime; in the early twentieth century, Sorel advocated proletarian violence to destroy the decadent bourgeois order, hoping that its exercise would ennoble the proletariat and make them worthy of triumph.

The assignment of punishment to the political order served to replace private vengeance with a public process. It also did away with the passion of vengeance and of the feeling of guilt and shame that followed execution of the accused. Yet the mystique that has surrounded political authority for so many centuries and has only recently begun to wane suggests that the substitution of a public for a private executioner has not eliminated the profound feeling that pollution threatens a community whenever there has been a murder. Instead, authority's burden is that it undertakes to do what is abhorrent to mankind; it shoulders the feelings of guilt that accompany the taking of life.[1] In the past, the impressive pomp of coronation rites and other solemn ceremonies of investiture were meant not only as symbolic ceremonies to legitimize authority but also as expiation rites to absolve the power holder of the defilement and pollution that would otherwise afflict both himself and the community when he was required, as he would inevitably be, to kill, maim and destroy.

Although the tradition of political theory has been a rationalistic one and most writers have sought other grounds for authority than the mystique suggested above, they have not been less sensitive to the fact that political authority will always have awesome powers at its disposal. The inevitable necessity to kill and destroy has been given its myths of absolution by the theorist as well. Violence has been justified in the service of the Good (Plato), or for evangelizing an obdurate world, rooting out heresy and implanting the true religion (Christian writers), or for ushering in a communist utopia or *das dritte Reich*. It is also important to note that thinkers as diverse as Plato, Machiavelli and Lenin have been emphatic, almost to the point of desperation, in insisting that anyone who would shoulder the burden of political authority should be exposed to a rigorous and prolonged education that would instill an ethic of selflessness and extirpate all traces of petty personal interests. All these writers realized that the dispensing of violence was far too serious an undertaking to be left to the untutored, however sincere they might be.

Historical development has not always taken counsel from philosophers, and it is not surprising that the relationship between the state and violence has owed rather less to theories than to the steady and unrelenting effort of rulers, or their agents, to establish a monopoly over the instruments of violence. Following the slow breakdown of the Roman Empire after the fifth century A.D., a complex and infinite fragmentation of power occurred. This condition persisted into the Middle Ages; everywhere in Europe the primary concern of political authorities was to maintain and, if possible, extend the precarious reign of law and order. This required an incessant campaign to eliminate the pockets of violence throughout Western Europe. The construction of the national, centralized state was the result of an unrelenting war, carried on over centuries, to divest local and parochial magnates of their authority to apply violence in their own bailiwicks. Feudalism had been not only a system of land tenure and a status structure of rights and duties but also a decentralized system for maintaining order. Feudal lords were expected to enforce law, allot punishment, levy taxes and maintain their own fighting forces.

Although it is easy to exaggerate the shortcomings of this system of governance, its absurdities seem blatant because we are the heirs of a long tradition of thought and practice which has accustomed us to believe that political governance automatically implies some authority or agency responsible for overall control, for enforcing and maintaining common laws and a uniform system of justice and for providing for the common defense. Yet, it is more illuminating to consider the modern centralized state with its concentrated ownership of the means of violence and compulsion, not as the inevitable and 'natural' successor to feudalism, but rather as an experiment in the centralized control of the instruments of violence. Feudalism had been an ill-fated attempt to provide a decentralized order without either the techniques of general control or the consciousness of a 'general' order transcending the local community. Still, the political lesson it taught was highly valuable, even if only in a negative sense. The lesson was that coercion and violence were not necessarily diminished if power was scattered and dispersed; the existence of many centers of control and of a variety of legal systems tended to increase the incidence of force. The very lack of system contributed to the unpredictability and inefficiency of political authorities.

To replace the confusions of feudalism, national rulers set about destroying the old instrumentalities of coercion and control. Private armies and bands of retainers were abolished; manorial courts were squeezed out of existence; local bodies of law were absorbed or overridden; local institutions, such as the jury or the sheriff, were geared to a slowly developing system of national institutions and bureaucracies. Although the pace of these developments differed in each of the major Western countries, the direction of events was unmistakable: The national political authorities were intent on establishing a monopoly over the forms of violence, or, stated differently, the exercise of violence was being converted into a national function. Once the means of violence devolved into the hands of the political order, systematic efforts were launched to develop trained specialists in the exercise and application of violence; energy, resources, and money began to flow in the direction of research into ever more effective and powerful means of destruction. In the end, the political order came to be the unchallenged master of violence, empowered *de facto* and *de jure* to dispense force on a scale as large as the interests and protection of society seemed to require.

The next important phase in the development of the theory and practice of violence was the attempt to delimit the exercise of force within the boundaries of national societies and, simultaneously, to eliminate the unpredictable element that seemed stubbornly to cling to all political power. For convenience, this phase may be called the Age of Liberal (or Constitutional) Democracy. It begins approximately in 1640, when the forces of parliamentarism and Puritanism first challenged the monarchy in England. It closes in 1940 with constitutional democracy fighting for its existence in a world already searching for radically different forms of political life.

The theory and practice of constitutional democracy have signified a concerted effort to restrict the application of violence by setting defined limits to power, by insisting on the observance of regularized procedures and by establishing strict methods for rendering those in power accountable for their actions. The paraphernalia of constitutionalism – the rule of law, due process, the separation of powers, checks and balances and the system of individual rights, with its significant emphasis on privileges and 'immunities' – have not eliminated power, but they have contributed to its regularization, to eradicating that unpredictable, sheerly destructive quality that epitomizes all violence.

Despite the success of constitutionalism in delimiting the role of violence in political life, the twentieth century has witnessed unprecedented experiments with violence. The number of victims, the magnitude of destruction and the ingenuity of the instruments are without historical parallel. This is the century of secret police, concentration camps, gas chambers, labor camps and the calculated 'liquidation' of specified classes, races and whole populations. Nor is the history of violence merely a chronicle of the wickedness of tyrants: Nagasaki and Hiroshima are the unforgettable burden of democracies as, on a smaller scale, are Montgomery, Johannesburg and Algeria. Moreover, there are some nagging doubts that the political order, for all its powerful weapons and dedicated, tight-lipped agents of the law, has wholly succeeded in eradicating private concentrations of violence. In daylight many of our city streets are busy avenues where human energy and motion are directed along orderly lines, but in darkness these same streets may temporarily lapse into a Hobbesian state of nature, a *bellum omnium contra omnes*, where gang warfare erupts or the innocent citizen is beaten, robbed or murdered. Or, again, side by side with the municipal government of duly elected officials, trained civil servants and all the other processes of 'public' government will exist another *imperium* now called 'the syndicate,' a secret and ill-defined system of governance with its own authoritative system of legality and enforcement, its own set of relations with the respectable elements above the surface.

It would be misleading to conclude from these illustrations that the problem is simply to devise more ingenious methods for controlling the unprecedented potential for violence now in existence. Techniques constitute a proper solution only when they are fitted to the problem. The changes of the past few centuries in Western political values and in certain cultural assumptions have been so profound that, unless we understand something of their nature, our techniques will be adapted to dealing with symptoms rather than causes. To grasp the contemporary problem of violence we need a somewhat unorthodox starting point. Instead of visualizing the problem as one whereby violence is directed at society, it might be fruitful to ask: Do the social and political forms of any given age constitute a particular method for adjusting to violence? Is it possible that political and social institutions help to establish a particular level of sensitivity toward violence so that individuals exposed to different types of political systems will differ markedly in their mode of adjustment to violence and their capacity to withstand it?

We often read documents from the past which reveal the sufferings and ordeals of various peoples and most of us, I suspect, have been astonished either by their capacities for enduring cruelty or matter-of-fact ways of inflicting it. At other times we may even have felt superior in reading about a nation or group that could not 'take it' or about some political leader's deep revulsion at having to break heads rather than count them.

With this rough conception of a 'tolerance level for violence,' let me advance a highly tentative observation apropos its political manifestation in contemporary Western societies: The *intensity* of violence in certain instances has increased, aside from the new scientific weapons of destruction, while our capacity for enduring violence has diminished. The intensity of violence has increased largely because of the effectiveness of established political institutions, practices and methods for combating violence. Owing to ingenious modern means of stamping out or containing private potentials for force and violence, civil life is no longer 'nasty, brutish, and short.' The police, bureaucracy, the courts, legislatures and executive agencies, together with the publicity given wrongdoing by modern communication media, have all contrived to restrict the unauthorized application of force and thereby to diminish the number of violent unpredictabilities in individual lives. In the same way, as has already been noted, the devices and practices of constitutional government have worked to reduce the unpredictabilities of state action. (For the classic, scholarly discussion of constitutionalism, see McIlwain.[viii]) One paradoxical result of these protective devices has been a magnification of the amount of force or violence needed for successful illegal activity: The protective walls thrown around society and the individual have proved so effective that the amount of violence needed to breach them is unprecedented. Crime must be organized into a vast imperium with its own resources, authority structure and even its own foreign relations. Society's defenses have been so strengthened that criminal elements must develop extraordinary power and cunning merely to attain a 'successful' level of criminality.[2]

Not only do illegal activities require a greater level of violence; our contemporary ideas of what constitutes a war reflect the same raised and intensified conception of the normal. That we demand more violence of war is evident in the slightly derogatory connotation of the term 'brush-war,' a so-called small-scale military operation, a sudden flare-up, which, hopefully, can be contained and prevented from spreading and which, prayerfully, may be fought with so-called conventional weapons. Yet the idea of such a war reveals how enlarged is our notion of the 'proper' scale for violence, proper with respect to our criteria for characterizing a specific outbreak of violence as a genuine war. Military operations in areas the size of Korea, Laos and the Congo have been considered small-scale. This implies that our conception of the truly abnormal and unpredictable has become so grotesquely enlarged that only continental, or intercontinental or even interplanetary warfare conducted with unimaginably devastating weapons and erupting with total surprise could produce violence of sufficient scope, intensity and unexpectedness to fulfill our stipulated criteria.

Man's attempt to violence also has its paradoxical side: The more successful a society is in restricting both public and private forms of violence, the more difficulty it has in coping with or enduring violence when it does crop up. This is partly because the protective devices of civilized society have succeeded in removing for most of its members the experience of violence. When violence does occur, fear is intensified by the element of the unknown. Our capacity to cope with violence has also been affected by the 'refinement' or 'hygenic fastidiousness' cultivated for several centuries. Oddly enough our century of brutality has also been the time when society has gone to notable lengths in shielding a substantial part of its members from some of the elemental facts of the human condition. All ugliness and hurt are whisked away before we can contemplate or grasp their meaning: The sick are quickly dispatched to hospitals, the incurables to nursing homes, retarded children to special institutions, the dead are consigned to morticians who are now experts in death rather than simple burial. Thus a whole subculture presided over by specialists and technicians has been created to protect us from contact with modes of our existence that earlier ages had experienced first-hand – it is only among lower-class immigrant groups that death is 'celebrated.'

By its very effectiveness, modern society has rendered man supremely unprepared for the ugly and violent things that inevitably succeed in penetrating the most ingenious of social warning systems. It has been said apropos of the experience of the French Resistance during World War II that men were not afraid to die, only afraid to suffer, a theme elaborated in Sartre's short story, *The Wall*. The implication is that men still expected to die, but deliberate cruelty and torture were assumed to be a thing of the remote past. One reason for the effectiveness of totalitarian systems in Italy and Germany was that deliberate and controlled violence was almost totally unexpected; when it was applied by the recognized agents of authority, the population's perplexity and bewilderment contributed greatly to successful manipulation by the new masters. When torture and sheer brutality are perpetrated by the very authority that previously has protected men against such acts, then society loses all sense of the painfully developed, centuries-old distinctions among authoritative acts, sheer force and unexpected violence.

The merest mention of totalitarianism and contemporary conceptions of warfare suggests that profound changes have occurred in Western man's way of thinking about violence. Obviously, the basic criteria are no longer wholly meaningful. The changes in our attitudes have been almost as dramatic as the changes in the technology of violence. Modern man's view of violence differs almost as greatly from pre-modern man's view as the nuclear warhead differs from the blunderbuss. These differences can be reduced to two general points. First, man is now prepared to look upon violence and its application with unparalleled detachment and scientific neutrality. This can be clearly seen by comparing Herman Kahn's recent book,[ix] the *locus classicus* for this set of attitudes, with Raymond Aron's *On War*,[x] which expresses a more traditional concern. Second, all discussions are colored by the growing assumption that, no matter what decision may be reached to localize the incidence of violence, the potential range of application is limitless.[3] The detachment with which violence is now viewed and the limitlessness of its scope are united by a common outlook. Detachment implies a spirit of looking at things with a clarity undistorted by ideologies, creeds or parochial loyalties; limitless violence implies that neither natural, nor theological, nor moral nor political barriers appreciably limit the application of forms of violence whose actual limits are still unknown. These two points require further elaboration.

Linguistic developments can illuminate important changes in the way a culture understands a persistent phenomenon. 'Violence' derives from the Latin *violentia*, which meant 'vehemence,' a passionate and uncontrolled force, the opposite of a calculated exertion of power.[4] Moreover, an ancient and enduring meaning of the word is that of a force working to pervert (rather than divert) some object, natural or human, from its 'natural' course of development or from the way it would otherwise express itself. Traces of this meaning are evident in the statement, 'This interpretation does violence to the text,' which implies that the meaning usually associated with a given passage, what we might call its 'proper' meaning, has been perverted, that is, 'injured' or prevented from communicating its accustomed meaning. Finally, the verb *violare*, which means 'to treat with violence,' carried the additional notion of exceeding some limit or norm. These meanings are reflected in our own verb 'to violate.'[5]

Classical thought of the fifth and fourth centuries B.C. abhorred any act that exceeded customary standards of moderation, or the mean. Accordingly, an act of violence was considered a breach of those natural and moral limits that the good man was duty-bound to observe. The finest expression of this position was the work of the political philosopher Aristotle, who had tutored Alexander the Great. Few military conquerors could equal Alexander's record of devastation or match his genuis for the organization of force and violence. Aristotle pondered long about this new breed of man who went about destroying old societies and creating new ones, who somehow combined a genius for smashing with an uncommon skill at uniting diverse peoples. What was the relation, Aristotle wondered, between the impulse for destruction and the traditional political impulse toward order. Beneath Alexander's restless urge for domination Aristotle perceived an unnattural passion that perverted the noble calling of the *politikos* or statesman. Mastery, Aristotle insisted in his *Politics* (VII. ii. 1324b 32), must never be confused with true statesmanship; there is something deeply wrong when a profession such as statesmanship is so practiced as to countenance deliberate killing and needless destruction as the legitimate measures of a skilled art. The unprecedented success of a conqueror does not place his acts beyond the limits set by nature and morality (VII. ii. 1324b 26). It is fundamentally wrong and unnatural that the conqueror employs violence to degrade a particular species, the political animal, which nature had not intended for domination or subjection. 'One does not hunt men to furnish a banquet or a festival: one hunts what is meant to be hunted for that purpose ...' (VII. ii 1324b 38–41).

The conviction that natural limits to violence existed and that violence was inherently wrong[6] persisted to the sixteenth century. The same cultural and historical forces that shattered the Aristotelian-Thomistic view of the cosmos and turned to reconstructing it in the name of mathematics and science were simultaneously at work in the field of political theory. Machiavelli was to political theory what Galileo was to modern physics, a dispeller of illusions who passionately wished to confront things 'as they really were.' Once Machiavelli's *Prince* achieved notoriety, the whole course of political theory was changed. For our purposes the most important change affected the outlook of the political theorists, who ceased to view violence as an expression of passion. They sought instead to treat it as a measured application of force, the study of which should aspire to be a precise science and the actual exercise of which should be in the hands of men of cool and calculating temperaments. Machiavelli had hoped that a true 'economy of violence' could be achieved – a system of maxims and rules of action that would assist rulers in adjusting the application of violence to the precise requirements of a situation. If the exercise of violence could be invested with truly surgical precision, it might be possible to confine injury, death and destruction to an absolute minimum. As envisaged by Machiavelli, the science of violence presupposed an extraordinary detachment on the part of both the theoretician and the political actor, a detachment insulating them from contact with the pain of those who were the objects of violence. This outlook was present in Machiavelli's *The Prince*, Chapter VIII; there he distinguishes between 'good' and 'bad' forms of cruelty, counseling that a ruler should prepare an inventory of necessary injuries before he seizes power and then quickly commit them so that his subjects 'may taste their bitterness but a short time.' Benefits, on the other hand, should be doled out slowly so that subjects will live in constant hope of future enjoyments and hence be submissive.

These changing attitudes toward violence were accompanied by still another, albeit quieter and less spectacular, revolution in thought, namely a drastic reduction in the estimate of what force and compulsion could achieve. Although there were exceptions,[7] the major political theorists of the seventeenth and eighteenth centuries, those who left the strongest imprint on later thinking, believed unanimously that mankind could not be improved by force. Citizens could not be terrorized into virtue or saintliness, nor could societies be forcibly transformed into prosperous and benevolent utopias. Although such theorists as Harrington, Locke, Montesquieu, Rousseau and Jefferson disagreed on a large number of political matters, they all agreed that violence could not regenerate man or society. This conclusion may seem a considerable advance over the position maintained by religious fanatics of the sixteenth and seventeenth century who had proclaimed the purifying effects of violence on the soul.

A more revealing contrast is provided by comparing the older views of Augustine or Plato with those of the modern writers mentioned above. Both the great Bishop of Hippo and the Greek philosopher justified the application of force to induce correct belief, yet a careful examination of both arguments shows that, however deplorable the policy they advocated, neither writer believed that force could actually create belief. Each believed that man was endowed with a nature, and that that nature ought to be perfected. And because each believed so profoundly in the perfectibility of man or, in Christian terms, his salvation, each was prepared to countenance what each had plainly and publicly rejected on numerous occasions, the use of force to correct belief. Both vacillated on the issue because they were firmly convinced that any exercise of violence constituted a threat to the inherent structure of man and that any sustained program of violence risked reducing man to a dehumanized and brutalized condition.[8]

But, beginning with Hobbes in the seventeenth century, the assumption that man had a structure and that this structure was known began to weaken. There were many reasons for this *crise de conscience*, as Paul Hazard has called it, but surely not the least important was the change that occurred in the implication of 'knowing.' Human nature, as men 'knew' it before the revolution of modern science, had come down in the form of the Christian conception of man. But the decline in religious conviction that had begun in the seventeenth century was accompanied by a new conception of what it meant to 'know.' The old structure of man that had become familiar through a reading of the Old and New Testaments, by listening to countless sermons in a thousand drafty churches and by an overwhelmingly religious system of education was abolished. But the new way of knowing inspired by modern science seemed less confident of its ability to 'know' the structure of man, much less to state with anything like the fervor of Christianity wherein the inherent value of that structure consisted. At the same time, the new way of knowing concentrated on understanding man through a very different method – in terms of his behavior. Although the psychology of the last hundred years has begun restoring a sense of structure to man, this new way of 'knowing' has not, and perhaps cannot, supply what the old way possessed, that is, a sense of the intrinsic value of man's internal structure. In the absence of such a belief, there is a corresponding absence of a sense of limit. The inhibitions that led Plato and Augustine to recoil from a policy of loosing violence upon the soul may still exist; if so, it is because we are still living off the moral capital of an earlier age. The precariousness of our condition is due, not to the growth of experimentation or even manipulation, but to the fact that these activities, scientific and political, are carried on in an atmosphere in which the sense of a structural limit to human personality and behavior has become steadily weaker.

The same movement toward 'limitlessness' and the same loss of a sense of structure, both of which encouraged a mentality favoring the unlimited application of violence, have reappeared in modern political and social theories. Greek and medieval political thought had been reared on the assumption that society possessed a natural structure, a 'constitution' or *politeuma*. Greek and medieval writers were aware that a particular political system might articulate its life virtuously or vulgarly,[9] but the determination whether a particular political system was adjudged bad centered around the question of whether a regime represented a 'perversion' of its particular form, that is, whether rule by one man was a genuine species of monarchy or the perversion of tyranny. Most of these earlier writers also believed that human action could assist, or inhibit or prevert the structure inherent in a given political form. More important, they also believed that a stateman was justified in establishing a new political order only when the old had proved itself beyond a doubt to be a perversion or monstrosity. Ancient writers were so sensitive to the structure of a polity that they were loath to prescribe a total plan for a new society except for the launching of a colony. Almost to a man they shied away from prescribing powerful measures for the reform of an old and established society, so great was their fear of injuring the inherent structure.[10]

Modern political thought has largely surrendered the conception of society informed by a natural structure. Beginning with Machiavelli and extending through Hobbes and Locke, gaining additional momentum from the French Revolution and the revolutionary movement of the nineteenth and twentieth centuries, the conviction has grown that society is an artifact, a pragmatic creation that men can design to meet their needs or wishes; there is no inherent structural principle in society standing in the way of what men want.[11] Once men ceased to think in terms of 'the nature of society,' it became increasingly easy to justify the use of violence to *create* a new society: Since society possessed no enduring nature, violence was being used merely to replace one contrivance by another. On this basis revolutionary parties were organized to serve as avowed instruments of violence, the striking force for inaugurating a new and totally unprecedented state of affairs. The modern theory of revolution thus formed an exact parallel to the modern theory of the individual: Neither individual nor society possesses an inherent structure, a nature articulated over time. Neither has what used to be called a natural biography or history. It follows that both the individual and society are pretty much what we choose to make of them; neither can be said to contain an inherent principle of protest against the use of violence.

Finally, the whole notion of limit as a restraint on the violence of international conflicts has been all but destroyed. As has already been noted, the Greeks had rejected the notion that a conqueror could utilize any means of force against an enemy. The early Christians expressed the notion of limit by trying to establish a distinction between the just and the unjust war. Our own age has obliterated all of these distinctions, first, by ignoring the distinction between civilians and soldiers, home front and battle front, and, second, by tacitly abolishing all limits to the amount of force allowable in gaining victory. If Hiroshima is the symbol of limitless violence, it is not the *ultima Thule* beyond which no state will press its claim of justifiable violence.

Today little vitality remains in the idea that force is justifiable only to the extent that it is used to protect the common interest or well-being of society. This norm has ceased to operate as a limit because the 'interest of society' no longer coincides with either the geographic boundaries of society or the foreign commitments of a society. Today the claim to use violence to protect society has been extended far beyond the borders of national society and far beyond the traditional meaning of foreign commitments. Those claims now literally approach infinity. President Kennedy has recently proclaimed that the space program of the nation is 'firmly based upon the awareness that space competence is as essential for national security as it is for national growth.'[xi] The redefinition of national interest to include outer space inevitably includes the claim that violence in interstellar regions is justifiable in defending and advancing that interest. And, in the same way that national or even international boundaries no longer set limits to the justifiable province of violence, so the older belief that the application of force ought to be directed at lawbreakers or at an easily definable 'enemy' has also been replaced by a notion that is limitless.

In the past, the idea of force was based on the assumption that those who should be punished or even destroyed could be isolated – singled out from the rest of humanity. It is now accepted as rational political thinking to contemplate the possible destruction of all, or most, of the inhabitants of the globe and to project violence in a way unparalleled in human thought except in theological terms. It has often given sceptics wry amusement that the God of the Calvinists and the Augustinians should have been so omnipotent as to be able to punish Adam's original sin by transmitting it as an inherited and ineradicable taint to all his progeny from generation to generation. Yet the genetic destruction potentially present in modern instruments of violence makes today's political man as omnipotent as the God of Christian theology. Man, too, can inflict a taint on generations yet unborn; he, too, can create an apocalypse that will render the earth uninhabitable. It remains to be seen whether he can match God's promise that the Day of Judgement will find the earth uninhabitable for the sinners alone.

Notes

1. For some interesting examples of the same theme in primitive kingship, see Frazer's *The Golden Bough.*[vii]

    The theme of the burden of monarchy in its relation to violence is beautifully brought out in Shakespeare's *Hamlet* when the Prince asks a captain why the army is marching on Poland. The captain replies (IV. 4. 14.): 'We go to gain a little patch of ground/That hath no profit but the name.'

    Hamlet muses (IV. 4. 47.): '... while, to my shame, I see/The imminent death of twenty thousand men,/That for a fantasy and trick of fame/Go to their graves like beds. ...'

2. It would be interesting to compare contemporary juvenile gangs and underworld organization with the same phenomena in eighteenth century England, a period of relative social and political tranquillity wherein the great constitutional gains of the seventeenth century were consolidated. The streets of London were terrorized by young toughs, 'The Mohawks,' and the underworld was a well-known and

powerful element in London life; Gay's *Beggars' Opera* is, of course, one glimpse of this world.

3. 'Limitless' is more appropriate than 'unlimited' in this context. The latter presupposes a choice between the limited and the unlimited, whereas the former implies that modern violence in the form of war is inherently limitless, that is, we cannot control the form in which it is carried out.

4. See Cicero's *Philippics*, 12.11.26.

5. These meanings were also present in the Greek *bia*. See Thucydides' reference to 'violation of the constitution,' in *History of the Peloponnesian War*, VIII.53.

6. This is in contrast to the superficial view often encountered in contemporary discussions; this claims that power itself is not bad, it all depends on how it is used. The difficulty is that this assertion presupposes a moral judgment, namely, that power is neutral. This cannot be allowed for, as soon as one abandons high abstractions and deals with concrete instances, it becomes obvious that power always means the ability to coerce or to apply control over others. In technical language, the concept of power 'contains' the element of compulsion; we may disagree about its value or use, but it is not neutral.

7. These exceptions were almost wholly religious fanatics, such as the Fifth Monarchy Men in England. After 1650 they had ceased to be a significant factor in European politics.

8. Augustine's views were most carefully worked out in his *Epistles*, especially 87, 93, 97, 185. See also J. N. Figgis, *Political Aspects of St. Augustine's 'City of God,'* London, 1921, Lectures III, IV; G. Combès, *La doctrine politique d'Augustin*, Paris, 1927, pp. 330 ff. For Plato's views see *Laws* X. 907D–912D.

9. The sense of structure appears in the fondness for organic metaphors displayed by classical and medieval thought. For examples, see Plato, *Republic* V. 461–2; John of Salisbury, *Policraticus* V. ii; Aquinas, *De Reqimine Principum*, I.i.

   The concern with the way a political system articulated its life is reflected in the classical concern for distinguishing between 'good' and 'bad' constitutions. See Plato, *Republic*, VIII. 543A *et seq.*; Aristotle, *Politics*, III. 1278b 11 *et seq.*; Polybius, *The Histories*, VI. 1–9.

10. Plato was more ambivalent in his attitude toward violence. In *Epistle VII*, 331D, he rejects the use of force or revolutionary methods. In the *Politlcus*, 309A, he justifies the application of force to expel undesirable elements from the population. It should be noted however, that here and in other passages Plato always likened the ruler to a skilled technician. This suggests his concern to restrict to a minimum the inevitable use of violence.

11. The clearest expression of this viewpoint is to be found in Hobbes' *Leviathan*, especially the Introduction.

References

i. Jones, J. W. 1956. *The Law and Legal Theory of the Greeks*. Oxford University Press. New York. N.Y. : 250. See also R. J. Bonner and G. Smith. 1938. *The Administration of Justice from Homer to Aristotle*. University of Chicago Press. Chicago, Ill. 1: 15–56.

ii. Dodds, E. R. 1951. *The Greeks and the Irrational*. University of California Press. Berkeley and Los Angeles, Calif.: 35–43.

iii. Guthrie, W. K. C. 1955. *The Greeks and Their Gods*. Beacon Press. Boston, Mass.: 191ff.

48   *Violence: A Philosophical Anthology*

  v. Brauer, J. C. 1954. *Reflections on the Nature of English Puritanism.* Church History 22: 102.
 vi. Ollivier. A. 1954. *Saint-Just et la Force des Choses.* 8th ed. Paris. France.
vii. Frazer, J. G. 1958. *The Golden Bough.* single-volume ed. Macmillan. New York, N.Y. : 194ff.
viii. McIlwain, C. H. 1940. *Constitutionalism Ancient and Modern.* Cornell University Press. Ithaca, N.Y.
 ix. Kahn, H. 1960. *On Thermonuclear War.* Princeton University Press. Princeton, N.J.
  x. Aron, R. 1959. *On War.* Doubleday. Garden City, N.Y.
 xi. *The New York Times.* Feb. 1, 1962 : 3.

COMMENTARY ON WOLIN

Sheldon Wolin is best known in political theory for his book *Politics and Vision*, first published in 1960, where he defends a radical account of democracy.[1] In this article, written in 1962 at a time when the civil rights movement was gaining momentum, and pro-civil rights demonstrations were on the rise, Wolin casts a critical eye on the relationship between Western civilization and man's disposition towards violence.[2]

From the opening paragraph, where the reader is reminded of man's unique talent, namely 'his capacity for systematically experimenting with violence and for justifying the results', Wolin sets out to discredit the widely held belief in a direct correlation between the forward march of civilization and the diminution of brutality and violence. After all, as Wolin rightly reminds us: 'the twentieth century has witnessed unprecedented experiments with violence. The number of victims, the magnitude of destruction and the ingenuity of the instruments are without historical parallel. This is the century of secret police, concentration camps, gas chambers, labour camps and the calculated 'liquidation' of specified classes, races and whole populations.' And for those who might still hang on to their rose-tinted vision, objecting that the culprits of the worst violence of the twentieth century were tyrants, Wolin has an unpleasant wake-up call: 'Nagasaki and Hiroshima are the unforgettable burden of democracies as, on a smaller scale, are Montgomery, Johannesburg and Algeria.' This list could be updated to include the massacre of Mai Lai in Vietnam in 1968, Bloody Sunday in Northern Ireland in 1972, the US military backing of many brutal dictatorships in Latin America between the 1960s and the 1990s, and many other events.[3]

What Wolin finds particularly interesting about man's relationship to violence is his ability to justify it, legitimize it, and therefore disguise it to such an extent that we almost forget that it is everywhere around us. As Wolin explains: 'Western societies have aimed not so much at eliminating violence as at concealing or softening its exercise and restricting extreme instances of force to a marginal existence.'

Here Wolin suggests that there are important differences between the concepts of violence and force. Unlike the use of force, violence is unexpected, unpredictable, and involves an unusual amount of destruction. The theory and practice of constitutional democracy has gone a long way towards eliminating the unexpected, unpredictable and utterly destructive nature of violence. As a result, violence is now highly regulated, even hygienic, and therefore when it occurs it appears to us justified and legitimate. We seem unable to think of the lawful exercise of power by a democratic authority as an act of violence, even though that is exactly what it is.

The modern state has not only established a monopoly over the forms and use of violence, but the exercise of violence has been converted into a national function. Today we train specialists in the exercise and application of violence, and invest heavily into ever more effective methods of destruction: 'In the end, the political order came to be the unchallenged master of violence, empowered *de facto* and *de jure* to dispense force on a scale as large as the interests and protection of society seemed to require.' What we don't always realize is just how often democratic authorities make use of such violence: 'each of these authorities, no matter how benign or democratic, is capable of dropping its stately and measured demeanour when it feels threatened; it will lash out at its critics, enemies or tormentors in an unexpected display of force and violence.'

Notes and further reading

1. Sheldon Wolin, *Politics and Vision: Continuity and Innovation in Western Political Thought*, expanded edn, Princeton, NJ: Princeton University Press, 2004.
2. For a similar view, which reflects what could be called the 'fable of civilization', see John Keane, *Reflections on Violence*, London: Verso, 1996.
3. See also Jonathan Glover, *Humanity: A Moral History of the 20th Century*, New Haven, CT: Yale University Press, 2001.

4
On Violence

Robert Paul Wolff

Everything I shall say in this essay has been said before, and much of it seems to me to be obvious as well as unoriginal. I offer two excuses for laying used goods before you. In the first place, I think that what I have to say about violence is true. Now, there are many ways to speak falsehood and only one way to speak truth. It follows, as Kierkegaard pointed out, that the truth is likely to become boring. On a subject as ancient and much discussed as ours today, we may probably assume that a novel – and, hence, interesting – view of violence is likely to be false.

But truth is not my sole excuse, for the subject before us suffers from the same difficulty that Kant discerned in the area of metaphysics. After refuting the various claims that had been made to transcendent rational knowledge of things-in-themselves, Kant remarked that the refutations had no lasting psychological effect on true believers. The human mind, he concluded, possessed a natural disposition to metaphysical speculation, which philosophy must perpetually keep in check. Somewhat analogously, men everywhere are prone to certain beliefs about the legitimacy of political authority, even though their beliefs are as groundless as metaphysical speculations. The most sophisticated of men persist in supposing that some valid distinction can be made between legitimate and illegitimate commands, on the basis of which they can draw a line, for example, between mere violence and the legitimate use of force. This lingering superstition is shared by those dissenters who call police actions or ghetto living conditions 'violent'; for they are merely advancing competing legitimacy claims.

I shall set forth and defend *three* propositions about violence:

First: The concept of violence is inherently confused, as is the correlative concept of nonviolence; these and related concepts depend for their meaning in political discussions on the fundamental notion of legitimate authority, which is also inherently incoherent.

Second: It follows that a number of familiar questions are also confusions to which no coherent answers could ever be given, such as: when it is permissible to resort to violence in politics; whether the black movement and the student movement should be nonviolent; and whether anything good in politics is ever accomplished by violence.

Finally: The dispute over violence and nonviolence in contemporary American politics is ideological rhetoric designed either to halt change and justify the existing distribution of power and privilege or to slow change and justify some features of the existing distribution of power and privilege or else to hasten change and justify a total redistribution of power and privilege.

Let us begin with the first proposition, which is essential to my entire discussion.

I

The fundamental concepts of political philosophy are the concepts of power and authority.[1] Power in general is the ability to make and enforce decisions. Political power is the ability to make and enforce decisions about matters of major social importance. Thus the ability to dispose of my private income as I choose is a form of power, whereas the ability to make and enforce a decision about the disposition of some sizable portion of the tax receipts of the federal government is a form of *political* power. (So too is the ability to direct the decisions of a large private corporation; for the exercise of political power is not confined to the sphere of government.) A complete analysis of the concept of political power would involve a classification both of the means employed in the enforcing of decisions and of the scope and variety of questions about which decisions can be made.[2] It would also require an examination of the kinds of opposition against which the decision could be enforced. There is a very considerable difference between the ability a parliamentary majority has to enforce its decisions against the will of the minority and the ability of a rebel military clique to enforce its decisions against the Parliament as a whole.

Authority, by contrast with power, is not an ability but a right. It is the right to command and, correlatively, the right to be obeyed. Claims to authority are made in virtually every area of social life, and, in a remarkably high proportion of cases, the claims are accepted and acquiesced in by those over whom they are made. Parents claim the right to be obeyed by their children; husbands until quite recently claimed the right to be obeyed by their wives; popes claim the right to be obeyed by the laity and clergy; and of course, most notably, virtually all existing governments claim the right to be obeyed by their subjects.

A claim to authority must be sharply differentiated both from a threat or enticement and from a piece of advice. When the state commands, it usually threatens punishment for disobedience, and it may even on occasion offer a reward for compliance, but the command cannot be reduced to the mere threat or reward. What characteristically distinguishes a state from an occupying army or private party is its insistence, either explicit or implicit, on its *right* to be obeyed. By the same token, an authoritative command is not a mere recommendation. Authority says, 'Do this!' not, 'Let me suggest this for your consideration.'

Claims to authority have been defended on a variety of grounds, most prominent among which are the appeal to God, to tradition, to expertise, to the laws of history, and to the consent of those commanded. We tend to forget that John Locke thought it worth while to devote the first of his *Two Treatises on Civil Government* to the claim that Europe's monarchs held their authority by right of primogenitural descent from Adam. It is common today to give lip service to the theory that authority derives from the consent of the governed, but most of us habitually accord *some* weight to any authority claim issuing from a group of men who regularly control the behavior of a population in a territory, particularly if the group tricks itself out with flags, uniforms, courts of law, and printed regulations.

Not all claims to authority are justified. Indeed, I shall suggest shortly that few if any are. Nevertheless, men regularly accept the authority claims asserted against them, and so we must distinguish a descriptive from a normative sense of the term. Let us use the term *'de facto* authority' to refer to *the ability to get one's authority claims accepted by those against whom they are asserted.* 'De jure authority', then, will refer to *the right to command and to be obeyed.* Obviously, the concept of *de jure* authority is primary, and the concept of *de facto* authority is derivative.

Thus understood, *de facto* authority is a form of power, for it is a means by which its possessor can enforce his decisions. Indeed, as Max Weber – from whom much of this analysis is taken – has pointed out, *de facto* authority is the *principal* means on which states rely to carry out their decisions. Threats and inducements play an exceedingly important role in the enforcement of political decisions, to be sure, but a state that must depend upon them entirely will very soon suffer a crippling reduction in its effectiveness, which is to say, in its political power. Modern states especially require for the successful prosecution of their programs an extremely high level of coordination of the behavior of large numbers of individuals. The myth of legitimacy is the only efficient means available to the state for achieving that coordination.

Force is the ability to work some change in the world by the expenditure of physical effort. A man may root up a tree, move a stalled car, drive a nail, or restrain another man, *by force*. Force, in and of itself, is morally neutral. Physically speaking, there may be very little difference between the physical effort of a doctor who resets a dislocated shoulder and that of the ruffian who dislocated it. Sometimes, of course, force is used to work some change in the body of another man – to punch him, shoot him, take out his appendix, hold his arms, or cut his hair. But there is in principle no significant distinction between these uses of force and those uses which involve changing some other part of the world about which he cares. A man who slips into a parking place for which I am heading inflicts an injury on me roughly as great as if he had jostled me in a crowd or stepped on my toe. If he destroys a work of art on which I have lavished my most intense creative efforts, he may harm me more than a physical assault would.

Force is a means to power, but it is not of course a guarantee of power. If I wish to elicit hard work from my employees, I can threaten them with the lash or tempt them with bonuses – both of which are employments of force – but if my workers prefer not to comply, my threats and inducements may be fruitless. It is a commonplace both of domestic and of international politics that the mere possession of a monopoly of force is no guarantee of political power. Those who fail to grasp this truth are repeatedly frustrated by the baffling inability of the strong to impose their will upon the weak.

There are, so far as I can see, *three* means or instruments by which power is exercised – three ways, that is to say, in which men enforce or carry out their social decisions. The first is *force*, the ability to rearrange the world in ways that other men find appealing or distasteful. In modern society, money is of course the principal measure, exchange medium, and symbol of force. The second instrument of power is *de facto* authority – the ability to elicit obedience, as opposed to mere compliance, from others. *De facto* authority frequently accrues to those with a preponderance of force, for men are fatally prone to suppose that he who can compel compliance deserves obedience. But *de facto* authority does not reduce to the possession of a preponderance of force, for men habitually obey commands they know could not effectively be enforced. The third instrument of power is social opinion, or what might be called the 'symbolic' use of force. When a runner competes in a race, he may want the first-prize money or the commercial endorsements that will come to the winner, or he may even just like blue ribbons – but he may also want the acclaim of the fans. Now, that acclaim is expressed by certain uses of force – by clapping of hands and cheering, which are physical acts. But its value to the runner is symbolic; he cherishes it as an expression of approval, not merely as a pleasing sound. To say that man is a social creature is not merely to say that he hangs out in groups, nor even to say that he engages in collective and cooperative enterprises for self-interested purposes; it is most importantly to say that he values symbolic interactions with other men and is influenced by them as well as by the ordinary exercise of force and by claims of authority. This point is important for our discussion, for, as we shall see, many persons who shrink from the use of force as an instrument of political power have no compunctions about the use of social opinion or what I have called the 'symbolic' use of force. Anyone who has observed a progressive classroom run by a teacher with scruples of this sort will know that a day 'in Coventry' can be a far crueler punishment for an unruly ten-year old than a sharp rap on the knuckles with a ruler.

We come, finally, to the concept of violence. Strictly speaking, *violence is the illegitimate or unauthorized use of force to effect decisions against the will or desire of others.* Thus, murder is an act of violence, but capital punishment *by a legitimate state* is not; theft or extortion is violent, but the collection of taxes *by a legitimate state* is not. Clearly, on this interpretation the concept of violence is normative as well as descriptive, for it involves an implicit appeal to the principle of *de jure* legitimate authority. There is an associated sense of the term which is purely descriptive, relying on the descriptive notion of *de facto* authority. Violence in this latter sense is the use of force in ways that are proscribed or unauthorized by those who are generally accepted as the legitimate authorities in the territory. Descriptively speaking, the attack on Hitler's life during the second World War was an act of violence, but one might perfectly well deny that it was violent in the strict sense, on the grounds that Hitler's regime was illegitimate. On similar grounds, it is frequently said that police behavior toward workers or ghetto dwellers or demonstrators is violent even when it is clearly within the law, for the authority issuing the law is illegitimate.

It is common, but I think wrong-headed, to restrict the term 'violence' to uses of force that involve bodily interference or the direct infliction of physical injury. Carrying a dean out of his office is said to be violent, but not seizing his office when he is absent and locking him out. Physically tearing a man's wallet from his pocket is 'violent,' but swindling him out of the same amount of money is not. There is a natural enough basis for this distinction. Most of us value our lives and physical well-being above other goods that we enjoy, and we tend therefore to view attacks or threats on our person as different in kind from other sorts of harm we might suffer. Nevertheless, the distinction is not sufficiently sharp to be of any analytical use, and, as we shall see later, it usually serves the ideological purpose of ruling out, as immoral or politically illegitimate, the only instrument of power that is available to certain social classes.

In its strict or normative sense, then, the concept of political violence depends upon the concept of *de jure*, or legitimate authority. If there is no such thing as legitimate political authority, then it is impossible to distinguish between legitimate and illegitimate uses of force. Now, of course, under any circumstances, we can distinguish between right and wrong, justified and unjustified, uses of force. Such a distinction belongs to moral philosophy in general, and our choice of the criteria by which we draw the distinction will depend on our theory of value and obligation. But the distinctive political concept of violence can be given a coherent meaning *only* by appeal to a doctrine of legitimate political authority.

On the basis of a lengthy reflection upon the concept of *de jure* legitimate authority, I have come to the conclusion that philosophical anarchism is true. That is to say, I believe that there is not, and there could not be, a state that has a right to command and whose subjects have a binding obligation to obey. I have defended this view in detail elsewhere, and I can only indicate here the grounds of my conviction.[3] Briefly, I think it can be shown that every man has a fundamental duty to be autonomous, in Kant's sense of the term. Each of us must make himself the author of his actions and take responsibility for them by refusing to act save on the basis of reasons he can see for himself to be good. Autonomy, thus understood, is in direct opposition to obedience, which is submission to the will of another, irrespective of reasons. Following Kant's usage, political obedience is heteronymy of the will.

Now, political theory offers us one great argument designed to make the autonomy of the individual compatible with submission to the putative authority of the state. In a democracy, it is claimed, the citizen is both law-giver and law-obeyer. Since he shares in the authorship of the laws, he submits to his own will in obeying them, and hence is autonomous, not heteronymous.

If this argument were valid, it would provide a genuine ground for a distinction between violent and nonviolent political actions. Violence would be a use of force proscribed by the laws or executive authority of a genuinely democratic state. The only possible justification of illegal or extralegal political acts would be a demonstration of the illegitimacy of the state, and this in turn would involve showing that the commands of the state were not expressions of the will of the people.

But the classic defense of democracy is *not* valid. For a variety of reasons, neither majority rule nor any other method of making decisions in the absence of unanimity can be shown to preserve the autonomy of the individual citizens. In a democracy, as in any state, obedience is heteronymy. The autonomous man is of necessity an anarchist. Consequently, there is no valid *political* criterion for the justified use of force. Legality is, by itself, no justification. Now, of course, there are all manner of utilitarian arguments for submitting to the state and its agents, even if the state's claim to legitimacy is unfounded. The laws may command actions that are in fact morally obligatory or whose effects promise to be beneficial. Widespread submission to law may bring about a high level of order, regularity, and predictability in social relationships which is valuable independently of the particular character of the acts commanded. But in and of themselves, the acts of police and the commands of legislatures have no peculiar legitimacy or sanction.

Men everywhere and always impute authority to established governments, and they are always wrong to do so.

II

The foregoing remarks are quite banal, to be sure. Very few serious students of politics will maintain either the democratic theory of legitimate authority or any alternatives to it. Nevertheless, like post-theological, demythologized Protestants who persist in raising prayers to a God they no longer believe in, modern men go on exhibiting a superstitious belief in the authority of the state. Consider, for example, a question now much debated: When is it permissible to resort to violence in politics? If 'violence' is taken to mean an *unjustified* use of force, then the answer to the question is obviously *never*. If the use of force were permissible, it would not, by definition, be violence, and if it were violent, it would not, by definition, be permissible. If 'violence' is taken in the strict sense to mean 'an illegitimate or unauthorized use of force,' then *every* political act, whether by private parties or by agents of the state, is violent, for there is no such thing as legitimate authority. If 'violence' is construed in the restricted sense as 'bodily interference or the direct infliction of physical harm,' then the obvious but correct rule is to resort to violence when less harmful or costly means fail, providing always that the balance of good and evil produced is superior to that promised by any available alternative.

These answers are all trivial, but that is precisely my point. Once the concept of violence is seen to rest on the unfounded distinction between legitimate and illegitimate political authority, the question of the appropriateness of violence simply dissolves. It is mere superstition to describe a policeman's beating of a helpless suspect as 'an excessive use of force' while characterizing an attack by a crowd on the policeman as 'a resort to violence.' The implication of such a distinction is that the policeman, as the duly appointed representative of a legitimate government, has a right to use physical force, although no right to use 'excessive' force, whereas the crowd of private citizens has no right at all to use even moderate physical force. But there are no legitimate governments, hence no special rights attaching to soldiers, policemen, magistrates, or other law-enforcement agents, hence no coherent distinction between violence and the legitimate use of force.

Consider, as a particular example, the occupation of buildings and the student strike at Columbia University during April and May of 1968. The consequences of those acts have not yet played themselves out, but I think certain general conclusions can be drawn. First, the total harm done by the students and their supporters was very small in comparison with the good results that were achieved. A month of classwork was lost, along with many tempers and a good deal of sleep. Someone – it is still not clear who – burned the research notes of a history professor, an act which, I am happy to say, produced a universal revulsion shared even by the SDS. In the following year, a number of classes were momentarily disrupted by SDS activists in an unsuccessful attempt to repeat the triumph of the previous spring.

Against this, what benefits flowed from the protest? A reactionary and thoroughly unresponsive administration was forced to resign; an all-university Senate of students, professors, and administrators was created, the first such body at Columbia. A callous and antisocial policy of university expansion into the surrounding neighborhood was reversed; some at least of the university's ties with the military were loosened or severed; and an entire community of students and professors were forced to confront moral and political issues which till then they had managed to ignore.

Could these benefits have been won at less cost? Considering the small cost of the uprising, the question seems to me a bit finicky; nevertheless, the answer is clearly, No. The history of administrative intransigence and faculty apathy at Columbia makes it quite clear that nothing short of a dramatic act such as the seizure of buildings could have deposed the university administration and produced a university senate. In retrospect, the affair seems to have been a quite prudent and restrained use of force.

Assuming this assessment to be correct, it is tempting to conclude, 'In the Columbia case, violence was justified.' But this conclusion is *totally wrong*, for it implies that a line can be drawn between legitimate and illegitimate forms of protest, the latter being justified only under special conditions and when all else has failed. We would all agree, I think, that, under a dictatorship, men have the right to defy the state or even to attack its representatives when their interests are denied and their needs ignored – the only rule that binds them is the general caution against doing more harm than they accomplish good. My purpose here is simply to argue that a modern industrial democracy, whatever merits it may have, is in this regard no different from a dictatorship. No special authority attaches to the laws of a representative, majoritarian state; it is only superstition and the myth of legitimacy that invests the judge, the policeman, or the official with an exclusive right to the exercise of certain kinds of force.

In the light of these arguments, it should be obvious that I see no merit in the doctrine of nonviolence, nor do I believe that any special and complex justification is needed for what is usually called 'civil disobedience.' A commitment to nonviolence can be understood in two different senses, depending on the interpretation given to the concept of violence. If violence is understood in the strict sense as the political use of force in ways proscribed by a legitimate government, then of course the doctrine of nonviolence depends upon the assumption that there *are* or *could be* legitimate governments. Since I believe this assumption to be false, I can attribute no coherent meaning to this first conception of nonviolence.

If violence is understood, on the other hand, as the use of force to interfere with someone in a direct, bodily way or to injure him physically, then the doctrine of nonviolence is merely a subjective queasiness having no moral rationale. When you occupy the seats at a lunch counter for hours on end, thereby depriving, the proprietor of the profits he would have made on ordinary sales during that time, you are taking money out of his pocket quite as effectively as if you had robbed his till or smashed his stock. If you persist in the sit-in until he goes into debt, loses his lunch counter, and takes a job as a day laborer, then you have done him a much greater injury than would be accomplished by a mere beating in a dark alley. He may deserve to be ruined, of course, but, if so, then he probably also deserves to be beaten. A penchant for such indirect coercion as a boycott or a sit-in is morally questionable, for it merely leaves the dirty work to the bank that forecloses on the mortgage or the policeman who carries out the eviction. Emotionally, the commitment to nonviolence is frequently a severely repressed expression of extreme hostility akin to the mortifications and self-flagellations of religious fanatics. Enough testimony has come from Black novelists and psychiatrists to make it clear that the philosophy of nonviolence is, for the American Negro, what Nietzsche called a 'slave morality' – the principal difference is that, in traditional Christianity, God bears the guilt for inflicting pain on the wicked; in the social gospel, the law acts as the scourge.

The doctrine of civil disobedience is an American peculiarity growing out of the conflict between the authority claims of the state and the directly contradictory claims of individual conscience. In a futile attempt to deny and affirm the authority of the state simultaneously, a number of conscientious dissenters have claimed the right to disobey what they believe to be immoral laws, so long as they are prepared to submit to punishment by the state. A willingness to go to jail for one's beliefs is widely viewed in this country as evidence of moral sincerity, and even as a sort of argument for the position one is defending.

Now, tactically speaking, there is much to be said for legal martyrdom. As tyrannical governments are perpetually discovering, the sight of one's leader nailed to a cross has a marvelously bracing effect on the faithful members of a dissident sect. When the rulers are afflicted by the very principles they are violating, even the *threat* of self-sacrifice may force a government to its knees. But leaving tactics aside, no one has any moral obligation whatsoever to resist an unjust government openly rather than clandestinely. Nor has anyone a duty to invite and then to suffer unjust punishment. The choice is simple: if the law is right, follow it. If the law is wrong, evade it.

I think it is possible to understand why conscientious and morally concerned men should feel a compulsion to seek punishment for acts they genuinely believe to be right. Conscience is the echo of society's voice within us. The men of strongest and most independent conscience are, in a manner of speaking, just those who have most completely internalized this social voice, so that they hear and obey its commands even when no policeman compels their compliance. Ironically, it is these same men who are most likely to set themselves against the government in the name of ideals and principles to which they feel a higher loyalty. When a society violates the very principles it claims to hold, these men of conscience experience a terrible conflict. They are deeply committed to the principles society has taught them, principles they have truly come to believe. But they can be true to their beliefs only by setting themselves against the laws of the very society that has been their teacher and with whose authority they identify themselves. Such a conflict never occurs in men of weak conscience, who merely obey the law, however much it violates the moral precepts they have only imperfectly learned.

The pain of the conflict is too great to be borne; somehow, it must be alleviated. If the commitment to principle is weak, the individual submits, though he feels morally unclean for doing so. If the identification with society is weak, he rejects the society and becomes alienated, perhaps identifying with some other society. But if both conscience and identification are too strong to be broken, the only solution is to expiate the guilt by seeking social punishment for the breach of society's laws. Oddly enough, the expiation, instead of bringing them back into the fold of law-obeyers, makes it psychologically all the easier for them to continue their defiance of the state.

III

The foregoing conclusions seem to reach far beyond what the argument warrants. The classical theory of political authority may indeed be inadequate; it may even be that the concept of legitimate authority is incoherent; but surely *some* genuine distinction can be drawn between a politics of reason, rules, and compromise on the one hand, and the resort to violent conflict on the other! Are the acts of a rioting mob different only in degree from the calm and orderly processes of a duly constituted court of law? Such a view partakes more of novelty than of truth!

Unless I very much misjudge my audience, most readers will respond roughly in this manner. There may be a few still willing to break a lance for sovereignty and legitimate authority, and a few, I hope, who agree immediately with what I have said, but the distinction between violence and nonviolence in politics is too familiar to be so easily discarded. In this third section of my essay, therefore, I shall try to discover what makes the distinction so plausible, even though it is – I insist – unfounded.

The customary distinction between violent and nonviolent modes of social interaction seems to me to rest on *two* genuine distinctions: the first is the *subjective* distinction between the regular or accepted and the irregular or unexpected uses of force; the second is the *objective* distinction between those interests which are central or vital to an individual and those which are secondary or peripheral.

Consider first the subjective distinction between regular and irregular uses of force in social interactions. It seems perfectly appropriate to us that a conflict between two men who desire the same piece of land should be settled in favor of the one who can pull more money out of his pocket. We consider it regular and orderly that the full weight of the police power of the state be placed behind that settlement in order to ensure that nothing upset it. On the other hand, we consider it violent and disorderly to resolve the dispute by a fist fight or a duel. Yet what is the difference between the use of money, which is one kind of force, and the use of fists, which is another? Well, if we do not appeal to the supposed legitimacy of financial transactions or to the putative authority of the law, then the principal difference is that we are accustomed to settling disputes with dollars and we are no longer accustomed to settling them with fists.

Imagine how barbaric, how unjust, how *violent;* it must seem, to someone unfamiliar with the beauties of capitalism, that a man's ability to obtain medical care for his children should depend solely on the contingency that some other man can make a profit from his productive labor! Is the Federal Government's seizure of my resources for the purpose of killing Asian peasants less violent than a bandit's extortion of tribute at gunpoint? Yet we are accustomed to the one and unaccustomed to the other.

The objective distinction between central and peripheral interests also shapes our conception of what is violent in politics. When my peripheral or secondary interests are at stake in a conflict, I quite naturally consider only a moderate use of force to be justified. Anything more, I will probably call 'violence.' What I tend to forget, of course, is that other parties to the conflict may find their primary interests challenged and, hence, may have a very different view of what is and is not violent. In the universities, for example, most of the student challenges have touched only on the peripheral interests of professors. No matter what is decided about ROTC, curriculum, the disposition of the endowment, or Black studies, the typical philosophy professor's life will be largely unchanged. His tenure, salary, working conditions, status, and family life remain the same. Hence he is likely to take a tolerant view of building seizures and sit-ins. But let a classroom be disrupted, and he cries out that violence has no place on campus. What he means is that force has been used in a way that touches one of his deeper concerns.

The concept of violence serves as a rhetorical device for proscribing those political uses of force which one considers inimical to one's central interests. Since different social groups have different central interests and can draw on different kinds of force, it follows that there are conflicting definitions of violence. Broadly speaking, in the United States today, there are four conceptions of violence corresponding to four distinct socioeconomic classes.

The first view is associated with the established financial and political interests in the country. It identifies the violent with the illegal, and condemns all challenges to the authority of the state and all assaults on the

rights of property as beyond the limits of permissible politics. The older segments of the business community adopt this view, along with the military
establishment and the local elites of middle America. Robert Taft was once a
perfect symbol of this sector of opinion.

The second view is associated with the affluent, educated, technical and
professional middle class in America, together with the new, rapidly growing, future-oriented sectors of the economy, such as the communications
industry, electronics, etc. They accept, even welcome, dissent, demonstration, ferment, and – within limits – attacks on property in ghetto areas. They
look with favor on civil disobedience and feel at ease with extralegal tactics
of social change. Their interests are identified with what is new in American
society, and they are confident of coming out on top in the competition for
wealth and status within an economy built on the principle of reward for
profitable performance.

The 'liberals,' as this group is normally called, can afford to encourage
modes of dissent or disruption that do not challenge the economic and social
arrangements on which their success is based. They will defend rent strikes,
grape boycotts, or lunch-counter sit-ins with the argument that unemployment and starvation are a form of violence also. Since they are themselves
in competition with the older elite for power and prestige, they tend to view
student rebels and black militants as their allies, up to the point at which
their own interests are attacked. But when tactics are used that threaten their
positions in universities, in corporations, or in affluent suburbs, then the
liberals cry *violence* also, and call for the police. A poignant example of this
class is the liberal professor who cheers the student rebels as they seize the
Administration building and then recoils in horror at the demand that he
share his authority to determine curriculum and decide promotions.

The third view of violence is that held by working-class and lower-middle-
class Americans, those most often referred to as the 'white backlash.' They
perceive the principal threat to their interests as coming from the bottom
class of ghetto dwellers, welfare clients, and nonunionized laborers who
demand more living space, admission to union jobs with union wages, and a
larger share of the social product. To this hard-pressed segment of American
society, 'violence' means street crime, ghetto riots, civil-rights marches into
all-white neighborhoods, and antiwar attacks on the patriotic symbols of
constituted authority with which backlash America identifies. Studies of the
petty bourgeoisie in Weimar Germany suggest, and George Wallace's pres-
idential campaign of 1968 confirms, that the lower middle class, when
it finds itself pressed between inflationary prices and demands from the
lower class, identifies its principal enemy as the lower class. So we find the
classic political alliance of old established wealth with right-wing populist
elements, both of which favor a repressive response to attacks on authority and a strong governmental policy toward the 'violence' of demands for
change.

The fourth view of violence is the revolutionary counterdefinition put forward by the outclass and its sympathizers within the liberal wing of the established order. Two complementary rhetorical devices are employed. First, the connotation of the term 'violence' is accepted, but the application of the term is reversed: police are violent, not rioters; employers, not strikers; the American army, not the enemy. In this way, an attack is mounted on the government's claim to possess the right to rule. Secondly, the denotation of the term is held constant and the connotation reversed. Violence is good, not bad; legitimate, not illegitimate. It is, in Stokely Carmichael's great rhetorical flourish, 'as American as cherry pie.' Since the outclass of rebels has scant access to the instruments of power used by established social classes – wealth, law, police power, legislation – it naturally seeks to legitimize the riots, harassments, and street crme which are its only weapons. Equally naturally, the rest of society labels such means 'violent' and suppresses them.

In the complex class struggle for wealth and power in America, each of us must decide for himself which group he will identify with. It is not my purpose here to urge one choice rather than another. My sole aim is to argue that the concept of violence has no useful role to play in the deliberations leading to that choice. Whatever other considerations of utility and social justice one appeals to, no weight should be given to the view that *some* uses of force are prima facie ruled out as illegitimate and hence 'violent' or that other uses of force are prima facie ruled in as legitimate, or legal. Furthermore, in the advancement of dissenting positions by illegal means, no special moral merit attaches to the avoiding, as it were, of body contact. Physical harm may be among the most serious injuries that can be done to an opponent, but, if so, it differs only in degree and not in kind from the injuries inflicted by so-called 'nonviolent' techniques of political action.

IV

The myth of legitimate authority is the secular reincarnation of that religious superstition which has finally ceased to play a significant role in the affairs of men. Like Christianity, the worship of the state has its fundamentalists, its revisionists, its ecumenicists (or world-Federalists), and its theological rationale. The philosophical anarchist is the atheist of politics, I began my discussion with the observation that the belief in legitimacy, like the penchant for transcendent metaphysics, is an ineradicable irrationality of the human experience. However, the slow extinction of religious faith over the past two centuries may encourage us to hope that in time anarchism, like atheism, will become the accepted conviction of enlightened and rational men.

Notes

1. What follows is a summary of analyses I have published elsewhere. The concept of political power is treated in Chapter III of *The Poverty of Liberalism* (Boston: Beacon Press, 1968). The concepts of legitimacy and authority are analyzed in my essay on 'Political Philosophy' in Arthur Danto, ed., *The Harper Guide to Philosophy* (New York: Harper & Row, 1970).
2. See Robert A. Dahl, 'The Concept of Power,' *Behavioral Science* (July 1957), for just such a classification.
3. See 'Political Philosophy,' in Danto, *op. cit.*

COMMENTARY ON WOLFF

This article was published as part of a symposium on 'Violence' held at the American Philosophical Association annual conference on 28 December 1969. The next article in this anthology, by Bernard Gert, was also part of this symposium.[1]

A scholar of Kant and Marx, in 1970 Robert Paul Wolff published his book *In Defense of Anarchism*, arguably the work he is still best known for.[2] In this book he puts forward a defence of philosophical anarchism; namely the belief that a state does not have a right to command and therefore we, as citizens, are not subject to a binding obligation to obey the state. Wolff suggests that every person has a fundamental duty to be autonomous, in Kant's sense of the term, and that autonomy is in direct opposition to obedience, which is submission to the will of another.

Wolff's anarchism forms the backdrop for his views on violence, hence in this article Wolff argues that 'men everywhere are prone to certain beliefs about the legitimacy of political authority, even though their beliefs are as groundless as metaphysical speculation.' It is exactly because Wolff refuses to acknowledge the legitimacy of political authority that he also rejects the distinction between mere violence and the legitimate use of force. It follows that, according to Wolff, there is no difference between murder and capital punishment, or between theft and the collection of taxes.[3]

On the basis of this account of violence, Wolff goes on to ponder the following question: When is it permissible to resort to violence in politics? If 'violence' is taken to mean an unjustified use of force, then violence in politics could never be justified: 'If the use of force were permissible, it would not, by definition, be violence, and if it were violent, it would not, by definition, be permissible.' But as we have seen, Wolff rejects the distinction between legitimate and illegitimate authority, or between *de jure* and *de facto* authority, or indeed between the legitimate use of force and the illegitimate use of violence. If the state does not have the right to command, as Wolff claims, every time it enforces its authority it is using violence, which opens up the possibility that it is always permissible to use violence in politics in response to violence.

Notes and further reading

1. For a critique of Wolff's account of violence, see Francis C. Wade, 'On Violence', *The Journal of Philosophy*, Vol. 68, No. 12, 1971, pp. 369–77.
2. Robert P. Wolff, *In Defense of Anarchism*, New York: Harper 1970.
3. Apart from anarchists, Wolff's work has also inspired many leading libertarians, including Robert Nozick, *Anarchy State and Utopia*, Oxford: Blackwell, 1974; and Hillel Steiner, *An Essay on Rights*, Oxford; Blackwell, 1994.

5
Justifying Violence

Bernard Gert

There are ten moral rules. They are:

Do not kill	Do not deceive
Do not cause pain	Keep your promise
Do not disable	Do not cheat
Do not deprive of freedom or opportunity	Obey the law
Do not deprive of pleasure	Do your duty

Some might define an 'act of violence' as an unwanted intentional violation of any one of the first three rules. They would then regard an unwanted intentional violation of the fourth or fifth rule as an 'act of force.' This distinction seems to have been employed by one of the Dartmouth students who occupied an administration building last spring. When the deans were being led out of the building, one asserted that the students were using violence on him, and a student replied that they were not using violence, they were using force. The distinction between an act of violence and an act of force may be valuable in some discussions; e.g., it may allow us to condemn institutional violence while allowing for institutional force.

For the purposes of this paper, however, I shall usually not distinguish between unwanted intentional violations of the first three rules and unwanted intentional violations of the next two. I do not deny that violence is more closely related to violations of the first three rules and force to violations of the next two, but there are so many exceptions and borderline cases that I shall, for the purpose of this paper, define an act of violence as an intentional violation of any of the first five rules toward someone who has no rational desire to have the rule violated with regard to himself. I realize that this definition does not correspond exactly to ordinary usage, but it is close enough so that there should be no serious distortion of the philosophically relevant points.

Some might prefer to call any unwanted intentional violation of any of the ten moral rules an act of violence. This would be a serious distortion

66

of the concept. It would make it logically impossible for there to be non-violent civil disobedience. There seems to be a general distinction between violent crimes and nonviolent ones. By and large I think this corresponds to unwanted intentional violations of the first five rules and unwanted intentional violations of the second five. But I do not think the correlation is exact, and nothing very much turns on it. One further point of clarification. Although it may be possible to commit an act of violence against oneself, suicide being common enough to have a name, when I talk of an act of violence in this paper, I shall mean an act of violence committed against another person.

Having defined what I mean by an act of violence, I can now proceed to what seems to me to be the philosophically interesting question: How are acts of violence justified? Since violence involves violating the moral rules, we must discuss not only the concept of justification, but also the nature of the moral rules.

The concept of justification depends upon the concept of reason, and thus some discussion of reason is necessary. It is irrational to desire death, pain, disability, or loss of freedom, opportunity, or pleasure for oneself, unless one has a reason. I call desires for these things 'irrational desires.' The objects of irrational desires, I call 'personal evils.' It is also irrational not to desire to avoid the personal evils. 'Reasons for acting' are beliefs that can make acting on an irrational desire, rational. The belief that having my right arm cut off will save my life is a reason for wanting my right arm cut off. Any belief that my action will decrease my chances of dying, of suffering pain or disability, or of losing freedom, opportunity, or pleasure are reasons for acting. Other reasons are beliefs that my action will increase my abilities, freedom, opportunity, or pleasure. In the basic sense of 'justify', to justify an action is to show that it is rational. (Moral justification will be discussed later.) Normally, one attempts to justify only those actions which would be irrational if one did not have a reason for doing them. In general, these are actions that one knows significantly increase one's chances of suffering some personal evil, i.e., dying, suffering pain or disability, or losing freedom, opportunity, or pleasure.

But not all reasons are adequate to justify all actions that would be irrational without a reason. Clearly, one will need a stronger reason for killing oneself than for depriving oneself of some pleasure. What counts as an adequate reason for a particular action is often a matter of dispute. When all rational men agree that an action needs a reason and that there is no adequate reason for doing it, I call that action 'prohibited by reason.' When all rational men agree that not performing some action needs a reason and that there is no adequate reason for not doing it, I call that action 'required by reason.' When neither doing nor omitting an action needs a reason or when rational men differ as to the adequacy of a reason for doing or omitting some action, I call that action 'allowed by reason.' Irrational actions are the same as actions prohibited by reason; rational actions include both actions required by reason and those allowed by reason.

It is a fair summary of the account given so far to say that it is prohibited by reason to act against one's self-interest; required by reason to act so as to prevent oneself from suffering significant personal evil; and allowed by reason to do anything else. But this account of reason is inadequate because there are other reasons in addition to those related to one's own self-interest. Beliefs that one's action will help others to avoid death, pain, disability, or loss of freedom, opportunity, or pleasure; or to gain further abilities, freedom, opportunity, or pleasure, are also reasons. For these beliefs can also make an action that would otherwise be irrational, rational. Thus it is allowed by reason to act contrary to one's self-interest, if one will thereby benefit another. However, it is also allowed by reason to sacrifice the interests of others in order to benefit oneself.

Some parents sacrifice their own interests in order to benefit their children, other parents do not; both courses of action are allowed by reason. All that reason prohibits is action or nonaction that both results in suffering evil oneself and fails to benefit anyone else. All that reason requires is the avoidance of irrational action (or nonaction). All other actions are allowed by reason. Reason thus does not offer much in the way of a guide to conduct.

Let us now consider the moral rules. Most of their characteristics are purely formal; they simply make clear what is meant by the universality of moral rules, viz., the irrelevance of considerations of person, place, group, or time. Moral rules apply to all and only those who can understand and guide their actions by them, i.e., to all rational men with the relevant voluntary abilities. This makes clear the independence of moral rules from the will or decision of any man or group of men and entails that moral rules are unchanging. It also guarantees that men without certain features are not subject to moral rules. But, though moral rules are universal, they are not absolute. That there are exceptions to the moral rules makes clear that it is impossible to apply the moral rules mechanically in deciding what to do or in making moral judgments.

The content of the moral rules is determined by the requirement that protection from evil, rather than the promotion of good, is their primary purpose. This leads to the final characteristic of a moral rule. All rational men must advocate obedience to it. Of course, the concept of a rational man is usually not made very clear. Nor is it clear in what manner or with what qualifications all rational men would advocate obedience to the moral rules. Nonetheless, in spite of the vagueness, there is no doubt that if a rule is to be a moral rule, all rational men must agree in taking a certain attitude toward it, an attitude that involves the view that it should be universally obeyed, though this is not meant to exclude exceptions.

If a rational man uses only those beliefs which are shared by all other rational men, e.g., that men are mortal, it turns out that he will share with all other rational men certain attitudes toward the first five moral rules. The beliefs must be specified in this way; for one's attitude is often determined by one's beliefs, and, since beliefs can vary so much, it would be extremely unlikely that without that specification we could reach any agreement in attitude. Limiting beliefs to those required by reason, we find that one attitude that all rational men would make toward the first five moral rules is the following:

> I want all other people to obey the rule with regard to anyone for whom I am concerned (including myself) except when they have a good specific reason for thinking that the person in question or myself (possibly the same) has a rational desire that the rule not be obeyed with regard to him.

Since violence is defined as an unwanted violation of the first five moral rules, it is no accident that all rational men generally condemn violence. But rational men need not condemn all violence; they may agree that some violence is justified.

In order to see why violence is sometimes justifiable, let us consider the attitude rational men would have toward the rules if they were required to take an attitude that they could advocate to all other rational men. This eliminates the egocentricity of the previous attitude and gives us an attitude toward the rules that very closely approaches what we now consider to be the appropriate attitude. When something is being advocated in order to reach agreement among all rational men, I shall say that it is being 'publicly advocated.' When an attitude is adopted in order to be publicly advocated, I shall call it a 'public attitude.' Public advocacy need not be sincere, though, of course, it can be. A rational man's public attitude toward the first five moral rules does not encourage blind obedience to them. On the contrary, it allows that quite often they need not be obeyed. Less often, all rational men may even publicly advocate that they should not be obeyed. Not only are there justified violations of the moral rules; there is even unjustified obedience to them. For a rational man does not have a fetish for neat, uncluttered obedience to rules; he desires, insofar as possible, to avoid the unwanted evils that result from violations of the moral rules. But sometimes violation of a moral rule may result in preventing significantly more evil than is caused by the violation.

In discussing reason we saw that only those actions which would be irrational if one did not have a reason for them need to be justified. Such actions can be justified by providing reasons that show either that the action is allowed by reason or, less frequently, that it is required by it. In a similar manner, only those actions that would be immoral if one did not have a reason, need to be morally justified. Generally, these are violations of the moral rules. And such violations can be justified by providing reasons that would result either in some rational men publicly advocating such a violation or, less frequently, in all rational men publicly advocating violation.

Those violations which all rational men would publicly advocate, I call violations 'required by public reason.' If a violation is required by public reason, then public reason prohibits obeying the rule in this situation. Obeying the rule is morally unjustified. Those violations which some rational men would publicly advocate I call violations 'allowed by public reason.' These kinds of violation cause most of the genuine moral controversy. A violation that no rational man would publicly advocate I call 'a violation prohibited by public reason.' Such violations are morally unjustified.

One kind of violation required by public reason is one in which one inflicts an evil on someone, with his consent, in order to prevent his suffering a significantly greater evil. This kind of violation is not an act of violence.

One kind of violation allowed by public reason is one in which significantly greater evil is prevented by breaking the rule than would be caused by the violation, though not for the same person. This is an act of violence.

One kind of violation prohibited by public reason is one in which the rule is broken simply in order to promote good for oneself or for someone for whom one is concerned. This is unjustified violence.

We want a formulation of a public attitude toward the moral rules that accounts for the different kinds of violations. The following formulation seems to be acceptable:

> Everyone is to obey the rule with regard to everyone except when he would publicly advocate violating it.

The 'except' clause does not mean that all rational men *agree* that one is *not to obey* the moral rule when one would publicly advocate violating it, only that they *do not agree* that one *is to obey* the rule when one would publicly advocate breaking it.

Though all rational men would publicly advocate the stated attitude toward the moral rules, not all rational men will obey the rules as the public attitude requires. Though reason requires adopting a certain public attitude, it does not require adopting this attitude as one's genuine attitude toward the rules. Reason only allows, it does not require that we act morally. It is a mark of a false theory to 'prove' that it is irrational to act immorally. The most one can hope to show is that reason requires a certain public attitude toward at least some of the moral rules. But all rational men are aware that agreement in public attitude does not guarantee that no one will violate a moral rule except when he would publicly advocate violating it. The rational man need not be a hypocrite, but all rational men are aware of the possibility of hypocrisy. Awareness of the possibility of unjustified violation of the rules requires us to consider the rational man's attitude toward such violations.

All rational men would publicly advocate that all those who unjustifiably violate the moral rules be liable to punishment. Failure to publicly advocate this would lessen the protection from violations that all rational men desire.

We can now state the rational man's public attitude toward each of the moral rules as follows:

> Everyone is to obey the rule with regard to everyone except when he would publicly advocate violating it. Anyone who violates the rule when he would not publicly advocate such a violation may be punished.

I call this attitude the 'moral attitude.' Only those rules toward which all rational men would publicly take this attitude count as genuine or basic or justifiable moral rules. It is clear that all rational men would publicly take the moral attitude toward the first five moral rules.

Since the moral attitude allows one to break the rule when one would publicly advocate breaking it, it is important to examine the circumstances in which a rational man might do this. Publicly advocating anything requires that all rational men be able to understand and to accept what you are advocating. This means that the circumstances in which one can publicly advocate violation of a rule must provide reasons that could be understood and regarded as adequate by all rational men. As noted earlier, sometimes these circumstances will be such that all rational men would publicly advocate violation of the rule. The clearest example of this kind of case is one in which the person toward whom one is violating the rule has a rational desire that the rule be violated with regard to him. But this kind of violation is not an act of violence. For example, a person wants a rabies shot because he knows that, even though it is very painful, failure to have it will result in significantly greater pain and death. In fact, in this example, given the extreme horror of death by rabies, even if the person, because of his fear of present pain, did not want the rabies shot, still public reason would require giving it to him. This is a case of justified violence. However, when the evil that a person would suffer if you did not break the rule with regard to him is not indisputably significantly greater than the evil he would suffer if you did, then public reason only allows breaking the rule with regard to him when he does not desire it. Public reason may also allow violence whenever this results in significantly less evil being suffered even when the evil is shifted from one person to another. However, it must be indisputable that the evil being prevented by the violence is significantly greater than the evil caused. But even when this is the case, rational men may still publicly advocate different courses of action.

Nonetheless, there are extreme cases in which all rational men would agree that, even if the evil is to be switched from one person to another, there is a point at which the amount of evil to be prevented by breaking the rule is so much greater than the amount of evil caused by breaking it, that one ought to break it. Thus, if an innocent child contracts some highly dangerous and infectious disease, similar to that which causes plagues, it will be justifiable to use violence against him in order to keep the plague from spreading.

Thus all rational men would publicly advocate some violence even when it is not for the benefit of the person with regard to whom the rule was violated. However, this would never be done lightly, and some rational men will demand an extremely high proportion of evil prevented to evil caused before they would publicly advocate violence. Further, all rational men will demand good specific reasons for believing that more evil is being prevented by violence than by obeying the moral rules.

'Punishment' is also a justifiable violation of the moral rules. Of course, one must be the appropriate person to administer the punishment. There also is a further limitation, namely, that more evil should not be inflicted than one would publicly advocate as punishment for this kind of violation. Violence in order to prevent violence would also be publicly advocated by some rational men. Provided, of course, that one had a good specific reason for thinking that an act of violence was going to be committed. However, one cannot inflict greater evil than would have been inflicted as the punishment for the violence unless significantly greater evil is being prevented. If these provisions are not met, then I do not see the possibility of any rational men still publicly advocating it. Any violence simply in order to obtain some good for someone for whom one is concerned, including oneself, is unjustifiable. No rational man would publicly advocate this kind of violence. Thus all killing and torturing for pleasure or profit is clearly immoral, whereas killing and torturing to prevent greater killing and torturing may sometimes be allowed by public reason.

Thus we now see that rational men may disagree about the justification of some violence. The disagreements will occur, however, within a larger framework of agreement. But this does not mean that, in genuine cases of moral disagreement, public reason requires taking one side and prohibits taking the other. For it is very likely that genuine moral disagreements concerning the justification of violence are those which occur within the larger framework, where it is allowed by reason to publicly advocate either alternative. It is here that each individual has to decide for himself what violence he would publicly advocate.

Providing a justification of some violations of the moral rules does not provide a mechanical decision procedure for moral questions. Very few if any genuine moral disputes can be settled by applying this set of justifications to the facts. All I have attempted to do is to provide a limit to genuine moral disputes: to show that there is a point beyond which rational men can no longer disagree about what morally should be done. Before this point is reached, no application of what I have said will settle the issue. Men must decide on their own what weight they will give to the various considerations. I have only shown what the morally relevant considerations are: the amount of evil to be caused, avoided, or prevented; the rational desires of the people toward whom the rule is to be broken; and the effect this kind of violation, if allowed, would have. So I have not provided anything that functions like an ideal observer to whom one can take any moral problem and who will then pronounce what ought to be done. The cases that can be answered clearly by what I have said are those cases in which most people have had no doubt about what is morally right.

Though all rational men publicly advocate that a man act morally, they need not publicly advocate that he act this way from certain motives. Some may reply to this, 'But sometimes it is the motive that determines the morality of the act.' They grant that some actions are immoral no matter what the motives, viz., those in which we know that our violation of the moral rule will cause more evil than it prevents. But they hold that the motive sometimes does determine the morality of the action. Killing an incurable cancer patient who had requested to be killed would be immoral if I did it in order to benefit myself or someone I cared for, but not if I did it in order to prevent his suffering.

Persuasive as this reasoning sounds, the conclusion is false. It is not the motive that determines the morality of the action; it is whether one would publicly advocate that sort of violation. If one would publicly advocate the violation, then the violation is not immoral no matter what the motive for it. If one would not, the violation is immoral, regardless of the motive. Two factors serve to obscure this point: (1) We do not distinguish carefully enough between our moral judgment on the act and the moral judgment we make on a person who acts from certain kinds of motives. (2) We believe that certain kinds of motives lead people to violate moral rules even when they would not publicly advocate such violations, whereas other kinds of motives naturally lead only to violations that one would publicly advocate. It is primarily this second belief, which is probably true, that accounts for the false view that the motive determines the morality of an act. The morality of a violation of the moral rules is determined by whether one would publicly advocate such a violation. The motive at most determines the moral worth of the action, i.e., how much it indicates about the moral character of the agent.

It is extremely important to realize that an action can be both immoral and contrary to one's self-interest. Failure to realize this, together with the view that all rational actions are either required by self-interest or required by morality, leads to the view that whenever a rational person sacrifices himself for others he is acting morally. But violating the moral rules when one would not publicly advocate such a violation is immoral even if one is willing to sacrifice one's life in performing the violation. Unjustified violations of the moral rules that are contrary to one's self-interest are not just a logical possibility. On the contrary, without underestimating the amount of evil caused by immoral actions done from motives of self-interest, I think that considerably more evil has been caused by immoral actions that were contrary to the self-interest of the agent. Religions have provided motives for men to act in ways that were both immoral and contrary to their self-interest. The amount of evil caused by self-sacrificing immoral actions for religious reasons is incredible. So many men have not only slaughtered others but risked their own lives in advancing the interests of their religion that it is impossible to hold that self-interest is the sole cause of immoral action.

But religion is only one of many sources of reasons for being immoral. One is often immoral in order to advance the interests of one's social or economic class. And sometimes these immoral actions require some sacrifice of self-interest. Men often act both immorally and contrary to their self-interest in order to advance the interests of their race or ethnic group. But today probably the greatest and most serious source of reasons for being immoral come from one's country. Many men are not only willing, but anxious to sacrifice their lives for their country even when their country is engaged in an immoral war. The evil caused by immoral actions due to nationalism probably outweighs the evil caused by the immoral actions due to all other reasons put together. Taking an interest in one's country need not lead to immoral actions. To be willing to do whatever is in the best interests of one's country except act immorally, is the mark of a patriot. A nationalist is one who is willing to advance the interests of his country even when this requires him to act immorally. To keep patriotism from degenerating into nationalism is impossible without a clear understanding of morality.

Usually one does not consider whether one would be willing to publicly advocate one's judgment on some moral matter, e.g., a violation of a moral rule. Sometimes a man may even believe that he would be willing to publicly advocate his judgment, but further reflection convinces him that he would not. It is this latter case that is most appropriately called 'making a mistaken moral judgment.' It is not surprising that people often make mistaken moral judgments. It is no easy matter to see what one would publicly advocate. One must consider what one would advocate if one did not know who the parties involved were, but knew only the morally relevant facts; for no beliefs about individuals can be used when publicly advocating an attitude. Sometimes considering the act with the two parties reversed is helpful. But not always. A judge should not consider what he would advocate if he were the criminal. What he must consider is what he would publicly advocate.

The distinction between moral judgments and judgments made on moral matters allows one to make a simple statement about moral progress. Moral progress occurs as judgments on moral matters become moral judgments. Assuming, of course, that these judgments are not hypocritical. It is generally not realized how many judgments on moral matters are not even intended to be moral judgments. Many people realize that their judgments cannot be publicly advocated, but do not care about this. They are not concerned with reaching agreement among all rational men, only with a limited number. In primitive societies this often includes only the other members of the society. In civilized societies, it may not even include this much. Some people make judgments that could be agreed to only by people with a similar social status. Some people make judgments that could be accepted only by people of the same race or religion. Indeed, in modern societies a man is usually considered a highly moral man if his judgments on moral matters could be agreed to by all members of his society. Since most of the moral matters one makes judgments upon are matters concerning only those people in one's society, it is easy to overestimate the extent of moral progress. A man whose judgments on domestic matters make him seem a most moral man often is seen not to be so when he makes judgments on foreign policy.

One of the lesser, but nonetheless significant evils of war is the reversing of moral progress. People, whose judgments on moral matters had been genuine moral judgments, no longer make the same judgments. Especially when the moral rules are violated by their country, they make judgments they could not possibly publicly advocate. They no longer care about reaching agreement among all rational men; they care only about reaching agreement among their fellow countrymen. They even condemn as unpatriotic those who continue to make genuine moral judgments on such matters. Thus nationalism overwhelms morality, not only as the basis for action, but also as the basis for judgment. Confusion about morality often allows nationalistic judgments to pass for moral ones, a confusion often not only supported by the leaders of the country but often shared by them. Sometimes, however, nationalism is explicitly put forward as superior to morality. 'My country, right or wrong' is a slogan war makes respectable even in the most civilized societies. Thus war often causes people to lose that decent respect for the opinion of mankind that morality demands.

To summarize and make relevant. Violence, i.e., an unwanted intentional violation of any of the first five moral rules, is justifiable only when one would publicly advocate such a violation. In most situations, a necessary condition for being able to publicly advocate such a violation is that there be good reason to believe that the violation will prevent more death, pain, etc., than it causes. Violence is not justified as a purely symbolic protest against injustice; one must believe this protest will have some beneficial effect. It is not better when it is all in vain, as some members of the Cyrano Left believe. Neither purity of heart nor willingness to sacrifice oneself justifies violence, and it is even clearer that attempts to ease one's conscience do not do so. However, these mistaken attempts to justify individual acts of violence do not result in as much death, pain, disability, etc., as the mistaken attempts to justify collective violence. National self-interest, except for self-defense, does not justify violence, nor does national honor. To use violence to defend honor is to do such violence to the concept of honor, that it will never survive the defense.

I do not deny that violence is sometimes even required by public reason and that considerably more violence is allowed by public reason, but I think there can be no doubt that the overwhelming majority of acts of violence are prohibited by public reason and thus completely unjustified.

COMMENTARY ON GERT

Moral philosopher Bernard Gert has spent the last 50 years investigating, clarifying and developing a moral theory grounded on the normative concept of impartiality.[1] In this paper, he attempts to answer two specific questions: What is an act of violence? And, how are acts of violence justified?

Gert defines an act of violence as an intentional violation of five fundamental moral rules towards someone who has no rational desire to have the rule violated with regard to himself or herself. The five rules are: do not kill; do not cause pain; do not disable; do not deprive of freedom of opportunity; do not deprive of pleasure.

What is particularly interesting about this definition is that violence is clearly not a neutral concept from a normative point of view. The fact that the idea of violence is defined in relation to the violation of moral rules suggests that violence is essentially intertwined with our sense of morality.

But Gert does not dwell on this definition of violence; instead, he is more interested in exploring the latter question, regarding the justification of violence. Gert's starting point is the notion of 'justification'. He explains that 'the concept of justification depends upon the concept of reason', therefore 'in the basic sense of "justify", to justify an action is to show that it is rational.' This suggests that the focus of our inquiry naturally shifts to a discussion of reason and rationality, although Gert warns us that reason does not offer much in the way of a guide to conduct, since to act against one's self-interest is both allowed and prohibited by reason.

Notwithstanding its limitations, what makes the concept of reason pivotal to our moral discourse is the fact that it underpins a certain understanding of justification. Thus, as Gert explains, 'when something is being advocated in order to reach agreement among all rational men, I shall say that it is being "publicly advocated".' Armed with this notion of justification, which may be described as contractarian, we can now turn to the specific question of justifying violence. Gert argues that violence is justifiable only when one would publicly advocate the violation of any of the five moral rules. That is to say, 'everyone is to obey the [moral rule] with regard to everyone except when he [or she] would publicly advocate violating it'.

Gert clearly allows for the justification of violence, at least in theory. As he explains: 'One kind of violation allowed by public reason is one in which significantly greater evil is prevented by breaking the rule than would be caused by the violation, though not for the same person.' It is interesting to note that under Gert's sophisticated theorizing, it seems possible to combine, without apparent contradiction, a contractarian account of justification with consequentialist reasoning.

Note and further reading

1. See his *The Moral Rules*, New York: Harper 1970; *Morality: A New Justification of the Moral Rules*, New York: Oxford 1988; *Morality: Its Nature and Justification*, New York: Oxford, 1998, revised edn 2005; *Common Morality*, New York: Oxford University Press, 2004.

6
Violence, Peace and Peace Research
Johan Galtung

1. Introduction

In the present paper we shall be using the word 'peace' very many times. Few words are so often used and abused – perhaps, it seems, because 'peace' serves as a means of obtaining verbal consensus – it is hard to be all-out against peace.[1] Thus, when efforts are made to plead almost any kind of policy – say technical assistance, increased trade, tourism, new forms of education, irrigation, industrialization, etc. – then it is often asserted that that policy, in addition to other merits, will also serve the cause of peace. This is done regardless of how tenuous the relation has been in the past or how dubious the theory justifying this as a reasonable expectation for the future. Such difficulties are avoided by excluding any reference to data from the past or to theories about the future.

The present article (PRIO–publication No. 23–9) is a revised version of talks originally presented by the author at the Oslo Conference on the plan for a peacemaker's academy, organized jointly by the Peacemakers' Academy Committee, Vermont and the International Peace Research Institute, Oslo, 14–17 November 1968; at the peace research seminar organized by the Gandhian Institute of Studies, Varanasi, 8–9 March 1969; at the meeting of the Japan Peace Research Group Tokyo, 27 March 1969; at a seminar organized by the Seminar for Peace and Conflict Research, Lund, 26 April 1969, and at the international seminar organized by the Centro Studi e Iniziative, Partinico, 3–4 May 1969. I am indebted to the organizers of these meetings, Randolph Major, Sugata Dasgupta, Hisako Ukita, Håkan Wiberg and Danilo Dolci and to many participants for highly stimulating comments and criticism. But special gratitude should be expressed to Herman Schmid, Lund University, Sweden, for his lucid and important criticism of some concepts of peace research, in *Journal of Peace Research*, 1968, pp. 217–32. Although I agree neither with his critique nor with his proposals, and feel that his way of presenting my own views is misleading, there are certainly few persons who have stimulated discussion and rethinking in this fundamental field so much. However, the present article is not a systematic answer to his arguments, but rather an effort, partly stimulated by him, to indicate what to the present author seems to be a fruitful way of thinking about violence, peace and peace research.

This practice is not necessarily harmful. The use of the term 'peace' may in itself be peace-productive, producing a common basis, a feeling of communality in purpose that may pave the ground for deeper ties later on. The use of more precise terms drawn from the vocabulary of one conflict group, and excluded from the vocabulary of the opponent group, may in itself cause dissent and lead to manifest conflict precisely because the term is so clearly understood. By projecting an image of harmony of interests the term 'peace' may also help bring about such a harmony. It provides opponents with a one-word language in which to express values of concern and togetherness because peace is on anybody's agenda.[2]

One may object that frequent use of the word 'peace' gives an unrealistic image of the world. Expressions like 'violence', 'strife', 'exploitation' or at least 'conflict', 'revolution' and 'war' should gain much higher frequency to mirror semantically a basically non-harmonious world. But leaving this major argument aside for the moment, it is obvious that some level of precision is necessary for the term to serve as a cognitive tool. At this point, of course, nobody has any monopoly on defining 'peace'. But those who use the term frequently in a research context, as peace researchers (will do) do, will at least have gained some experience when it comes to definitions that should be *avoided* for one reason or another.

To discuss the idea of peace we shall start from three simple principles:

1. The term 'peace' shall be used for social goals at least verbally agreed to by many, if not necessarily by most.
2. These social goals may be complex and difficult, but not impossible, to attain.
3. The statement *peace is absence of violence* shall be retained as valid.

The third principle is not a definition, since it is a clear case of *obscurum per obscurius*. What we intend is only that the terms 'peace' and 'violence' be linked to each other such that 'peace' can be regarded as 'absence of violence'. The reasons at this early point in our semantical excursion, are twofold: the statement is simple and in agreement with common usage, *and* defines a peaceful social order not as a point but as region – as the vast region of social orders from which violence is absent. Within this region a tremendous amount of variation is still possible, making an orientation in favor of peace compatible with a number of ideologies outlining other aspects of social orders.

Everything now hinges on making a definition of 'violence'. This is a highly unenviable task, and the suggestions will hardly be satisfactory to many readers. However, it is not so important to arrive at anything like *the* definition, or *the* typology – for there are obviously many types of violence. More important is to indicate theoretically significant dimensions of violence that can lead thinking, research and, potentially, action, towards the most important problems. If peace action is to be regarded highly because it is action against violence, then the concept of violence must be broad enough to include the most significant varieties, yet specific enough to serve as a basis for concrete action.

Thus, the definition of 'peace' becomes a major part of a scientific strategy. It may depart from common usage by not being agreed to 'by most' (consensus not required), yet should not be entirely subjectivistic ('agreed to by many'). It should depict a state of affairs the realization of which is not utopian ('not impossible to obtain'), yet not on the immediate political agenda ('complex and bifficult'). And it should immediately steer one's attention towards problems that are on the political, intellectual, and scientific agenda of today, and tomorrow.

2.   On the definition and dimensions of 'violence'

As a point of departure, let us say that *violence is present when human beings are being influenced so that their actual somatic and mental realizations are below their potential realizations.* This statement may lead to more problems than it solves. However, it will soon be clear why we are rejecting the narrow concept of violence – according to which violence is *somatic* incapacitation, or deprivation of health, alone (with killing as the extreme form), at the hands of an *actor* who *intends* this to be the consequence. If this were all violence is about, and peace is seen as its negation, then too little is rejected when peace is held up as an ideal. Highly unacceptable social orders would still be compatible with peace. Hence, *an extended concept of violence is indispensable* but that concept should be a logical extension, not merely a list of undesirables.

The definition points to at least six important dimensions of violence. But first some remarks about the use of the key words above, 'actual' and 'potential'. *Violence is here defined as the cause of the difference between the potential and the actual,* between what could have been and what is. Violence is that which increases the distance between the potential and the actual, and that which impedes the decrease of this distance. Thus, if a person died from tuberculosis in the eighteenth century it would be hard to conceive of this as violence since it might have been quite unavoidable, but if he dies from it today, despite all the medical resources in the world, then violence is present according to our definition. Correspondingly, the case of people dying from earthquakes today would not warrant an analysis in terms of violence,[3] but the day after tomorrow, when earthquakes may become avoidable, such deaths may be seen as the result of violence. In other words, when the potential is higher than the actual is by definition *avoidable* and when it is avoidable, then violence is present.

When the actual is unavoidable, then violence is not present even if the actual is at a very low level. A life expectancy of thirty years only, during the neolithic period, was not an expression of violence, but the same life-expectancy today (whether due to wars, or social injustice, or both) would be seen as violence according to our definition.

Thus, the potential level of realization is that which is possible with a given level of insight and resources. If insight and/or resources are *monopolized* by a group or class or are *used for other purposes*, then the actual level falls below the potential level, and violence is present in the system. In addition to these types of *indirect* violence there is also the *direct* violence where means of realization are not withheld, but directly destroyed. Thus, when a war is fought there is direct violence since killing or hurting a person certainly puts his 'actual somatic realization' below his 'potential somatic realization'. But there is also indirect violence insofar as insight and resources are channelled away from constructive efforts to bring the actual closer to the potential.[4]

The meaning of 'potential realizations' is highly problematic, especially when we move from somatic aspects of human life, where consensus is more readily obtained,[5] to mental aspects. Our guide here would probably often have to be whether the value to be realized is fairly consensual or not, although this is by no means satisfactory. For example, literacy is held in high regard almost everywhere, whereas the value of being Christian is highly controversial. Hence, we would talk about violence if the level of literacy is lower than what it could have been, not if the level of Christianity is lower than what it could have been. We shall not try to explore this difficult point further in this context, but turn to the dimensions of violence.

To discuss them, it is useful to conceive of violence in terms of influence, as indicated in the statement we used as a point of departure above. A complete influence relation presupposes an influencer, an influencee, and a mode of influencing.[6] In the case of persons, we can put it very simply: a *subject*, an *object*, and an *action*. But this conception of violence in terms of a *complete* interpersonal influence relation will lead us astray by focussing on a very special type of violence only; also *truncated* versions where either subject or object or both are absent are highly significant. To approach this we shall start with two dimensions characterizing the violent action itself, or the mode of influence.

The *first distinction* to be made is between *physical* and *psychological* violence. The distinction is trite but important mainly because the narrow concept of violence mentioned above concentrates on physical violence only. Under physical violence human beings are hurt somatically, to the point of killing. It is useful to distinguish further between 'biological violence', which reduces somatic capability (below what is potentially possible), and 'physical violence as such', which increases the constraint on human movements[7] – as when a person is imprisoned or put in chains, but also when access to transportation is very unevenly distributed, keeping large segments of a population at the same place with mobility a monopoly of the selected few. But that distinction is less important than the basic distinction between violence that works on the body, and violence that works on the soul; where the latter would include lies, brainwashing, indoctrination of various kinds, threats, etc. that serve to decrease mental potentialities. (Incidentally, it is interesting that such English words as 'hurt' and 'hit' can be used to express psychological as well as physical violence: this doubleness is already built into the language.)

The *second distinction* is between the *negative* and *positive* approach to influence.[8] Thus, a person can be influenced not only by punishing him when he does what the influencer considers wrong, but also by rewarding him when he does what the influencer considers right. Instead of increasing the constraints on his movements the constraints may be decreased instead of increased, and somatic capabilities extended instead of reduced. This may be readily agreed to, but does it have anything to do with violence? Yes, because the net result may still be that human beings are effectively prevented from realizing their potentialities. Thus, many contemporary thinkers[9] emphasize that the consumer's society rewards amply he who goes in for consumption, while not positively punishing him who does not. The system is reward-oriented, based on promises of euphoria, but in so being also narrows down the ranges of action. It may be disputed whether this is better or worse than a system that limits the range of action because of the dysphoric consequences of staying outside the permitted range. It is perhaps better in terms of giving pleasure rather than pain, worse in terms of being more manipulatory, less overt. But the important point is, the awareness of the concept of violence can be extended in this direction, since it yields a much richer basis for discussion.

The *third distinction* to be made is on the object side: *whether or not there is an object that is hurt*. Can we talk about violence when no physical or biological object is hurt? This would be a case of what is referred to above as truncated violence, but nevertheless highly meaningful. When a person, a group, a nation is displaying the means of physical violence, whether throwing stones around or testing nuclear arms, there may not be violence in the sense that anyone is hit or hurt, but there is nevertheless the *threat of physical violence* and indirect threat of mental violence that may even be characterized as some type of psychological violence since it constrains human action. Indeed, this is also the intention: the famous balance of power doctrine is based on efforts to obtain precisely this effect. And correspondingly with psychological violence that does not reach any object: a lie does not become more of a truth because nobody believes in the lie. Untruthfulness is violence according to this kind of thinking under any condition, which does not mean that it cannot be the least evil under some widely discussed circumstances.

Is destruction of things violence? Again, it would not be violence according to the complete definition above, but possibly some 'degenerate' form. But in at least two senses it can be seen as psychological violence: the destruction of things as a foreboding or threat of possible destruction of persons,[10] and the destruction of things as destruction of something very dear to persons referred to as consumers or *owners*.[11]

The *fourth distinction* to be made and the most important one is on the subject side: *whether or not there is a subject (person) who acts*. Again it may be asked: can we talk about violence when nobody is committing direct violence, is acting? This would also be a case of what is referred to above as truncated violence, but again highly meaningful. We shall refer to the type of violence where there is an actor that commits the violence as *personal* or *direct*, and to violence where there is no such actor as *structural* or *indirect*.[12] In both cases individuals may be killed or mutilated, hit or hurt in both senses of these words, and manipulated by means of stick or carrot strategies. But whereas in the first case these consequences can be traced back to concrete persons as actors, in the second case this is no longer meaningful. There may not be any person who directly harms another person in the structure. The violence is built into the structure and shows up as unequal power and consequently as unequal life chances.[13]

Resources are unevenly distributed, as when income distributions are heavily skewed, literacy/education unevenly distributed, medical services existent in some districts and for some groups only, and so on.[14] Above all the *power to decide over the distribution of resources* is unevenly distributed.[15] The situation is aggravated further if the persons low on income are also low in education, low on health, and low on power – as is frequently the case because these rank dimensions tend to be heavily correlated due to the way they are tied together in the social structure.[16] Marxist criticism of capitalist society emphasizes how the power to decide over the surplus from the production process is reserved for the owners of the means of production, who then can buy themselves into top positions on all other rank dimensions because money is highly convertible in a capitalist society – if you have money to convert, that is. Liberal criticism of socialist society similarly emphasizes how power to decide is monopolized by a small group who convert power in one field into power in another field simply because the opposition cannot reach the stage of effective articulation.

The important point here is that if people are starving when this is objectively avoidable, then violence is committed, regardless of whether there is a clear subject-action-object relation, as during a siege yesterday or no such clear relation, as in the way world economic relations are organized today.[17] We have baptized the distinction in two different ways, using the word-pairs personal-structural and direct-indirect respectively. Violence with a clear subject-object relation is manifest because it is visible as *action*. It corresponds to our ideas of what *drama* is, and it is personal because there are persons committing the violence. It is easily captured and expressed verbally since it has the same structure as elementary sentences in (at least Indo-European) *languages*: subject-verb-object, with both subject and object being persons. Violence without this relation is structural, built into structure. Thus, when one husband beats his wife there is a clear case of personal violence, but when one million husbands keep one million wives in ignorance there is structural violence. Correspondingly, in a society where life expectancy is twice as high in the upper as in the lower classes, violence is exercised even if there are no concrete actors one can point to directly attacking others, as when one person kills another.

In order not to overwork the word violence we shall sometimes refer to the condition of structural violence as *social injustice*.[18] The term 'exploitation' will not be used, for several reasons. First, it belongs to a political vocabulary, and has so many political and emotional overtones that the use of this term will hardly facilitate communication. Second, the term lends itself too easily to expressions involving the verb exploit, which in turn may lead attention away from the structural as opposed to the personal nature of this phenomenon – and even lead to often unfounded accusations about intended structural violence.[19]

The *fifth distinction* to be made is between violence that is *intended* or *unintended*. This distinction is important when *guilt* is to be decided, since the concept of guilt has been tied more to *intention*, both in Judaeo-Christian ethics and in Roman jurisprudence, than to *consequence* (whereas the present definition of violence is entirely located on the consequence side). This connection is important because it brings into focus a bias present in so much thinking about violence, peace, and related concepts: ethical systems directed against *intended* violence will easily fail to capture structural violence in their nets – and may hence be catching the small fry and letting the big fish loose. From this fallacy it does not follow, in our mind, that the opposite fallacy of directing all attention against structural violence is elevated into wisdom. If the concern is with peace, and peace is absence of violence, then action should be directed against personal as well as structural violence; a point to be developed below.

Sixth, there is the traditional distinction between two levels of violence, the *manifest* and the *latent*.[20] Manifest violence, whether personal or structural, is observable; although not directly since the theoretical entity of 'potential realization' also enters the picture. Latent violence is something which is not there, yet might easily come about. Since violence by definition is the cause of the difference (or of maintaining the non-decrease) between actual and potential realization, increased violence may come about by increases in the potential as well as by decreases in the actual levels. However, we shall limit ourselves to the latter and say that there is latent violence when the situation is so unstable that the actual realization level 'easily' decreases. For personal violence this would mean a situation where a little challenge would trigger considerable killing and atrocity, as is often the case in connection with racial fights. In such cases we need a way of expressing that the personal violence is

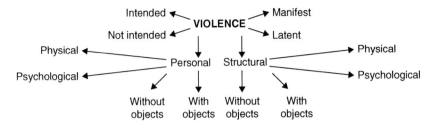

Figure 1.   A Typology of Violence

also there the day, hour, minute, second before the first bomb, shot, fist-fight, cry – and this is what the concept of latent, personal violence does for us. It indicates a situation of unstable equilibrium, where the level of actual realization is not sufficiently protected against deterioration by upholding mechanisms.

Similarly with structural violence: we could imagine a relatively egalitarian structure insufficiently protected against sudden feudalization, against crystallization into a much more stable, even petrified, hierarchical structure. A revolution brought about by means of a highly hierarchical military organization may after a brilliant period of egaliatarianism, and after major challenge, revert to a hierarchical structure. One way of avoiding this, of course, is to avoid hierarchical group struggle organizations in the first run, and use nonviolent nonhierarchical guerrilla organizations in the fight so as to let the means be a preview of the egalitarian goal.[21]

That concludes our list of dimensions of violence, although many more could be included. One question that immediately arises is whether any combinations from these six dichotomies can be ruled out *a priori*, but there seems to be no such case. Structural violence without objects is also meaningful; truncation of the complete violence relation can go so far as to eliminate both subjects and objects. Personal violence is meaningful as a threat, a demonstration even when nobody is hit, and structural violence is also meaningful as a blueprint, as an abstract form without social life, used to threaten people into subordination: if you do not behave, we shall have to reintroduce all the disagreeable structures we had before.

Disregarding the negative-positive distinction as less important in this context, we end up, essentially, with the typology illustrated in Figure 1.

If peace now is regarded as absence of violence, then thinking about peace (and consequently peace research and peace action) will be structured the same way as thinking about violence. And the violence cake can evidently be cut a number of ways. Tradition has been to think about violence as personal violence only, with one important subdivision in terms of 'violence vs. the threat of violence', another in terms of 'physical vs. psychological war', still another (important in ethical and legal thinking) about 'intended

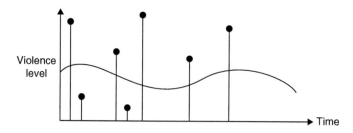

Figure 2.   Time and the Two Types of Violence

vs. unintended', and so on. The choice is here to make the distinction between personal and structural violence the basic one; justification has been presented (1) in terms of a unifying perspective (the cause of the difference between potential and actual realization) and (2) by indicating that there is no reason to assume that structural violence amounts to less suffering than personal violence.

On the other hand, it is not strange that attention has been focussed more on personal than on structural violence. Personal violence *shows*.[22] The object of personal violence perceives the violence, usually, and may complain – the object of structural violence may be persuaded not to perceive this at all. Personal violence represents change and dynamism – not only ripples on waves, but waves on otherwise tranquil waters. Structural violence is silent, it does not show – it is essentially static, it *is* the tranquil waters. In a *static* society, personal violence will be registered, whereas structural violence may be seen as about as natural as the air around us. Conversely: in a highly *dynamic* society, personal violence may be seen as wrong and harmful but still somehow congruent with the order of things, whereas structural violence becomes apparent because it stands out like an enormous rock in a creek, impeding the free flow, creating all kinds of eddies and turbulences. Thus, perhaps it is not so strange that the thinking about personal violence (in the Judaeo–Christian–Roman tradition) took on much of its present form in what we today would regard as essentially static social orders, whereas thinking about structural violence (in the Marxist tradition) was formulated in highly dynamic northwest-European societies.

In other words, we conceive of structural violence as something that shows a certain stability, whereas personal violence (e.g. as measured by the tolls caused by group conflict in general and war in particular) shows tremendous fluctuations over time. This is illustrated in Figure 2.

This is to a large extent tautological. A type of violence built into the social structure should exhibit a certain stability: social structures may perhaps sometimes be changed over night, but they may not very often be changed that quickly. Personal violence, which to a larger extent is seen as subject to the whims and wishes of individuals, should show less stability. Hence personal violence may more easily be noticed, even though the 'tranquil waters' of structural violence may contain much more violence. For this reason we would expect a focus on personal violence in after-war periods lest they should become between-war periods; and if the periods protracts sufficiently for the major outburst of personal violence to be partly forgotten, we would expect a concentration on structural violence, provided the societies are dynamic enough to make any stability stand out as somehow unnatural.[23]

3. The means of personal and structural violence

To make this distinction less abstract, let us now explore how personal and structural violence, are, in fact, carried out. Starting with personal violence, concentration on 'actual somatic realization': how can it be reduced or kept low at the hands of somebody else? The question is simple, as are the answers since they suggest an instrumental approach to the problem of violence. There is a well-specified task to be done, that of doing bodily harm unto others, and there are persons available to do it. But this is a production relation, suggesting a 'development' much like in the economic sector of society, with the introduction of increasingly refined tools and differentiated social organization – only that the tools in this case are referred to as weapons or arms, and the organization is not called a workshop or a factory, but a gang or an army.

A typology of personal, physical violence can now be developed focussing on the *tools* used, starting with the human body itself (in the elementary forms of fist fights and the more advanced forms, such as *Karate* and *Aikido*), proceeding towards all kinds of arms culminating, so far, with ABC weapons. Another approach would use the form of *organization*, starting with the lone individual, proceeding via mobs and crowds ending up with the organizations of modern guerrilla or army warfare. These two approaches are related: just as in economic organizations the means and mode of production (here direct bodily violence) depend on each other, and if one is lagging behind a conflict will arise. Together these two approaches would yield the history of military warfare as a special case, since much bodily violence is not military. The approach would be cumulative for a weapon or technique, and a form of organization once developed may become obsolete but not erased; hence this typology would not be systematic, but always open to record new developments.

A more systematic approach can be obtained by looking at the target; the human being. He is relatively known anatomically (structurally) and physiologically (functionally), so typologies can be developed on that basis. One primitive typology might be as shown in Table 1. The basic distinction is not water-tight, but nevertheless useful: for one thing is to try to destroy the machine (the human body) itself, another to try to prevent the machine from functioning. The latter can be done in two ways: denial of *input* (sources of

Table 1   A Typology of Personal Somatic Violence

Focussed on the anatomy	Focussed on the physiology
1. *crushing* (fist fight, catapults)	1. *denial of air* (choking, strangulation)
2. *tearing* (hanging, stretching, cutting)	2. *denial of water* (dehydration)
3. *piercing* (knives, spears, bullets)	3. *denial of food* (starvation due to siege, embargo)
4. *burning* (arson, flame thrower)	4. *denial of movement*
5. *poisoning* (in water and food, in gases)	a. by body constraint (chains, gas)
6. *evaporation* (as in nuclear explosion)	b. by space constraint (prison, detention, exile)
	c. by brain control (nerve gases, 'brain-washing')

energy in general, air, water, and food in the case of the body), and denial of *output* (movement). The human output can be *somatic*, recorded by the outside as movement (with standstill as a limiting case) or *mental* not recorded directly from the outside (only by indicators in the form of movements, including movements of vocal chords). The borderline between physical and psychological personal violence is not very clear, since it is possible to influence physical movements by means of psychological techniques, and vice versa: physical constraints certainly have mental implications.

In Table 1 some of the techniques have been indicated in parenthesis. A note should be added here about *explosions*. In principle they are of two kinds: to propel some missile, and to work directly on human bodies. Explosions are much used for the latter purpose because they combine the anatomical methods: a standard bomb would combine 1 and 2; add some shrapnel and 3 is also taken care of; add some simple chemicals so as to make it a fire bomb and 4 is taken into account; some gases would include 5 and if in addition the contraption is made nuclear the crowning achievement, 6, is there – presumably for ever, at least in principle, since it is difficult systematically to unmake an invention, it can only be suppressed. New weapons can always be invented, based on one or any combination of the principles in the Table. But there is also room for the more basic innovation: the introduction of a new principle.

Is it now possible to construct a corresponding typology for structural violence? If we accept that the general formula behind structural violence is inequality, above all in the distribution of power, then this can be measured; and inequality seems to have a high survival capacity despite tremendous changes elsewhere.[24] But if inequality persists, then we may ask: which factors, apart from personal violence and the threat of personal violence, tend to uphold inequality? Obviously, just as military science and related subjects would be indispensable for the understanding of personal violence, so is the science of social structure, and particularly of stratification, indispensable for the understanding of structural violence.

This is not the occasion to develop general theories of social structure, but some ideas are necessary to arrive at some of the mechanisms. Most fundamental are the ideas of *actor, system, structure, rank* and *level*. Actors seek goals, and are organized in systems in the sense that they interact with each other. But two actors, e.g. two nations, can usually be seen as interacting in more than one system; they not only cooperate politically, e.g. by trading votes in the UN, but also economically by trading goods, and culturally by trading ideas. The set of all such systems of interaction, for a given set of actors, can then be referred to as a structure. And in a structure an actor may have high rank in one system, low in the next, and then high in the third one; or actors may have either consistently high ranks or consistently low ranks.

However, if we look more closely at an actor, e. g. a nation, we shall very often be able to see it as a structure in its own right, but an integrated structure since it is able to appear as an actor. This 'Chinese boxes' view of actors is very important, and leads to the concept of level of actors. There are three major interpretations:[25]

- in terms of *territories*: a nation can be seen as a set of districts, in turn seen as a set of municipalities, and these are then seen as a set of individuals;
- in terms of *organizations*: a factory can often be seen as an assembly line with sub-factories feeding into the assembly-line with their products, finally coming down to the individual worker.
- in terms of *associations*: they can often be seen as consisting of local chapters, ending up with individual members.

Thus, the image of the social order or disorder can be presented as in Figure 3.

In all these systems there is interaction, and where there is interaction, value is somehow exchanged. It then makes very much sense to study what the value-distribution is after the system has been operating for some time, and the gross distinction has been made between egalitarian and inegalitarian distributions.

We can now mention six factors that serve to maintain inegalitarian distributions, and consequently can be seen as mechanisms of structural violence:

1. *Linear ranking order* – the ranking is complete, leaving no doubt as to who is higher in any pair of actors;
2. *Acyclical interaction pattern* – all actors are connected, but only one way – there is only one 'correct' path of interaction;
3. *Correlation between rank and centrality* – the higher the rank of the actor in the system, the more central his position in the interaction network;

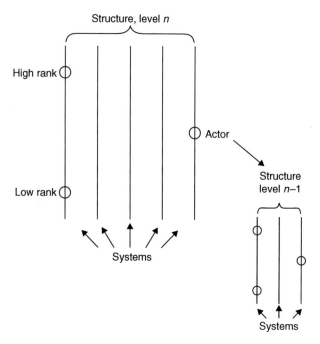

Figure 3.   An Image of the Social Order

4. *Congruence between the systems* – the interaction networks are structurally similar.
5. *Concordance between the ranks* – if an actor is high in one system then he also tends to be high in another system where he participates and
6. *High rank coupling between levels* – so that the actor at level n–1 is represented at level n through the highest ranking actor at level n–1.

The factors can best be understood by examining to some extent their negation, starting with the last one.

Thus, imagine that a nation is dominated by an economic and cultural capital, but has a much smaller political capital through which most political interaction in the international system is carried out. This would tend to distribute the power at the level of cities since the coupling is not at the highest point. Similarly, we could imagine that the major road from the capital to a district did not connect directly with the district point of gravity but with some peripheral point; as when a government is represented abroad not by the president or prime minister but by the foreign minister – or a sub-factory not by the manager but by his deputy. But very often the top actor at level n–1 is made the representative at level n – with a number of implications.[26]

Similarly, imagine there is considerable rank discordance, even to the point where the summated rankings of the actors tend to be relatively equal. In that case, patterns of inequality would be less consistent and less reinforcing, and the amount of disequilibrium in the system would also tend to upset any stability. Moreover, if the systems are not congruent but differ in structure, actors will not so easily generalize interaction patterns but be more flexible, less frozen into one way of acting (for instance servility). And if the actor with highest rank did not necessarily have the most central position in the network this would diminish his power, which would also be diminished if actors with lower ranks were to a larger extent permitted direct interaction (not only interaction mediated through the actors with high rank). Finally: non-linear, pyramidal (also known as partial) ranking order permits more leeway, more flexibility in the system.[27]

Many propositions can now be developed about this, a basic one being that social systems will have a tendency to develop all six mechanisms unless deliberately *and persistently* prevented from doing so. Thus the pattern is set for an aggravation of inequality, in some structures so much so that the lowest-ranking actors are deprived not only relative to the potential, but indeed below subsistence minimum. Inequality then shows up in differential morbidity and mortality rates, between individuals in a district, between districts in a nation, and between nations in the international system – in a chain of interlocking feudal relationships. They are deprived because the structure deprives them of chances to organize and bring their power to bear against the topdogs, as voting power, bargaining power, striking power, violent power – partly because they are atomized and disintegrated, partly because they are overawed by all the authority the topdogs present.

Thus, the net result may be bodily harm in both cases, but structural violence will probably just as often be recorded as psychological violence. Hence, highly different means may lead to highly similar results – a conclusion to be explored later.

4. The relation between personal and structural violence

In this section some comments will be offered on this relationship, following this outline:

1. Is there really a distinction between personal and structural violence at all?
2. If there is, does not one type of violence presuppose the manifest presence of the other?
3. If pure types exist, could it not nevertheless be said that they have a prehistory of the other type?
4. If this is not generally the case, could it not be that one type of violence presupposes the latent presence of the other?

5. If this is not the case, could it not be that one is the price we have to pay for the absence of the other?
6. If this is not generally the case, could it not be that one type is much more important in its consequences than the other?

Let us start with the first question.

It may be argued that this distinction is not clear at all: it disregards slights of the structural element in personal violence and the personal element in structural violence. These important perspectives are regained if a person is seen as making his decision to act violently not only on the basis of individual deliberations but (also) on the basis of expectations impinging on him as norms contained in roles contained in statuses through which he enacts his social self; *and*, if one sees a violent structure as something that is a mere abstraction unless upheld by the actions, expected from the social environment or not, of individuals. But then: does not this mean that there is no real distinction at all? Cannot a person engaging in personal violence always use expectations from the structure as an excuse, and does not a person upholding an exploitative social structure have responsibility for this?

The distinction that nevertheless remains is between violence that hits human beings as a *direct* result of Figure 4 type actions of others, and violence that hits them *indirectly* because repressive structures (as analyzed in preceding section) are upheld by the summated and concerted action of human beings. The qualitative difference between these actions is the answer. The question of guilt is certainly not a metaphysical question; guilt is as real as any other feeling, but a less interesting one. The question is rather whether violence is structured in such a way that it constitutes a direct, personal link between a subject and an object, or an indirect structural one, not how

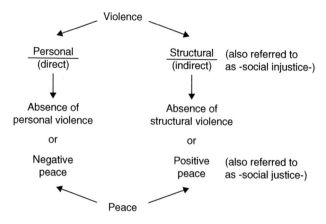

Figure 4.   The Extended Concepts of Violence and Peace

this link is perceived by the persons at either end of the violence channel. The objective consequences, not the subjective intentions are the primary concern.

But are personal and structural violence empirically, not only logically, independent of each other? Granted that there may be a correlation so that structures richly endowed with structural violence often may also display above average incidence of personal violence, it is possible to have them in pure forms, to have one without the other? are there *structures where violence is person-invariant* in the sense that structural violence persists regardless of changes in persons? And conversely, are there *persons where violence is structure-invariant* in the sense that personal violence persists regardless of changes in structural context?

The answer seems to be yes in either case. The typical feudal structure, with a succession of encapsulating hierarchies of metropole-satellite relationships is clearly structurally violent regardless of who staffs it and regardless of the level of awareness of the participants: the violence is built into the structures. No personal violence or threat of personal violence are needed. And there are persons who seem to be violent in (almost) any setting – often referred to as 'bullies'. Characteristic of them is precisely that they carry their violent propensity with them far outside any structural context deemed reasonable by society at large, for which reason they will often be institutionalized (in prison or mental hospital, depending on which basic norms they infract first and most clearly). Hence, we may conclude that the two forms of violence are empirically independent: the one does not presuppose the other.

But from this alone it cannot be concluded that there is no necessary (not only sufficient) *causal relationship* between the two types of violence, or that the even stronger condition of *one-way reductionism* is not fulfilled. One may argue that all cases of structural violence can, by closer scrutiny, be traced back to personal violence in their *pre-history*. An exploitative caste system or race society would be seen as the consequence of a large-scale invasion leaving a thin, but powerful top layer of the victorious group after the noise of fighting is over. A bully would be seen as the inevitable product of socialization into a violent structure: he is the rebel, systematically untrained in other ways of coping with his conflicts and frustrations because the structure leaves him with no alternatives. That structural violence often breeds structural violence, and personal violence often breeds personal violence nobody would dispute – but the point here would be the cross-breeding between the two. In other words: pure cases are only pure as long as the pre-history of the case or even the structural context are conveniently forgotten.

Far from denying that these may be fruitful perspectives both for research into the past and the etiology of violence as well as for search into the future and therapy for violence we would tend to reject the position that violence presupposes a pre-history of violence of the same or opposite kinds. This view is a breeding theory, and like all breeding theories it fails to answer two questions: how did the process come into being at all? and is spontaneous generation of violence impossible, or are all cases of violence the legitimate offspring of other cases of violence – handed down through some kind of apostolic succession, the content being more like 'original sin' though?

Take the case of structural violence first. Here it may be argued we will never get the perfect test-case. Imagine we based our thinking on something like this: people, when left to themselves in isolation (in a discussion group, stranded on an isolated island, etc.) will tend to form systems where rank, or differential evaluation of relatively stable interaction patterns referred to as status, will emerge; high ranks tend to cluster on persons who already have some high ranks, and interaction tends to flow in their direction – hence the net result is sooner or later a feudal structure. One might then object: yes, because these persons are already socialized into such structures, and all they do is to project their experiences and their habits so as to give life to an embryonic structure. And there is no way around it: human beings, to be human, have to be rated by humans, hence there will always be an element of succession.

Maybe, but, we also suspect that the reasoning above holds true even under *tabula rasa* conditions because it probably is connected with the fact (1) that individuals are different and (2) that these differences somehow are relevant for their interaction behavior. Hence, special measures are needed to prevent the formation of feudal structures: structural violence seems to be more 'natural' than structural peace. And similarly with personal violence: it is difficult to see how even the most egalitarian structure would be sufficient to prevent cases of violence, whether they result from conflicts or not. Personal violence is perhaps more 'natural' than personal peace. It could also be argued that an inegalitarian structure is a built-in mechanism of conflict control, precisely because it is hierarchical, and that an egalitarian structure would bring out in the open many new conflicts that are kept latent in a feudal structure.

One could now proceed by saying that even if one type of violence does not presuppose the manifest presence of the other, neither synchronically, nor diachronically, there is nevertheless the possibility that manifest structural violence presupposes latent personal violence. When the structure is threatened, those who benefit from structural violence, above all those who are at the top, will try to preserve the status quo so well geared to protect their interests. By observing the activities of various groups and persons when a structure is threatened, and more particularly by noticing who comes to the rescue of the structure, an operational test is introduced that can be used to rank the members of the structure in terms of their interest in maintaining the structure. The involvement that does not show clearly in times of unimpeded persistence is brought up to the surface when there is turbulence. But one has to observe carefully, for those most interested in the maintenance of status quo may not come openly to the defence of the structure: they may push their mercenaries in front of them.[28] In other words, they may mobilize the police, the army, the thugs, the general social underbrush against the sources of the disturbance, and remain themselves in more discrete, remote seclusion from the turmoil of personal violence. And they can do this as an extrapolation of the structural violence: the violence committed by the police is personal by our definition, yet they are called into action by expectations deeply rooted in the structure – there is no need to assume an intervening variable of intention. They simply do their job.

This view is probably generally very valid, even if it may underestimate the significance of a number of factors:

1. the extent to which the 'tools of oppression' may have internalized the repressive structure so that their personal violence is an expression of internalized, not only institutionalized norms;
2. the extent to which those who benefit from the structural violence may themselves have severe and sincere doubts about that structure and prefer to see it changed, even at their own expense;
3. the extent to which the 'challenge of the structure' may be a personal confrontation with the police etc. more than with the structure, and reveal more about the dynamics of interpersonal relations than about the structure.[29]
4. the extent to which all members in a violent structure, not only the top-dogs, contribute to its operation and hence are all responsible as they can all shake it through their non-cooperation.

But these are minor points; social affairs always refuse to be captured in simplistic formulations. More important is whether one can also turn the proposition around and gain some insight by saying that manifest personal violence presupposes latent structural violence – which is not the same as saying that it presupposes manifest structural violence. The idea would be that of an egalitarian structure maintained by means of personal violence, so that when this pattern of violence is challenged to the point of abolition there will be an emergence of structural violence.

The proposition is interesting because it may open for some possible insights in structures yet unknown to us. It does not seem *a priori* unreasonable to state that if the absence of personal violence is combined with a pattern of structural violence, then personal violence is nevertheless around the corner – and correspondingly that if absence of structural violence is combined with personal violence, then structural violence is also around the corner. All we are saying is only that the sum of violence is constant, only that one has to take into account the latent variety of the type of violence 'abolished' to see more clearly how that type is in a standby position, ready to step in once the other type crumbles. Absence of one type of violence is bought at the expense of the threat of the other.

But, however insight-stimulating this may be in certain situations we refuse to accept this pessimistic view for two reasons. First, the two propositions seem simply not to be true. It is not at all difficult to imagine a structure so purely structural in its violence that all means of personal violence have been abolished, so that when the structure is threatened there is no second trench defense by mobilizing latent personal violence. Similarly, a structure may be completely unprepared for freezing the released forces stemming from a reduction of personal violence into a hierarchical order. Empirically such cases may be rare, but yet significant.

Second, the assumption would be that human beings somehow need violence to be kept in line; if not of the personal type, then of the structural variety. The argument would be that if there is no personal violence or threat of personal violence then a very strong hierarchical order is needed to maintain order and to control conflict; and if there is no structural violence or threat of structural violence, then personal violence will easily serve as a substitute. But even if this may be a reasonable theory to explain possible empirical regularities, that in itself is not sufficient argument for reifying a regularity into a principle supposedly eternally valid. On the contrary, this would be a highly pessimistic view of the human condition, and to accept it fully would even be a capitulationist view.

From the problem of whether one type of violence is necessary to *obtain* or *sustain* the other type, whether at the manifest or the latent levels, it is not far to the opposite problem: is one type of violence necessary or sufficient to *abolish* the other type? The question, which actually splits into four questions, brings us directly into the center of contemporary political debate. Let us examine briefly some of the arguments.

1. *Structural violence is sufficient to abolish personal violence.* This thesis seems to have a certain limited and short-term validity. If all the methods mentioned above for sustaining structural violence are implemented, then it seems quite possible that personal violence *between the groups segregated by the structure* is abolished. The underdogs are too isolated and too awed by the topdogs, the topdogs have nothing to fear. But this only holds between those groups; within the groups the feudal structure is not practised. And although the structure probably is among the most stable social structures imaginable, it is not stable in perpetuity. There are many ways in which it may be upset, and result in tremendous outbursts of personal violence. Hence, it may perhaps be said to be a structure that serves to compartmentalize personal violence in time, leading to successions of periods of absence and presence of personal violence.

2. *Structural violence is necessary to abolish personal violence.* This is obviously not true, since personal violence will cease the moment the decision not to practise it is taken. But this is of course begging the question: under what condition is that decision made and really sustained? That structural

violence represents an alternative in the sense that much of the 'order' obtained by means of (the threat of) personal violence can also be obtained by (the threat of) structural violence is clear enough. But to state a relation of *necessity* is to go far outside our limited empirical experience.

3. *Personal violence is sufficient to abolish structural violence.* Again, this thesis seems to have a certain limited short-term validity. Personal violence directed against the topdogs in a feudal structure incapacitating them bodily by means of the techniques in Table 1, used singly or combined. When the topdogs are no longer there to exercise their roles the feudal structure can clearly no longer function. Hence, just as under 1 above *between*-group structural violence *may* be abolished by this process. But to abolish the *topdogs* in a violent structure is one thing, to abolish the violent *structure* quite another, and it is this *fallacy of misplaced concreteness* that is one of the strongest arguments against the proposition. The new power group may immediately fill the vacancies, retaining the structure, only changing the names of the incumbents and possibly the rationalization of the structure, in which case the structural violence is not even abolished for a short term. Or the structure may re-emerge after some time, because of internal dynamism or because it has after all been firmly imprinted on the minds of the new power-holders and has thus been present all the time in latent form.

4. *Personal violence is necessary to abolish structural violence.* This is, of course, a famous revolutionary proposition with a certain currency. One may argue against it on three grounds: empirically, theoretically and axiologically. *Empirically* one would point to all the cases of structural change decreasing structural violence that seem to take place without personal violence. The counter-argument will be that there were cases with no basic change of the structure, for if there had been a fundamental threat to the power-holders then they would have resorted to personal violence. *Theoretically* one would point to the qualitative difference between the means of personal and structural violence and ask: even if personal violence *may* lead to the abolition of structural violence, is it not likely that some, and possibly also more effective means of changing a structure would be structural, for instance systematic changes of interaction networks, rank profiles etc.? In other words, the belief in the *indispensability of personal violence* could be said, on theoretical grounds, to be a case of *fetishization* of personal violence. And then there is the *axiological* argument: even if personal violence could be seen as indispensable up till today, on empirical and/or theoretical grounds, this would be one more good reason for a systematic search for the conditions under which this indispensability would disappear.

Again our search seems to fail to uncover any absolutes. It is hard to sustain a belief in sufficiency or necessity one way or the other. The two types of violence simply do not seem to be more tightly connected empirically than logically – and as to the latter, the whole exercise is an effort to show that they may be seen as logically independent even though they are continuous with each other: one shades into the other.

But even if one now rejects reductionism one way or the other there would still be good reason for focussing research attention more on one kind of violence than on the other: it may always be argued that one is much more important in its consequences than the other. Thus, imagine we were able to calculate the losses incurred by the two forms of violence, or the gains that would accrue to mankind if they could be eliminated. In principle this should not be quite impossible, at least not for the simpler physical forms of violence that show up in terms of mortality, and possibly also in terms of morbidity. Mortality and morbidity rates under the condition of absence of war can usually be calculated relatively well by extrapolation from pre-war and post-war data. It is more difficult for the case of absence of exploitation, but not impossible: we could calculate the levels attained if all available resources were used for the purpose of extending and improving the biological life-span and in addition were distributed in an egalitarian fashion in social space. The costs incurred by violence of one form or the other would then appear as the difference between the potential and the actual, as the definition requires, and the costs can then be compared. One could also imagine calculations of the costs of the joint operation of the two forms of violence.

One significant feature of such calculations, that definitely should have a high priority on the research program of peace research institutes, is that the door would be opened for answers to questions such as whether the costs in terms of personal violence were higher or lower than the gains in reduction of structural violence in, say, the Cuban revolution. The present author would say that they were definitely lower, using comparable Latin American countries as a basis for evaluating the costs of the structural violence under Batista, but in the equation one would of course also have to include the personal violence under Batista and the structural violence under Castro, e.g. in the form of almost complete alienation of the former bourgeoisie, not only as status holders, but as persons. Such statements are impressionistic however, they should be backed up empirically.

But however attractive such calculations may be – for reasons of intellectual curiosity about the dynamics of violence, structural and personal, even to develop much higher levels of theoretical insights into these phenomena than we possess today – this is not the same as accepting cost-benefit analysis in this field as a basis for political action. The point here is not so much that one may have objections to projecting the mathematical 'one human life-year = one human life-year', regardless how it is lost or gained, on to the stage of political action, but rather that this type of analysis leads to much too modest goals for political action. Imagine that the general norm were formulated 'you shall act politically so as to decrease violence, taking into account both before and after levels of personal and structural violence'.

A norm of that kind would be blind to possible differences in structural and personal violence when it comes to their potential for getting more violence in the future. But it would also condone action as long as there is any decrease, and only steer political action *downwards* on the violence surface, not lead to a systematic search for the *steepest* gradient possible, even for a descent route hitherto unknown to man.

But equally important is to recall that it is hardly possible to arrive at any general judgment, independent of time and space, as to which type of violence is more important. In space, today, it may certainly be argued that research in the Americas should focus on structural violence, between nations as well as between individuals, and that peace research in Europe should have a similar focus on personal violence. Latent personal violence in Europe may erupt into nuclear war, but the manifest structural violence in the Americas (and not only there) already causes an annual toll of nuclear magnitudes. In saying this, we are of course not neglecting the structural components of the European situation, (such as the big power dominance and the traditional exploitation of Eastern Europe by Western Europe) nor are we forgetful of the high level of personal violence in the Americas even though it does not take the form of international warfare (but sometimes the form of interventionist aggression).

5. On the definition of 'peace' and 'peace research'

With the distinction between personal and structural violence as basic, violence becomes two-sided, and so does peace conceived of as the absence of violence. *An extended concept of violence leads to an extended concept of peace.* Just as a coin has two sides, one side alone being only one aspect of the coin, not the complete coin, peace also has two sides: *absence of personal violence*, and *absence of structural violence*.[30] We shall refer to them as *negative peace* and *positive peace* respectively.[31]

For brevity the formulations 'absence of violence' and 'social justice' may perhaps be preferred, using one negative and one positive formulation. The reason for the use of the terms 'negative' and 'positive' is easily seen: the absence of personal violence does not lead to a positively defined condition, whereas the absence of structural violence is what we have referred to as social justice, which is a positively defined condition (egalitarian distribution of power and resources). Thus, peace conceived this way is not only a matter of control and reduction of the overt use of violence, but of what we have elsewhere referred to as 'vertical development'.[32] And this means that peace theory is intimately connected not only with conflict theory, but equally with development theory. And peace research, defined as research into the conditions – past, present and future – of realizing peace, will be equally intimately connected with conflict research and development research; the former often more relevant for negative peace and the latter more relevant for positive peace, but with highly important overlaps.

To justify this way of looking at peace and peace research, let us see where the many efforts to conceive of peace in terms of only *one* of these 'sides' or aspects leads us. Such efforts are likely to bring into focus, in theory and indeed in practice, the onesidedness on which they are based and to highlight the need for richer concepts of peace. Here only a very sketchy outline of this type of analysis will be presented, particularly since relations between personal and structural violence were to some extent explored in the preceding section.

Thus, a research emphasis on the reduction of personal violence at the expense of a tacit or open neglect of research on structural violence leads, very easily, to acceptance of 'law and order' societies.[33] Personal violence is built into the system as work is built into a compressed spring in a mattress: it only shows when the mattress is disintegrating. And on the other hand there may be a research emphasis on righting social wrongs on obtaining social justice at the expense of a tacit or open acceptance and use of personal violence. The short-term costs of personal violence appear as small relative to the costs of continued structural violence. But personal violence tends to breed manifest physical violence, not only from the opponent but also inside one's own group – and the aftermath of violent revolutions generally seems to testify to this.

We may summarize by saying that too much research emphasis on one aspect of peace tends to rationalize extremism to the right or extremism to the left, depending on whether onesided emphasis is put on 'absence of personal violence' or on 'social justice'. And these two types of extremism are of course not only formally, but also socially closely related and in a dialectic manner: one is often a reaction to the other. When put into practice both may easily develop into well-known social orders where neither of the two aspects of peace are realized: gross social injustice is maintained *by means of* highly manifest personal violence. The regime usually tries to maintain a *status quo*, whether it means forceful maintenance of traditional social injustice that may have lasted for generations, or the forceful maintenance of some new type of injustice brought in by an attempt to overthrow the old system.

If 'peace' now is to be interpreted as an effort to play on both, one may ask: does this not simply mean some kind of 'moderate' course, some effort to appear 'objective' by steering carefully between the two types of extremism outlined above? There is no doubt a danger in this direction. Efforts to avoid both personal and structural violence may easily lead to accept one of them, or even both. Thus, if the choice is between righting a social wrong by means of personal violence or doing nothing, the latter may in fact mean that one supports the forces behind social injustice. And conversely: the use of personal violence may easily mean that one gets neither long-term absence of violence nor justice.

Or, we can put the argument in a slightly different framework. If we are interested in e.g. social justice but also in the avoidance of personal violence, does this not constrain our choice of means so much that it becomes meaningful only in certain societies? And particularly in societies that have already realized many social-liberal values, so that there is considerable freedom of speech and assembly, and organizations for effective articulation of political interests? Whereas we are literally immobilized in highly repressive societies, or 'more openly repressive societies' as modern critics of liberalism might say? Thus, if our choice of means in the fight against structural violence is so limited by the non-use of personal violence that we are left without anything to do in highly repressive societies, whether the repression is latent or manifest, then how valuable is this recipe for peace?

To this we may answer along many lines.

One answer would be to reject the definition given above of peace, because we want 'peace' to refer to something attainable and also in fact attained, not to something as utopian as *both* absence of personal violence *and* social justice. We may then slant the definition of 'peace' in the direction of absence of personal violence, *or* absence of structural violence, depending on where our priorities are. In our definition above we have suggested that the two enter in a completely symmetrial manner: there is no temporal, logical or evaluative preference given to one or the other. Social justice is not seen as an adornment to peace as absence of personal violence, nor is absence of personal violence seen as an adornment to peace as social justice. Unfortunately, on the printed page, one has to appear before the other or above the other, and this is often interpreted as priority (compare the recent debate on whether a certain group's political slogan should be 'peace and freedom' or 'freedom and peace'). Actually, somebody should invent some way of printing so that absolutely no connotation of priority is implied.

This approach presupposes that we somehow are attracted by the term 'peace' and would like to let that word express our goal rather than some other word. But another answer would be to give up the word 'peace' and simply state our interest in one or both of the two values and then try to do our best along both dimensions, so to speak. This appears less satisfactory, because of the generally widespread use of the term 'peace' – so widespread and so generally acknowledged that it possibly presents some kind of substitute in this secular age for feelings of devotion and community that in former ages were invoked by reference to religious concepts. In fact, 'peace' has indeed religious overtones to many, and that this probably contributes to the use of the word 'peace' as a carrier of feelings of universal love and brotherhood in our days. Hence, in spite of the many possibilities for semantic confusion, we would argue in favor of retaining the term 'peace'.

A third answer would be to combine the first two approaches, to talk little or at least not very loudly about peace – for fear of blushing, among other reasons – and to give up one of the two goals, absence of violence and social justice. This attitude, found today in several circles, may be commended for its honesty and lack of hypocrisy. Neither the 'law and order' racist or primitive capitalist society, nor the openly repressive post-revolutionary society is presented as realizations of 'peace', but as social orders where one made a choice between two evils, direct violence or social injustice, using what was seen as the lesser evil to drive out the greater evil (possibly ending up with both).

And then there is a fourth approach which will be preferred in this context. It may be expressed as follows:

Both values, *both* goals are significant, and it is probably a disservice to man to try, in any abstract way, to say that one is more important than the other. As mentioned, it is difficult to compare the amount of suffering and harm that has been caused by personal or structural violence; they are *both* of such an order of magnitude that comparisons appear meaningless. Moreover, they *seem* often to be coupled in such a way that it is very difficult to get rid of both evils; more likely the Devil is driven out with Beelzebub. In view of this difficulty, so amply testified through human history, we should be very careful in passing moral judgements too readily on those who fail to realize both goals. To realize one of them is no mean achievement either, particularly if we consider the number of social orders and regimes that realize neither.

But the view that one cannot meaningfully work for both absence of personal violence and for social justice can also be seen as essentially pessimistic, as some sort of intellectual and moral capitulationism.[34] First of all, there are many forms of social action available today that combine both in a highly meaningful way. We are thinking of the tremendously rapid growth in the field of nonviolent action, both in dissociative nonviolence that serves to keep parties apart so that the weaker party can establish autonomy and identity of its own, and associative nonviolence that can serve to bring them together when a basis for equal non-exploitative partnership exists.[35] We are thinking of all that is known about the theories of symmetric, egalitarian organization in general.[36] We are thinking of the expanding theory of vertical development, of participation, decentralization, codecision. And we are thinking of the various approaches to arms control and disarmament issues, although they are perhaps of more marginal significance.[37] This is not the place to develop these themes; that will be done in other contexts. But secondly, once the double goal has been stated – that peace research is concerned with the conditions for promoting both aspects of peace – there is no reason to believe that the future will not bring us richer concepts and more forms of social action that combine absence of personal violence with fight against social injustice once sufficient activity is put into research and practice.[38] There are more than enough people willing to sacrifice one for the other – it is by aiming for both that peace research can make a real contribution.

Notes

1. This point is elaborated further in *Theories of Peace* (forthcoming), Chapter 1.1.
2. This, of course, is not strictly true. It was not on Fascist or nazi agendas, nor is it on the agenda of contemporary revolutionary thinking. However, even for these cases violence is not an end, but rather a means to overcome obstacles impeding the realization of a future order, the millennium, the communist society, etc; these future orders do not seem to contain violence. But this is hardly a universal human invariant. The Viking paradise looks violent, and warlike tribes/societies like the Pathans would probably put complete absence of violence last on the agenda, if at all.
3. But what if a social order is such that some people live well in solid, concrete houses and others in shacks that crumble under the first quake, killing the inhabitants? In other words, even if the natural disaster is unavoidable, differential social impact may have been avoidable. This may certainly justify the use of the term 'structural violence' for such differential housing standards, not only because of differential exposure to earthquakes (as in the earthquake zone in Western Sicily), but because of implications for differential health standards in general, educational possibilities, and so on and so forth. Whether it justifies the use of such epithets as 'violent' or 'assassin' to the people sustaining such social structures, or (which is not quite the same) to the people on top of such social structures, is another matter.
4. Since the potential level depends not only on the use and distribution of available resources, but also on insight, a crucial person in this picture is the scientist or anyone who opens for new insights into how old, or new, resources may be utilized. In other words, anyone who makes possible what was formerly not feasible raises the level of potentiality. But the level may also be lowered, perhaps not so often because insight is forgotten (although history is full of such cases too) as because resources become more scarce – for instance due to pollution, hoarding, over-utilization, etc. In short, we make no assumption about the shape of the potential realization curve through time, nor do we make any assumption about the corresponding curve for actual realization. In particular we reject the optimistic assumption according to which both curves are monotonously increasing and with a decreasing gap so that there is asymptotic convergence of the actual to the potential, 'until the potentialities of man are fully realized'. This is an ideology, usually in the form of an underlying assumption, not a description or reality. As Bertrand Russell writes (Autobiography, Vol. III; p. 221): 'When I was young, Victorian optimism was taken for granted. It was thought that freedom and prosperity would spread gradually throughout the world by an orderly process, and it was hoped that cruelty, tyranny and injustice would continually diminish. Hardly anyone was haunted by the fear of great wars. Hardly anyone thought of the nineteenth century as a brief interlude between past and future barbarism –.' In short, let us make no assumptions, but focus on the causes for a discrepancy between the curves, admitting for a lag in the application and distribution of new insights; whether they are called technological or social.
5. However, it is by no means obvious how potential life-span should be defined. One cannot use the age at death of the oldest person dying today or this year; this may be too low because he does not benefit from possible advances in hygiene etc. made too late to have an impact on him, or not yet made, and it may be too high because he is specially advantaged genetically. But the average of the p% of the social order benefiting fully from insight and resources already available should at least yield a basis for an estimate of what is possible today.

6. In an article 'On the Meaning of Nonviolence', *Journal of Peace Research*, 1965, pp. 228–57 the concept of influence is basic in an effort to analyze the difference between violence and non-violence, and positive and negative versions of the latter. In the present article the focus is on a typology of violence, not on a typology of non-violence.
7. Ibid., pp. 230–4.
8. Loc. cit.
9. This is a recurrent theme in Herbert Marcsue, *One-dimensional Man* (Boston Press, 1968), especially Part I, 'One-dimensional Society',
10. This is a recurrent theme in much of the analysis of violence in the US. Violence against property is seen as training, the first window–pane crushed to pieces is also a blow against the bourgeois in oneself, a liberation from former constraints, an act of communication signalling to either camp a new belongingness and above all a rejection of tacit rules of the game. 'If they can do that to property, what can they do to persons –'
11. It was pointed out by Herman Kahn (at a seminar at PRIO, May 1969) that middle class students and lower class police may have highly different relations to property: as something highly replaceable for the middle class student in an affluent society, as something difficult to attain for a lower class Irish cop. What to one is a relatively unproblematic act of communication may to the other be sacrilegeous, particularly since students probably aspire to mobility and freedom unfettered by property ties.
12. The term 'institutional violence' is often sometimes used, but we have preferred 'structural' since it is often of a more abstract nature and not anything that can be traced down to a particular institution. Thus, if the police are highly biased the term institutionalized violence may be appropriate, but this is a highly concrete case. There may be violence built into a structure without any police institution at all, as will be developed in the next section.
13. This is clearly expressed by Stokeley Carmichael in 'Black Power' (*The Dialectics of Liberation*, David Cooper ed., London Penguin, p. 151,1968):

> 'It is important to this discussion of racism to make a distinction between the two types: individual racism and institutional racism. The first type consists of overt acts by individuals, with usually immediate results of the death of victims, or the traumatic and violent destruction of property. This type can be recorded on TV cameras and can frequently be observed in the process of commission.
>
> The second type is less overt, far more subtle, less identifiable in terms of specific individuals committing the acts, but is no less destructive of human life. The second type is more the overall operation of established and respected forces in the society and thus does not receive the condemnation that the first type receives.

His distinction individual/institutional is the same as our personal/structural. But we prefer the term 'personal' because the person sometimes acts on behalf of groups, whereas 'individual' may be interpreted as the opposite of 'group'. But particularly in the context Carmichael discusses group violence is immensely important – the mob lynching as opposed to the individual murderer – but that does not make the violence institutional. It still satisfies all the other criteria, e.g. it consists of 'overt acts by individuals', 'can be recorded on TV-cameras' (as in a war), etc.

14. The difficulty here, as often pointed out, is that international statistics usually reflect averages and not dispersions, ranking nations in order of average achievement, not in terms of degree of equality achieved in distribution. One reason is of course that such data are not readily available, but that is only begging the question *why* they are not available. One reason for that again may be that it upsets ranking orders and reveals less positive aspects of social orders used to define themselves as world leaders, but that is hardly a sufficient explanation. Another reason might be that the problem is simply not sufficiently clearly defined, nor is it regarded as sufficiently feasible or indeed desirable to decrease dispersions. When this becomes sufficiently crystallized it will also find expressions in international statistics.

15. The remark in the preceding note holds *a fortiori* here: not only is it difficult to present any measure of dispersion of power, it is difficult enough to measure power at all, except in the purely formal sense of voting rights. He who comes up with a really meaningful measure in this field will contribute greatly to crystallization of political fighting as well as administrative endeavors.

16. Again the same: the publications of these correlations would contribute significantly to increased awareness, since the current ideology is precisely that correlations between achieved and ascribed ranks should be as low as possible, preferably zero.

17. Economic sanctions occupy interesting middle position here. They are clearly violent in their ultimate consequences, which are starvation etc., but the hope is of course that they are slow enough to permit capitulation much before that. At the same time they are clearly also built into the structure, for the most vulnerable countries are also the countries that tend to be at the bottom of the international stratification in general: high in dependence on trade, low in commodity dispersion and low on trade partner dispersion. See Johan Galtung, 'On the Effects of International Economic Sanctions, With Examples from the Case of Rhodesia', *World Politics*, 1967, pp. 387–416.

18. One expression of what is meant by social justice is found in declarations of human rights, where a number of norms about equality are stated. However, they very often suffer from the deficiency that they are personal more than structural. They refer to what individuals can do or can have, not to who or what decides what they can do or have; they refer to distribution of resources, not to power over the distribution of resources. In other words, human rights as usually conceived of are quite compatible with paternalism whereby power-holders distribute anything but ultimate power over the distributions, so that equalization without any change in the power structure is obtained. It is almost painful to see how few seem to realize that much of the current anti-establishment anti-authority revolt is precisely about this: concessions are not enough, not even equality is enough, it is the way in which decisions about distribution are arrived at and implemented that is basic. But there is little reason to believe that this will not also in due time crystallize into some kind of human right and be added to that list of philosophical and political battlefields.

19. Exploitation also has an ambiguity which we actually have exploited in this section. There seems to be a liberal interpretation in terms of distribution and inequality, and a Marxist interpretation in terms of power, particularly over the use of the surplus produced by others (in a capitalist economy). Clearly one can have one type of exploitation without the other.

20. I am indebted to Hans Rieger and other participants in the seminar at the Gandhian Institute of Studies for pointing out the possibility of using the manifest-latent distinction in connection with both personal and structural violence.

21. This is a point where Gandhi and Mao Tse–Tung would agree in theory, although in practice they are both so dominant in their organizations that it probably was not too meaningful to speak of real egalitarianism.

22. See Note 13 for Carmichael's analysis. The basic point in our communication structure is of course that personal violence much more easily 'can be recorded on TV cameras', although this is not correct strictly speaking. There is no intrinsic reason why structural violence should not be registered on TV cameras; in fact, really good cameramen delight in doing exactly this. But the concept of *news* is against its prominent display; that concept is in itself geared to personal rather than structural violence. For an analysis, see Johan Galtung and Mari Holmboe Ruge, 'The Structure of Foreign News', *Journal of Peace Research*, 1965, pp. 64–91, especially on person-vs Structure-oriented news.

23. Herman Schmid seems to be very correct when he points out (op. cit., p. 217) that peace research grew out of a certain historical condition and the basic concepts were colored by that condition. No doubt this explains some of the emphasis on *symmetric conflict*, and we would add, on personal violence both because of war memories and war threats. However, the threats of a major war in the North Atlantic area failed to materialize, economic growth continued, but exploitation remained constant or increased. So, towards the end of the 'sixties the focus changes;' for some persons to a completely new focus (as when Schmid and others would argue in favor of conflict creation research, of polarization and revolution research), for others (as the present author) to an extension of focus, as argued in the present article.

24. Thus, it is almost unbelievable how little the gap between rich and poor seems to be affected by the general increase, within nations and between nations.

25. This is the general theme in Johan Galtung, 'A structural Theory of Integration', *Journal of Peace Research*, 1968, pp. 375–95.

26. One of these implications is of course that it enhances his power: he monopolizes information from the level above and can convert this into power at his own level. Another implication is that he is very often untrained for or unfit for the task to be performed at the higher level since his frame of reference all the time has been level $n-1$. The manager of a certain type of products suddenly finds himself on the board of a big business corporation doing quite different things; the leading nation in a regional alliance suddenly finds itself responsible for world affairs and forced to think within a completely new frame of reference, and so on.

27. We have not discussed the possibility of denying rank differences completely by making everybody equal, since there seem always to be some differences that elude equalization attempts and these differences tend to become significant. Make everybody citizens with equal voting rights, and differences in style of life become overwhelming, abolish class differences on trains and the upper classes go by plane, and so on.

28. Few have expressed this image as well as Eldridge Cleaver in *Soul on Ice* (London: Cape, 1969, p. 92):

    'Both police and the armed forces follow orders. Orders. Orders flow from the top down. Up there, behind closed doors, in antechambers, in conference rooms, gavels bang on the tables, the tinkling of silver decanters can be heard as ice water is poured by well fed, conservatively dressed men in horn-rimmed glasses, fashionably dressed American widows with rejuvenated faces and tinted hair, the air permeated with the square humor of Bob Hope jokes. Here all the talking is done, all the thinking, all the deciding.

Gray rabbits of men scurry forth from the conference room to spread decisions throughout the city, as News. Carrying out orders is a job, a way of meeting the payments on the house, a way of providing for one's kiddies. In the armed forces it is also a duty, patriotism' Not to do so is treason.'

29. See Note 11 for Kahn's analysis, where he added that fighting with fists would be about as natural for the Irish cops as it is unnatural for the upper middle class student, and fighting with words as natural for that student as it is unnatural for the cop. Hence, when the student destroys property and heaps abuse on the police he challenges the police much beyond the tolerance level, and the police respond with the reaction they know, violence; a reaction for which the students are untrained. One does not need structural explanations to account for an outburst of violence in such cases. But one could ask why such people are in the police department, and one explanation can supplement rather than supersede another.

30. This coin metaphor, of course, is not to suggest that one side excludes the other. Indeed, as pointed out so many times in the preceding section: a given social order may exhibit both, one or (perhaps) neither of them. The metaphor applies to the conceptualization of peace, not to the empirical world.

31. Of course, I am very much aware of changes in my own presentation of these concepts, just as I am confident that new formulations will follow in the wake of those presented here. Whereas 'negative peace' remains fairly constant, meaning 'absence of violence', I think it gains from the precision given to 'violence' in that context, a 'personal violence'. But 'positive peace' is constantly changing (as is 'positive health' in medical science). I used to see it in terms of integration and cooperation ('An Editorial', *JPR*, 1964, pp. 1–4), but now agree fully with Herman Schmid that this expresses a much too integrated and symmetric view of conflict groups, and probably reflects the East–West conflict or a certain ideology in connection with that conflict. I would now identify 'positive peace' mainly with 'social justice', the latter taken in the double sense of this article – but I think one could also be open to other candidates for inclusion since the definition given of violence is broad enough also to point in other directions. This is to some extent attempted in section 1.3 of *Theories of Peace*. Moreover, I think Schmid is basically right (op. cit. p. 221) in saying that there is a tendency to focus on negative peace because consensus is more easily obtained – but I share his rejection of that tendency. To reveal and unmask the subtle mechanisms of structural violence and explore the conditions for their removal or neutralization is at least as important, although comparisons of the two types of violence in terms of priorities seems a little bit like discussing whether medical research should focus on cancer or heart diseases. And to this should be added, emphatically, that a discipline fully satisfied with its own foundations and definition is probably a dead discipline. Fundamental debate and debate over fundamentals are the signs of health, not of disease. These issues are difficult, and we shall make progress only through more practice in analyzing them and more praxis in working with them.

32. In *Theories of Development*, forthcoming.

33. Thus, there is little doubt that in general peace research (Schmid, op. cit., p. 222) in this decade that has passed since it was launched has met with more approval from the north–western establishment in the world than from other quarters, but so has cancer research. From this it does not follow that peace research is meaningless to the third world and to revolutionary forces. The same skewed distribution can be found almost anywhere, due to the skewed distribution of world resources and the generally feudal structure of the world. But Schmid is certainly right in setting peace research in a social setting: 'who will pay for it', and 'who will be able to implement advice from peace researcher' are basic questions. I only fail to see that there should be any implicit reason why peace research should fall into the arms of the establishment more than into other arms not to mention be able to retain considerable autonomy in its pursuits. This presupposes an academic structure that does not steer all research into the arms of the power-holders, left or right, but leaves the road open for pursuits of insights into the mechanisms behind any kind of violence, any kind of obstacle to human self realization.

34. Thus, peace research is seen here as an effort to promote the realization of *values*. To what extent these values coincide or not with the interests of certain *groups* is another matter. Hence, peace research could not be identified with the ideology of a group unless that group professed the same values. It is also an open question whether group identification with these values will in fact serve to promote these values.

35. Some of this is explored in 'On the Meaning of Nonviolence', and infinitely much more can be done in this direction. However, the important thing seems to be that there is no reason whatsoever why peace research should be tied to study of symmetric conflict only, and to integrative, or as we prefer to say, 'associative' (integrative being too strong a term) approaches. Any effort to explore structural violence will lead to awareness of asymmetric conflict, between parties highly unequal in capabilities – and I think it is unfair to state that this is neglected in the type of peace research carried out at the International Peace Research Institute in Oslo. The terms 'topdog-underdog' may be unfamiliar and even be resented by those who prefer to do this research in a Marxist tradition and jargon, but it is nevertheless an effort. More precisely, the effort has been to understand better the *structure* of structural violence, one little indication of which is given in section 3 of this article. And there is no implicit reason why the remedy should be in associative policies only. On the contrary, I tend to feel in general that associative policies are for equals, i.e. for symmetric conflict, whereas polarization and dissociative policies are much better strategies for exploited groups. This is also reflected in the doubleness of non-violent strategies, all themes to be more fully developed in *Theories of Conflict* (forthcoming). When Schmid says (op. cit., p. 219) that peace research 'should explain … how latent conflicts are manifested – /and/how the present international system is seriously challenged or even broken down' he seems to betray the same type of onesidedness that he accuses peace research of – interest in controlling manifest conflicts only, in bringing about integration, in formulating problems in terms meaningful to international and supranational institutions. But this onesidedness will almost inevitably result if research shall be geared to serve the interests of specific groups, high or low, instead of the promotion of values. It is as hard to believe that disintegration, polarization, dissociation is always the best strategy as it is to believe the opposite.

But this seems to be closely related to Schmid's conflictology (op. cit., pp. 224–8), where he seems to believe that I have a subjectivistic conception of conflict. If there is anything the conflict triangle purports to achieve it is exactly the opposite: the definition of conflict independently of attitudes and behavior, and also independently of perceptions of the situation held by the parties (as different from their attitudes to each other). To me, conflict is incompatibility of goals, but how these goals are established is a quite different matter. To ask the parties for their perception of what they pursue and what, if anything, stands in the way is one, but only one approach. I have nothing against definitions in terms of 'interests' the concept of 'goal' is wide enough to encompass. The difficulty is, as Schmid readily and frankly admits (op. cit., p. 227) to 'decide what the interests are' and I share with him the idea that 'this is a challenge rather than a reason to abandon the idea of an interest definition of conflict'. But I feel these interests have to be postulated, as I think Marx to a large extent did, and then one has to explore the implications. I also think they can be seen as expressions of values, but not necessarily held by the actor, nor necessarily held by the investigator, just as postulated values. Thus, if one feels it is contrary to the interests of children, as autonomous human beings, to accept the tie as the children *of* their biological parents, then there is certainly an incompatibility in the present family system: parents have interests as owners incompatible with the children's interests as self-owners. The only difference between this example and Schmid's master-slave example is that he gives a paradigm for a conflict of the past, I a paradigm for a conflict of the future, and moreover for a conflict I think will be manifested fairly soon, in line with the general wave towards defeudalization of the social order. And I certainly agree with Schmid that polarization will here be a part of the solution.

36. For an effort in this direction, see Johan Galtung, *Cooperation in Europe* (Strasbourg: Council of Europe, 1968).
37. An effort to give some reasons why are found in 'Two Approaches to Disarmament: The Legalist and the Structuralist', *Journal of Peace Research* 1967, pp. 161–95.
38. And it is of course not necessary that all or most or much of this sails under the flag of 'peace research' or any other flag for that matter – only the slightly totalitarian minded would be inclined to feel so. What is important is that it is done, and that there is contact between different approaches so that they and others can benefit from ideological and institutional pluralism.

COMMENTARY ON GALTUNG

Johan Galtung is the founder of Peace Studies as a major academic discipline. This article, published in 1969 in the *Journal of Peace Research*, is perhaps not only the most influential single contribution to a discipline that Galtung helped to define and shape, but also arguably the piece that Galtung is still, after more than 50 years of activism, best known for.[1]

Galtung starts by giving us two definitions; of 'peace' and 'violence'. Peace is defined not merely as absence of war but, instead, as 'absence of violence', where violence 'is present when human beings are being influenced so that their actual somatic and mental realizations are below their potential realizations'. From this definition we learn that Galtung favours a broader definition of violence than the narrow conception, according to which violence is reduced to an intentional act of causing physical harm. Instead, Galtung wants to highlight the difference between the potential and the actual, by stressing how violence can take the form of avoidable restrictions on an individual's ability to fulfil his or her potential. Thus Galtung reminds us that violence can be both physical and psychological; that it can take the form of both negative and positive influences; that no person needs to be physically hurt for violence to occur; that violence can be intended or unintended, manifest or latent.

By putting together all these dimensions of violence, Galtung is then able to construct his celebrated distinction between *personal* or *direct* violence (where there is an actor that commits the violence) and *structural* violence (where there is no such actor). It is precisely this idea of structural violence that has brought fame to Galtung amongst students of peace and violence. As Galtung explains, in the case of structural violence: 'there may not be any person who directly harms another person in the structure. The violence is built into the structure and shows up as unequal power and consequently as unequal life chances.'

Exactly what the 'structure' is in structural violence remains a fiercely debated issue. The examples Galtung uses to illuminate this question provide us with important hints, from 'the way world economic relations are organized today' to culturally defined power relations: 'thus, when one husband beats his wife there is a clear case of personal violence, but when one million husbands keep one million wives in ignorance there is structural violence.'

It is Galtung's intention to bring closer the ideas of violence and social injustice. Indeed, he even goes so far as to define structural violence *as* social injustice, a claim that has attracted much criticism for stretching the meaning of violence beyond meaningful recognition.[2] Nevertheless, Galtung's notion that there is violence in the uneven distribution of resources, and in particular in the chronic inequality in the power to decide over the distribution of resources, is a major contribution to the literature on violence, and therefore to peace research. As Galtung explains, an extended concept of violence leads to an extended concept of peace, thus peace has two sides: absence of personal violence and absence of structural violence.[3]

Notes and further reading

1. In 1959, Galtung founded the International Peace Research Institute (PRIO) in Oslo.
2. See John Keane, *Reflections on Violence*, London: Verso, 1996, p. 66.
3. See also Johan Galtung's *Peace by Peaceful Means: Peace and Conflict, Development and Civilization*, London: Sage, 1996; and *Transcend and Transform: An Introduction to Conflict Work*, London: Pluto, 2004. For an overview of Galtung's philosophy of peace, see Peter Lawler, *A Question of Values: Johan Galtung's Peace Research*, Boulder, CO: Lynne Rienner, 1995.

7
What is Wrong with Violence

Gerald C. MacCallum

This paper does not consider possible accounts of why we should *never* countenance or bring about violence, but only accounts of why we should never do so without some special justification or excuse. The problem of when, if

---

This paper was discovered among MacCallum's papers when work on this collection was already considerably advanced. Although it is not possible to date it with precision, it appears to have been worked on in the period 1968–70, especially in 1969–70 when MacCallum was in Europe on an ACLS fellowship, to have been put aside to be continued at some later date, and then to have been worked on only intermittently. MacCallum's curriculum vitae of 1971 and 1972 indicates that 'What Is Wrong with Violence?' was given as a public lecture at Aarhüs University in April 1970 and as a seminar to the Philosophy Institute at the University of Bergen in May 1970, though we cannot tell whether the paper here published for the first time is the paper so identified. In April 1970, MacCallum also lectured on 'Reform and Violence' at Aarhüs University and gave a seminar 'On Violence' to the Filosofiska Institutionen at Stockholm University; in May 1970 he gave a lecture entitled 'Violence and Morality' at the Philosophy Institute of Oslo University, and in June 1970 a talk on 'Violence' to the Philosophy Faculties of the University of London. His fellowship year was clearly occupied with this topic. But we have not found among his papers anything to determine the exact content of the talks, papers, lectures, and seminars MacCallum gave in these places in spring 1970. MacCallum became chair of the Department of Philosophy at the University of Wisconsin in the fall of 1970, serving for two years. This was a particularly busy and stressful period, which included among other things planning for and supervising a move of the department from Bascom Hall and several other buildings to its present home in Helen C. White Hall, and this could partially explain the paper's being put aside at that time. He could have had little time then for *any* philosophical work. However, in May 1971 MacCallum found the time to give a talk on 'Reform and Violence' at the Waukesha Campus of the University of Wisconsin and on 'Philosophical Work on Violence' to the Philosophy Faculty at Temple University. The present paper is referred to above, in Chapter 11, 'Violence and Appeals to Conscience,' at p. 178. Largely for these reasons it was decided to include the paper in this volume – it can be thought of as a sort of appendix to the collection. Though it is in somewhat rough and unfinished form, and undoubtedly would have taken on quite a different aspect if MacCallum had been able to work on it further himself, it is

ever, violence would be excusable or justifiable is surely important to discuss eventually, but one can hardly do so in a sound way until he understands precisely why excuses or justifications are called for, and it is quite enough for the moment to consider that. So far as I can see, violence has not been discussed in this fundamental way. The focus of attention has been on when violence is justifiable or excusable – or, as it is often put, on when and whether violence is ever a 'necessary evil.' Few if any persons seem to have considered seriously why it is an evil at all. Thus, there is work here that needs doing.

I

When asked what is wrong with violence, our readiest answer seems to lie in citation of the connection of violence with injury, damage, and destruction, and, via these, on at least some occasions with pain and discomfort. But the connection is not a simple one.

It is not simple in part because the notion of violence is itself complex. Violence appears sometimes to be treated as an impulse or force or stock of psychic or physical energy (as in 'Violence raged within him'), sometimes as a form or kind of action or activity (as the activity of wind or waves suggested in 'The violence of the storm was shattering'), sometimes as a tool or instrument for the achievement of a purpose (as in 'He didn't use violence'), and sometimes as a result of a certain sort, perhaps one brought about in a certain way (as in 'Look at the violence that was done here').

These appearances of difference can of course be rationalized by reference to one central notion. But a great deal depends on the central notion one chooses, and there may be no one unmistakably 'correct' choice. One could, for example, treat violence as most basically a form or kind of action or

---

not, in our judgment, 'unpublishable,' as MacCallum called it. There are a number of passages, amounting in some instances to whole paragraphs or even whole groups of pages, that were marked off in brackets, perhaps signifying places where MacCallum felt a serious problem lurked, perhaps portions he planned to revise, perhaps sections he omitted when reading the paper to some group or other. We have found no way of telling, though we do know, on the testimony of Professor Michael Pritchard, that the paper was circulated to and read by some participants in the Buffalo Conference on Violence of 1974, where MacCallum presented his paper on 'Violence and Appeals to Conscience,' and that these two papers supplement each other well. After some consideration it was decided not to mar the text by incorporating these brackets. Other changes, such as corrections of obvious typing errors, have been silently made. Words in brackets were inserted by the editors as emendations obviously needed. The author's notes were taken out of the text proper and incorporated into footnotes, with the various references filled in by the editors, as with some previous papers in this volume.

Following the paper itself there is a set of 'Notes for "What Is Wrong with Violence?",' MacCallum's own title (which MacCallum had attached to his working copy of the paper), which provide the author's own abstract of the paper and an account of at least some of its deficiencies. See p. 255 and pp. xxxi–xxxii. Eds.

activity, and consequently regard such an expression as 'Look at the violence that was done here' to be an elliptical way of saying 'Look at the results of the violence (i.e., the violent action or activity) that took place here.'

Proceeding in this fashion, one might see the connection between violence, on the one hand, and injury, damage, and destruction, on the other hand, as this: violence has only a *tendency* to bring about injury, damage, destruction, or, better, violence has a tendency to do this with respect to certain possible objects or objects within certain ranges. The restriction is better because, to take an example, the violence of a storm on top of Mount Everest may have been shattering though nothing up there was in the slightest danger of injury, damage or destruction, there being no people up there, etc., though if there had been people up there, they and their tents would have been in considerable danger. Taking this approach, one would have the burden of somehow characterizing the ranges of objects or things that violence, perhaps definitionally, has a tendency to injure, etc. One would need to allow for the possible importance of shifts of context (e.g., the lower threshold of activity qualifying as violence in a nursery *might* (I am not saying 'would') be lower than the lower threshold on the high seas). And, since one's concern would be principally with characterizing this lower threshold, one would not wish to include within the range either things that are too tough (e.g., Mount Everest itself) or things that are too tender (e.g., orchids, which may be damaged or destroyed when subjected to rough handling that falls short of violence). Furthermore, in rationalizing the relationship of this central notion of violence to the others suggested, one would have, for example, the related but embarrassing problem of explaining why, if such an expression as 'Look at the violence that was done here' is an elliptical way of saying 'Look at the results of the violence (i.e., the violent action or activity) that took place here,' one could not always point to the results and say 'Look at the violence that was done'; for example, one could not do this in the case of our storm on top of Mount Everest (sans people and tents) because, when the storm is over, there is nothing appropriate to which one can point.

Confronted with this latter problem, we might consider starting out in a different way. One could treat as most fundamental the view of violence established in 'Look at the violence that was done here,' and understand a person who utters 'The violence of the storm was shattering,' to be saying that the activities of wind or wave constituting the storm were shattering, these activities being called 'the violence of the storm' because they were such as likely to wreak violence on certain kinds of things that were or might have been in their path. (Our basic task would then be to characterize what it is for violence to be done to something. Violence as a kind of activity would then be characterized as activity of a sort that would be likely to do violence to things within a roughly delineated range of things if any such things were in its path, etc.)

I favor this latter approach. As providing a central notion by reference to which the other idioms may be rationalized, it presents no specially difficult problems. More importantly, it seems to me to provide the firmest and least troubling basis for characterizing the whole family of notions and for a coherent and intuitively fitting account of why people commonly think there is something wrong with violence. Rather than arguing these points, however, I shall simply lay out some of what can be done once this choice is made.

II

One can sometimes be taken to see 'the violence that was done' though this is not always clearly so. One might find it strange to be told that he was being taken to see the violence a speaker had done to language, or the violence a commentator had done to another man's thought. But being taken to see the violence that was done is clearly sometimes possible, and cases where it is possible are, I believe, central to our understanding of what it is for violence to be done. One cannot base a sharply delineated metaphysic of violence on these cases, but analysis of them can provide a reasonably secure basis for comprehending the network of not-very-sharply-bounded concepts in this area. It can at least provide us with a reference point from which we may reasonably see other cases as extensions and elaborations of these cases.

When we are taken to see 'the violence that was done' we expect to see manifestations of injury, damage, or destruction. If we do not find them, we are likely to ask, 'Where is the violence that was done?' Perhaps it has been cleaned up or repaired, or perhaps it is not readily observable (the damage was deep; the injury was not what we had been looking for), or perhaps it is not what we are prepared to call injury, damage, or destruction, though the person taking us to it and so-calling it believed it to be so. But some such explanation of the defeat of our expectations must be forthcoming for the claim that violence was done to remain intelligible.

This is the clearest and tightest connection I have found between violence, on the one hand, and injury, etc., on the other. When one moves to other cases of 'violence done,' cases where we cannot clearly 'be taken to see' the violence that was done, either one will need to expand one's notions of what is to count as injury, etc., well past the 'brute' notions of these with which we ordinarily operate – expand them in ways that make their application more debatable, more 'metaphysical,' and all the same highly interesting and possibly important – or one will need to shift to a notion of 'harm' that doesn't clearly involve them. Furthermore, when one moves from our 'basic' idiom ('the violence that was done') to a discussion of some of the other idioms – e.g., 'the violence of the storm was shattering' and 'Violence raged within him' – one will find that, though the threads of connection with injury, damage, and destruction, or at least with 'harm,' are still there, they will not be so thick, and he will find that he can pick them up in variously different ways.

Showing all this is too big a job for the present paper, though some of it will emerge in what follows. For the present, we might pause and ask whether, given the restricted but clear connection just exposed, we can yet say much about the wrongness of violence even in that restricted setting. When violence has been done, and is of a sort that we can be taken to see, then something has thereby been injured, damaged, or destroyed. Our further views on this fact, however, will depend on what we think about the disvalue of injury, damage, and destruction per se.

One way of putting the matter is to say that we must show violence connected with those cases of injury, damage, and destruction that are disvaluable. But there is a deeper point here. Suppose that we judged injuries, etc., harmless in certain cases because we thought that what was injured, etc., was of no account or even positively noxious. Should we conclude from this that countenancing or bringing about violence, insofar as it amounts to countenancing or bringing about injury, etc., is not always but only sometimes in need of special justification or excuse? One may find two significantly different reactions to the suggestion, each exposing a highly general world-view. One [reaction] is to think, 'Yes, that's right. The countenancing or bringing about of violence, and thus of injury, etc., is surely not in need of any special justification or excuse; for this, in itself, is not wrong. It is only wrong when what is thereby injured, etc., is of some account. As many things are inconsequential and many other things are clearly noxious, it is silly to think of needing generally a special excuse or justification; the question does not become important until we have some special reason to think that the things in question are of account.' The other reaction is to think, 'No, that's wrong. The general presumption must be in favor of supposing everything to be of some account, and a showing that something is inconsequential or noxious will simply constitute a form of the excuse or justification one needs for countenancing violence and thus, injury, etc., to it.'

Which of these reactions is right? Or, if neither is unquestionably right, which is most reasonable? The answer one gives will make a significant difference in his account of the wrongness of violence. I find both these reactions in myself, and perhaps you do also. There seem to be historical, economic, and sociologic – or quasi-sociologic – explanations of this. For example, the view that much in the world is inconsequential and that, while many things may show on their faces that they are consequential (e.g., humans, or at least members of one's own community), one must generally have some special reason to believe that various other things are consequential before becoming concerned about their injury, etc.: this view may have established itself because of its congeniality to ambitious, hardy, and (very beneficially) none-too-reflective inhabitants of a frontier such as John Locke thought the New World to be, viz., a place where, no matter how much a man 'took' there was as much and more left for others. It would be less congenial, however, to persons who think of the planet as a place where essential resources are rapidly disappearing, and who are full of doubts stemming from realization of the faultiness of past judgments concerning what on that planet was important and what was not. It might also be less congenial to persons who thought, as Locke also thought, that the world and its contents are God's property and that we are but stewards set to watch over it in God's interests.

Such 'explanations' as these may be thought to expose reasons, or at least the beginnings of reasons, for holding one or the other of the two views in question. Doubtless this is so. But I am not at all certain what the outcome should be, and cannot explore the matter further here. I seek merely to expose it to view so that one may see precisely how it lies in waiting for one who wishes to explore the wrongness of violence.

III

In pushing more broadly into the discussion of what is wrong with violence, we must sooner or later consider what is supposed or presupposed about the way injuries, etc., are produced when we consider them to be 'the violence done.' For, from the fact that something has been injured, damaged or destroyed, it does not follow that violence was done. One's leg may be injured when he [*sic*] slips and falls on an icy path. The finish on a valuable table may be damaged when rain is blown on it through an open window. One's liver may be destroyed over a period of years by a slow-acting disease. None of these is clearly a case where violence has been done. If we are to grasp what is or may be wrong with violence and, in the instant case, with 'violence done' (where we can be 'taken to see it'), we must, therefore, consider not only what is or may be wrong with injury, etc., per se, but also whether there may be something wrong with them produced in the way characteristic of 'violence done' in addition to what, if anything, is wrong with them per se.

What is the way in question? There seems no clearly marked boundary between that way and other ways. But the following considerations figure in our willingness to view injuries, etc., as cases of violence done.

1. *External imposition.* To the extent that the change whose outcome is injury, damage, or destruction has been recognizably effected by forces external to the thing injured, damaged, or destroyed, we are willing, if certain other conditions listed below are also met or approximated, to regard the outcome as violence done. If, for example, a tornado uproots a tree which then strikes a man, breaking his leg, his broken leg, as well as the uprooted tree, would easily count as part of the violence done by the tornado. But if the man's leg has been broken in a fall on an icy path on a calm and sunny day while he was proceeding unhurriedly to the post office, the injury would not so clearly count as a case of violence done, the reason being that we have

in this latter case no clearly acceptable candidate for the external force or forces effecting the change whose outcome was this injury.

In order to forestall some criticisms of this conclusion, a few caveats seem necessary. (a) The icy condition of the path certainly played a role in bringing about the fall resulting in a broken leg. Indeed, we might in some circumstances say that the man slipped and fell because the path was icy (though we might not say this if the path had been icy all winter and the man had been walking it daily without accident; in such circumstances we might think it more appropriate to say that the man slipped and fell because he got careless). But even where we are inclined to say that he slipped and fell because the path was icy, here, unlike the case of the uprooted tree, the man's own behavior has so obviously played a role in bringing about this injury that we might justifiably object, unless the circumstances were extraordinary, to saying that the injury had been effected by the icy path. (b) One might find momentarily attractive the idea that the forces effecting the fall were located in the man and perhaps in nature but not in the leg that was injured, and hence that they were external to the leg. But the necessary argument to an embarrassing conclusion here can hardly be very strong. When a man's leg has been broken, for example, we can equally well say that the injury was to him and that it was to his leg, that he is now injured and that his leg is now injured, that we now have an injured man and that he now has an injured leg, etc. Apart from concerns we may have when on the scene of the actual event and trying to cope with it, in the light of which we may, e.g., want to locate who was injured or locate where he was injured, there is no clear reason for choosing only one of these lines of description of the outcome. (c) One might be brought up short by the idiom 'violence to oneself.' If one can indeed do violence to oneself, then perhaps the forces effecting the change resulting in violence done need not be external to what is thereby injured, damaged or destroyed. The difficulty with this hypothesis, however, is that the notion of self-inflicted violence is one of a set of notions – including those of self-mastery, self-indulgence and self-deception – all of which are widely recognized to be problematic for the same reason, viz., they seem to require for their intelligibility the dichotomizing of the self into two elements or aspects – the master and the mastered, the indulger and the indulged, the deceiver and the deceived, and, in our case, the perpetrator and the victim. It is true that heroic attempts have been made to avoid this result. But none of those I know have succeeded. In the last paragraph of Sartre's famous chapter on self-deception in *Being and Nothingness*, for example, I, at least, do not find the dichotomizing avoided in his summing-up of the matter. (Consider the way he there hypostatizes self-deception itself as a thinking, willing agent.) I conclude that, rather man being a countercase to my claim about externality, the problematic character of 'violence to oneself' would, if anything, confirm the point.

2. *Suddenness of change.* Suppose a change whose outcome has been injury, damage, or destruction to have been recognizably effected by forces external

to the thing so changed. If so, then, to the extent that the change has been a sudden one, we are, subject perhaps to one further condition mentioned below, willing to regard the outcome as violence done. Roughly stated, the point of this consideration is merely that some changes occur too slowly for their outcomes to count easily as violence done, even though the outcomes clearly involve injury, etc. The outcome of a gradual or corrosive change such as would be brought about by 'painting' a steel door daily with a weak acid solution until the door is destroyed or at least obviously damaged is difficult to see as violence done because the process of change toward the critical outcome (patent damage or destruction) lacks the characteristic abruptness of cases of violence done.

3. *Radicalness of change.* Given that a change whose outcome is injury or damage is fairly rapid and recognizably effected by forces external to the thing changed, the more radical the change is, the more willing we are to count the result as violence done. If, for example, the only recognizable change is an injury that is very slight (e.g., a slightly cut finger), we are relatively unwilling, but if it is relatively severe we *are* willing, to recognize the result as violence done. A *fortiori*, when the result is destruction we are willing.

In sum, when injuries, etc., count as 'the violence done,' we know, suppose, or presuppose that they have been effected by forces external to the thing so affected, that they were brought about fairly suddenly, and that the resulting changes in the thing are more or less marked or notable. The first of these conditions seems to me strong enough to qualify as a necessary condition. The other two do not, unless one interprets them as requiring that the change be not too slow and not too slight; but interpreting them in this way gives them a spurious definiteness.

One can begin providing a rationale for the operation of these three conditions, and also carry on directly the exploration of what is wrong with violence, by noting the following remarkable fact: Quite apart from any initial identification of the outcome of a change as injury, damage, or destruction, we are in some of our moods inclined to suppose that change preeminently satisfying the three conditions just mentioned is wrong, and wrong simply by virtue of its having satisfied these conditions. We think it wrong because, if it satisfies these conditions, it damages, destroys, or violates the integrity of the things so changed.

I say that we think this in 'some of our moods' because (1) we are not always prepared to see the subjects of change preeminently satisfying our three conditions as having integrities that could be damaged, etc., and (2) even when we do so see them, we are not always prepared to regard the damage, etc. [as] disvaluable. We are most strongly inclined to think both of these when the subject of the change in question is a human being; but embedded in our cultural (e.g., theological) history are considerations supporting us strongly in extending these views to things that are not human beings, and even to 'the whole of our environment' or 'all of creation.' Some of the considerations supporting and subverting these extensions have already been suggested. The matter is difficult to discuss because the concepts involved are not sufficiently well-bounded to lend themselves to precise treatment. But it is important to venture on the discussion because the common undifferentiated view that violence is wrong draws considerable support (and perhaps rightly) from these extensions, as well as from the central cases of violence done to human beings.

IV

Even in the case of human beings, however, there are difficulties. One must familiarize himself with these difficulties in order to develop a sense of proportion about the later difficulties with the extensions, and also in order to expose portions of the conceptual networks to which appeal must be made in working out the difficulties in both cases.

Suppose, for example, I give permission to a surgeon to amputate my leg in a high-speed but also presumably highly-skilled operation, and suppose that the operation goes as planned. The change has been sudden, radical; and apparently effected by an external force. Has my integrity been damaged, destroyed or violated, or only the integrity of my body, or not even that?

If the integrity of my body were merely its wholeness or completeness as a normal human body, this integrity would seem to have been damaged, destroyed, or violated by the operation. But suppose that quite a few years earlier my arm had been amputated. My body would not, at the time leading up to this latest operation, have had any wholeness or completeness as a normal human body. Nevertheless, supposing that no more surprising facts are to be revealed, the integrity of my body was damaged, destroyed, or violated by this latest operation; or so, at least, we might be inclined to say. What supports this inclination is a view of the integrity of my body as consisting of its wholeness or completeness as *my* body, and pursuit of this point will reveal why the amputation *violated* as well as damaged or destroyed the integrity of my body.

The human body is normally viewed as not merely an assemblage of parts, but a system of more or less harmoniously integrated parts. When speaking of its integrity we can thus be speaking of its completeness or wholeness as such a system. When so viewed, the integrity of the body will have both inward-looking and outward-looking aspects. The inward-looking aspect will emphasize the integration of the body's parts that supports our view of them as parts of a system. The more harmoniously the parts are related to each other, the more completely systematic the body is seen to be, and the easier it is to identify as one complete thing rather than many things. The outward-looking aspect will emphasize the importance of the boundaries in the light of which we may determine what is a part of this system and what is not.

The system is seen as a bounded domain having inertia or principle(s) of organization and operation of its own, and thus as one complete or whole thing in an environment of other things. The upshot is that the integrity of the body is seen to be a function both of the relations of its parts to each other and of its relations to other things. The more harmoniously the parts are related to each other, the greater the integrity of the system because the easier it is to identify as one complete thing rather than many things; likewise, the more completely the state of the system is determined by its own inertia or principle(s) of operation, the greater its integrity because the easier it is to identify as one distinct thing among other things.

When the situation is so conceived, one can see that the integrity of my body was probably violated as well as damaged by this latest amputation, just as it probably also was by the earlier amputation many years ago. Each amputation removed a part from the bodily system, thus, expectably, throwing the remainder of the system into a state of at least temporary disequilibrium from which it must have recovered in order for me to survive. I obviously did recover in the earlier case, and the remainder of my body, in establishing new equilibriums, reconstituted – or, better, constituted – itself as a system; the integrity of this system was, in turn, violated by the second amputation. The part removed in each case was an important one, and thus the system-change needed for recovery was expectably great. The removal was furthermore very sudden, and thus the disequilibrium produced in the remainder of the system was presumptively significant; there was no question of a series of adjustments to small disequilibriums produced by gradual removal or atrophying of a part. Lastly, the removal was effected by an external force and thus was an effect of an intrusion upon the system. Thus, with regard to its inward-looking aspect, the integrity of the body-system was significantly damaged if not destroyed, both by simply the removal of a significantly integral part of the system (thus destroying its wholeness or completeness as *that* system), and by the consequent disequilibriums making difficult the identification of the remainder as (at least yet) a (complete) system. With regard to its outward-looking aspect, the integrity of the body-system was violated by the intrusion of external force in effecting a significant change within the domain of the system – an intrusion interfering with the determination of the state of the system simply by its own inertia or principle(s) of operation. (We could assimilate this either to cases of violating someone's privacy – viz., intruding upon it – or if we see the system's inertia or principle(s) of operation as constituting the 'law' of the system, to cases of violating a law.)

The notions suggested here by such terms as 'system,' 'equilibrium,' and 'harmonious integration' are certainly not well-bounded and are potentially treacherous. They cannot here be given the examination they deserve, but they are surely not nonsensical and, I will simply claim, have not been used here unreasonably. What seems to have been shown by using them is what can be meant by saying that the integrity of my body has been damaged and violated, how it was both damaged and violated by the amputations in question, and how this was so because those admittedly very radical changes in my body were produced very suddenly and were effected by an external force.

I say that these things 'seem to have been shown' because, if we contemplate the possible *occasions* of the amputations (e.g., if we ask why I gave the surgeon my permission for the last one), we may begin to have doubts about the analysis. In what state was the leg when I gave permission? Was it badly mangled, or gangrenous? Or was it a perfectly healthy leg that I wanted removed for cosmetic affect[1] (e.g., to complete my planned pose as a war hero)? The analysis works most smoothly in the latter case, but that of course is also the least likely case. The difficulties with the other cases are roughly of two sorts: (1) They suggest that, from the inward-looking point of view of integrity, the leg or at least part of it was already not integrated very well into the rest of the system or that there were already serious disequilibriums traceable to the condition of the leg. This makes the amputation itself seem less a disruption of the system. (2) They also suggest that in one way or another the amputation was necessary to *save* the system or at least what would be left of it. These considerations are forceful, though if one were to press on them they might not in the end appear decisive (consider that the amputation of the whole leg removes a source of disruption and a threat, but it also removes more than that). But they are directed at best to whether the integrity of my body was *damaged* by the amputation. Their focus is thus on the inward-looking aspect of integrity. Even if they were decisive, we would need to consider still whether the integrity of my body had been *violated* by the amputation – a matter resting principally on consideration of the outward-looking aspect. If either of the two difficulties is thought to disturb my claim about that, it must, I fear, [be] only because violating integrities is generally thought to be bad, and it is difficult to see the amputation as a bad thing if it were necessary to save the system (or what would be left of it). But surely, beneficial or not, the amputation does constitute an intrusion into the domain of the body-system – an intrusion interfering with the determination of the state of the system by its own inertia or principle(s) of operation. It thus violates the integrity of that system. Though I agree that if it were introduced precisely in order to remedy the effects of previous and perhaps catastrophic intrusions (e.g., the mangling of my leg in an accident) it might look more like an interference with the self-determination of the states of the system, nevertheless it still itself constitutes an interference – as witness what would happen if the operation were not performed; the results might not be happy ones, but they would constitute the playing out of the effects of the operation of the system's own inertias and principles of operation. That we would think it best for the integrity of the system to be violated in this way merely shows that we do not always think such a thing to be bad, given certain circumstances. But citation of those circumstances constitutes here precisely the justification for something that would, in their absence, surely be counted bad in the present range of cases. (One must of course discuss why it would be counted bad, and something will be said of this later.)

Turning now to the more interesting and complicated question of whether *my* integrity, and not merely that of my body, has been damaged or violated by the amputation, we might start by asking whether the former doesn't follow from the latter.

In a new sense of 'integrity' that now appears on the scene, it clearly does not. The integrity of persons is often considered to be their rectitude – their uprightness and honesty. Surely, on this understanding, damage to and violation of the integrity of my body need not involve similar effects on my integrity. The amputation in itself surely did not damage or violate my integrity so conceived, and indeed it is difficult to see how this integrity could be violated or even straightforwardly damaged at all, though it could be lost or compromised or just never developed.

But this vision of integrity is connected to, or is perhaps but an aspect of another – one having, as with the notion of the integrity of the body, both inward- and outward-looking aspects. And when this further vision of integrity is operating, damage to and violation of the integrity of persons may indeed by connected with similar effects on the integrity of their bodies.

The inward-looking aspect of this vision focuses on the person as a locus of various drives, impulses, needs, wants, thoughts, etc. These are not by any means clearly seen as *parts* of the person, and neither is it at all clear that their relationships to each other are systematic enough to support a view of them as clearly constituting a system; further, and even more crucially for the question just asked, it is not clear precisely how they are related to the body, though some relationships are surely often supposed (one need mention only the so-called 'mind-body problem' to conjure up visions of the issues that must be met here). Nevertheless, in the face of all these unclarities, it is clear enough that the inward-looking aspect of a person's integrity is thought to be a function of the extent to which his impulses, needs, wants, thoughts, etc. are harmoniously and 'coherently' integrated *vis-à-vis* each other. And the rationale for this is strikingly similar to that found in the inward-looking view of the integrity of the body. The question is whether we are being presented with one thing or with many things, one person or – so to speak – many persons.

This vision of the integrity of persons has of course been richly troubling. Given the generally favorable attitude toward striving for and protecting the integrity of persons, the emphasis on completeness and wholeness may be thought, for example, to enforce a disturbingly closed-off view of something so quicksilvery and open-ended as men sometimes seem to be. Plato might approve, but Walt Whitman would not; consider Plato's criticism of actors in the *Republic* on the grounds that one should be one person and not many;

and consider the following quote from George Kateb utilizing Whitman's view:

> Proteus could become the symbol of the tone of Utopian life. The aim would be . . . to allow individuals to assume various 'personae' without fear of social penalty, . . . to strive to have each self be able to say, in the words of Walt Whitman's 'Song of Myself': 'I am large, I contain multitudes.'[2]

And the matter has certainly disturbed Sartre and, less directly, John Dewey, as well as other modern philosophers before and since. Sartre, for example, was critical of people who long to be something 'solid,' something inescapable, though it is not clear how far he would be able to avoid the view of integrity used above. In his famous lecture 'Existentialism is a Humanism,' he sums things up by saying, 'What we mean to say is that a man is no other than a series of undertakings, that he is the sum, the organization, the set of relations that constitute these undertakings.'[3] This does not seem to me to escape the view of integrity just used.

The connection of this inward-looking view of integrity with integrity-as-rectitude is via the notion of honesty, and is especially clear in the interesting and paradoxical cases of honesty to oneself. I spoke earlier of the difficulty with the notion of self-deception and of Sartre's attempt to cope with the dichotomizing of the self that the intelligibility of the notion seems to require. The difficulty is precisely that self-deception seems to involve the disintegration of the self. Listen to Sartre attempting to sum-up the results of the discussion in his famous chapter:

> the first act of self-deception is to flee what it cannot flee, to flee what it is. The very project of flight reveals to self-deception an inner disintegration in the heart of being, and it is this disintegration which it wishes to be.[4]

Much can be made of these two sentences, and I don't wish to suggest that I accept them entirely (insofar as I understand them), but they certainly show the way to connecting integrity-as-rectitude with integrity as the internal coherence and integration of the self.

Concerning whether damage to or violation of the integrity of the body, such as the amputation we have been considering, will amount also to a damaging or destruction of this inner integrity of the person, the issue seems in the first place to depend on how we resolve problems of the mind-body type mentioned earlier. Apart from that, the upshot seems at best a contingent matter. Will the amputation in itself, for example, amount to a disruption or lessening of the harmony and coherence of my impulses, needs, wants, drives, thoughts, etc.? Perhaps not. But it may lead to such a disruption or lessening so clearly and immediately that we would be tempted to count that, along with absence of the leg, as unqualifiedly one of the outcomes of the surgery. This would be especially tempting if the person had or was preparing for a career in which the leg was essential.

The claim that the integrity of something (in this case a person) has been *violated* will, as before, be hinged principally to the outward-looking aspect of the integrity of the thing. And, as before, this aspect will emphasize the importance of the boundaries in the light of which we determine where the thing ends and other things begin. The thing is again seen as a bounded domain having an inertia or principle of operation of its own, and thus as one complete or whole thing in an environment of other things. The thing's integrity is violated when this domain is intruded upon and changes are produced within the domain that interfere with and counter or 'overcome' the effects of the thing's own inertia or principles of operation. The less this happens and the more completely the state of the thing is determined by the operation of its own inertia, etc., the greater will be its integrity.

The integrity of a person is thus, on the outward-looking view, a function of what is commonly called the autonomy of the person. A thing's autonomy, or the extent to which it has autonomy or is autonomous, is in part a function of the extent to which it is in need or want of nothing not already contained in itself. It is also a function of the extent to which what happens to the thing is self-determined. (These two aspects of autonomy are connected in ways that could be explored if one had the time and space.) Not surprisingly, the concept of autonomy is not a very clear one because we are not clear on whether we want to understand it so that it has realistic applications to things of this world, or rather so that it is a limit which the situations of such things might approach but never reach. The difficulty here of course lurks close-by even in the outward-looking view of the integrities of bodies. But its connection with the integrities of persons has always been more prominent and has always most excited philosophers.

The connection of the integrities of persons with their autonomy raises a host of metaphysical, moral, social and psychological issues. Compare the Kantian and post-Kantian discussions up through Sartre of the autonomy and, not incidentally, the freedom of persons. And, to mention matters even more widely associated with social philosophy, consider the way recent social thinkers have been made uncomfortable by the view of men as somewhat autonomous, and thus viable, domains. When they most dislike it, they call it 'atomistic individualism,' and there have been numerous recent attempts, whether in the name of overcoming loneliness or alienation or whatever, or merely in the name of a more nearly correct account of the metaphysics of the situation of men, to break down these boundaries (or, as they are sometimes called, 'barriers') between self and other. In some social movements, this appears in attempts to establish 'gemeinschaft' or tribal styles of communal life. But one also finds hesitation about the rigidity of the boundaries supposed to exist between persons and their non-human environments; the newer views of some speculative biologists (cf. Waddington) on the profound effects on men of their immediate physical and biological environments may suggest to some that far too much importance has been attached to the distinction between what is inside and what is outside these boundaries. In both cases, the internal-external distinction in the light of which we see persons as well-bounded entities is under attack. The attacks will surely have enormous ramifications for our thinking about men and the world if we take them seriously. We should not be surprised to find these issues lying in wait for us when we discuss the possible wrongness of violence.

It is difficult to proceed in the face of them, but perhaps we could push on for the moment with a somewhat modest notion of autonomy. The aspect of autonomy generally most at issue in discussions of the integrity of persons is that concerned with the self-determination of what happens to one. It connects easily with integrity-as-rectitude, as is evidenced in the usefulness of 'uprightness' in characterizing rectitude; 'uprightness' suggests a certain strength underwriting independence from external pressures and blandishments in determining what one shall do and what shall become of one. It seems safe to say that we can operate with a fairly crude notion of this side of autonomy in view of the particular and rather special problem with which we are concerned at this stage of the discussion. We are interested in whether the amputation of my leg, to which I by hypothesis gave permission, constitutes a violation of my integrity. We are interested in this because the amputation constitutes a preeminently sudden and radical externally effected change at least in my body and perhaps also in me, and I have argued that such change has occurred whenever violence has been done, that we are in some of our moods inclined to believe such changes wrong because they damage, destroy or violate the integrities of what is so changed, and that this reaction is at least part of what underlies the common opinion that violence is wrong. I am now exploring what supports and what subverts the reasonableness of this substructure of the common view. We have so far seen that the amputation in question – an instance of such change though not *thereby* a case of violence done – did indeed damage and violate the integrity of my body. The question is now whether it damaged or violated my integrity, though we have already seen that there are reasons to worry about the full relevance of this because, since it is not clear just how I am connected to my body, we must be at least slightly unclear about whether the amputation brought about a change in me as well as a change in my body. The effect of all this on the concept of integrity that we may reasonably use here is that the range of changes we are considering (preeminently sudden, radical, and externally effected) consists of such relatively dramatic changes that we may not need a very subtle or far-reaching notion of autonomy-as-self-determination to deal with them.

Turning to the amputation and its connection with my autonomy, if it did indeed produce a change in me as well as in my body (and when confronted with this issue I feel like a person confronted with an optical illusion that looks now concave, now convex), and if the change counted as a radical change in me as well as in my body (and, indeed, this might be dubious though the rest be clear), then the case is worth exploring further. The problem now is whether the radical change in me was simply that I no longer had my leg. If so, then, because I gave permission to the surgeon, the amputation did not violate my integrity as an autonomous decider of what is to happen to me – at least on common understandings of what this means, and on the presumption that I was not coerced, tricked, or beguiled into giving permission. But precisely in this case the status of the amputation as effected by an external force (and thus also its status as a case of violence done to me) may muddy because I seem to have played a bit too much of a role in its occurrence. Compare here the case of the man whose leg was broken in a fall on an icy path, and the man whose leg was broken when he was struck by a tree uprooted by a tornado.

If the radical change produced in me by the amputation was not, or was not solely, the loss of my leg, then my permission to amputate my leg may not have been so clearly permission to produce that further change in me, and the question of whether the amputation violated my integrity as decider of what would happen to me would have to be re-raised. (And in either case, if I had been coerced, tricked, or beguiled into giving permission, we might rightly be uncomfortable in various ways about whether my integrity-as-decider had been violated. If pursued further, this uncomfortableness would reveal an underlying network of mixed and controversial views on what men are and what they ought to be – e.g., views, some of which have already been mentioned, about the interplay of intellect, will, and environment.) Further, if I had not given permission at all to the surgeon, then no conclusion would be immediately obvious. For, it would depend on whether the amputation occurred against my expressed wishes, or took place without my being asked because I was unconscious or delirious, or took place without my being asked simply because, though I was in condition to respond, nobody asked me – either through an oversight or as a part of somebody's scheme. Only in the first case would it be perfectly clear that my integrity-as-decider had been violated. (And, again, the other cases would, if we pursued them and tried to rationalize our reactions to them, lead us to an underlying network of highly debatable views on the nature and state of men.)

Through all these difficulties, the important thing to notice for our present purposes is the central role played by the view that persons are well-bounded entities in the common and still developing sentiment that there is something wrong with violence to persons. If it is going to be necessary to re-think the former, then it is going to be necessary to re-think at least part of the latter. The view of persons as bounded and at least somewhat autonomous entities contributes to our sense of a *person* (as distinct from merely a person's body) as something violable, and thus something on which change may be externally imposed. It thus supports our increasing tendency to think that violence may be done to persons in ways distinct from merely doing violence to the bodies of persons.

V

Do things other than persons and the bodies of persons have integrities that could be damaged, destroyed, or violated? We are in some of our moods inclined to think so, though we are inconstant and unclear about how far the idea should be extended. Whether everything which has been subjected to sudden, radical, and externally effected change has an integrity that could be violated is an issue that could take us far afield. Such questions cannot be discussed now, though they must eventually be discussed, and we might expect to find when we do so the reappearance of at least some portions of the networks of concepts and problems just exposed.

And of course new concepts and problems will appear. For example, matters are often unclear with the extensions just suggested because (i) we are not accustomed to thinking of what has been changed as a thing and thus do not readily think in terms of 'its' autonomy or integrity (as with an area devastated by a storm cutting across political boundaries and across boundaries between town and country and between tilled and untilled, tended and untended, land), or (ii) we see the thing in question as so clearly noxious or of no account that we find it idle to have an interest in its autonomy or integrity.

Extensions of the notion of integrity to things other than persons and their bodies draw support at many points, as is well known, from analogies with persons and persons' bodies – analogies strongest in the case of higher animals, weaker in the case of lower animals, plants, etc.

But the extension from the human to the non-human is also often guided by consideration of human interests and fundamentally based on connections between the things in question and human autonomy. This is most obvious with things in which we, as Locke would say, 'have a property,' or contemplate having a property, things which we have built, things on which we have lavished or contemplate lavishing attention and labor. The extension can be complex in such cases – sometimes involving a view of the things as having integrities of their own, and sometimes instead or as well a view of them as somehow a part of oneself or as somehow tied in their fate, actually or potentially, to one's own integrity.

We also find extensions underwritten by considerations connected to but more remote from notions of personal property. The non-human contents of the world are sometimes thought of, collectively or individually, as a 'heritage' 'left' to us by preceding generations or by God, or a heritage simply presented to us by 'Nature,' to be husbanded and held in trust for the use and benefit of present and future generations. This view is currently popular in the U.S., which rightly feels itself confronted with critical ecological issues, preeminently including so-called environmental 'pollution.' The view leads us to think of the state in which we 'received' the world as having special importance (as though the world were an estate for whose management we might eventually be praised or reproached or damned, the judgement being based on the condition of the world when we 'turn it over to others' as compared with its condition when we 'received' it). Or cf. de Jouvenal: 'While any farmer or industrialist knows that he must provide for the upkeep of his plant, the basic "plant" we have received, the Earth, seems to us to call for no stewardship.'[5] We ourselves are then, at least for purposes of this judgment, seen as external to this world, and our own behavior toward it counts, at least when we are active toward it, as an impingement of external forces upon it, and thus, if our action is precipitous and dramatic, as violating its integrity vis-a-vis its initial state. (Cf., 'When anything becomes extinct, there is an uncanny feeling that somewhere a hole has been made in the fabric of creation.'[6])

And one might find extensions underwritten by more abstract considerations such as those brought forward in the following argument: Imagining change is imagining a subject or subjects of change, and is thus to operate with at least some (however indefinite) notion of the boundaries of what has been changed. To imagine further that the change has been effected by a force or forces clearly (by hypothesis in the statement of the issue) external to what has been changed, is to give those boundaries sufficient firmness to support at least the beginnings of thinking in terms of our further requirement. For, in order to imagine the forces clearly external, one must grasp, more or less, the contrasts giving the case its sense. One must have at least a primitive grasp of the difference between forces that are external and forces that are not, and thus must have some notion of what it would have been like if no external forces had operated and, to put the matter crudely, what had been changed had been 'left undisturbed' or 'left alone.' And the latter, which is consistent both with change and with absence of change just so long as neither is effected by external forces, solidifies a notion of the boundaries of what has been changed as enclosing a domain within which events could proceed more or less autonomously and thus a domain the integrity of which could be violated.

These are examples of lines of thought we would have to examine if we were to pursue further the aspects of the common views that extend to non-humans the idea that things have integrities that might be damaged, destroyed, or violated when subject to the sort of change we've had in mind.

VI

If all this discussion is to play a role in a general account of the disvalue of violence, done and the at least *prima facie* wrongness of countenancing or bringing about such violence, one must sooner or later carry further the two lines of investigation suggested by this paper – viz., the connection of violence done with injury, damage, and destruction straightforwardly conceived in their more or less 'brute' forms, and its connection with a broader notion of harm to things stemming from consideration of damage to, destruction of, or violations of their integrities. One must push further into claims about the wrongness of these. Whether or not one is inclined to find the matter problematic, one might agree that it would be nice to be able to *show* these things, and at least that understanding them thoroughly is essential for sound reasoning about when, if ever, violence is excusable or justifiable.

This paper has, of course, been concerned with only some aspects of the possible wrongness of violence. The discussion has been confined to the possible wrongness of violence having been done to something in cases where we can be taken to see the violence done, and to what problems are met in attempts to give perfectly general accounts of this. We did not reach other cases of violence, for example, cases where violence has been done to language or to a man's thought. And since, to take only some obvious examples, violence even of the sort we can be taken to see is often done to things by wind and waves as well as by people, we did not reach, except in a most casual way, matters concerned with the possible wrongness of *engaging-in* or *using* violence. Nothing, for example, was said about the possibly[7] deleterious effects of engaging-in violence or[8] made here between whether their engagement was deliberate or inadvertent or even unconscious, and whether if deliberate it was aimless or purposeful. Nor was anything said about the possibly[7] deleterious effects of such violence on persons or societies or segments of societies which, even though not the perpetrators and perhaps not even the subjects of the violence in question, are affected by their witnessing or hearing of it and are led thereby, according to some hypotheses, either to indulge in their own tendencies toward violence or to engage in 'prudential' or morally righteous counter-violence or abandonment of social techniques abstaining from the use of violence.

Such things are on the minds of many people concerned about the possible wrongness of violence. My justification for not reaching them is that I have been fully occupied elsewhere, and occupied with matters I think more basic to an account of the wrongness of violence.

Notes for 'What Is Wrong with Violence?'*

The Problem: Why is countenancing or bringing about violence in need of any special justification or excuse?

Two Preliminary Claims:

1. The notion of violence is complex (and therefore correct accounts of its wrongness may be expected also to be complex). Some views of violence:
   (a) violence as an impulse or force or stock of psychic or physical energy
   (b) violence as a form or kind of action or activity
   (c) violence as a tool or instrument for the achievement of a purpose
   (d) violence as a result of a certain sort (achieved, perhaps, in a certain way)
      (i) sometimes a result that we cannot clearly 'be taken to see' (e.g., violence done to language or to a man's thought)
      (ii) sometimes a result that we can clearly 'be taken to see' (e.g., violence done to a park or to a forest).

2. Though none of these may be inescapably the fundamental notion, choice of the last (dii) as central provides a foundation for the most coherent and least troubling account of why violence is generally considered wrong.

Some Central Claims About (dii):

1. If violence (dii) has occurred, then something has been injured, damaged or destroyed.
   Comment: But is there anything wrong per se with injury or damage to or destruction of things? I touch on this issue, but hardly pursue it.
2. If violence (dii) has occurred, then something has been changed, and the change has been
   (i)   effected by external force(s)
   (ii) fairly sudden [and]
   (iii) fairly radical.

3. If change preeminently satisfying these three conditions has occurred, then we are in some moods inclined to think that the integrity of

---

* These notes were appended to MacCallum's working copy of 'What Is Wrong with Violence?' They are included here as providing both an abstract of the paper provided by the author and also an account by the author of some of the defects of the paper. Whether this addendum was provided for some audience, for people to whom MacCallum circulated the paper for comments, or simply for MacCallum's own use – perhaps in some never pursued revision – does not appear from the information available to the editors.

what has been so changed has thereby been damaged, destroyed, or violated.

Comments: (a) Therefore, if violence (dii) has occurred, then we are in some moods inclined to think that the integrity of something has been damaged, destroyed, or violated.

          (b) But are we right when we think this way about the connection between violence and integrity? I try to explore rationales for thinking this way – to find reasons that could be offered for it (focusing on the connection suggested in claim 3, and providing a fairly extensive explication of 'integrity').

          (c) But, even if, or insofar as, we are right in thinking this way, would this be enough to show something wrong with violence (dii)? Is there anything wrong per se with damage to or destruction or violation of the integrities of things? I touch on this issue (with special reference to the notions of autonomy and, incidentally, freedom), but hardly pursue it.

Bare-Bones Results: We can show that countenancing or bring[ing] about violence (dii) is in need of special justification or excuse if we can show (a) that there is something wrong per se with injury and damage to and destruction of things, or (b) that there is something wrong per se with damage to and destruction and violation of the integrities of things, *and* that change satisfying the three conditions mentioned above (2i, ii, iii) always damages, destroys, or violates the integrity of what is so changed.

Matters not touched upon in the paper:

1. Is there anything else that might, non-derivatively, be wrong with violence (dii)?
2. Precisely what might, derivatively or not, be wrong with violence of other sorts (e.g., violence to language or to a man's thought) or with violence when differently conceived (e.g., as a form or kind of activity)?

Notes

1. It is not clear to the editors whether MacCallum wanted this word to be 'affect,' in the sense, say, of *affectation*, or 'effect.' Eds.
2. George Kateb, 'Utopia and the Good Life.' In *Utopias and Utopian Thought*, edited by Frank E. Manuel (Boston: Houghton Mifflin, 1966), p. 256.
3. Jean-Paul Sartre, 'Existentialism is a Humanism,' translated by Philip Mairet. In *Existentialism from Dostoevsky to Sartre*, edited by Walter Kaufman (Cleveland & New York: Meridian Books, 1956), p. 301.

4. Sartre, 'Self-deception,' in Kaufman, ed., *Existentialism from Dostoevsky to Sartre*, p. 270.
5. Bertrand de Jouvenal, 'Utopia for Practical Purposes.' In Manuel, *Utopias*, p. 231.
6. A quote from *Time* magazine, 'Letters Column,' European edition, 16 February 1970, p. 2.
7. At both these places 'possible' appears in the original. The editors have changed this to 'possibly.' Eds.
8. This 'or' was 'on' in the original. A line or two may have been omitted in the typescript available to us. Eds.

COMMENTARY ON MACCALLUM

Gerald C. MacCallum (1925–1987) is best known to political philosophers for his work on negative and positive freedom, in particular for his account of freedom as a triadic relation involving an agent, certain preventing conditions, and certain doings or becomings of the agent.[1]

This piece by MacCallum on 'What is Wrong with Violence' appeared in print for the first time in 1993, although MacCallum wrote it sometime between 1969 and 1970. It was never published by MacCallum during his lifetime, in part because it is an unfinished piece of work. The 'Notes for "What Is Wrong with Violence?"' reproduced at the end of the essay suggest that MacCallum was clearly aware of areas in his argument where more work was needed. This piece, with the attached 'Notes', was eventually published posthumously for the first time in a collection of MacCallum's essays edited by Marcus G. Singer and Rex Martin.

In this article, MacCallum does not ask himself if or when violence could be justified. Instead, he investigates the even more basic question of why we consider violence to be an evil – after all, if there was nothing wrong with violence, there would not be any need for a justification.[2]

MacCallum examines, and eventually refutes, the standard line that violence is wrong because of its connection with injury, damage, or destruction. As MacCallum says, this connection is not a simple one. From the fact that something has been injured, damaged or destroyed, it does not follow that violence was done. Furthermore, it is not as easy as it seems to assess the injury, damage or destruction done by violence since it is not always possible to see manifestations of injury, damage or destruction.

MacCallum highlights three considerations which figure in our willingness to view injury, damage or destruction as cases of violence done: external imposition (when the injury, damage or destruction have been recognizably effected by forces external to the thing injured, damaged or destroyed); suddenness of change; radicalness of change. MacCallum argues that only 'external imposition' qualifies as a necessary condition, although he is aware of the limitations of this approach.

Finally, MacCallum analyses what could constitute the disvalue of injury, damage or destruction. Thus, he devotes the last pages of his piece to looking into the notion of 'integrity'. This is arguably one of the most original insights into the nature of violence. According to MacCallum, integrity is to be understood not only in terms of the physical integrity of the body, but also the metaphysical, moral, social and psychological issues related to what it means to be an autonomous person.

In the 'Notes' attached to this piece, MacCallum asks himself: 'Is there anything wrong per se with damage to or destruction or violation of the integrities of things? I touch on this issue (with special reference to the notion of autonomy and, incidently, freedom), but hardly pursue it.' Although Mac-Callum never answered these questions, he is indicating the way to some extremely relevant issues intrinsic to the evil of violence.

Notes and further reading

1. G. C. MacCallum, Jr., 'Negative and Positive Freedom', *Philosophical Review*, Vol. 76, 1967, pp. 312–34.
2. For an attempt to answer a similar question, see V. Bufacchi, 'Why is Violence Bad?', *American Philosophical Quarterly*, Vol. 41, No. 2, 2004.

8

On the Meaning and Justification of Violence

Robert Audi

I The philosophical importance of violence

In every major period of human history, some men have used violence to achieve certain of their ends. Moreover, in a great many cases in which men have used violence, they have thought themselves morally justified in doing so. On the other hand, history has long had its opponents of violence, and ancient traditions as diverse as those of Buddhism and Christianity seem to forswear it – officially, at least – almost without qualification. Today, violence is perhaps more controversial than ever; and though most people believe that sometimes men are morally justified in using it, a good many have put forward plausible arguments against it and have shown impressive courage in their use of nonviolent means of moral protest. Even those who advocate certain uses of violence tend to speak of the need to 'resort' to it, and almost everyone believes that *violence is in itself undesirable* and must therefore be used only when some powerful, usually moral, justification can be given.

These points suggest that the subject of violence holds considerable philosophical interest, and surely violence is of particular philosophical interest today: both its nature and its justifiability are frequently debated; it is at once inevitable and deplorable; and it raises questions of the most pressing sort about what means men are morally justified in using to achieve their ends. The present age, moreover, is an age of militancy, perhaps in part because its unprecedented wealth has led to an understandable impatience for reforms whose need has long been widely acknowledged. The Black Panther Party in the United States, for instance, counsels in its newspaper, 'Black People: Keep Your Guns'; and radicals in many countries, including the United States, very commonly affirm that the pervasive injustices they face can be cured only through a revolution. But although the subject of violence is philosophically important, it has not been given sufficient philosophical attention. While many philosophers have remarked on the subject, no major philosopher has produced a thorough analysis of the concept of violence or a rigorous and detailed answer to the question of what conditions, if any, would justify the use of violence. To be sure, Marx, Engels, and later Marxists have given various arguments for certain uses of violence; but so far as I know their writings do not contain either a sustained attempt to work out an analysis of violence or a systematic discussion of the moral issues surrounding its justification. The French philosopher, Georges Sorel, for example, does not offer a careful definition of 'violence' in his *Reflections on Violence*, and the book remains a compilation of rather loosely related essays on topics sometimes only distantly connected with violence.

Much is now being written on violence, but I believe that a thorough analysis of the concept is still needed, and there seems to be almost as great a need for detailed discussion of the issues concerning the justification of violence, especially insofar as it can be regarded a strategy for achieving social reform. Accordingly, in this essay[1] I shall first develop a definition of the concept of violence, and then proceed to examine what seem the most important issues surrounding the question of the conditions, if any, under which the use of violence might be morally justified. My concern is not, however, to produce a set of precise recommendations about where and when violence should be used in any actual situation, whether for defensive purposes, or to achieve reforms, or to carry out a revolution. I do not think that making this kind of specific recommendation of conduct is the business of the philosopher as such. I would insist, however, that his task is not irrelevant to the task of responsibly working out such recommendations. For I take it that if we are to make reasonable and morally justifiable decisions about whether to use violence in a given case, it is essential that we have a clear notion of what violence is, what forms of violence should be distinguished, and what sorts of considerations are pertinent to justifying its use and to deciding in what form it might be warranted. Perhaps my discussion will also be relevant in another way to the task of deciding whether violence should ever be used and, if so, in what form; for in making clear how we might reasonably deal with this task, I shall try to dispose of a number of plausible but mistaken views about the nature and justification of violence.

II Analysis of the concept of violence

Perhaps I should acknowledge immediately that it is in some ways misleading to speak of 'the' concept of violence. For while there seems to be a concept of violence shared by the vast majority of those who use the term, there are other concepts of violence that are quite different, some idiosyncratic, some rather widely shared. We sometimes speak of the violence of a storm, or of an edition's doing violence to a text, and here we are not using 'violence' in the sense that concerns me. Nor shall I be concerned with violence as a quality of temperament, though violence of temperament can perhaps be understood as largely a disposition to exhibit violence in the sense that does concern me. Speaking very broadly, I am concerned with violence as a kind of human action or activity (or occasionally action or activity of other animate beings). Violence in this sense is always *done*, and it is always done *to* something typically a person, animal, or piece of property. We should distinguish, then, between the doing of violence and merely acting violently: a frenzied lunatic might act violently by swinging his fists in the air and screaming inarticulately into the night; he would not, in this case, be doing violence, though perhaps acting violently can be analyzed in terms of its similarity to, and the potential it implies for, the doing of violence. Indeed, perhaps the notion of violence as something done is fundamental, in the sense that the other notions of violence can be analyzed in terms of it or conceived as extensions of it. In any case, it seems clear that violence as a kind of action or activity is of greatest moral and philosophical significance, and it is with violence in this sense that I shall be concerned. In developing an analysis of violence in this sense, I shall be working toward a kind of definition, one which should help us to understand violence – not in the sense that it tells us something about its causes or effects, but in the sense that it makes explicit what is normally meant by 'violence' in certain important contexts.

It should be fruitful to begin with a diverse group of examples of the kind of violence in question. This will serve not only to clarify the sense of 'violence' with which I am concerned but also to anchor the discussion in some concrete cases whose importance for the subject of violence will be immediately apparent. Moreover, this procedure will provide us with a way of testing the definition that emerges; for the kind of definition of 'violence' I am seeking will not be a stipulation of a new sense of the term, but an explication of the term as it is now used to refer to the kinds of morally significant actions and activities I shall illustrate. This is not to assume that the concept of violence is a very precise one or that there are no cases which some would call violence and some not; but there is a wide range of cases to which every (or virtually every) competent speaker of English would apply the term 'violence,' and I shall try to frame a definition which fits these, in the sense that it requires us neither to include any cases which we would ordinarily be unwilling to include nor to exclude any which we would ordinarily be unwilling to exclude. Because the term 'violence' is vague, however, there will of course remain borderline cases. But I shall try to develop my definition in such a way that, in discussing whether or not these should be considered violence, we at least have a clear idea what sorts of questions it is relevant to ask in order to make a reasonable decision.

Let us begin with the following cases. Nearly all of these would, under any conditions whatever, be clear cases of violence; and all of them would under most conditions be clear cases: beating a person up, punching, striking, or wrestling with him; trampling him, vigorously pushing him around, and sharply and forcefully slapping his face; burning someone, stabbing him, flogging or flaying him; raping someone, shooting him, running him over with a motor vehicle, and dragging him behind a horse or vehicle; dropping bombs or napalm on people, their dwellings, or crops; storming a house or any populated area, and armed attacking of any person or persons; beating, torturing, or maliciously slaughtering an animal; breaking windows by throwing stones through them, and breaking down the door of someone's dwelling; destroying furniture, and burning or wrecking automobiles, dwellings, or places of business. Other cases of violence, not quite as clear as the above, are these: screaming menacingly or abusively at someone; beating one's head against the wall in a fit of madness; and 'tearing someone apart' psychologically by provoking him, through verbal cruelty, to hysterical breakdown or explosive rage. Lastly, we should mention some cases which seem under certain conditions to be clear cases of violence and under others to be at best borderline cases. Murder, for example, is a clear case of violence if carried out by drubbing, but at best a borderline case if carried out by calm and unresisted poisoning resulting in rapid, fearless, and painless death. Similar remarks seem to apply to armed holdup and to the use of poisonous gases and deadly bacteria.

It is true that murder and armed holdup are usually considered 'crimes of violence'; but this may be because they are in the vast majority of cases violent rather than because those who use the terminology think that murder and armed holdup must be violent. I am not claiming, however, that sometimes murder and the use of poisonous gases or deadly bacteria are clearly not violent; my point here is simply that in some cases they seem neither clearly cases of violence nor clearly not cases of violence. I shall assume, then, that in the course of our discussion we must be on guard against the now very common blanket term, 'crime of violence,' and others like it, such as 'crime in the streets': although these terms obviously cover many paradigm cases of violence, they are also used to refer to borderline cases or even very doubtful cases.[2] We are thus best off if we concentrate, at least initially, on unmistakably clear cases of violence.

In the light of the foregoing examples, we can begin to work toward an analysis of the concept of violence. We might first consider a rather simple view that may be suggested by some of the most common examples of violence: that violence is the infliction of physical injury on some person. What I want to say about this is simply that although violence very often involves the infliction of physical injury on someone, it need not; someone could push a person around and even strike him quite hard, without physically injuring him. It is not easy to say what constitutes physical injury; but whatever physical injury is, it is clear that a person in very good physical condition might be pushed around and struck a good deal without sustaining such injury. For one thing, provided he was struck only in certain places he might emerge without even a bruise. Moreover, if someone negligently but accidentally steps on and breaks one's toe, he has inflicted a physical injury, yet we could not normally charge him with being violent. These considerations show that even if we revise the definition to read, 'Violence is the infliction on someone of physical suffering,' it will still be inadequate: in the case just mentioned, one might suffer a good deal from a person's stepping on one's toe, without in the least having been the object of violence. We must also grant that although in wrestling and boxing people may be the objects of considerable violence, they need not suffer. Moreover, presumably there are such people as masochists; and they should be able, without suffering, to withstand considerable violence.

Another inadequacy in these two definitions is that they fail to mention something which is very important, though it is often overlooked in discussions of violence: that violence may be psychological. Perhaps it is true that psychological violence never constitutes a paradigm case of violence; but there seem to be instances in which few would withhold the term, though in these cases no physical contact occurs between the perpetrator and the sufferer. Suppose a man screams abusive epithets at his wife, humiliates her, and provokes her to a hysterical breakdown, which he exacerbates by continuing his vilification. Surely he would be doing her violence, though he might leave her physically untouched. Or consider a savage verbal attack upon someone, such as we find in Albee's *Who's Afraid of Virginia Woolf?* The attacker might be thought of as doing violence to his victims, perhaps even without screaming. It may be that where we speak of violence in reference to cases in which no physical contact is made with the person suffering it, we must be able to imagine a clear potential for physical violence, or some important similarity to physical violence; but violence may nonetheless occur without there actually being any physical contact with the person who suffers it.

Once we recognize the existence of psychological violence, we must complicate our definition further. We might say that violence is the physical or psychological abuse of a person; and it is important to add that such abuse tends to result in injury or suffering or both. For it seems to be part of our concept of violence to persons – and we could even include this point in our definition – that it tends to result in suffering or injury; under typical conditions, when the violence is neither very slight nor the victims very resistant to pain and injury, the violence does result in suffering or injury or both. This definition is superior to the previous two in that it includes the notion of psychological violence and allows for the possibility that violence does not result in suffering or injury. Nevertheless, the definition is quite inadequate; while there is some plausibility in holding that physical abuse of a person is a sufficient condition for doing him violence, there are clearly forms of psychological abuse that do not constitute violence. Insulting, embarrassing, or humiliating a person would sometimes constitute psychological abuse but usually not violence. Perhaps, however, we can take care of this difficulty by supplementing the notion of abuse; it would be better to say, for example, that violence is the physical, or the sharp, caustic, psychological abuse of a person. By requiring that the psychological abuse in question be sharp and caustic, which suggests the psychological counterparts of cutting and burning the body, we might rule out those insults and other psychological abuses whose delivery would very often not constitute violence. But whether these notions would rule out, say, a father's severe but less than violent rebuke of a delinquent son, is not clear. In any case, before refining this definition further we should try to meet some more pressing problems.

We have not so far taken into account those examples of violence characterized by the destruction of various kinds of property. The most obvious step to take, then, is to add to the last of the above definitions, 'or the destruction of property.' But because such things as orderly, routine demolitions of old buildings are the destruction of property, we need a more complicated notion. We might now try substituting, for 'the destruction of property,' 'the unjustified destruction of property.' But although most violence in the destruction of property is probably unjustified, there might be cases in which violent destruction is justified; dynamite might have to be used for the rapid destruction of an obsolete structure to make way quickly for a new one. Moreover, there are certainly instances in which nonviolent destruction is unjustified; a person might, with consummate nonviolence, destroy an automobile by disassembling it and dissolving its parts in aqua regia.

Thus it might be better to substitute, for the notion of the mere destruction of property, the notion of the highly vigorous, or incendiary, or vigorous and malicious destruction or damaging of property. By 'incendiary destruction or damaging' I mean, very roughly, 'destruction or damaging through the malicious use of fire,' and it should be added that usually the object in question is fairly large, at least the size of a typical item of furniture. This vague restriction as to size is necessary; for although in certain situations we could perhaps reasonably consider the burning of, say, a small photograph, a case of incendiarism, it would distort the meaning of 'incendiary' to consider the malicious burning of items of this size as a clear or typical case. The notion of damage is intended to allow for the obvious fact that violence to property need not always result in its destruction; and though the notion of vigor resists precise definition it may help to say that, typically, what is done vigorously is done with a substantially greater expenditure of energy than is usual or necessary for the action or activity in question, and in most cases also faster than is usual or necessary.

We are now closer to the concept of violence with which we are concerned; but the notion of vigorous or incendiary destruction or damaging is of course vague, and even if we now have a necessary condition for violence to property, it is perhaps questionable whether we have a sufficient condition. If, needing firewood, one destroys an old cabinet that nobody wants, using rapid strokes with a heavy sledge hammer, one's destruction of it might be considered highly vigorous; but though some would call this a case of violence, I think there might be as many who would not be sure whether to label it thus.

Another difficulty we must face is the omission of any mention of violence to animals. To deal with this, we might expand the definition we have so far arrived at to read, 'Violence is the physical, or the sharp, caustic psychological, abuse of a person or animal (tending to result in his suffering or injury or both); or the highly vigorous, or incendiary, or vigorous and malicious destruction or damaging of property.' It might be thought that the notion of psychological violence has no application to animals, but by screaming at certain animals and in various ways frightening them, one might, particularly where they show signs of suffering, be properly said to be doing them violence. Indeed, just as we sometimes speak of a person's reacting violently to what another person does, even if he does him no physical violence, we occasionally speak of people's reacting violently to something an animal has done, especially where, though no physical violence is done to the animal, it is the object of persistent and frightening shouts.

It is more difficult, however, to meet the objection that the physical abuse of animals is not a sufficient condition for doing them violence; for it would seem that overworking a pack horse might well be physically abusing him, yet would not be doing him violence. Indeed, though overworking a human being at a physically taxing job is not the sort of thing one would think of if asked for an example of physical abuse, it does not seem wholly unnatural to consider it such. Perhaps, then, we need some other notion than that of mere physical abuse in order to capture the concept of physical violence.

Before attempting to deal with this problem, however, there is another important question we should discuss: Must violence be done intentionally? It is not implausible to maintain that it must be. We might note, for instance, that most of the examples of violence on the above list are actions and activities that are inconceivable except as intentional, for example, raping, beating up, and storming a city. Moreover, if someone punches another person unintentionally, though not through carelessness, in mock boxing, or if someone shoots another person unintentionally in an unavoidable hunting accident, it would probably not be correct to say he had done him violence. But even if the vast majority of actual cases of violence, and all the paradigm cases, are intentional, it nevertheless seems possible for violence to be unintentional. If in a rage one inadvertently and unintentionally tramples three children and knocks over two old ladies, one would still be guilty of violence; and if a pilot unintentionally released his bombs over a crowded city, he would surely be responsible for doing violence to the people below. Thus, although there are ways of doing violence which can be conceived only as intentional, not all violence need be intentional. One might think we could at least say that nothing can count as doing violence unless one is morally responsible for it. This certainly applies to the great majority of cases in which people do violence; but if we alter the above case to one in which a victim of some serious psychosis, provoked into rage, does the trampling, we can see that it is possible for someone to do considerable violence without being morally responsible for it.

Very similar considerations are relevant to the question whether violence entails the *violation* of at least one moral right. Again, in the most usual cases violence involves the violation of some moral right; and if we accept the plausible view that there are some inalienable rights, such as the right to humane treatment, then some kinds of violence – torturing someone to death or brutally flogging him – are inconceivable apart from the violation of a moral right. But there are also some cases, like wrestling and boxing, in which even paradigmatic violence can occur without the violation of any moral right. This is one reason why, although the use of the term 'violence' usually conveys some disapproval, the term is sometimes used with no such force. There is an important relation between the concept of violence and that of the violation of moral rights; but the relation is too complex to permit the conclusion that either entails the other. If violence entailed the violation of at least one moral right, or if it were 'by definition' unjustifiable, we should have to accept the absurd consequence that, if we witness things like one man's forcefully punching another man in the face, or the rapid, fiery, and thunderous dynamiting of a row of beautiful old houses, or the atomic bombing of Hiroshima, we cannot know whether violence has been done until we have enough information – and this is often a great deal indeed – to make a perhaps very difficult moral judgment on the situation in question.

On the basis of the foregoing discussion, it seems reasonable to propose the following three-part definition: Violence is the physical attack upon, or the vigorous physical abuse of, or vigorous physical struggle against, a person or animal; or the highly vigorous psychological abuse of, or the sharp, caustic psychological attack upon, a person or animal; or the highly vigorous, or incendiary, or malicious and vigorous, destruction or damaging of property or potential property. In addition, let me emphasize an important point which I take to be implicit in the terms of the definition: that violence to animate beings tends to involve or cause their suffering or injury or both.

Before raising the question whether this definition is adequate, I want to indicate how it is an improvement over the previous definition. First, it substitutes 'attack upon, or the vigorous physical abuse of, or vigorous physical struggle against' for 'physical abuse.' This seems to be an improvement, since it is reasonable to suppose that when a person or animal is physically attacked, *vigorously* abused physically, or vigorously struggled against physically, we have a case of physical violence. It seems almost equally clear that when a person is subjected to sharp and caustic psychological attack or to highly *vigorous* psychological abuse, we have a case of psychological violence. I shall not attempt to give a definition of 'vigorous abuse,' but it should be of some help to say that, typically, vigorous abuse of persons is very rough treatment, especially shoving, punching, dragging, slapping, stabbing, slashing, trampling, crushing, burning, and shooting. Vigorous psychological abuse may be thought of, in rough terms, as the psychological counterpart of these abuses, and it is usually accompanied by sharp tones and screaming and often by insults and threats; but the definition allows for the possibility that psychological violence may be perpetrated without words, as where only inarticulate screams and threatening gestures are used, or in writing, as in the case of a scathing and strident diatribe. Both kinds of abuse are examples of what is typically a kind of 'improper use'; but the case of self-defense shows that what is typically improper may be justified in special circumstances, and the cases of wrestling and boxing show that what would in some situations be improper is in other situations perfectly proper. Secondly, whereas the rider to the previous definitions required that violence to animate beings usually 'result' in suffering or injury, this definition is to be understood as making the broader requirement that such violence tend to 'involve or cause' suffering or injury. This is an improvement because there are certain kinds of violence that essentially involve suffering or injury in such a way that they cannot be correctly said to cause or result in it: blowing a man's leg open does not cause the blowing open of his leg, for this particular violence is logically impossible in the strictest sense without this injury; and savagely torturing a man does not cause or result in the suffering constituted by the torturing, though it may cause him suffering for the rest of his life. Where the violence we are talking about is specified as torturing, suffering is essentially involved, else there could not be torture. Thirdly, whereas the former definition referred to the destruction or damaging of property, the definition we are now considering refers to the destruction or damaging of property *or* potential property. This has the obvious advantage of acknowledging as violence certain kinds of destruction or damaging of inanimate objects that are not anyone's property.

If we now turn to the question whether the definition I have proposed is adequate, we face a number of problems. For one thing, the definition says nothing about who must do violence. I have already acknowledged that violence can be done by animals; but can we rule out the possibility of say, nonhuman rational beings doing violence? I think not. Yet it does not follow that, in a definition of 'violence,' we should explicitly mention what seems so remote a possibility. The best course is to admit that the term is open-textured. This is not to say that it is vague, though it is vague because there are certainly actual cases in which there is no clear answer to the question whether the term applies. The point is that our concept of violence, like a great many concepts, is such that we are simply not prepared to say that no hitherto unimagined cases could arise in which we would be uncertain whether the concept applies. To be sure, if we were confronted with, say, non-human rational beings and could observe their behavior, it might be quite clear whether the term 'violence' could reasonably be applied to some of the things they do. But even if we could draw up some sort of catalogue of all the cases of violence now imaginable, as well as all borderline cases, we would be misrepresenting the logic of the concept of violence if we maintained that no other cases of violence, or borderline cases, could ever arise. These remarks also bear on the question whether violence can be done only *to* people, animals, and inanimate objects. Without mentioning these three groups one could not have an adequate analysis of violence; but I do not mean to suggest that we could not, without overturning the concept of violence, apply the term to the doings of nonhuman rational beings that so far can be only vaguely imagined.

Another problem that deserves mention arises if one asks what physical violence, psychological violence, and violence to inanimate objects have in common in virtue of which they may all be considered violence. One might be tempted to say that my definition does not capture the 'essence' of violence, but merely introduces three subsidiary concepts of violence. This objection seems to me mistaken. First, surely the correct thing to say here is that the definition makes explicit the three fundamental aspects, or perhaps kinds, of violence, rather than three different concepts of it, though in any case it does not seem very important whether we speak of one concept of violence that includes three closely related kinds of violence, or of three closely related concepts of violence. Secondly, while I do not wish to affirm the view that all instances of a concept must have at least one thing in common, I believe that in the case of the concept of violence it is apparent that the notion of vigorous abuse comes very close to forming a kind of core; for virtually all instances of violence involve vigorous abuse, and those that do not can be seen to exhibit important resemblances to it or a clear potential for it. Thus, the concept of violence, as expressed in the three-part definition I have proposed, certainly does not lack unity. That a concept may be exemplified by importantly different things does not entail that it is 'really' a set of different concepts misleadingly lumped under a unitary heading.

It may also be objected that my definition of 'violence' is inadequate because there are contexts in which we could not, without oddity, substitute the defining expression for 'violence': for instance, where we speak of physical violence. But the reason for the oddity of this substitution is that the defining expression, like the concept of violence itself, is disjunctive; hence, where 'violence' is modified by 'physical,' whose very point in this case is to rule out psychological violence and violence to inanimate objects, we of course cannot substitute for 'violence' the entire defining expression, which specifies all three kinds of violence. The substitution which it would be relevant to consider here would be to put, in place of 'physical violence,' the part of the definition specifying the meaning of 'physical violence'; and this substitution would always, or nearly always, be acceptable. In any case, even if the sort of substitution which is envisaged in the above objection must be possible if the defining expression is synonymous with the expression being defined (and I doubt whether this must be so), for the sort of definition provided by a philosophical analysis, synonymy in this sense may be too strict a condition to impose. A more reasonable condition – and one which I believe my definition meets – is that it be a conceptual truth that for any x, x is an instance of the concept being defined if and only if x is an instance of the concept represented by the defining expression.

Other difficulties that should be discussed are the vagueness of most of the terms in the definition, and the possibility of its failing to provide a sufficient condition, perhaps even a necessary condition, for violence. Regarding the first difficulty, I doubt whether anyone would deny that the term 'violence' is vague; and because it is, it should not be surprising if even an adequate definition is also vague: for if a definition clearly applied, or clearly failed to apply, to a great many kinds of cases to which the term being defined neither clearly applied nor clearly failed to apply, we might justifiably doubt its adequacy as a definition, though it might, as a rational reconstruction or as a precising definition, be eminently successful.[3] With these points about definition in mind, let us consider an example. Suppose that after blowing up at his wife and storming out of the house a man returns calm and seeks entry. Suppose he also answers her question, 'You aren't going to be violent?' in the negative, but then calmly, stealthily, and without causing her any suffering, poisons her to death while she sleeps. It is tempting to say that he lied to her and did do her violence. But while he certainly lied in that he implied he would not *harm* her, what he did is surely at best a borderline case with respect to the concept of violence; and legally as well as morally it would probably be regarded as even more reprehensible than a violent murder. Thus, although my definition does seem to rule out this case, its doing so is not a serious objection to it, nor do there appear to be many cases in which it would be clear whether or not the definition applied, yet unclear whether or not we would apply the term 'violence.' Moreover, it is worth noting that the definition calls our attention to what seem the right considerations to appeal to in deciding whether to apply the term in a borderline case. If, for example, the question arises of whether a certain poisoning represents violence, one important consideration that would naturally occur to us is *how* it was carried out, especially whether it was carried out with vigorous physical abuse of the victim. Had the man imagined above forced the poison down his wife's throat, he would have exhibited violence, because he would then have both attacked and vigorously abused her.

What may be a more serious difficulty for the definition than its vagueness is the existence of cases in which it does not appear to provide a sufficient condition for violence. Suppose that a man vigorously abuses a horse by riding him at full speed almost to the point of exhaustion. Assuming that he does not whip him in doing so, we can still regard the case as one of vigorous physical abuse, but need we conclude that he does the horse violence? I suspect that here people would disagree, depending on their views regarding the proper treatment of horses; and this makes the example doubly interesting because it brings out that violence, being widely considered

typically wrong, is like many other things of which people usually disapprove (or approve) in that, in certain cases, whether they believe it is present
depends heavily on their attitudes toward the cases in question. Nevertheless,
clear cases of violence easily outnumber the borderline cases; and perception
of the former is normally independent of the moral attitudes of the person judging. But even if we try to take the point of view of someone who
does not care about horses, it would not be unreasonable to say that the
rider we are envisaging has done his horse violence. At the very least we
can say that we have here what many people would regard as a borderline
case, and that the clearer it becomes that what was done qualifies as *vigorous*
physical abuse, the more natural it is to speak of violence. Let me emphasize that in acknowledging some cases in which people's attitudes, including
their moral attitudes, may sometimes affect their use of 'violence,' I am not
suggesting that moral attitudes affect their use of it in all cases. As my definition suggests, I believe that in most instances, and certainly in the most
important ones, the question whether violence has occurred can be reasonably answered independently of the moral attitudes of those who answer
it. But my definition also suggests that, although violence does not entail
the violation of any moral rights, it is, in most cases at least, *prima facie*
wrong.

It is also worth mentioning in this connection that some people, especially
some with a strongly Marxist orientation, speak of violence where my definition would rule it out. Some speak of American society as doing violence
to the Negro, referring to pervasive discrimination and exclusion, however
peacefully maintained. Perhaps this should be regarded as a metaphorical way
of expressing disapproval, and many are inclined to be sympathetic with it
as such. But taken literally it would reveal conceptual confusion. To be sure,
if enough people came to use 'violence' to refer to what in standard usage
would now be called (nonviolent) infringement of certain rights, we would
have to acknowledge a new sense of 'violence.' But it is difficult to see how
we would gain by this. We would increase the risk of ambiguity and equivocation; and we would also increase the temptation, to which too many
already succumb, of substituting a vague general term of disapproval for one
which, like 'discriminatory hiring,' describes the specific grievance needing
attention.

A more difficult case for the definition would be one in which, in rebuking
an employee, a man subjects him to highly vigorous psychological abuse,
or to a sharp and caustic psychological attack, yet never actually screams or
makes threatening gestures. Must we conclude that he has done the employee
violence? Once again, one's view of what is proper in the situation will in part
determine one's judgment; yet I believe that if we take seriously the words
we are considering, we can see that they would not apply except to what
it would be not unreasonable to call violence; if the employer is guilty of
highly *vigorous* abuse, then even if he is not screaming, he is at least speaking

in quite harsh tones; or if what he says constitutes a sharp, caustic *attack*, it surely would have to include such things as humiliating criticisms, biting insults, and rude or disrespectful words, as well as various kinds of attacks or slights upon the person, such as allegations of incompetence, deprecations of past performances, and stinging prophecies of future failures. I believe that if such abuses are thought of as vigorously delivered, or as constituting a sharp, caustic attack, then at worst the definition would require us in a few cases to regard as violence what most would regard as a borderline case.

We can test the definition from another point of view by seeing whether it helps us to make plausible distinctions between violence and things that have something in common with it and are in a good many cases likely to be confused with it. In considering these distinctions, I shall not be attempting to give any definitions; my concern is simply to show some of the ways in which violence, conceived according to the definition I have proposed, differs from certain other concepts. Contrasting it with these other concepts should also help to clarify it further.

Consider first the concept of force, in the sense illustrated by the idea of using force to get someone *to do* (or abstain from doing) something. One important point is that force can be used without violence or even the threat of violence, as when, on pain of having his salary attached, a man is forced to sell something to pay a debt; blackmail, moreover, may involve no violence yet is a kind of force. Secondly, while violence may always involve force in the sense of the expenditure of energy, one may do someone violence – by striking him, for example – without forcing him to do anything; and clearly one need not force anyone to do anything in order to do violence to inanimate objects. Nevertheless, it is very important to see that in a huge number of the typical cases, violence involves at least forcing someone to submit to something against his will, as when a person is beaten by thugs. In these cases violence is also, in a perhaps figurative sense, *violation* of a person, though not necessarily of his moral rights: a homicidal maniac forfeits his right to nonviolent treatment if he leaves the authorities no nonviolent way of bringing him to trial.

The case with terror is similar: clearly violence, as in a wrestling match or the destruction of houses, does not entail that anyone be terrorized or in any way afflicted with terror; and though the infliction of terror upon people and the use of terror as a political or military strategy are almost always accompanied by some violence, terror could be thus used without violence and possibly even without the threat of it. Superstitious people, for example, can probably be terrorized by certain myths, such as tales of a lurking eternity of Sisyphean, though nonviolent, toil. Broadly speaking, whereas violence, in the sense that concerns us here, is a kind of action or activity, terror is either a frightened psychological condition or, by extension, a set of tactics that tend to produce that condition; and though these tactics are typically violent they need not be.

Brutality, on the other hand, in the sense in which it characterizes actions and activities as opposed to temperament, perhaps does entail violence, though possibly one might talk of a man's brutal slaying of his infant child, even if, without any struggle or other movement on the part of the child, the man gently drowned him. But clearly violence, as in the case of justified demolition, need not be brutal. It does seem, however, that most of the paradigm cases of violence involve brutality, and this is one reason why we think of violence as typically wrong.

Violence also need not be cruel, as various of the cases discussed above will show; and there are certainly forms of cruelty, such as deprivation of food, that are not violent. But in the vast majority of clear cases of violence there is some cruelty, and we seem to conceive of all cases of violence as at least potentially cruel. What is cruel, however, need not be the sort of thing that is at least potentially violent, as we can see if we consider subtle humiliations, tactfully executed frustrations, and hushed enkindlements of already poignant jealousy.

Aggression, on the other hand, is usually violent, though people can exhibit some aggression in conversation, business, and international affairs without actually becoming violent. Although there may be some question about whether violence to living things must constitute aggression, I think it need not: both the possibility of roughly but restrainedly tossing around a masochist, and the possibility of 'clean' wrestling merely for enjoyment, would show this. Moreover, it is obvious that not all violence to inanimate objects would constitute aggression, as certain cases of justified demolition show.

The case of political oppression is perhaps more difficult: not only has there probably never been an oppressive regime that did no violence to its subjects, but one might wonder whether a people could be truly oppressed if no violence were used. As the example of superstitious people suggests, however, I do think that oppression, whether political or nonpolitical, is possible without violence, perhaps even without the threat of it, but certainly when the threat of it is present. For it is well known that people may be deprived of their liberties by threats; and it seems possible that if they were imbued with certain kinds of fanatical zeal they might eventually be oppressed through their adherence to a paralyzing but psychologically comforting body of myths. On the other hand, it should now be obvious that violence may occur without anyone's being even temporarily oppressed.

Now even if what I have said so far is accepted, some, including some philosophers, might raise the following objection: Suppose we accept your definition of 'violence,' and your accompanying remarks, as making explicit what is ordinarily meant by the term and thus as providing a kind of analysis of the ordinary concept of violence. Why should we accept your definition as in any way important, or as telling us what violence really is, as opposed to what people think it is? And why should we operate with your concept of violence rather than our own? To take first the question why we should accept the definition as telling us what violence really is, I should like to dispel any suggestion that I have been attempting to summarize what people think, or would say, violence is: there is a great deal of difference between asking what people mean by a term and asking what they think, or would say, they mean by it; and the briefest investigation will show that people are generally unable to give adequate definitions of what they mean even by terms which are very familiar to them and whose use they have unquestionably mastered. Thus, articulating what is meant by a philosophically interesting term is by no means a matter of somehow synthesizing the definitions people would give.

As for the question of what it is to say what violence really is, there could be several answers. One of them is especially relevant here: to say what violence really is, is to say what we really mean by the term when we use it in everyday life, as opposed to what various people, especially many philosophers and most moralists, say it means. This point is particularly important where the theoreticians or others in question have some special bias or blindness which affects their views about violence. Another answer is that to say what violence really is, is to give a psychological account of its causes, its effects, and the typical details of its occurrence. Many have been disappointed with philosophical accounts because they have been hoping for psychological accounts. The two are of course different, though it is worth mentioning that until we have at least a rough concept of something, say violence, we cannot even identify it for scientific study; hence the philosophical task of conceptual analysis need by no means be irrelevant to the tasks of empirical science, especially social science. If, for instance, a sociologist's concept of violence does not include psychological violence, he may never think to study this even though it might shed much light on the nature and causes of other kinds of violence.

Regarding the question of why someone with a concept of violence different from the one analyzed above should operate with the latter rather than with his own, I want to begin by saying that of course he may define 'violence' so as to express his own concept and he may use the term accordingly. In some cases, moreover, it may be desirable to do this. But *if* he wishes to communicate clearly with those who do not share his concept – and in most cases few will share his special concept – he runs various risks. Suppose he regards violence as the unjustified use of force.[4] If he wishes to be understood by most people, he must not only announce that this is what he means but is likely to have to repeat this often as a reminder to himself and others. For with the vast majority of people meaning one thing and him another, the dangers of confusion would be great. He must also find a way of re-expressing what others mean when they use the term 'violence,' and this is likely to be difficult and unnatural; the natural thing would be for him to fall into using 'violence' in at least two senses, and it is common for philosophers who do the sort of thing I am envisaging to lapse into equivocal argument. He might reason as follows, especially if he is not careful to spell out what he means at each step: violence is (by definition) the unjustified use of force; rioting is clearly a case of violence (in the ordinary sense); so rioting is unjustified. Whatever one thinks about the justifiability of rioting, this argument would be a question-begging equivocation. Finally, it is important to realize that although by exercising great care one could use some terms as one pleased without confusion, it is not clear how far this could go without a serious breakdown in communication. Suppose, for example, that the philosopher we were imagining used 'force' in some esoteric sense; he would then have to make clear not only what he meant by 'violence,' but also what he meant by 'force,' and presumably he must somewhere stop if he is ever to get around to communicating anything. Thus, although I would not deny anyone the freedom to use the term 'violence' as he likes provided he finds a way to make himself clear, and though we should certainly welcome the coining of new terms for concepts not already expressible by a current term, I think that usually the risks of using well-established terms in new senses are likely to outweigh the advantages.

Clarification, on the other hand, seems highly desirable; and I hope that the definition for which I have argued clarifies the concept of violence both in the sense that it makes explicit what is ordinarily meant by 'violence,' and in the sense that it helps us to decide, in a reasonable way, whether certain borderline cases should or should not be called violence. The definition is admittedly somewhat vague; but I think that it is by no means hopelessly so, nor any more so than necessary given the vagueness of the concept being defined; and surely the examples discussed above serve to reduce its vagueness appreciably. In any case, the definition seems to me to be sufficiently accurate and clear to enable us to embark upon a fruitful discussion of the issues surrounding the justification of violence.

III Preliminary theoretical considerations concerning the justification of violence

In discussing the justification of violence I shall be primarily concerned with the sorts of considerations relevant to deciding whether its use is morally justified. After outlining what some of these considerations are, I shall go on in the next section to show some of their implications for various important views, most of them well known, about the conditions under which violence is morally justified.

The moral position I shall propose will be quite general. This should not be surprising: if I have been correct about how many ways there are in which people can do violence, then we should not ask about the justification of violence in the abstract; we must consider what kind of violence is in question, and this forces us to examine a very wide range of actions and activities.

I shall be primarily concerned, however, with violence contemplated as a strategy for achieving social reform, particularly where the reform envisaged is regarded as the rectification of grave moral wrongs, and even where revolution is considered necessary to achieve this reform. At the present time, violence of this sort is perhaps more controversial than any other sort, though the question of the conditions, if any, under which one nation is justified in making war on another is also important and difficult. The position I shall take on the justification of violence will, I hope, provide a way of dealing with this latter question; but I shall not have space to address it explicitly. The question of the justification of violence in purely personal affairs is also an important one; but I shall only outline how my position would lead us to deal with the question.

In discussing the justification of violence as a strategy for achieving social reform, we must first recognize considerations of justice: as virtually everyone would grant, to say that a strategy, policy, or course of action would be unjust is to produce a moral consideration against it, one which is normally – and perhaps always – morally conclusive. It is equally clear that to say that something would be just is to produce a moral consideration in favor of it. Yet if we seek to formulate a principle of justice indicating what, in general, justice requires, we can no longer secure such wide agreement. Nearly all writers on the subject of distributive justice, which is our concern here, hold that justice, in the distribution of what has been aptly called benefits and burdens, requires that we treat people equally except under special conditions. R. B. Brandt, for example, maintains that to act justly is to treat persons equally 'in some matter that involves the distribution of things that are good or bad, except as ... inequality is required by moral considerations [principles] with substantial weight in the circumstances.'[5] But a good many writers on the subject of justice take it to require more than equality. Frankena, for instance, has maintained that justice also requires us to observe the principles of 'non-injury, non-interference, and non-impoverishment.' Thus, 'If a ruler were to boil his subjects in oil, jumping in afterwards himself, it would be an injustice but there would be no inequality of treatment.'[6]

I cannot now try to settle the question of which of these conceptions of justice is preferable; but my present sympathies lie more with the broader conception expressed by Frankena. For one thing, if we are to speak at all of the just state and of just laws, it seems that we must grant that a state can be just only if it abstains from injuring, impoverishing, or interfering with its subjects. For instance, we would regard as injustices certain interferences, such as arbitrary curfews and highly confining travel restrictions, and certain deprivations and injuries, even if a government imposed them through the due enactment of laws and with scrupulous impartiality.

Regarding the notion of equality, which is clearly central to the notion of justice, it is important to see that there is room for a good deal of disagreement concerning what constitutes equality of distribution. Consider a group of factory workers who do the same sort of job. Would equal pay for them be the same money per unit of time on the premises, per unit of time on the job, per unit of effort, per unit of output, per unit of need, per unit of time on the job given a certain educational level or level of seniority, or would equal pay represent some combination of these factors, or something involving factors different from any of them? Most of these notions of equal pay have had their advocates, and the difficult moral question of what notion of equality is appropriate in a given case becomes even more refractory for situations more complicated than the above. Concerning the notion of a morally justified exception to the principle that people should be treated equally, I cannot go into detail; but normally such exceptions should be of clear benefit to the community as a whole. Thus, letting only certain officials sign treaties with other countries, and allowing people in certain emergencies to violate speed limits, constitute justifiable exceptions; but excluding people from the franchise on the basis of their sex, and barring them from the use of public facilities on the basis of their color, do not.

In addition to considerations of justice we must also recognize, in discussing the justification of violence as a strategy for achieving social reform, considerations of freedom: whether the use of violence would enhance or diminish human freedom. It may seem that such considerations are encompassed by the broad principle of justice already mentioned: if we consider freedom a benefit or some kind of good, then if we both distribute benefits equally and abstain from interfering with people, what more need we do to guarantee people all the freedom to which they have a moral right? Perhaps it is reasonable to answer, 'nothing,' particularly if we are sufficiently scrupulous in the difficult task of deciding what constitutes a morally justified exception to the requirement that people be treated equally. But as I interpret the principle of non-interference, it would not lead us to go far enough to guarantee the degree of freedom to which people have a moral right, though one could of course stipulate that it is to have whatever breadth is required for this purpose. What I would suggest is that, particularly in formulating social policies, we observe the principle of maximization of freedom, which requires that people have, or at least that reasonable steps be taken to give them, the most extensive freedom possible within the limits of justice – the most extensive freedom which, within the limits of non-injury, non-impoverishment, and non-interference, can be extended equally to everyone in the society in question.

The reason why it is doubtful whether the broad principle of justice mentioned above entails this principle of maximization of freedom is that there seem to be cases in which one might, particularly on the level of nationwide legislation, abstain from interfering with people yet fail to maximize their freedom within the limits of justice. Consider a case in which a government makes no attempt to establish diplomatic relations with a certain other country, even though it does not ban travel to the country in question. This might create a situation in which citizens of the first country are in practice not free to travel to the second, since the authorities in the latter will probably not admit them. In some cases like this we might reasonably say that their government discourages them from traveling to the country in question; but provided diplomatic relations had not existed and then been broken, the case could be such that we would not be justified in saying that the government is guilty of interference with people's freedom. Or, take a case in which a government simply provides no legal status to contracts and wills. Once again, assuming these had never been deprived of legal status in the society we are imagining, and that no one in the society is attempting to institute them, we could not reasonably speak here of interference, though there could not in this society be such things as legally enforcing contracts or waiving one's legal right to enforce a provision of a will; and *a fortiori* there could be no such thing as being free to enforce a contract legally or to waive one's legal right to enforce a provision of a will. To be sure, it would be misleading in this case to speak of people's not being free to enforce contracts or waive their legal rights to enforce wills; but I believe it is reasonable to interpret the notion of maximization of freedom to apply not only to removing existing barriers to certain actions, but also to rendering possible certain actions which are inconceivable apart from certain rules. These examples illustrate that we cannot think of freedom simply as a matter of non-interference, even though interference is perhaps the most common and most serious breach of freedom. There are multitudinous things we do which are very important to us and which presuppose not only that the state abstain from interfering with us but that it make provisions for us in very positive ways; and one kind of case in which violence might be contemplated occurs when, even without positively interfering with the freedom of its citizens, a government seems remiss in providing for the enhancement of their freedom.

Other examples should also show that non-interference does not exhaust our obligations concerning freedom. If we recognize that – as the fairly common phrases, 'prisoner of ignorance' and 'slave to prejudice' imply – there may be psychological and social, as well as physical and legal, barriers to freedom, then we can again see that there may be instances in which people ought to have certain freedoms they lack not because of outside interference but because of psychological barriers to action. Is an ignorant, superstitious person free to go to places he believes haunted by murderous demons? Can a man so prejudiced against socialism that his finding it unmitigatedly evil is a foregone conclusion make an assessment of it as an alternative to capitalism? It does not seem unreasonable to answer that people like this are not free to do the things in question; but their inability to do them need not be attributable to anyone's interfering with their liberty.

It may be objected that the principle of maximization of freedom here proposed would require both governments and individuals to treat as obligations actions and programs of action that are at most laudable. In replying to this I would emphasize that of course some limits must be recognized on what must be done to augment human freedom; but some limitation is already present in the requirement that what we do to augment one freedom must not interfere with some other, though of course the incompatibility of two freedoms would pose a problem here, as it would for almost any set of moral principles, and we must try to determine such things as what rights and freedoms are fundamental. Moreover, the principle of maximization of freedom is flexible in that where people do not have a freedom they ought to have, it requires only that, if they cannot be given it immediately, those with authority in the relevant domain take reasonable steps to bring it about.

The third consideration relevant to the justification of violence as a strategy for achieving social reform, is what we may roughly call welfare: that some action or program of action increases human happiness, and especially that it reduces human suffering, is a consideration which is nearly always relevant to any moral assessment of it. To try to define 'happiness' or 'suffering' here is out of the question, but it may help to say that being happy, in large part at least, consists in doing things one wants to do, or finds satisfying, or both; and suffering consists largely in doing, or having to submit to, things which one very much does not want or which cause pain or frustration. Another problem is that measuring happiness and suffering is difficult and in some cases apparently impossible. Fortunately, we can often say with justified confidence that one law will relieve more suffering – for example, hunger – than another, and that a certain program of reform will do more for the people's welfare – by creating more jobs – than another program. Finally, it seems reasonable to hold that, with certain exceptions which need not detain us here, the reduction of suffering should have priority over a 'comparable' increase in happiness; that is, even if we could by legislation increase income for one group from a comfortable to a more comfortable level, it would be preferable to reduce by a comparable amount the suffering due to poverty of an about equally large group. Moreover, it seems reasonable to hold that another strong obligation we have with respect to the welfare of those for whom we are responsible is to guarantee them a certain minimum level of well-being, though it is usually impossible to say exactly what constitutes this minimum. Thus, I suggest the principle that we take all reasonable steps to maximize the proportion of happiness to suffering, giving priority to the reduction of suffering over the increase of happiness, and to the increase of happiness below the minimum acceptable level of well-being, over comparable increases above it.

Here one may be inclined to say: Even if the principle of justice does not entail the principle of maximization of freedom, is it not entailed by the principle of justice together with the principle of maximization of welfare? I am inclined to doubt that it is, though clearly in practice fulfilling the requirements of the principles of justice and maximization of welfare would be very likely to fulfill the requirements of maximization of freedom. But the examples given earlier strongly suggest that the former two principles do not entail the latter. For one thing, it seems possible that granting people certain new freedoms would fail to enhance their happiness, and might even decrease it. Secondly, even if enhancements of freedom beyond what is required by non-interference would always result in increased happiness for all concerned, this does not seem to be the only kind of morally relevant *reason* for such enhancements. Thus, I am still inclined to hold that there are three independent moral principles.

One may justifiably wonder what we should do in case of conflicts among these principles. The question is a very difficult one, but I shall say only this: the principle of justice and the principle of maximization of freedom fortunately cannot come into conflict because it is essential to the latter, as I have formulated it, that it require only what is compatible with the former; the principle of maximization of welfare, as we might call it, can conceivably conflict with either of the other principles (though it can be plausibly argued that in practice it never will), and I would argue, as I think almost anyone would, that should such a conflict occur the former principles should virtually always have priority. This is not to say that a huge gain in welfare, especially a huge reduction in human suffering, can never outweigh a very minor injustice, though in cases like this some would tend to say it would be an injustice *not* to choose the huge gain in welfare.

I propose, then, that we consider the issue of the justification of violence, particularly large-scale violence intended to achieve social reform, in the light of the above three principles. I shall not argue for them; yet surely they or something very similar will seem reasonable to anyone who reflects carefully enough on how he might reasonably deal with moral problems having the broad social dimensions of the kind of violence with which I am primarily concerned. More work certainly needs to be done to render the principles less vague. But the openendedness and complexity of our ordinary moral problems strongly suggest that very great precision in this case would probably lead to rendering the principles inflexible; they would then be open to numerous counterexamples, and would often be inapplicable to cases not anticipated in their formulation.

IV   The justification of violence

If I have been at least roughly correct about what violence is and what sorts of considerations are relevant to justifying its use, then we should now be able to discuss fruitfully some of the issues surrounding its justification. We might begin by distinguishing several kinds of violence, each of which seems clearly to fit the definition of violence given in Section II. It is worth making at least a very rough distinction between personal and social violence: personal violence has nonpolitical motives and is perpetrated by a single person or small group of persons against another person or small group; social violence is violence by a group of people, almost always directed against the state or against another group of people, and usually perpetrated for political reasons. A person's shooting an acquaintance would usually be a paradigm of personal violence; a large riot resulting in extensive personal injury would be a paradigm of social violence. It seems somewhat unnatural to speak of violence done by one army to another as social violence, and it is probably better to call this simply military violence, though it is certainly social as opposed to personal. We also need to distinguish between violence to persons and violence to property or other inanimate things; and it is important to distinguish homicidal from nonhomicidal violence; and morally injurious violence – violence which violates someone's rights – from morally excusable violence, that is, violence which does not violate anyone's rights, as in the case of most violent athletic contests. Perhaps we should also distinguish hand-to-hand violence, as in the case of a fist fight, from violence 'at a distance' – such as sniping, shelling, and bombing. There also seems to be an important difference between defensive and offensive violence, the former being violence undertaken on a reasonable belief that using it is necessary to protect one's moral rights, the latter being violence undertaken in order to subjugate someone or otherwise violate his moral rights. But this is a very difficult distinction to draw, nor do defensive and offensive violence seem to exhaust the possibilities of violence, since spontaneous violence might well be of neither kind.

What seems of greatest philosophical interest at present among the kinds of violence just mentioned is social violence, both to people and to property, homicidal and nonhomicidal, defensive and offensive, and whether hand-to-hand or done at a distance. In particular, I am concerned with the justifiability of such forms of violence in civil disobedience, in resistance, in revolution, and in attempts to achieve social progress that cannot be placed in any of these three categories. In discussing each case I shall appeal primarily to the three moral principles outlined above, and I shall proceed from arguing the inadequacy of various mistaken views about the justifiability of violence to some constructive suggestions about its use in civil disobedience, resistance, revolution, and social reform. Although the discussion will be focused on violence, what I have to say will have important application to questions concerning the justification of force as a strategy for achieving social reform and to various other moral questions concerning policies of social action.

This is not meant to suggest that the principles proposed have no application to the justification of personal violence; as moral principles of the most general sort, at least one of them should have an indirect bearing on any moral issue. But in a great many cases, particularly in deciding what moral obligations one individual has to another individual of his acquaintance, their bearing is very often only indirect: they may be appealed to in justifying the subsidiary moral principles which 'govern' much of our conduct toward other individuals; but a great many of our typical obligations toward other individuals, for example, to do what we have promised to do, have their immediate basis in these more specific principles. To apply this to a case of personal violence, imagine a man who is contemplating beating his wife. My position does not imply that in deciding whether it would be right to do this he is free to appeal directly to the three general principles; as the wording of the principles suggests, they are intended to apply primarily to policies, strategies, practices, and other general prescriptions of conduct. Their rigorous application to the kind of case imagined would, I think, support the principle that (possibly with a few very special exceptions) we ought not to beat people. I would also hold, though I cannot argue for it here, that my principles would support both some form of the ordinary moral principles requiring truth-telling and promise-keeping, and the ordinary moral conviction that people in certain special relations to others, such as parents and children, acquire special obligations. None of this implies that it is never morally right to call ordinary moral principles into question; the point is simply that in deciding what is morally obligatory or permissible in our relations with other individuals, we cannot bypass moral principles ordinarily relevant to the kind of situation in question, though where two such principles conflict, we may in most cases appeal to one or more of the three general principles.

Let us take first the extreme view that no one is ever justified in using violence. The natural thing to say here is that if violence is necessary to stop a Hitler from carrying out his planned atrocities, then it should be used. Most people would find it hard to deny this, but advocates of nonviolence might well argue that in fact it is never necessary to use violence, even to stop a man like Hitler, particularly if nonviolent protests are used at the first signs of evil. Although I find this claim highly implausible, neither a philosopher nor anyone else can assess it, as applied to an actual case, without a thorough analysis of the facts regarding various societies. But what chiefly needs to be said here is that it is certainly conceivable that a man like Hitler might be stopped only through violence; and insofar as there is good reason to think that only violence can stop him, the use of at least some violence, especially nonhomicidal violence aimed at bringing about a coup or forcing the needed change in social policy, might obviously be justified by the moral principles to which I am appealing.

Another extreme position would be that violence is always justified if it is the most efficient means of throwing off oppression or rectifying some other form of injustice. This position seems almost as implausible as the first: clearly injustice and suffering created by the violence might substantially outweigh the burden of using a less efficient means of reform. Suppose that nonviolent protest could bring down an oppressive but unstable regime in a somewhat longer time than would be required by the use of violence. If it were evident that the violence would probably involve suffering and deaths, the nonviolent protest would almost certainly be preferable. Here it is important to mention something which seems both obvious and important, but which is much too rarely taken into account in discussions of violence and revolution: that there is simply no way to compare with any precision the moral 'cost' of taking a man's life, especially an innocent man's life, with the moral value of reducing suffering or eliminating oppression or some other form of injustice. No doubt there is a level of atrocity at which almost anyone would say – and could justifiably say – that there is so much oppression, injustice, or suffering that if, in order to improve the situation substantially, we have to do something that might well take an innocent man's life we ought still to do it. To be sure, if it is a certainty that some innocent person must die, particularly if his identity is known, the situation becomes even more problematic and violence would be much more difficult – perhaps impossible – to justify. It seems clear that in deciding whether to use violence that might result in death, especially the death of someone not guilty of whatever wrong must justify the use of violence in the first place, we have to make every possible effort to find a nondeadly alternative; and we should be extremely careful not to exaggerate the moral outrage that requires rectification, particularly if we regard ourselves as the victims. But there is no simple way, perhaps no way at all, to answer the question how to weigh the taking of lives, especially of people innocent or largely innocent of the moral wrongs we want to rectify, against the moral gains we might make through their rectification. The principles of justice, maximization of freedom, and maximization of welfare suggest why this should be so; for how can we say how much injustice we do to a man in taking his life, or how much freedom or happiness we deprive him of? Given that the preservation of human life is of very great moral value on almost any moral outlook, and certainly on the principles proposed above, this is surely one of the most powerful arguments that can be brought against most of the typical uses of violence.

Two other views that deserve mention are (a) that violence of the sort we are concerned with – social violence done out of a genuinely moral desire to achieve social change – cannot be justified unless all channels of nonviolent protest have been exhausted, and (b) that violence is never justified in a democratic society. Regarding (a), it is not clear that there usually *is* any definite number of channels of nonviolent protest, or what it takes to exhaust a channel of protest. Yet even assuming that there were a definite number and that we could exhaust them, this might take so long and allow so much moral wrong in the meantime that some degree of nonhomicidal violence, and especially violence to property, would be warranted if it could be reasonably argued to be necessary to rectifying the moral wrongs in question. If nonviolent means of eliminating oppressive curfews and arbitrary travel restrictions, or of providing a minority group with the rights of citizens, would take many years, whereas damaging a few nonresidential buildings could achieve the needed changes in a few months or a year, the latter course could perhaps be justified by the principles of justice, maximization of freedom, and maximization of welfare. This point depends, of course, not only on the view that violence is not 'by definition' unjustifiable, but also on the view that certain kinds of damage to property constitute violence; yet I believe I have argued adequately for these views in defending my analysis of the concept of violence. I would not claim, however, that a situation of the sort envisaged here is probable; more important, I am certainly not denying that there is a strong prima facie obligation to try a reasonable amount of nonviolent protest before using violence, nor would I claim that we can usually be at all sure that social violence can be prevented from becoming homicidal. But even the minimal claims I have made suggest that we cannot reasonably hold that violence is never justified unless all channels of nonviolent protest have been exhausted.

Regarding (b), the thesis that social violence of the sort that concerns us is never justified in a democratic society, I would first want to say that much depends on what we mean by 'democratic.' If it means something like 'such that political power lies in the hands of the people,' then the thesis is surely false. For the majority of people in a society could be, and indeed at times have been, deceived into accepting or voting for measures whose injustice might in some cases be eradicable only by violent, though not necessarily homicidal, protest. If, on the other hand, 'democratic' is used, as it often is nowadays, in such a way that a society is not considered democratic unless certain moral rights are guaranteed and the government has a certain minimum concern for the welfare of the citizens, then there is no clear answer to the question whether violence is ever justified in a democratic society. For it is not clear that the term 'democratic,' used this way, would ever apply to a society in which the three principles I am appealing to are seriously violated. In any case, the general position I want now to propose should enable us to deal with the issues concerning the justification of violence regardless of the kind of political system with respect to which they arise.

What I propose is that in deciding whether violence would be justified in a given case in which it is being considered as a means of correcting certain grave moral wrongs, we should ascertain its probable consequences for justice, freedom, and human welfare, and compare these with the probable consequences of the most promising nonviolent alternative(s) we can think of on careful reflection, choosing the course of action which satisfies, or comes closest to satisfying, the requirements of the principles of justice, maximization of freedom, and maximization of welfare. The restriction to cases in which violence is being considered as a means of correcting certain grave moral wrongs is important: these would have to be cases in which a serious attempt has been made, or at least considered, to solve the problem through legal or other nonviolent procedures; and they would usually be cases of serious injustice, such as deprivations of freedom, though certain other serious moral wrongs – such as a government's neglecting the welfare of its people – might sometimes justify the consideration of some forms of violence. It would certainly not do to say that, regardless of the moral grievance and regardless of whether nonviolent means have been tried, it is morally legitimate to consider using violence; and while I believe this sort of restriction would follow from the principles I am using, it seems best to include it at the outset in the interest of explicitness and brevity.

It is important to reemphasize my position that considerations of justice and freedom have priority over considerations of welfare. In comparing violent and nonviolent strategies of reform, our first concern should be to determine what would establish, or come closest to establishing, justice and the maximum freedom possible within the limits of justice. Secondarily, we should consider the consequences for welfare of adopting a violent as opposed to a nonviolent strategy; but these considerations could be decisive only where the more fundamental considerations weighed equally in favor of some violent and some nonviolent strategy, or perhaps, with the qualifications suggested earlier, where a huge gain in welfare is balanced against a minor injustice. Suppose that a group of young men who have vigorously protested the Vietnam War have very good evidence that records of their public protests are being kept by their draft boards and will be used unfairly against them, say in drafting them as a punitive measure. They might face the alternatives of violently breaking into the office and burning all its records or, on the other hand, taking the case to the courts. My point here would be that the most important consideration should be what is required by the principles of justice and freedom; and as I see it they would here require, assuming there is legal recourse for the grievance, that efforts be made to take the case to the courts: for the men to violate laws which the great majority of others respect and obey, often with considerable sacrifice, would be a prima facie violation of the requirement that benefits and burdens be distributed equally, and hence a prima facie injustice; and breaking into the office would be, prima facie, an unjustified violation of others' rights and an interference with their freedom to carry out their regular jobs. Even if it could be shown that all concerned would be happier if the men simply broke into the office and burned the records, this would not be a substantial consideration in favor of the violent alternative, and it is worth pointing out that the publicity which injustice receives from court proceedings is often an important step toward reform, even if the case is initially lost and sometimes when it is lost in the highest courts.

Let us now complicate the example by supposing that the men go to the very highest court and lose. What now should they do? Much depends on whether they lost the principle that punitive use of the draft is unjust or simply failed to win the point that their draft board was planning it. Suppose they lose the latter point. What then? For one thing, this may indicate some weakness in their evidence against their draft board; secondly, in many societies, nonviolent resistance would in this case be both the morally courageous course of action and most likely to arouse the conscience of people who might help. If, on the other hand, we suppose that the men's evidence against their draft board is of the sort a reasonable man would consider conclusive, but that they lost because their witnesses were afraid to testify, then the case becomes even more problematic. One consideration not yet mentioned would be the kind and degree of immorality of the war for which they were to be drafted; another would be what they might be able to do by some new nonviolent attempt to expose those who have perpetrated the injustice against them and their witnesses. There are other considerations, and I cannot now go into sufficient detail to try to settle the question, though perhaps enough has been said to suggest that the kind of limited violence envisaged here is not obviously impossible to justify under any circumstances whatever, even if it does appear that in a country like America today nonviolent protest would be morally preferable. The case would have been equally complicated had we supposed that, in the highest court of the land, the men had lost the principle that punitive use of the draft, especially against political dissenters, is unjust. Here we would have an even larger issue which might well warrant the consideration, though not necessarily the adoption, of revolution.

There are, of course, a number of difficulties confronting the view I propose regarding the justification of violence. I have already mentioned the impossibility of weighing with any precision the moral cost of taking a human life, especially an innocent life, against moral gains in justice, freedom, and welfare. But this is likely to be a serious problem for any plausible position on the justification of violence, and we can at least say that there is one kind of case in which some weighing might be possible: when the risks to human life of undertaking violence can be compared with the risks to it of abstaining from violence. Thus, if violence that would probably cost about a hundred lives could be shown necessary to save thousands, it would presumably be justified if it did not have certain other morally undesirable consequences such as the brutalization of a large number of people.

Secondly, there are profound difficulties in measuring justice or injustice, freedom or its curtailment, and happiness or suffering. It would be wrong to conclude, however, that there are not even rough standards which are in practice very useful. While the notions of equality and of a justified exception to the principle that men should be treated equally are vague, it is nonetheless clear that denying various civil liberties on grounds of color is not a justified inequality, whereas denying voting privileges to children is; and a great many injustices, particularly those serious enough to warrant the consideration of violence, are equally obvious. Moreover, even if we grant that there is an area of reasonable disagreement concerning a large number of freedoms, there is wide agreement on such fundamental freedoms as freedom of speech, freedom of worship, and freedom of personal movement; and these are the sorts of freedoms whose curtailment would be appealed to in most cases in which considerations of freedom might warrant the use of violence.

Finally, it is clear that there are rough indices of suffering and happiness which make possible at least judgments about the suffering or happiness of one person or group as compared to that of another or to their own suffering or happiness at different times: we can consider disease as opposed to physical well-being; psychological well-being (insofar as this can be measured without indulging any moral prejudice); poverty as opposed to comfortable income; observations and subjective reports of pain, tension, and malaise, as opposed to observations and subjective reports of zest, comfort, and satisfaction; and proportion of things done or submitted to that are wanted as opposed to unwanted.

Let me now comment briefly on the implications of my position for the use of violence in civil disobedience, resistance, revolution, and social reform. To begin with civil disobedience, one may reasonably question whether there is any kind of violence with which it is logically compatible. Certainly in the clear cases of civil disobedience the protest is both nonviolent and orderly; and if we think of civil disobedience as undertaken in protest against some particular law(s), but out of respect for law as an institution, one may well question whether violence could be a part of it. Suppose, however, that a group of students decided to block the pathway of some unarmed fellow students engaging in military drill and soon to go to war; and suppose the protesters were unarmed and planned not to use violence. If violence broke out but remained on the level of mild fisticuffs, with the protesters fighting only defensively, and if the protesters were willing to accept punishment if the courts demanded it, would we have to say that they had not succeeded in practicing civil disobedience? The answer to this question does not seem to be simply that they did not succeed, though it perhaps would be if, even without having planned to use violence, the protesters did initiate it. Civil disobedience requires that those practicing it be making a reasoned attempt to appeal to the conscience of others; they must not be attempting to impose their will on others through the use of force, which they would certainly be doing if violence were a calculated part of civil disobedience. On the other hand, if violence 'spontaneously' breaks out, particularly where the protesters fight only defensively, it is entirely possible that we could speak of their having succeeded in committing civil disobedience. Perhaps we could say that in certain cases civil disobedience may be accompanied by violence, even on the part of those committing the disobedience, but the violence must not have been calculated; nor can a protest count as civil disobedience if the protesters respond to violence with substantially greater violence than is required for self-defense. If violence has any place in civil disobedience, then, it seems to be a very minor and restricted one.

The case with resistance is different, and what chiefly needs to be said here is that there is no moral justification for the use of large-scale social violence except where injustice or some other form of moral wrong is very serious and where nonviolent means of rectification have been carefully considered and, if possible, attempted. It seems reasonable to maintain that justice, maximization of freedom, and maximization of welfare should be the guiding principles; and they should be applied in the light of questions like the following: What are the chances of death and in how many cases? How many are likely to suffer violence, and what sort of violence would it be – bodily violence or violence to property? To what extent are those who use violence likely to be brutalized by it or to come to use it indiscriminately, either at the time in question or at a later time? How much violence is likely to be evoked as a *response* to the violence being considered? Of those who may suffer violence, how many are guilty of creating or perpetuating the moral wrongs which might justify the violence, and how many are innocent or largely innocent in this respect? How effective will the contemplated violence be in rectifying the wrongs it is meant to reduce or remove? Is the immorality which might warrant violence getting worse or better, and what is the likelihood of dealing with it nonviolently in a reasonable length of time? Is violence to be definitely planned, or is it simply to be approved should certain circumstances arise?

Questions like these seem to be equally relevant to the justifiability of attempting a revolution. But since revolution almost necessarily requires very extensive violence, even greater care must be taken in attempting to justify it. The questions I suggest we ask in considering whether to use violence are very difficult; and it is not surprising that many of them have not been faced, much less answered, by advocates of violence. Yet it is only through rigorously pursuing these and similar questions that we can weigh the consequences for justice, freedom, and welfare, of using a violent as opposed to a nonviolent method of moral rectification, and decide whether the best course of action would be non-violent protest within the law, civil disobedience, resistance, or revolution, which is likely to require widespread and deadly violence.

Regarding the use of violence to achieve social reforms that do not qualify as the correction of injustice – such as certain improvements in state services or in the material well-being of large groups of people – it seems reasonable to say that particularly where material well-being is already at a level representing a secure and not uncomfortable life, any appreciable violence to persons could not be justified. For even assuming that there is no legal or other nonviolent way of achieving the goal, violence would probably require injustice to someone, and I am supposing that the gains in happiness that might result would not outweigh the injustice done. Suppose that a highway, which was a mere convenience to a large number of people, would have to go through a place where some American Indians who had been living there for generations were determined to stay unless bodily ejected. If we assume that neither they nor the larger community has a clear right in the dispute, probably the state would not be justified in using violence (or even force) to remove them, even if the convenience to the community could be reasonably claimed to outweigh substantially the inconvenience to them. Of course, if the disparity between what the community stands to gain and what a few stand to lose in being forced, violently if necessary, to comply with the community's wishes, becomes very great, the issue becomes more complex and we may begin to ask how much convenience a small group has a *right* to deny to a much larger group, especially to the community as a whole. In this case the minority's insistence on what it wants could be unjust, since it could be an interference with the community's freedom to do what it has a right to do; but it still seems clear that, with perhaps very few exceptions, if gains in happiness which do not represent what anyone has a right to should require violence to persons, the violence should not be used. For surely it is reasonable to give considerations of justice very high priority over considerations of welfare, as I have already suggested in discussing possible conflicts among the three moral principles proposed; and doing violence to someone, at least violence of the sort relevant here, unless it can be shown to be required to rectify some serious injustice, is certainly doing him an injustice.

V Conclusion

A great deal more remains to be said about violence. But if the position put forward in this essay is essentially correct, then at least a beginning has been made toward a reasonable view on the meaning and justification of violence. I have argued that violence is the physical attack upon, or the vigorous physical abuse of, or vigorous physical struggle against, a person or animal; or the highly vigorous psychological abuse of, or the sharp, caustic psychological attack upon, a person or animal; or the highly vigorous, or incendiary, or malicious and vigorous, destruction or damaging of property or potential property. This definition is certainly not without vagueness, but I hope that through qualifications, through examples, and through contrasting violence with force and other concepts with which it may be confused I have gone some distance toward reducing the vagueness of the definition. There is also a good deal of indeterminacy surrounding the principles of justice, maximization of freedom, and maximization of welfare; but again, by discussing possible conflicts among these principles, by adding important restrictions, and by considering the application of the principles to particular cases, I have sought to clarify them as much as possible within the limits of an essay of this length. They of course do not provide a mechanical computation procedure for deciding whether violence in a given case is justified. But to expect this would be to misunderstand moral reasoning and to demand virtually inflexible moral rules that would surely be inadequate to the unpredictable diversity of actual situations in which moral decisions are called for.

It may appear that this essay is conservative. Some contemporary advocates of violence might object either that I have in effect ruled out the use of social violence completely, or that I have imposed such severe restrictions on

166 Violence: A Philosophical Anthology

its use that no one who rigorously applied my position would ever use such violence. Both of these objections seem to me mistaken. There is one common consequence of violence about which I am certainly conservative: the taking of human life, especially the life of an innocent person. But I believe that there have doubtless been and will probably be in the future instances of both personal and social violence, as in certain cases of self-defense, which could be morally justified. Moreover, I have emphasized (though I have not had space to explain in detail) that typically violence to property is morally on a different footing from violence to persons, especially homicidal violence; and it seems clear that in some cases considerable violence to property might be justified by sufficiently pressing moral considerations. For these reasons, I would deny that no one who rigorously applied my position could ever use violence. It is true that the position forces the person contemplating violence to ask some very difficult questions and to gather a good deal of data for the calculation of some important probabilities. A reasonable answer to such questions is not likely to come in a moment's reflection. What people consider a reasonable answer will depend largely on the strictness of their moral and epistemological upbringing; but if I would tend to reject as hasty the reasonings of hotheaded and self-righteous saviors of humanity, I would also stoutly reject the demand, often made as a conservative maneuver, for what is virtually the kind of certainty philosophers have often sought for such rock-solid propositions as that there is an external world. Still, if we are considering something with such high moral cost, and such incalculable effects, as social violence, it is surely not too much to ask that our reasoning be careful, repeated, and subjected to the criticisms of those who argue for nonviolent alternatives.

Notes

1. For helpful comments on an earlier version of this essay, I am grateful to several friends and colleagues, especially Joseph Bien, Douglas Browning, Robert Causey, Philip Hugly, Samuel Richmond, and Alan Tucker.
2. In a *New York Times* editorial for July 13, 1969, Tom Wicker refers to armed robbery as a 'crime of violence.' But suppose an armed thief lets himself into a house with a key and, in full view of the owner, who calmly cooperates, quietly walks off with some jewelry. Has he been in any way violent?
3. There is not, I would grant, a sharp distinction between definitions that provide an analysis and those that provide a rational reconstruction, or those that simply reduce the vagueness of the term being defined. Indeed, because an analysis is likely to be unhelpful if it is not in a sense more explicit than the expression being analyzed, we should usually suspect that the class of borderline cases for the expression being defined is smaller than, and not merely a subset of, that for the expression proposed as an analysis. Thus, I would not be disturbed if my definition should be a good deal less vague than 'violence,' or even if it contains whatever element of rational reconstruction might be implied by its deciding borderline cases in a way

that can be supported by appeal to the use of the term to refer to clear cases of violence.

4. It is interesting to note that the second edition of *Webster's New International Dictionary* defines 'violence' as 'the unjustified or unwarranted exercise of force, usually with the accompaniment of vehemence, outrage, or fury.' That a good dictionary should be this far off – and I think that this degree of inaccuracy is not uncommon in dictionaries – should be some indication that the sorts of definitions philosophers seek are neither likely to be found in dictionaries nor even likely to be discoverable using traditional lexicographical techniques.

5. R. B. Brandt, *Ethical Theory* (Englewood Cliffs, N. J.: Prentice-Hall, 1959), p. 410.

6. William K. Frankena, 'The Concept of Social Justice,' in *Social Justice*, ed. R. B. Brandt (Englewood Cliffs, N. J.: Prentice-Hall, 1962), pp. 14, 17.

COMMENTARY ON AUDI

Robert Audi, a distinguished philosopher in the analytical tradition, is perhaps best known for his important contributions to epistemology, ethics and philosophy of religion.[1] His article 'On the Meaning and Justification of Violence', first published in 1971, is one of the most influential philosophical accounts of violence in recent years.[2] As Audi explains, 'although the subject of violence is philosophically important, it has not been given sufficient philosophical attention.' In this article, Audi attempts to provide us not only with an exemplary, thorough analysis of the concept of violence, but also with a rigorous investigation into the conditions that would, possibly, justify the use of violence.

After acknowledging the difficulty, if not impossibility, of capturing every type of violence into one all-purpose definition, Audi proposes the following three-part definition of violence: 'Violence is the physical attack upon, or the vigorous physical abuse of, or vigorous physical struggle against, a person or animal; or the highly vigorous psychological abuse of, or the sharp caustic psychological attack upon, a person or animal; or the highly vigorous, or incendiary, or malicious and vigorous, destruction or damaging of property or potential property.'

As a single, comprehensive definition of violence, what Audi is proposing deserves much praise. By suggesting that 'the notion of vigorous abuse comes very close to forming a kind of core', Audi allows not only for the fact that at the receiving end of an act of violence we find either animate beings or inanimate objects, but that the act of violence itself can be measured in either physical or psychological terms.

Furthermore, in the process of constructing this definition, Audi makes a number of important points: that violence to animate beings tends to involve or cause their suffering or injury or both; that although in the vast majority of cases violence is done intentionally, it nevertheless seems possible for violence to be done unintentionally; and that while in the most usual cases violence involves the violation of a moral right, there are cases in which violence can occur without the violation of any moral right. It is also worth pointing out that while Audi's definition of violence is considerably broader than standard definitions, he wants to avoid the temptation to equate the concept of violence with just any instance of social injustice, discrimination or social exclusion – a widespread practice that, according to Audi, 'would increases the risk of ambiguity and equivocation'.[3]

Regarding the justification of violence, Audi restricts his analysis to violence contemplated as a strategy for achieving social reform, in particular for the rectification of injustice. Thus, in the specific case of civil disobedience, resistance or revolution, Audi does not think that social violence is by definition unjustifiable, nevertheless he argues that the burden is on those advocating the use of violence to make a compelling case.

In helping us to navigate this potentially deadly moral maze, Audi appeals to three guiding moral principles: justice, the maximization of freedom, and the maximization of welfare: anyone contemplating the use of violence ought to weigh the consequences for justice, freedom and welfare, of using a violent as opposed to a non-violent method of moral rectification.

Notes and further reading

1. See his *Action, Intention, and Reason*, Ithaca, NY: Cornell University Press, 1993; *The Architecture of Reason*, New York: Oxford University Press, 2001; *Epistemology: A Contemporary Introduction to the Theory of Knowledge*, London: Routledge, 1998; *The Good in the Right: A Theory of Intuition and Intrinsic Value*, Princeton, NJ: Princeton University Press, 2005; *Moral Knowledge and Ethical Character*, New York: Oxford University Press, 1997; *Religious Commitment and Secular Reason*, Cambridge: Cambridge University Press, 2000.
2. This essay was first published in Jerome A. Shaffer (ed.), *Violence*, New York: David McKay, 1971. The other essays in that volume are: Ronald B. Miller, 'Violence, Force and Coercion'; Robert L. Holmes, 'Violence and Nonviolence'; Bernard Harrison, 'Violence and the Rule of Law'.
3. On this issue, see also Robert Audi, 'Violence, Legal Sanctions, and Law Enforcement', in Sherman M. Stanage (ed.), *Reason and Violence: Philosophical Investigations*, Oxford: Blackwell, 1974.

9
What Violence Is

Newton Garver

I

Most people deplore violence, many people embrace violence (perhaps
reluctantly), and a few people renounce violence. But through all these postures there runs a certain obscurity, and it is never entirely clear just what
violence is.

Those who deplore violence loudest and most publicly are usually identified with the status quo – school principals, businessmen, politicians,
ministers. What they deplore is generally overt attacks on property or against
the 'good order of society.' They rarely see violence in defense of the status
quo in the same light as violence directed against it. At the time of the Watts
riots in 1965 President Johnson urged Negroes to realize that nothing of any
value can be won through violent means – an idea which may be true but
which Johnson himself seemed to ignore in connection with the escalation
of the Vietnam war he was simultaneously embarking upon. But the President [Johnson] is not the only one of us who deplores violence while at the
same time perpetrating it, and a little more clarity about what exactly we
deplore might help all around.

Those who renounce violence are equally hard to follow. Tolstoy, Gandhi,
and Muste stand out among the advocates of nonviolence of the past century,
and as one reads them it becomes clear that they do not all renounce exactly
the same thing. There is much that is concrete and detailed in the writings
of these men, but nonetheless it is not easy to avoid the impression that
'nonviolence' is really just morality itself rather than a specific commitment
to eschew a certain well-defined sort of behavior.

Those who embrace violence are in a much better position, for they stand
ready to embrace whatever is 'inevitable' or 'necessary' in the circumstances,
and hence the question of just where violence begins or leaves off does not

---

Source: The Nation, June 24,1968, pp. 817–22, (Revised by author.) Reprinted by
permission of the author.

arise for them. But if we want to know about the nature and varieties of violence, it does not help to be told that violence is unavoidable or that it is a
necessary means to some end. There is a question about understanding violence before we come to adopt a posture toward it, and it is to that question
we now turn.

II

What I want to do is to present a kind of typology of violence. I want, that is,
to try to make clear what some of the different types and kinds and forms of
violence are, and thereby to give a perspective of the richness of this topic.
Unfortunately, I can't begin saying what the types of violence are without
saying first what it is I'm giving you a typology of. So let's begin with a
definition of violence.

What is violence? That is a typical philosophical question. The psychiatrists
and the sociologists are interested in the questions: why is there violence?
what causes violence? That's not my concern – at least not my professional
concern nor my concern here. What I'm interested in is the old-fashioned
philosophical question: What is the nature or essence of violence? We can
make a good start etymologically. The word 'violence' comes, of course, from
the French, prior to that from the Latin, and you can find Greek roots if you're
up to it – which I'm not. The Latin root of the word 'violence' is a combination
of two Latin words – the word '*vis*' (force) and the past participle '*latus*' of
the word '*fero*' (to carry). The Latin word '*violare*' is itself a combination of
these two words, and its present participle '*violans*' is a plausible source for
the word 'violence' – so that the word 'violence,' in its etymological origin,
has the sense of to carry force at or toward. An interesting feature of the
etymology is that the word 'violation' comes from this very same source as
the word 'violence,' which suggests to us the interesting idea that violence
is somehow a violation of something: that carrying force against something
constitutes in one way or another a violation of it.

The idea of force being connected with violence is a very powerful one.
There is no question at all that in many contexts the word 'force' is a synonym
for the word 'violence.' This is particularly true if you talk about, for example,
a violent blizzard: a violent blizzard is nothing but a blizzard with very great
force. The same is true of a violent sea and other bits of violence in nature. It is
simply some aspect of nature manifested to us with especially great force. But
I don't want to talk about natural phenomena – certainly not meteorological
phenomena. I want to talk instead about human phenomena. In human
affairs violence cannot be equated with force.

One of the very first things to understand about violence in human affairs
is that it is not the same thing as force. It is clear that force is often used
on another person's body and there is no violence done. For example,
if a man is drowning – thrashing around and apparently unable to save

himself – and you use the standard Red Cross life-saving techniques, you will use force against his body although certainly you won't be doing any violence to him. You will, in fact, be saving his life instead. To think so rigidly of force and violence being identical with one another that you call this sort of life-saving an act of violence is to have lost sight entirely of the significance of the concept. Similarly, surgeons and dentists use force on our bodies without doing violence to us.

The idea of violence in human affairs is much more closely connected with the idea of violation than it is with the idea of force. What is fundamental about violence in human affairs is that a person is violated. Now that is a tough notion to explain. It is easy enough to understand how you can violate a moral rule or a parking regulation, but what in the world does it mean to talk about 'violating a person'? That, I think, is a very important question, and because it can give a fresh perspective on what it means to be human it deserves fuller consideration than I can give it in this context. If it makes sense to talk about violating a person, that just is because a person has certain rights which are undeniably, indissolubly, connected with his being a person. The very idea of natural rights is controversial since it is redolent of Scholasticism, but I find myself forced to accept natural rights in order to understand the moral dimension of violence. One of the most fundamental rights a person has is a right to his body – to determine what his body does and what is done to his body – because without his body he wouldn't be a person anymore. The most common way a person ceases to exist is that his body stops functioning – a point which appeals especially forcefully if you think of a person as a living, growing thing rather than as something static or as a substance in the traditional sense. Apart from a body what is essential to one's being a person is dignity in something like the existentialist sense. The dignity of a person does not consist in his remaining prim and proper or dignified and unruffled, but rather in his making his own decisions. In this respect what is fundamental about a person is radically different from what is fundamental, for example, about a dog. I have a dog. I don't expect him to make decisions: When I tell him to sit or to stay I expect him just to do it, not to decide. And, indeed, the way I have treated my dog, which seems to be a good way to treat a dog, is to train him to respond in a more or less mechanical way to certain commands. Now that, it seems to me, is to give a dog a very good place in life, at least as we have arranged it. However, to treat a human being that way is an affront to his dignity as a human being, just because it is essential to a human being that he have a kind of dignity or 'autonomy,' as Kant put it.

The right to one's body and the right to autonomy are undoubtedly the most fundamental natural rights of persons, but there are subsidiary ones that deserve mention as part of the background for our discussion of violence. One of these stems from the right to autonomy. It is characteristic of human action to be purposive and to have results and consequences, and freedom therefore is normally conceived as involving not only the right to decide what to do but also the right to dispose of or cope with the consequences of one's action. One aspect of this right is the right to the product of one's labor, which has played an important role in the theory of both capitalism and communism. Both Marx and Locke, in two entirely different traditions as we think of it nowadays, have a labor theory of economic value: that the inherent value of something is determined by the amount of labor that is required to produce it. It is one of the ironies of intellectual history that the right of persons to the product of their labor constitutes the basis for both Locke's defense of private property and Marx's attack on it. If we follow this line of thought to the extent that we consider one's property as an extension of his person the scope of the concept of violence becomes greatly enlarged, perhaps in harmony with popular thought on the subject, at least on the part of propertied persons; but one should always bear in mind that a person can reconcile himself much more readily to loss of property than he can to loss of life.

If we say that the results of what a person does belongs to him, we should have in mind not only this kind of labor theory of value but also the more or less natural and expectable consequences of a person's action. One of Jean-Paul Sartre's most interesting plays, *Altona*, develops this theme. In this play Sartre depicts a young man who does things that would normally have very serious consequences' probably his death. At one time he defies the Nazis, at another time the American Military Government that is occupying the country. On both occasions his father intervenes and cuts him off from the normal, expected consequences of his actions consequences which anybody else would have suffered. Sartre shows what an awful impact it has upon this man, as a person, to have the consequences of his actions cut off in this way. In the end this victim of paternalism is one of Sartre's rather hideous characters, sequestered in a room in the center of his father's grand mansion having hallucinations of crabs and visions of expiation.

Here then is an indication of what is involved in talking about the violation of a person, and it seems to me that violence in human affairs comes down to violating persons. With that in mind, let me turn now to discussion of the different types and forms of violence. Violence can be usefully classified into four different kinds based on two criteria, whether the violence is personal or institutionalized and whether the violence is overt or a kind of covert or quiet violence.

III

Overt physical assault of one person on the body of another is the most obvious form of violence. Mugging, rape, and murder are the flagrant 'crimes of violence,' and when people speak of the danger of violence in the streets it is usually visions of these flagrant cases that float before their minds. I share the general concern over the rising rate of these crimes, but at the same time I deplore the tendency to cast our image of violence just in the mold of these flagrant cases. These are cases where an attack on a human body is also clearly an attack on a person and clearly illegal. We must not tie these characteristics in too tight a package, for some acts of violence are intended as a defense of law or a benefit to the person whose body is beaten – e.g. ordinary police activity (not 'police brutality')[1] and the corporal punishment of children by parents and teachers. The humbler cases are violence too, although the fact that policemen, teachers, and parents have socially defined roles which they invoke when they resort to violence indicates that these cases have institutional aspects that overshadow the purely personal ones. These institutional overtones make a great deal of difference but they cannot erase that there is violence done. Of course not all cases are so clear: I leave to the reader to ponder whether all sex acts are acts of violence, or just how to distinguish in practical terms those that are from those that are not. Whenever you do something to another person's body without his consent you are attacking not just a physical entity – you are attacking a person. You are doing something by force, so the violence in this case is something that is easily visible, has long been recognized as violence, and is a case of overt, personal violence.

In cases of war, what one group tries to do to another group is what happens to individuals in cases of mugging and murder. The soldiers involved in a war are responsible for acts of violence against 'the enemy,' at least in the sense that the violence would not have occurred if the soldiers had refused to act. (Of course some other violence might have occurred. But in any case I do not wish to try to assess blame or lesser evils.) The Nuremberg trials after World War II attempted to establish that individual soldiers are responsible morally and legally too, but this attempt overlooked the extent to which the institutionalization of violence changes its moral dimension. On the one hand an individual soldier is not acting on his own initiative and responsibility, and with the enormous difficulty in obtaining reliable information and making a timely confrontation of government claims, not even U.S. Senators, let alone soldiers and private citizens, are in a good position to make the necessary judgments about the justice of a military engagement. On the other hand a group does not have a soul and cannot act except through the agency of individual men. Thus there is a real difficulty in assigning responsibility for such institutional violence. The other side of the violence, its object, is equally ambiguous, for 'the enemy' are being attacked as an organized political force rather than as individuals, and yet since a group does not have a body any more than 'it has a soul 'the enemy' is attacked by attacking the bodies of individual men (and women and children). Warfare, therefore, because it is an institutionalized form of violence, differs from murder in certain fundamental respects.

Riots are another form of institutionalized violence, although their warlike character was not widely recognized until the publication of the report of the President's National Advisory Commission on Civil Disorders (the 'Riot' Commission). In a riot, as in a war, there are many instances of personal violence, and some persons maintain that the civil disorders are basically massive crime waves. But on the other hand there is also much of a warlike character. One of the characteristics of the Watts riot, as any will know who have read Robert Conot's very interesting book, *The Rivers of Blood, Years of Darkness*, is that in that riot the people who were supposed to be controlling the situation, the Los Angeles police and their various reinforcements, simply did not know basic facts about the community. In particular they did not know who was the person who could exercise a sort of leadership if the group were left alone and that person's hand was strengthened. One incident illustrates the sort of thing that happened. A Negro policeman was sent in plain clothes into the riot area and told to call back into the precinct whenever there was anything to report. He was told, furthermore, not to identify himself as a policeman under any conditions for fear of jeopardizing himself. At one point, he tried to intervene when some cops were picking on just altogether the wrong person and he ended up getting cursed and having his head bashed in by one of his fellow members of the Los Angeles police force. The police were in such a state that they couldn't even refrain from hitting a Negro policeman who was sent on a plain-clothes assignment into that area. In effect, the Los Angeles police and their various allies conducted what amounted to a kind of a war campaign. They acted like an army going out to occupy a foreign territory where they didn't know the people and didn't speak the language. The result was that their actions had the effect of breaking down whatever social structure there might have been. And the breakdown of the social structure then had the effect of releasing more and more overt violence. The military flavor of our urban disturbances has increased over the years, and 1967 saw the appearance not only of machine guns and automatic rifles but also of tanks and armored personnel carriers in Newark and Detroit, in what the Kerner Commission characterized as 'indiscriminate and excessive use of force.' For that reason the urban disorders that we've been having in recent summers are really a kind of institutionalized violence where there are two sides in combat with one another. It is quite different from a normal criminal situation where police act against individual miscreants.

Since these overt forms of violence are, on the whole, fairly easily recognized, let us go on to consider the other forms of violence, the quiet forms which do not necessarily involve any overt physical assault on anybody's person or property. There are both personal and institutional forms of quiet violence, and I would like to begin with a case of what we might call psychological violence, where individuals are involved as individuals and there are not social institutions responsible for the violation of persons that takes place. Consider the following news item:[2]

PHOENIX, Ariz., Feb. 6 (AP) – Linda Marie Ault killed herself, policemen said today, rather than make her dog Beauty pay for her night with a married man.

The police quoted her parents, Mr. and Mrs. Joseph Ault, as giving this account:

Linda failed to return home from a dance in Tempe Friday night On Saturday she admitted she had spent the night with an Air Force lieutenant.

The Aults decided on a punishment that would 'wake Linda up.' They ordered her to shoot the dog she had owned about two years.

On Sunday, the Aults and Linda took the dog into the desert near their home. They had the girl dig a shallow grave. Then Mrs. Ault grasped the dog between her hands, and Mr. Ault gave his daughter a .22-caliber pistol and told her to shoot the dog.

Instead, the girl put the pistol to her right temple and shot herself.

The police said there were no charges that could be filed against the parents except possibly cruelty to animals.

Obviously, the reason there can be no charges is that the parents did no physical damage to Linda. But I think your reaction might be the same as mine – that they really did terrible violence to the girl by the way they behaved in this situation. Of course one must agree that Linda did violence to herself, but that is not the whole account of the violence in this case. The parents did far more violence to the girl than the lieutenant, and the father recognized that when he said to a detective, 'I killed her. I killed her. It's just like I killed her myself.' If we fail to recognize that there is really a kind of psychological violence that can be perpetrated on people, a real violation of their autonomy, their dignity, their right to determine things for themselves, their right to be humans rather than dogs, then we fail to realize the full dimension of what it is to do violence to one another.

One of the most obvious transition cases between overt personal violence and quiet personal violence is the case of a threat. Suppose a robber comes into a bank with a pistol, threatens to shoot one of the tellers, and walks out with money or a hostage or both. This is a case of armed robbery, and we rightly lump it together with cases of mugging and assault, morally and legally speaking, even if everybody emerges from the situation without any bruises or wounds. The reason is that there is a clear threat to do overt physical violence. By means of such a threat a person very often accomplishes what he might otherwise accomplish by actual overt violence. In this case the robber not only gets as much loot but he also accomplishes pretty much the same thing with respect to degrading the persons he is dealing with. A person who is threatened with being shot and then does something which he certainly would never otherwise do is degraded by losing his own autonomy as a person. We recognize that in law and morals: If a person who is threatened with a revolver takes money out of a safe and hands it to the robber we don't say that the person who has taken the money out of the safe has stolen it. We say that the person acted under compulsion, and hence the responsibility for what is done does not lie with him but with the person who threatened him.

It is very clear, and very important, that in cases where there is a threat of overt physical violence that we acknowledge that a person acting under that sort of a threat loses his autonomy. Of course, he needn't surrender his autonomy: he could just refuse to hand over the loot. There can be a great deal of dignity in such a refusal, and one of the messages of Sartre's moral philosophy, his existentialism, is that whenever you act other than with full responsibility yourself for your own actions that you are acting in bad faith. Now that is a very demanding philosophy, but it is one which puts a great deal of emphasis upon autonomy and dignity in human action and is not to be lightly dismissed. Nevertheless we do not expect that people will act with such uncompromising strength and dignity. To recognize that people can be broken down by threats and other psychological pressures, as well as by physical attack, and that to have acted under threat or duress is as good an excuse before the law as physical restraints – these recognitions constitute acknowledgement of the pertinence of the concept of psychological violence.

Psychological violence often involves manipulating people. It often involves degrading people. It often involves a kind of terrorism one way or another. Perhaps these forms that involve manipulation, degradation and terror are best presented in George Orwell's book, *1984*. In that book the hero is deathly afraid of being bitten by a rat. He never is bitten by the rat, but he is threatened with the rat and the threat is such as to break down his character in an extraordinary way. Here what might be called the phenomenology of psychological violence is presented in as convincing a form as I know.

Apart from these cases of terror and manipulation and degradation there are certain other forms of psychological violence. One of the most insidious is what might be called the 'Freudian rebuff.'[3] The Freudian rebuff works something like this. A person makes a comment on the Vietnam war or on civil rights or on some other current topic. The person he is talking to then says, 'Well, you're just saying that because of your Oedipal relations with your father.' The original speaker naturally objects, 'Don't be silly. Of course I had a father and all that. But look at the facts.' And then he starts bringing out the journals and newspapers and presents facts and statistics from them. 'You must have a terrible Oedipal complex; you're getting so excited about this.' And the person then says, 'Look, I've had some fights with my father, but I'm not hung-up on him, I just have normal spats and affection. I've read the paper and I have an independent interest in the civil rights question. It has nothing to do with my relations with my father.' To which the response is, 'Well, your denial just proves how deep your Oedipal complex is.' This type of Freudian rebuff has the effect of what John Henry Newman[4] called 'poisoning the wells.' It gives its victim just no ground to stand on. If he tries to stand on facts and statistics, they are discounted and his involvement is attributed to Freudian factors. If he tries to prove that he doesn't have the kind of psychological aberration in question, his very attempt to prove that he doesn't have it is taken to be evidence that he does. He can't get out of the predicament. It is like a quagmire in which the victim sinks deeper no matter which way he moves. So long as the proffered definition of the situation is imposed on him, a person has no way to turn: there is no possible sort of response that can extricate him from that charge laid upon him. To structure a situation against a person in such a manner does violence to him by depriving him of his dignity: no matter what he does there is no way at all, so long as he accepts the problem in the terms in which it is presented, for him to make a response that will allow him to emerge with honor.

Although this sort of cocktail-party Freudianism is not very serious in casual conversations where the definition of the situation can be challenged or the whole matter just shrugged off, it must be kept in mind that there are many forms of this ploy and that sometimes the whole life and character of a person may be involved. A classic literary and religious version is the dispute between Charles Kingsley and John Henry Newman in the 19th century, in which Kingsley challenged Newman's integrity and ended up losing his stature as a Protestant spokesman, and which is written up in fascinating detail in Newman's *Apologia*. A political variation is the Marxian rebuff where, of course, it is because of your class standing that you have such and such a view, and if you deny that the class standing is influencing you in that way your very denial shows how imbued you are with the class ideology. Between parent and child as well as between husband and wife there are variations of this ploy which turn around the identification (by one insistent party) of love with some particular action or other, so that the other party must either surrender his autonomy or acknowledge his faithlessness.

The cases where this sort of psychological violence are damaging are those where the person structuring the situation is in some position of special authority. Another form particularly virulent in urban schools – and probably suburban schools too – is the teacher's rebuff. An imaginative child does something out of the ordinary, and the teacher's response is that he is a discipline problem. It now becomes impossible for the child to get out of being a problem. If he tries to do something creative he will be getting out of line and thereby 'confirm' that he is a discipline problem. If he stays in line he will be a scholastic problem, thereby 'confirming' that he did not have potential for anything but mischief. The result is a kind of stunted person typical of schools in large urban areas, where it is common for a child to enter the public schools half a year behind according to standard tests. Such a child has undoubtedly been a discipline problem during this time and the teacher has spent her effort trying to solve the discipline problem and keep him from getting out of line – that is, from learning anything.[5]

This last variation of the psychological rebuff brings us to the fourth general category of violence, institutionalized quiet violence. The schools are an institution, and teachers are hired not so much to act on their own in the classroom as to fulfill a predetermined role. Violence done by the teacher in the classroom may therefore not be personal but institutional, done while acting as a faithful agent of the educational system. The idea of such institutional violence is a very important one.

A clearer example of quiet institutional violence might be a well-established system of slavery or colonial oppression, or the life of contemporary American ghettos. Once established such a system may require relatively little overt violence to maintain it. It is legendary that Southerners used to boast, 'We understand our nigras. They are happy here and wouldn't want any other kind of life,' – and there is no reason to doubt that many a Southerner, raised in the system and sheltered from the recurrent lynchings, believed it quite sincerely. In that sort of situation it is possible for an institution to go along placidly, as we might say, with no overt disturbances and yet for that institution to be one that is terribly brutal and that does great harm to its victims and which, incidentally, at the same time brutalizes people who are on top, since they lose a certain measure of their human sensitivity.

There is more violence in the black ghettos than there is anywhere else in America – even when they are quiet. At the time of the Harlem riots in 1964 the Negro psychologist, Kenneth Clark, said that there was more ordinary, day-to-day violence in the life of the ghettos than there was in any day of those disturbances. I'm not sure exactly what he meant. The urban ghettos are places where there is a great deal of overt violence, much of it a kind of reaction to the frustrations of ghetto life. Fanon describes the similar phenomenon of the growth of violence within the oppressed community in the colonial situation in Algeria.[6] When people are suppressed by a colonial regime, when they lack the opportunities which they see other people, white people, around them enjoying, then they become frustrated and have great propensities to violence. The safest target for such angry, frustrated people are their own kind. The Algerians did their first violence to other Algerians, in part because it wasn't safe to do it to a Frenchman. And the same is largely true of the situation that has developed in our urban ghettos. It isn't safe for a person living in the ghettos, if he is feeling frustrated and at the point of explosion, to explode against somebody outside the ghetto; but he can do it to his kids, his wife, his brother and his neighbor, and society will tend to look the other way. So there is a good deal of overt violence in the black ghettos. Perhaps, that is what Clark meant.

But we also have to recognize that there is sometimes a kind of quiet violence in the very operation of the system. Bernard Lafayette, who has worked in urban areas for both the American Friends Service Committee and the Southern Christian Leadership Conference, speaks angrily of the violence of the status quo: 'The real issue is that part of the 'good order of society' is the routine oppression and racism committed against millions of Americans every day. That is where the real violence is.'[7] The fact that there is a black ghetto in most American cities which operates very like any system of slavery. Relatively little violence is needed to keep the institution going and yet the institution entails a real violation of the human beings involved, because they are systematically denied the options which are obviously open to the vast majority of the members of the society in which they live. A systematic denial of options is one way to deprive men of autonomy. If I systematically deprive a person of the options that are normal in our society, then he is no longer in a position to decide for himself what to do. Any institution which systematically robs certain people of rightful options generally available to others does violence to those people.

Perhaps denying options would not do violence to people if each individual person was an island unto himself and individuality were the full truth about human life. But it is not. We are social beings. Our whole sense of what we are is dependent on the fact that we live in society and have open to us socially determined options. I am now writing. As I write I make many choices about what to say, some having to do with whole paragraphs, some with single words, and some with punctuation. These choices are dependent upon a social institution, language. Unless I knew the language, and unless there were a society of language speakers, I would have no options at all about what to say. The options opened to us by language are very important, but language is only one part of our society. There are many sorts of options which are open to us and important to us as individuals. It is how we act, how we choose with respect to socially defined options, that constitutes what we really are as human beings.

What we choose to do with respect to our socially defined options is much more important than which language or which system of property rights we inherit at birth – provided we have access to the options defined in the system. By suppressing options you deprive a person of the opportunity to be somebody because you deprive him of choices. The institutional form of quiet violence operates when people are deprived of choices in a systematic way by the very manner in which transactions normally take place, without any individual act being violent in itself or any individual decision being responsible for the system.

These, then, are the main types of violence that I see. By recognizing those types of violence we begin to get the whole question of violence into a much richer perspective than when we hear the Chief of Police deplore violence. Such a richer perspective is vitally necessary, because we cannot do anything about the violence in our society unless we can see it, and most of us do not see it very well. Conceptions and perceptions are closely dependent on one another, and perhaps having a better idea of what violence is will enable us to recognize more readily the many sorts of violence that surround our lives.

IV

In concluding I would like to call attention to two aspects of violence. The first is that the concept of violence is a moral concept, but not one of absolute condemnation. Very often psychologists and sociologists and other scientists and students of animal behavior avoid the word 'violence' just because it does have a moral connotation. The word 'aggression' is sometimes used instead in some of the literature in psychology, and it is prominent in the title of Konrad Lorenz's recent book on animal behavior and aggression.[8] They choose this word 'aggression' because it lacks the moral connotations of the term 'violence.' I think it is important to recognize that the concept of violence is a moral concept, and that the moral elements come in through the fact that an act of violence is a violation of a person. I think that it is also important to recognize that the normal pattern of moral discourse allows for excuses and rationalization. We don't expect people never to do anything which is at all wrong: we allow for excuses.[9] Sartre's very hard line, that excuses undermine the dignity and moral strength of the person being excused, has not really won the day in law courts or in the general moral view; or perhaps what Sartre meant is that we should never allow ourselves excuses rather than that we should never allow them to others. When a person commits an act of violence he is not necessarily to be condemned, though he does have some explaining to do. The fact that we would require an excuse from him, or some justification of his behavior, indicates that a person's doing an act of violence puts the burden of proof on him; but it doesn't suffice to show that the case has gone against him yet.

The second thing I want to say is that it is entirely clear to me that there are degrees of violence. All these various forms of violence are indeed violence, but if I simply say of an act or an institution that it is violent I have not yet said enough to give a clear evaluation of that act. I must also take account of how *much* violence it does to persons affected. Unfortunately this is easier said than done. It might at first be thought that overt violence is always worse than quiet violence, but that rule does not hold generally except in the case of murder; in fact, physical injury often heals more readily than psychological damage. It is more plausible to argue that institutional violence is always of greater harm than personal violence, but that obviously depends on the degree of violence on each side – which means that we must be able to judge the degree of violence in an act or an institution independent of the kind of violence involved; What we need is a scale for measuring degrees of violence, and we don't have one. Still there are degrees of violence, and it is possible to achieve considerable intersubjective agreement about comparisons of pairs of cases.

Notes

1. A persuasive account of the extent to which law itself can be a form of violence, rather than an alternative to it, is to be found in E. Z. Friedenberg's essay 'A Violent Country' in the *New York Review*, October 20, 1966.

2. *New York Times*, February 7, 1968.
3. Of course this is an aspect of cocktail-party Freudianism rather than of psychoanalytic theory, and what Freud invented was not this little ploy but the concepts that were later distorted into it.
4. In his famous debate with Charles Kingsley. See his *Apologia Pro Vita Sua*, conveniently available in a paperback edition, Garden City, Doubleday, 1956.
5. Among the many works commenting on this aspect of public education, I have found those of Edgar Friedenberg and Paul Goodman most instructive. See Paul Goodman, *Compulsory Miseducation*, New York, Horizon, 1964; Edgar Z. Friedenberg, *The Vanishing Adolescent*, Boston, Beacon Press, 1959, and *Coming of Age in America*, New York, Knopf, 1963.
6. Frantz Fanon. *The Wretched of the Earth*, New York, Grove Press, 1966.
7. In *Soul Force,* February 15, 1968.
8. A classic study in psychology is John Dollard *et al. Frustration and Aggression*, New Haven, Yale, 1939. See also A. Buss, *The Psychology of Aggression*, New York, Wiley, 1961; K. Lorenz, *On Aggression*, New York, Harcourt Brace, 1966.
9. The late Prof. John L. Austin called the attention of moral philosophers to the importance of excuses in moral discourse. See 'A Plea for Excuses,' *Philosophical Papers*, London, Oxford University Press, 1961.

COMMENTARY ON GARVER

Newton Garver, a Quaker and political activist as well as distinguished philosopher, is one of the most radical voices on violence and nonviolence.[1] In this seminal article, a slightly revised version of a piece first published in *The Nation* on 24 June 1968, Garver presents us with an original and immensely popular definition and typology of violence.[2]

Although Garver acknowledges that the idea of force being connected with violence is a very powerful one, he argues that in human affairs (unlike natural phenomena) violence cannot be equated with force. Instead, the idea of violence in human affairs is much more closely connected with the idea of violation than it is with the idea of force: 'what is fundamental about violence in human affairs is that a person is violated'.

Garver goes on to elaborate in greater detail what it means for a person to be violated. He explains that a person has certain rights which are undeniably, indissolubly, connected with his being a person. In particular, Garver highlights the right a person has to their body, and to their dignity, or 'autonomy' in the Kantian sense of the word.

On the basis of this definition, Garver suggests that there are four main types or forms of violence, based on two criteria: first, whether the violence is personal or institutional; second, whether the violence is overt or covert (or 'quiet').

Physical, overt assault is what we normally associate with the idea of violence. Thus, physical assault of one person on the body of another, as in the case of mugging, rape and murder, are obvious examples of personal, overt violence. Warfare and riots are examples of institutionalized, overt violence. But Garver is more interested in exploring the other forms of violence, where violence is not overt but covert. This is what Garver refers to as the 'quiet forms of violence', which do not necessarily involve any overt physical assault on anybody's person or property.

Like overt violence, covert or quiet violence can also be either personal or institutional. In terms of personal, covert violence, Garver discusses the example of psychological violence, which includes threats, terror, manipulation and degradation. But most of all Garver wants to expose the type of violence that is institutional and covert. This is the most illusive, almost invisible, type of violence. It is also arguably the most destructive and pervasive type of violence: 'a clearer example of quiet institutional violence might be a well-established system of slavery or colonial oppression, or the life of contemporary American ghettos'. It is a feature of institutional, quiet violence that relatively little physical, overt violence is needed to maintain the status quo, according to which some people are systematically denied the dignity and autonomy which are enjoyed by the vast majority of the members of the society in which they live.

Notes and further reading

1. See his *This Complicated Form of Life: Essays on Wittgenstein*, Chicago: Open Court, 1994; *Wittgenstein and Approaches to Clarity*, Amherst, NY: Humanity Press, 2006; *Limits to Power: Some Friendly Reminders*, Buffalo, NY: Center Working Papers, 2007.
2. This article was reprinted seven times between 1968 and 1975.

10
The Marxist Conception of Violence
John Harris

The idea that if we are able to change things, to elect not to do so is also to determine what will happen in the world, is very old indeed. For obvious reasons, the idea is only employed when the things that happen are of some significance. The importance of the idea and its history stem from those cases where harm occurs which might have been averted or in which harm will occur unless it is averted. In such cases, many men have found it natural not only to blame those who could have prevented the harm, but did not do so, but also to think of such men as having brought the harm about, as being its cause.

I do not know when this idea first occurred. Plutarch makes use of it; John Bromyard, a fourteenth-century Chancellor of Cambridge, gives it most eloquent expression; and it is, of course, one of the main themes of Shakespeare's *Measure for Measure*. In modern times it has been associated most strongly with Marx, Engels, and Marxist thinkers, In their hands it has been used as a weapon in the controversy about 'violence.' Marxists have argued that deaths caused by the indifference and neglect of society or its rulers must be seen as being as much a part of human violence as the violent acts of revolutionaries.

In this paper I will defend two theses. The first is the idea that men are causally responsible for harm they could have prevented. The second is the view that such harm may properly be regarded as a form of violence. It is characteristic of those I shall loosely call 'Marxists' to combine both theses. I shall therefore, for convenience, call this combined view 'the Marxist conception of violence.' This loose use of the term 'Marxist' is, I think, justified on the grounds that the ideas with which I here associate it are to be found in the writings of both Marx and Engels, and because such ideas are characteristic of thinkers who either consider themselves to be, in some broad sense, followers of Marx, or who are called 'Marxists' by their opponents.

In Part I of this essay I shall give a number of examples of the Marxist conception of violence. I have chosen so many examples for three reasons: for their intrinsic interest, because they illustrate both the force and the character of the Marxist view, and finally because their number and variety help to defend the view from the charge that it violates ordinary usage or 'turns the language upside down.' Part II is devoted to a defense of the first thesis, and Part III to a defense of the second.

I

What I call 'the Marxist conception of violence' is probably as old as any thinking on responsibility. Plutarch, for example, makes the point that a man who fails to protect another from a death he was able to prevent, is just as guilty of that man's death as if he had wielded the sword himself. Talking of the revenge of the Triumvirs in his life of Mark Antony, Plutarch states: 'At the end of all this bartering of one death for another, they [the Triumvirs] were just as guilty of the deaths of those whom they abandoned as of those whom they seized.'[1]

In his guide for preachers, John Bromyard imagines the last judgment:

> On the left, before the supreme Judge's throne stand 'the harsh lords, who plundered the people of God with grievous fines, amercements and exactions, ... the wicked ecclesiastics, who failed to nourish the poor with the goods of Christ ... as they should have done. ... Then the oppressed bring a fearful indictment against their oppressors. ...' We hungered and thirsted and were afflicted with cold and nakedness. And those robbers yonder gave not our own goods to us when we were in want, neither did they feed and clothe us out of them. But their hounds and horses and apes, the rich, the powerful, the abounding, the gluttons, the drunkards and their prostitutes they fed and clothed with them, and allowed us to languish in want. ...
>
> 'O just God, mighty judge, the game was not fairly divided between them and us. Their satiety was our famine; their merriment was our wretchedness; their jousts and tournaments were our torments. ... Their feasts, delectations, pomps, vanities, excesses and superfluities were our fastings, penalties, wants, calamities and spoliation. The love-ditties and laughter of their dances were our mockery, our groanings and remonstrations. They used to sing – 'well enough! well enough l' – and we groaned, saying – 'Woe to us! Woe to us!' ...'[2]

The most compelling and coherent statement of the Marxist view occurs in Engels's book *The Condition of the Working Class in England*. It is worth quoting at some length:

> If one individual inflicts a bodily injury upon another which leads to the death of the person attacked we call it manslaughter; on the other hand, if the attacker knows beforehand that the blow will be fatal we call it murder. Murder has also been committed if society places hundreds of workers in

such a position that they inevitably come to premature and unnatural ends. Their death is as violent as if they had been stabbed or shot. Murder has been committed if thousands of workers have been deprived of the necessities of life or if they have been forced into a situation in which it is impossible for them to survive. Murder has been committed if the workers have been forced by the strong arm of the law to go on living under such conditions until death inevitably releases them. Murder has been committed if society knows perfectly well that thousands of workers cannot avoid being sacrificed so long as these conditions are allowed to continue. Murder of this sort is just as culpable as the murder committed by an individual. But if society murders a worker it is a treacherous stab in the back against which a worker cannot defend himself. At first sight it does not appear to be murder at all because responsibility for the death of the victim cannot be pinned on any individual assailant. Everyone is responsible and yet no one is responsible, because it appears as if the victim has died from natural causes. If a worker dies no one places the responsibility for his death on society, though some would realise that society has failed to take steps to prevent the victim from dying. But it is murder all the same.[3]

Christopher Caudwell, writing in 1938, makes use of a similar analysis of social relations:

Thus, just as much as in slave-owning society, bourgeois society turns out to be a society built on violent coercion of men by men, the more violent in that while the master must feed and protect his slave, whether he works or not, the bourgeois employer owes no obligation to the free labourer.[4]

Caudwell concludes, in agreement with Engels, that the absence of an individual assailant cannot affect responsibility:

The fact that one participates passively in bourgeois economy, that one does not oneself wield the bludgeon or fire the cannon, so far from being a defence really makes one's position more disgusting. ...[5]

Ten years later Harold Orlans summed up his experience of conditions in an American mental hospital, in which he had worked as a conscientious objector during the Second World War, as follows:

It is in the murder by neglect of decrepit old men that I believe the closest analogy is to be found with the death camp murders. The asylum murders are passive; the Auschwitz murders active ... but otherwise their logic is the same.[6]

Barrington Moore, Jr., warned that the death toll of the French revolutionary terror must be seen as a response to 'the prevailing social
order,' which 'always grinds out its toll of unnecessary death year after
year.' 'It would be enlightening,' Moore continues, 'to calculate the death
rate of the *ancien régime* from such factors as preventable starvation and
injustice.' Moore's point is that 'to dwell on the horrors of revolutionary violence while forgetting that of 'normal' times is merely partisan
hypocrisy.'[7]

Marx himself gives repeated examples of the injury, shame, degradation,
and death suffered every day by the working class and directly caused by the
capitalist economy. In the chapter entitled 'Machinery and Modern Industry' in volume I of *Capital*[8] he spends most of his time pointing out the
'antagonistic and murderous side' of modern manufacture. 'One of the most
shameful, the most dirty, and the worst paid kinds of labour' is that of the rag-
sorters who 'are the medium for the spread of small-pox and other infectious
diseases and are themselves the first victims.' We learn that 'it is impossible
for a child to pass through the purgatory of a tile field without great moral
degradation.' We are shown how the increase in the incidence of consumption among lace makers rose from one in forty-five in 1852 to one in eight
in 1860, and that the 'fearful increase in death from starvation during the
last ten years in London runs parallel with the extension of machine-sewing.'
'In one scutching mill at Kildinan, near Cork,' we are told, 'there occurred
between 1852 and 1856, six fatal accidents and sixty mutilations; every one
of which might have been prevented by the simplest appliances, at the cost
of a few shillings.' These mutilations 'are of the most fearful nature. In many
cases a quarter of the body is torn from the trunk, and either involves death,
or a future of wretched incapacity and suffering.' Marx's emphasis is on the
harm caused to human beings by their being forced to work in injurious conditions and by the failure of the employers or society generally to prevent
suffering and death that could easily and at little cost be prevented. Whenever harm comes to workers in any way connected with their employment
or the conditions of their lives that their work or lack of work forces upon
them, the employers and society at large treat the harm as a natural calamity
about which it is impossible to do anything. Marx believes that where human
intervention could prevent this harm, then failure to prevent the harm must
be seen as a cause:

Wherever there is a working day without restriction as to length, wherever there is night work and unrestricted waste of human life, there
the slightest obstacle presented by the nature of the work to a change
for the better is soon looked upon as an everlasting barrier erected by
Nature. No poison kills vermin with more certainty than the Factory Act
removes such everlasting barriers. No one made a greater outcry over
'impossibilities' than our friends the earthenware manufacturers. In 1864

however they were brought under the Act, and within sixteen months every 'impossibility' had vanished.[9]

Finally, I should like to cite the brief statement of an anonymous witness to a contemporary tragedy. Michael Elkins, broadcasting from Jerusalem for B.B.C. Radio News, reported that an eyewitness to the suicide squad massacre at Jerusalem airport said: 'Don't tell me anyone searched the suitcases of those men – whoever let those men on the plane is also guilty of murder.' I do not, of course, know whether this witness was a Marxist, even of any kind.

The Marxists emphasize both that the 'normal' conditions of society are vicious and injurious and that responsibility rests as much with those who allow such states of affairs to continue as with those who brought them about. It will be obvious that all these examples depend at some point on recognition of the causal efficacy of omissions: workers are murdered because conditions in which they cannot survive are 'allowed to continue,' one 'participates passively' in violent coercion, decrepit old men are murdered 'by neglect,' the *ancien régime* has a high death rate because of 'preventable starvation and injustice,' death and mutilation 'might have been prevented by the simplest appliances at the cost of a few shillings.' I shall next concentrate on the problem of how far we are causally responsible for harm we could have prevented, for if the Marxist claims about causal responsibility for such harm can be made out, then not only does their conception of violence move from rhetoric towards reality (because, of course, one of the essential elements of acts of violence is that there should be an agent), but a radical revision of our views about responsibility becomes imperative.

II

Jeremy Bentham called omissions which have consequences 'negative actions,' presumably because, like Engels, he was impressed by the fact that a failure to act can be as effective a way of doing something as an action traditionally understood. The great problem with omissions is to give an account of when a failure to act has consequences, and when it does not. Bentham obviously experienced this difficulty when he stated that 'to strike is a positive act; not to strike on a certain occasion a negative one,'[10] but failed to give any account of how to distinguish the occasions on which not to strike is a negative action from those on which it is not.

Since Bentham's time, several attempts have been made to give an adequate account of when a failure to act has consequences, and when it does not. In what follows, I shall consider three of the most influential of such attempts and argue that their deficiencies point the way to a more satisfactory account of negative actions, an account, moreover, which is clearly the one upon which the Marxist conception of violence relies.

The crucial question is: In what circumstances is it appropriate to say that Y is a consequence of not doing X? Eric D'Arcy asks this question, and answers that Y is called a consequence of A's not doing X only when:

(1) Doing X is a standard way of preventing Y.
(2) A is in some way expected to do X.
(3) X is required of A in order that something such as Y should not happen.[11]

D'Arcy makes it clear that A may be expected to do X, in the requisite sense of 'expected,' if either, (a) 'X is something that A usually does, or people usually do, in the situation in question,' or (b) 'X is required of him by some rule with which he is expected to comply.' 'This may of course be some moral rule, precept, or principle; but it will often be a non-moral rule.' The rule which requires X of A will often be, on D'Arcy's account, a catch-all Benthamite duty of beneficence which will cover 'things which we should, or ought to do or not do to others, even when they are not required by virtue of office, voluntary undertaking, or special relationship.'

D'Arcy explains his set of conditions under which Y will be a consequence of A's not doing X, as follows:

> A can ... be held responsible for Y only to the extent that some rela-tionship of cause and consequence exists between them; the only such relationship is that which exists by virtue of the connexion of each with X; and, by hypothesis, X connects them only to this extent, that X is enjoined upon A in order that something such as Y should not happen.[12]

And he concludes that 'in moral investigations, at least, the charge that A did not do X with the result that Y happened will ... be successfully rebutted if it can be shown, not only that doing X was something which was not required of A: but even that it was not required of him in order that things such as Y might not happen.'[13]

On D'Arcy's view, before we can say that A's failure to do X caused any result whatsoever, it must *already* be the case that X is expected or required of A. For if A is not already connected with X by some duty, then when X is not performed with the consequence that Y happens, A will not be connected to X, and therefore not to Y either.

D'Arcy has put his model together back-to-front, for his condition that 'X is required of A in order that something such as Y should not happen' would be pointless if it did not exploit our understanding of the causal connection between the failure of X and the occurrence of Y. D'Arcy's own explication of the notion of beneficence confirms this. Beneficence it will be remembered, covers 'things which we should, or ought to, do or not do to others.' One of D'Arcy's examples (derived from Bentham) of the exercise of this duty is the following: 'if a drunkard falls face downwards into a puddle, and is in danger of drowning, a bystander has a duty at least to lift his head a little to one side and so save him.' But our duty is not to go around lifting the heads of drunks, *and so save them*, our duty *is* to save them if we can. And we have this duty, because to fail to save someone we could save would be the death of him. It would not be the death of him because we have the duty; it would be the death of him because we fail to save him. His death results from our failure, whether we have a duty to save him or not (we might have a duty to kill this particular man and discharge it by failing to save him). It is not the existence of the duty that makes the death of the drunk a consequence of our failure to save him, rather it is the fact that unless we save him he will die that makes it our duty to save him.

If ever the duty of beneficence was owed, it was owed surely to the man who fell among thieves on the Jericho road. The thieves left him half dead, and he would perhaps have perished had the Samaritan followed the priest and the Levite and left him untended. The probable consequence of passing by on the other side would be the death of the man. To see this is to see a causal connection between the failure to tend the man and his death. And it is because we understand this connection that we see the point of the parable, that we realize why it is that the priest and the Levite ought to have tended the man. We do not need to postulate a duty of beneficence to explain how the neglect of the passersby might well have resulted in the man's death, rather we need to understand the causal connection between *neglect and death* to see why anyone might be required to tend to him.

John Casey, in a recent discussion of this problem, notes that 'the introduction of a statement which claims to give the *cause* of some event presupposes a pattern of normal expectations such that what will count as the cause of the event is, as it were, an intrusion into the pattern of expectations.'[14] Casey goes on to state the conditions under which failure to act can have causal status in terms similar to D'Arcy's. 'If a man does not do X, we cannot properly say that his not doing X is the cause of some result Y unless, in the normal course of events, he could have been expected to do X.' Casey then argues that a man can be held 'personally responsible' for something (and Casey means by this term roughly what Hart means by his term 'moral liability-responsibility,' namely, that the person is responsible in some way for which he may appropriately be praised or blamed) if (and only if):

(a) His actions (or omissions) are causally responsible for it.
(b) The outcome has some importance in terms of what he might be expected to do; in general, that is, in terms of a pattern of role responsibilities, in the context of which he acts.
(c) Normal conditions (i.e., no excusing conditions).[15]

Casey notes that 'the correctness of saying that condition (a) is satisfied rests on a rule of conversational propriety which is equivalent to the assertion of condition (b).' This note is necessary because, if 'the introduction of a statement which claims to give the *cause* of some event presupposes a pattern of normal expectations such that what will count as the cause of the event is ... an intrusion into the pattern of expectations,' we must have some idea of what our normal expectations are. And if a failure to act is to be identified and given causal status, the normal conditions in the light of which it is a *failure* to act must be known. In knowing what a man is expected to do, we know the normal conditions; when a man fails to do what is expected of him, we can see that the failure is an intrusion into the pattern of normal expectations, and we are then able to say that certain events are the *results* of his failure. Furthermore, Casey believes that what he calls 'a man's role' defines what sort of agent he is, and what are his responsibilities and obligations, *prior* to any particular case. This is, of course, sometimes true. The cultivation of his own garden is, if he does not employ a gardener, part of a man's 'role responsibilities' in the broad sense in which Casey uses the term. If the garden grows to seed and becomes possessed by things rank and gross in nature, the owner is responsible, and we know this prior to the deterioration of the garden, because we know who is responsible for its upkeep. But sometimes we know what a man's responsibilities and obligations are only *because* we see that failure to act in a certain way will result in the occurrence of the sort of thing that we expect or require people to prevent. And where this is so, Casey's notion of a man's role will fail to provide a way of specifying what a man's obligations are which is independent of the consequences of his not fulfilling them. In these cases it is not the fact that X is expected of a man that allows us to say that his not doing X makes him causally responsible for Y, but rather, the fact that we see him to be causally responsible for Y shows us that X was expected of him.

In their book *Causation in the Law*, Hart and Honoré deal extensively with the question of the causal status of omissions.[16] Their account relies heavily on some idea of normalcy. 'When things go wrong and we ask the cause, we ask this on the assumption that the environment persists unchanged, and something has 'made the difference' between what normally happens in it and what has happened on this occasion.' On their account, when an omission has causal status, it has that status because it constitutes a departure from what normally happens.

> What is taken as normal for the purpose of the distinction between cause and mere conditions is very often an artefact of human habit, custom and convention. This is so because men have discovered that nature is not only sometimes harmful *if* we intervene, but is also sometimes harmful unless we intervene, and have developed customary techniques, procedures and routines to counteract such harm. These have become a second 'nature'

and so a second 'norm.' The effect of drought is regularly neutralized by government precautions in preserving water or food; disease is neutralized by inoculation; rain by the use of umbrellas. When such man-made normal conditions are established, deviation from them will be regarded as exceptional and so rank as the cause of harm.

Hart and Honoré emphasize that deviation from customary techniques will rank as a cause, not because harm always results from such deviation, but because the 'omitted precaution would have arrested the harm.' This is certainly so, and it is an important point, but must the techniques have become *customary*, the procedures and routines *normal*, the method of prevention *standard*, before we can say that their omission caused some outcome?

At what point does the failure to neutralize the harmful effects of disease come to rank as the cause of those harmful effects? On the Hart-Honoré view this happens only when the practice of inoculation has become 'a second "nature" and so a second "norm." ' Let us suppose that a vaccine against cancer is developed, tried, and tested at a university or by a drug manufacturer, that its discovery is made known by the firm which developed it, but that no one takes steps to make it generally available or to provide money for its mass production. Are we not entitled, indeed required, to conclude that a government, for example, or a drug company, which continues to allow people to die of cancer, when they could so easily be saved, is causally responsible for their deaths? And are we not entitled to say this even though no customary practice of vaccination against cancer has become second nature to the society in question? Hart and Honoré might reply that while vaccination against cancer has not become customary, the practice of inoculation is a standard method of prevention of disease, and that it is this practice which makes it possible to say that the failure to make available any new vaccine may involve causal responsibility for the continuing prevalence of the disease.

But we can push our inquiry further back and ask whether, when it had become clear that Jenner's vaccine was successful in preventing smallpox, it would have been necessary to wait until the practice of inoculation had become standard *before* it would be correct to cite failure to vaccinate as a cause, perhaps the most significant cause, of an epidemic.[17]

When in 1939 Howard Florey and his team concentrated and purified Fleming's antibiotic penicillin and demonstrated its curative properties, it would surely have been ludicrous to suggest that it was necessary to wait until its use had become standard before anyone was in a position to realize that any failure to put it into mass production would cost thousands of lives. Indeed, its use could not become standard until it was put into mass production, and there would be no reason to put it into mass production and thus make its use standard, if it were not already obvious that to fail to do so would *cost* lives.

When is it true to say that Y is a consequence of A's not doing X? The idea that a prerequisite of our saying that A's failure to do X caused Y is that X be somehow expected of A, which is employed by Hart and Honoré, D'Arcy and Casey, is probably correct for the majority of negative actions. The fact that someone normally does X, or that it is expected for some other reason that someone will do X, makes the nonoccurrence of X on a particular occasion something that calls for explanation. Or again, if A is required to do X, we have a reason for wanting to know if X has happened, and if it has not happened, for wondering why not. In either case, we first expect X of A, and whatever reason we have for so doing also shows why the non-occurrence of X calls for an explanation at all, and indicates the direction in which to look for an answer. If we know it is the porter's job to raise the college flag at daybreak and at noon the college flagstaff is naked, we may want to know why the flag has not been raised, and the somnolence of the porter satisfies our curiosity. But the nakedness of flagpoles is unproblematic unless, *because* we know the porter's duties, we have some reason for expecting to see them clothed in flags. Where harm to human beings is concerned, however, our interest needs no special occasion. We are always interested in the causes of harm to ourselves and our fellow men.

The discussion of the theories of Hart and Honoré, D'Arcy, and Casey seems to indicate that the moment we realize that harm to human beings could be prevented, we are entitled to see the failure to prevent it as a cause of harm. As it stands, this statement seems too comprehensive in scope. We do not usually think of the man who fails to give money to save the victims of famine abroad as causing the deaths of some of the victims, even though we know that even a small donation would save lives. Still less, perhaps, do we think of society as guilty of massive carnage because it continues to allow the use of motor vehicles, although we know that were motor vehicles or most of them, to be banned, thousands of lives would be saved each year. That we do not usually speak of causes in these cases seems to show that there is something wrong with saying that the moment we realize that harm could be avoided, we are entitled to see the failure to prevent it as a cause of the harm. What appears to be wrong with the statement, and certainly the criticism that Hart and Honoré would level at it, is that it involves a confusion between causes and mere conditions. Wherever there is a possibility of preventing harm, its non-prevention is a necessary condition of the harm's occurring, but is something more required for a necessary condition to become a cause?

Hart and Honoré give a detailed account of just what more this is. They distinguish 'mere conditions' from 'causes' properly so called. Mere conditions are 'just those [factors] which are present alike both in the case where such accidents occur and in the cases where they do not, and it is this consideration that leads us to reject them as the cause of the accident, even though it is true that without them the accident would not have occurred.' It is plain, of course, that to cite factors which are present both in the case of disaster and of normal functioning would explain nothing; such factors do not 'make the difference' between disaster and normal functioning. Hart and Honoré emphasize that what is or is not normal functioning can be relative to the context of any given enquiry in two ways: either because some feature which pervades most contexts has been specifically excluded in a particular case, or because 'in one and the same case ... the distinction between cause and condition can be drawn in different ways. The cause of a great famine in India may be identified by the Indian peasant as the drought, but the World Food Authority may identify the Indian government's failure to build up reserves as the cause and the drought as a mere condition.' Hart and Honoré suppose that what we want to know, when we ask for a causal explanation in cases like this, is what made *these* people die of starvation when normally *they* would have lived? And the answer given is that one can say that what made this difference was the Indian government's failure to build up reserves – 'an abnormal failure of a normal condition.'

But what if normal functioning is always a disaster? Every year, just like clockwork, the poor and the jobless, the aged and the infirm, suffer terribly, and many of them die. What is the cause? The myopic view is that they die because they are poor and jobless, aged and infirm, that this is what distinguishes them from those who do not suffer, from those who do not die. But the 'World Moral Authority' may identify the neglect of other members of society or of the government as the cause, and the other features as mere conditions. And surely the 'World Moral Authority's' causal explanation is not upset by the discovery that this society normally neglects its weakest members, that there is no difference between what they did this year and what they always do, that caring for their needy is by no means an established procedure with them. Of course, Hart and Honoré can retreat to a second line of defense which their account prudently affords. They can say that, while this society may be callous, provision for the needy is none the less a well-established procedure among men, and it is this that allows us to cite neglect as the cause of suffering in the case; or in the case of the Indian famine, that building up reserves is a technique for preventing famine established at least since the time of Moses. This can only be a temporary line of defense, because there was a time when these precautions against harm were not the normal practice, and at that time, when men were wondering what was the cause of all the misery they saw about them, they did not ask themselves: why are these people suffering when *normally* they would not suffer? but, why are these people suffering *when they could have been spared* their suffering?

When we are seeking a causal explanation of the disasters that overtake human beings, we are often not seeking to explain why a disaster occurred on this occasion when normally it would not have occurred, but why it occurred on this occasion when it need not have done. Human life is often such a chapter of disasters that what we want explained is why these disasters happen when they could have been prevented. In these cases the question that interests us and the question that must interest anyone who wishes to explain why human beings so often needlessly come to grief, is not: *what made the difference*, but, *what might have made the difference*? In the case of the Indian famine the 'mere' conditions will be the drought, the failure of the crops, and so on; the cause will be the failure of the Indian government to build up reserves or perhaps the failure of other governments to send speedy and sufficient aid. When we are looking for what might make the difference between harm's occurring and its not occurring, anything that could have been done to prevent the harm in question is a likely candidate for causal status.

So far, we have been interested in the question of when a failure to act has consequences and when it doesn't, in when Y is a consequence of A's failure to do X and when it isn't. Our interest has been quite undiscriminating between the circumstances in which it is correct to say that Y is a *consequence* of A's actions or omissions and those in which one can say that A *caused* Y or that A is *responsible* for Y. But when we say that someone was the cause of harm to human beings, we are singling him out as the author of the harm (or at least as *one of* the authors), we are saying that he is responsible for it and probably that he is to blame (or if, for some reason, we feel that the harm was well-deserved, those responsible might be praised). Praise or blame is usually appropriate where harm to human beings is knowingly caused. If we think that a particular method of preventing a particular harm is for some reason ineligible, then we are unlikely to blame people for not using it, and if it is the only way that the harm could have been averted, we are unlikely to cite the failure to use the method as a *cause* of the harm, even though the fact that the harm occurred is, of course, a *consequence* of the failure to prevent it.

But what do these facts about the words we usually choose in different situations indicate about negative causation? If we think that a possible method of preventing harm is ineligible, that its use is for some reason completely out of the question, then we are unlikely to see it as something that might have made the difference (or that made the difference) between the harm's occurring and its not occurring. We just do not think of it as something that 'could have been done' to avert the disaster.

But people are likely to differ crucially about just how viable options of saving others are. Suffering people are likely to see the possibility of their sufferings being relieved as highly eligible, but those who would have to make sacrifices to bring relief are likely to think differently, especially if they have interests which would be permanently prejudiced by any change in the status quo.

Of course, if someone claims out of the blue that people who fail to do something that has hitherto been almost universally judged to be quite out of the question are causally responsible for the deaths of human beings, then some explanation at least is owed. But the legitimacy of claiming that a failure to exercise a particular option is causing death does not depend on our agreeing that the option should be, or should have been, exercised.

I have suggested that where Y involves harm to human beings, then Y will be a consequence of A's not doing X simply where X would have prevented Y and A could have done X. Where the doing of X is considered to be out of the question, we tend to act and talk as though the condition that A could have done X is not satisfied. People will differ as to just how 'impossible' the doing of X really is, different principles and interests will pull in different directions: what is out of the question for A, B will do without a second thought. If a doctor believes that he must never deliberately take life and so refuses to perform an abortion, even though the mother will die if the abortion is not performed, he does not see himself as causing the mother's death, rather he believes himself to have no choice. It is significant that such a man is often described as following the dictates of the divine law, or of his conscience, 'whatever the consequences,' and that discussions of the problems raised by such dilemmas are discussions of whether absolutist moral principles which ignore consequences can be justified. The point is not that one has to be a consequentialist, but that the adoption of principles or values, or even ways of life or ways of organizing society, which makes the prevention of certain sorts of harm by certain means 'out of the question,' does not prevent the harm being a consequence of the maintenance of those principles or that way of life. If we decide that preventing particular harm by particular means is 'out of the question,' we are unlikely to talk as though the harm were a consequence of our failure to prevent it. But the occurrence of such harm is the price we pay for the maintenance of our principles or of our way of life. Maybe it's worth it, maybe it isn't; that is another question. We can never rule out the possibility of hungry people in the third world, or even the victims of motor accidents in our own society claiming, with justice, that we are causally responsible for their plight because we decline to arrange things so that they may be preserved from harm.

To sum up, we must emphasize a distinction that has been implicit in the foregoing discussion: that between A causing Y by his failure to do X and his bringing about of Y by his failure to do X. That is, the distinction between *negative causation* and *negative action*. We can state formally the difference between the two as follows:

(a) Negative Causation: *A's failure to do X caused Y where A could have done X and X would have prevented Y, and where either: X is somehow expected or required of A, or Y involves harm to human beings.*

As many thinkers have observed, it seems inappropriate, even silly, to talk of a man being causally responsible for everything and anything he might have made different. There must be some reason for his interference, some point to it. There must be some feature of the situation that raises the issue of A's preventing Y by doing X. This feature, whatever it is, will make it appropriate to talk both of A's failing to do X, and of A's thereby causing Y. And this will be so even where we neither expect nor require A to do X, nor to prevent Y. Thus, either our expecting or requiring A to do X, or the fact that Y involves harm to human beings, are features of a situation that make it appropriate to talk of A's failure to prevent Y by doing X, as his causing Y. I don't intend this to be an exhaustive list of the conditions under which A's failure to do X can be said to cause Y. There may be situations in which quite different features may give reasons for interference and so make talk of causes appropriate.

(b) Negative Action: *A's failure to do X with the result Y will make the bringing about of Y a negative action of A's, only where A's doing X would have prevented Y and A knew or ought reasonably to have known this, and where A could have done X and knew, or ought reasonably to have known, this.*

We must here again note the distinction (pointed out by H.L.A. Hart)[18] between causal responsibility and 'moral liability-responsibility'; that is, between causing some outcome and being liable, accountable in some way that makes praise or blame appropriate. We are usually accountable for some outcome because we are causally responsible for it, but not simply because we are. It is only if the bringing about of Y is a negative action of A's that his causal responsibility for Y will raise the question of whether or not he might also be morally responsible for Y. And of course, whether A is morally responsible, whether he is to be held to account for bringing about Y, will depend on a number of other considerations, as indeed it would if he had brought Y about by positive actions.

If the argument so far is right, it presents us with a choice between only two consistent views about negative causation. We can deny that anyone is ever responsible for things he could have prevented or changed. This would go against many of our intuitions and common-sense judgments, and would deny a whole realm of discourse long established and firmly entrenched both in our practice and in our habits of speech. The second alternative will be even less attractive to many, for if we admit the concept of negative causation, if we allow that anyone is ever responsible for something he could have prevented or changed, then we must accept a drastic revision of our views about agency and responsibility.

In this section I have concentrated on showing that the Marxist conception of violence depends upon some theory of negative action. I have attempted to show that the accepted views about the causal efficacy of omissions are inadequate and to provide a consistent theory which not only accounts for the cases covered by the accepted view, but has the additional merit of explaining and underpinning the claims that Marxists and others wish to make about our responsibility for what happens in the world. This theory shows that the claims of the Marxists are not merely empty rhetoric, but are based on a solid and defensible theory of action.

I will conclude by trying very briefly to indicate the extent to which we are, I believe, morally responsible for our negative actions, and so make clearer why the theory of negative action developed in this section forces on us a radical revision of our views about responsibility.

If we take what is possibly the most generally recognized duty, that of refraining from killing, injuring or otherwise inflicting suffering on our fellow men, we see that this duty has both a positive and a negative form. We have the *duty not to injure anyone by performing harmful actions we could avoid.* This is the active voice of the duty which may be expressed in passive voice as the *duty not to injure anyone by failing to perform actions which we could perform and which, if performed, would prevent the injury from occurring.* If we sometimes take comfort from the reflection that no man is an island, we may sometimes also ponder just how, or how far, we are involved in mankind. If we accept the prohibition against killing or injuring other people, the theory of negative actions developed in this section shows us that, whereas we may have thought that whatever we do to allay the sufferings of others is mere charity, we are in most cases bound to help by the strongest of obligations. What possible basis could there be for distinguishing between active and passive forms of the duty not to injure others on moral, or any other grounds, that would make one form of the duty less binding than the other? If we have a duty not to kill others, it would be strange indeed if the duty not to kill by positive actions was somehow stronger than the duty not to kill by negative actions. I do not see how we can escape the conclusion that in whatever sense we are morally responsible for our positive actions, in that same sense we are morally responsible for our negative actions. And the corollary of this is, of course, that whatever considerations mitigate our moral responsibility for particular positive acts, considerations of equal moral force are needed to mitigate our responsibility for negative acts with the same consequences.

The morality to which our equal responsibility for positive and negative acts with the same consequences would commit us is clearly a very demanding one, but I think equally clearly a more moral one than is current. It would oblige us to work actively and, in the present state of the world, unremittingly for the relief and prevention of suffering. Whether or not all of us whose negative actions make us responsible for harm to others should be blamed, I am not sure. One should not perhaps blame people too severely for not rising much above the standards of their time. But whether or not we choose to blame people for all the harmful consequences of their negative actions, does not affect the question of their blameworthiness, and it does not affect their moral responsibility for their actions. We might have to accept for some while a discrepancy between most people's practice and the standards set by this morality.[19] I am sure, however, that we should recognize that this is a morality towards which we ought to work, and one of the ways to do this is to make people aware of what they are *doing.*

The view that to bring about harmful consequences through negative actions is every bit as bad as to do so through positive actions, has of course been challenged, particularly in the debates about the moral difference between killing and letting die. To defend this view against all the attacks that have been or might be leveled against it and to show how it would apply to some of the most controversial or paradoxical cases would require more space than I have here, and is therefore a task for another day.[20] We must now return to the question of violence. If the claims that the Marxists make about violence can be made out, it looks as though those who condemn violence are committed to oppose more than they imagine. I will now try to show that this is so.

III

The Marxists are pointing out that much of the harm that has been thought to be part of the natural hazards of life is not at all natural, and that if we ask why this harm is occurring when it might have been prevented, we will find that it is in fact attributable to the machinations of men. Far from being the result of the operation of gratuitous and impersonal forces, much harm must be seen as the work of assignable agents. Now what is the justification for calling the infliction of such harm 'violence'? Well, what is the objection?

The argument against the Marxist view goes roughly like this: The Marxists are attempting to call any harm caused by men to one another 'violence,' but violence is just one of the ways of doing harm – not all of them. Moreover, the Marxist view would obscure on collapse the traditional distinction between violence and nonviolence. We can, and do, tell the difference between clubbing a man to death and peacefully enjoying a good meal while he starves to death outside, or between burning down a man's house and evicting him. The distinction between violent and nonviolent ways of doing things is clear and useful for evaluating actions, and it allows us to try to understand and explain just what it is about violence that makes it such a fearful thing, so fearful a thing, indeed, that many men have been led to renounce violence absolutely (or at least as much as is convenient). The maintenance of the violent-nonviolent distinction, so far from begging any questions, as Marxists sometimes argue, leaves open all questions as to whether violent means are, for example, better or worse than nonviolent means. The distinction merely allows us to reserve the name of violence for those fearful acts upon which the traditional abhorrence of violence is founded.

This objection to the Marxist view is twofold. The claim is first that the Marxists simply use the concept of violence inappropriately, that they stretch its meaning beyond the breaking point and use it in a way which ignores distinctions that are ordinarily made. The second objection is more subtle. It is that the Marxists wish to claim that the distinction between positive and negative ways of contributing to someone else's injury is a morally insignificant distinction, and that they support the point by applying the word violence to both types of case. The objection, then, is that to apply the word violence to both types of case is self-defeating, for it concedes the moral importance of the distinction, in relying on the rhetorical force the word violence has because it standardly describes a certain kind of positive direct action.

To take the second point first: it is, of course, true that violence gets its rhetorical force from the sorts of cases which spring to mind when the word is mentioned. But just what are the cases from which violence derives its rhetorical potency? They are, surely, the cases which come closest to what we might call the rape, murder, fire, and sword paradigm, the terrible cases of violent infliction of death or serious injury. Of course, sack and pillage are not exactly everyday events, and even murder and grievous bodily harm make up only a small proportion of human violence. Much, perhaps most, of the violence which the anti-Marxists are willing to recognize is of a minor, even trivial nature; e.g., petty assaults, punch-ups outside bars, incidents in football crowds and on the field, and scuffles in demonstrations, breakings of windows and minor damage to property. Clearly the rhetorical force of 'violence' does not derive from these! And the Marxists do not rely on the fact that violence standardly describes certain types of positive direct action. They do rely on violence conjuring up pictures of tragic death, mutilation, or other serious injury. But there seems to be no compelling reason why these should have been inflicted only by positive direct rather than negative or indirect actions. The point is that it would be absurd to suppose that the moral importance of the distinction between acts of violence and acts which do not involve violence consists solely or even principally in their being positive rather than negative. Of course, the Marxists are relying on the rhetorical force the word violence has because of the cases with which it is standardly associated, but what is it about these cases which they rely on? Not, certainly, on the trivial contingency that they involve positive actions, but surely on the vital fact that they involve serious injury attributable to assignable agents.

So, the Marxist conception of violence cannot be regarded as self-defeating. It does not concede the moral importance of a distinction it wishes to demolish when it makes use of the rhetorical force of the word violence, nor does it rely on that distinction. Rather, the Marxists rely on the fact that the word violence derives its rhetorical force from its conjuring up pictures of the fearful injuries inflicted on men by men, and the Marxists claim that in this respect the cases they wish to call violence are isomorphic with those the anti-Marxists recognize.

Now, what of the claim that, whether or not the Marxist conception of violence is self-defeating, it none the less involves a mistake, the simple conceptual error of confusing violent methods of harming people with methods which are not violent? But how, in fact, do we distinguish violent methods from those which are not violent, and acts of violence from acts that are not acts of violence? The first thing to note is that there is an important difference between these two ways of posing the distinction. 'Violent' is an adjective, and a violent act an act appropriately qualified by that adjective. An act of violence, on the other hand, is an act belonging to a particular category or class of actions not coextensive with violent acts.

We can state the distinction between violent acts and acts of violence in this way: Almost any action a human being can perform can be performed violently. Mr. Wilson slicing viciously into a bunker, or Mr. Gladstone denuding the countryside of trees, are both performing violent acts. Even a cup of tea may be stirred violently. For those who dislike the circularity of saying that a violent act is an act performed violently, we can say simply that a violent act is any act appropriately characterized by the following sorts of words taken from the 'Violence' entry in *Roget's Thesaurus*: 'inclemency, vehemence, might, impetuosity, boisterousness, turbulence, bluster, uproar, riot, row, rumpus, fury, brute force, outrage, shock, explosion. ...' The considerations which lead us to classify acts as acts of violence are clearly of a different sort. When trying, for example, to assess the prevalence and the causes of violence in human affairs we are clearly not concerned with a well-hit golf ball; we might say that what concerns us here is what is left when we subtract a violent act from an act of violence. It is important to note that the words 'violent' and 'violence' and the phrases 'act of violence' and 'violent act' are often used indiscriminately between the two senses I have distinguished. In each case, the context must make clear whether the descriptive or classificatory sense of the term is intended.

What principles then determine the classification of acts as acts of violence for those who regard the Marxist view as conceptually confused?

To define with any sort of clarity the concept of violence upon which the anti-Marxists rely is no easy matter. Clearly they have in mind the rape, murder, fire and sword paradigm which involves the sudden forceful, and perhaps unexpected, infliction of painful physical injury upon an unwilling victim. Nowadays terrorists who machine-gun or bomb their victims are the classic case. But if the terrorists poison the water supply or gas their victims while they sleep, or brick them up in their houses to die of starvation or suffocation, we would not, I think, regard it as mistaken or confused if people continued to speak of 'terrorist violence.' And the terrorists could hardly claim to have renounced violence if they adopted such methods. If it is not inapposite to talk of violence in these cases, the door is already open to the Marxists.

We were told recently that children in Belfast adopt the following tactic against British soldiers.[21] Here is one of the children describing the method: 'That's the street right? These are the lamp-posts and that's the Army Land-Rover coming up the street. You tie your cheese-wire between two of the lamp-posts about six feet up. There's always a soldier standing on the back of the jeep; even with the search lights he can't see the wire in the dark. It's just at the right height to catch his throat.' No violent act on the part of the child, but clearly an act of violence. So long as such tactics are employed no one would call Belfast a violence-free city.

If a man is stabbed to death, we do not doubt that he has been the victim of a violent assault. Would we have to alter our judgment if we later learn that the stiletto slid between his ribs as easily as you please? This stiletto point is the thin end of the wedge. For if we are interested in the question of the prevalence of violence in human affairs, or in comparing the scale of violence in different societies, in different eras, or in assessing the violence of opposing factions, it would be absurd to ignore or exclude methods men find of killing or injuring their fellows that do not happen to involve vigorous direct actions.

If, for example, instead of bombs and guns, poison, nerve gas, and exposure to radiation became standard ways of eliminating our fellow men, we would not, I think, be inclined to claim that men had become less violent in their dealings with each other even though such methods do not involve physical assault or violent actions of any kind. If we are interested in the question of whether a particular society does or does not use violence as a method of settling differences or resolving disputes, we would certainly not ignore the fact that the society eliminated an opposition group or an unpopular minority by herding them into ghettos where they were left to die of starvation or disease. While such things go on, the claim that mankind is becoming less violent will be viewed with skepticism.

The questions that interest us about violence – questions about its prevalence, its causes, its prevention, questions about when it should be used and why, about whether or not it has been used in particular cases, whether it is on the increase, whether some societies or periods are or were more violent than others – would be trivial questions if all that they are about is whether or not actions of a particular description are used. Trivial also because much of our interest in these questions stems from our concern to solve the problem of violence, to minimize its use or even remove it entirely from human affairs, and this we might succeed in doing and yet leave intact all the features of the problem of violence that make a solution desirable. Death, injury and suffering might be just as common as before, only the characteristic complex of actions by which they are inflicted would have changed.

Surely our interest in all these questions about violence reflects a concern with the phenomenon of men inflicting injury, suffering, or death on one another? We are not so much interested in the particular methods men use to do this, or in the look, the physical character of the actions they use. We are interested in violence because it is a particular kind of activity – the activity in which men cause each other injury and suffering.

The point of contention between the Marxists and those who object to their conception of violence concerns what feature is constitutive of the concept. The Marxists claim that violence is the phenomenon of men inflicting injury on one another. The anti-Marxists might concede that this is part of the concept, but would insist that it is a necessary condition that those injuries be inflicted by vigorous, direct action. The question then arises as to whether the Marxists and their opponents are pointing to different forms of the same activity or to different activities. Are they using different conceptions of the same concept or different concepts? This question forces us to answer the question with which we started: what is the justification for calling the infliction of harm by negative actions 'violence'?

We have seen that a distinction must be made in our use of the terms violent and violence between what I have called the purely descriptive use of violence and its classificatory sense. I have shown that the classificatory sense of violence cannot be made parasitic on the descriptive sense without trivializing all the questions that most interest us. The justification for calling the infliction of harm by negative actions 'violence' is that when we classify an act as an act of violence we are saying that it is part of a single phenomenon, that all men who use violence are involved, in some sense, in the same activity. If we ask what this activity is, the answer that forces itself upon us is that it must be the infliction of injury or suffering upon others. It is this that makes the Marxist conception of violence one conception of the same concept which captures the rape, murder, fire, and sword paradigm.

For Thomas Hobbes, the first and fundamental reason for establishing the state was to protect men from the disasters of the war of every man against every man. Man's natural propensity to violence caused the worst features of this war, which were 'continual fear and danger of violent death, and the life of man solitary, poor, nasty, brutish and short.'[22] The Marxists did not need to create a fictional state of nature to see men in this condition, they just looked around. At the sight of men causing others to lead lives in fear and danger, poor, nasty, brutish and short, the Marxists naturally spoke of violence, for they were faced with an activity of essentially the same kind as that which Hobbes most feared. For Hobbes the remedy was the social contract; for the Marxists, the social revolution.

I have been concerned in this section to defend a particular use of a particular word against the charge that it is conceptually confused, self-defeating and likely to lead to ambiguity and equivocation. Defense, I think, must be the best form of attack, for it shows a way to turn the tables on this form of criticism and argue that it, in turn, is based on a confusion – that of failing to distinguish acts of violence and violent acts. One would then say that it is this confusion that has tempted a number of philosophers to criticize certain definitions of violence on the grounds that they class actions as acts of violence which do not involve violent acts.

Amidst all this confusion it would be very easy to miss the point, which is, surely, that the differences between the followers of what I have called the Marxist conception of violence and their critics are not due to confusion of any kind. The Marxists are not unaware of the many different sorts of harm that human beings can suffer, nor are their critics necessarily ignorant of the fact that vigorous direct action is not a sufficient condition of violence.

The dispute between Marxists and their opponents over the definition of violence is not to be explained by reference to the conceptual confusion of the protagonists.

The extreme intractability of the controversy over this definition is, of course, in part the result of the unwillingness of the various parties to renounce the right to use one of the most powerful terms of political rhetoric. But there are other things at stake. When we remember that violence is commonly thought of as a problem of world proportions requiring urgent solution, we uncover another motive for defining violence in a particular way. For to define violence is, in a sense, to determine the scope of this problem. In disputes over which features are constitutive of the concept of violence both political and philosophical motives play a part, and it may be that there is no final answer, no definitive analysis. Different features of the phenomenon of violence will loom larger as the form of the phenomenon varies, or as the political perspective of the theorists changes. Where muggings and violent demonstrations are the fear and the theorists speak for the fearful, vigorous direct actions will seem the most important features of violence. Where the streets are quiet, but people who could be saved are left to die of neglect or cold or hunger, or are crippled or killed by their living or working conditions, a different group of people may surfer, and other theorists may see their suffering as attributable to human agency, and so class it as part of man's violence to man.

If I am right that when we talk of violence we are not simply interested in the means whereby particular harm is inflicted, but rather in some characteristic activity or phenomenon, then there may be different distinctive features which are the hallmark of this activity, and reasonable men may differ as to what those features are. In this paper I have shown that the Marxist conception of violence isolates a feature of violence which, on any account must be central, and which is shared by the paradigm cases. I have argued that this conception in fact captures the activity which is constitutive of the concept of violence. About this, of course, there may be argument, but I believe that I have said enough to establish the Marxist conception of violence, at the very least, as one coherent conception of violence.

Notes

I am greatly indebted to Ronald Dworkin with whom I have discussed most of the topics treated in this essay. Thanks are also due to Alan Ryan and to the Editors of *Philosophy & Public Affairs* for helpful comments.

1. Plutarch, *Life of Mark Antony*, trans. Ian Scott-Kilvert (Harmondsworth, 1965), p. 287.
2. Quoted in Norman Cohn, *The Pursuit of the Millennium* (London, 1957; repr. 1970), p. 202.

3. Frederick Engels, *The Condition of the Working Class in England*, trans. and ed. Henderson and Chaloner (Oxford, 1958), p. 108.
4. Christopher Caudwell, *Studies in a Dying Culture* (London, 1938), p. 102.
5. *Ibid.*, p. 116.
6. Harold Orlans, 'An American Death Camp,' in Rosenberg, Gerver, and Howton, eds., *Mass Society in Crisis: Social Problems and Social Pathology* (New York, 1964).
7. Barrington Moore, Jr., *The Social Origins of Dictatorship and Democracy* (Boston, 1966; repr. 1969), p. 103.
8. Karl Marx, *Capital*, 1, ed. Engels, trans. Moore and Aveling (London, 1887; repr. 1957). chap. xv, sec. 8.c., pp. 466ff.
9. *Ibid.*, p. 480.
10. Jeremy Bentham, *Introduction to the Principles of Morals and Legislation*, ed. Harrison (Oxford 1947; repr. 1967), chap. viii, par. 8.
11. Eric D'Arcy, *Human Acts* (Oxford, 1963), pp. 47–49, 55.
12. *Ibid.*, p. 49.
13. *Ibid.*, p. 50.
14. John Casey, 'Actions and Consequences,' in *Morality and Moral Reasoning*, ed. John Casey (London, 1971), p. 180.
15. *Ibid.*, p. 187.
16. H. L. A. Hart and A. M. Honoré, *Causation in the Law* (Oxford, 1959), pp. 34–35, 37.
17. This is not perhaps the best example since it did not become clear that vaccination against smallpox was effective until the practice had become reasonably widespread. But with the modern practice of clinical trials we can easily imagine cases in which a completely new method of preventing or curing disease might be developed and proved effective before their use was at all general, let alone a second nature.
18. H. L. A. Hart, 'Postscript: Responsibility and Punishment,' in *Punishment and Responsibility* (Oxford, 1968), pp. 212–230.
19. This way of dealing charitably with the problem of blame I owe to Jonathan Glover.
20. My paper 'The Survival Lottery,' shortly to appear in *Philosophy*, argues for this view by examining in detail one such case.
21. Morris Fraser, 'Children of Violence,' *Sunday Times Weekly Review*, 29 April 1973, p. 33.
22. Thomas Hobbes, *Leviathan*, pt. 1, chap. 13.

COMMENTARY ON HARRIS

John Harris, who is best known for his work in medical and bioethics,[1] and in particular for defending the principle of consequentialism on all issues of applied ethics, worked on the concepts of violence and responsibility throughout the 1970s. This article, which was first published in 1974, forms the backbone of his book *Violence and Responsibility*.[2]

A conception of violence is 'Marxist' in the sense that any harm caused by indifference and neglect is as much a part of human violence as the violent acts of revolutionaries. Harris quotes Friedrich Engels, who wrote in *The Condition of the Working Class in England*: 'murder has also been committed if society places hundreds of workers in such a position that they inevitably come to premature and unnatural ends. Their death is as violent as if they had been stabbed or shot.'[3] In this article, Harris argues that we are causally responsible for harm that could have been prevented, and that this harm may properly be regarded as a form of violence.

Omissions which have consequences are referred to as Negative Actions. Harris suggests the following definition of Negative Action: 'A's failure to do X with the result of Y will make the bringing about of Y a negative action of A's, only where A's doing X would have prevented Y and A knew or ought reasonably to have known this, and where A could have done X and knew, or ought reasonably to have known, this.'

But Harris does more than provide us with a technical definition of Negative Actions; he wants to argue that to bring about harmful consequences through negative actions is every bit as bad as to do so through positive actions. Violence can be the result of either positive or negative actions; furthermore, from a moral point of view there is no difference between violence that results from positive action and violence that results from negative action.[4]

In light of what he says about violence and Negative Action, in his book *Violence and Responsibility*, Harris puts forward the following definition of violence: 'an act of violence occurs when injury or suffering is inflicted upon a person or persons by an agent who knows (or ought reasonably to have known), that his actions would result in the harm in question' (1980: 19). In this definition there is no mention of intentionality but only of foreseeable consequences, which, as we have seen, can be caused by either positive or negative actions.

Notes and further reading

1. See his *The Value of Life: Introduction to Medical Ethics*, London: Routledge, 1985; *Bioethics*, Oxford: Oxford University Press, 2001; *On Cloning*, London: Routledge, 2004.

2. John Harris, *Violence and Responsibility*, London: Routledge, 1980.
3. F. Engles, *Conditions of the Working Class in England*, Oxford: Oxford University Press, 1999.
4. For a similar view on acts and omissions, see T. Honderich, *Violence for Equality*, London: Routledge, 1989; and Jonathan Glover, *Causing Death and Saving Lives*, Harmondsworth: Penguin, 1977.

11
On Justifying Violence
Kai Nielsen

I discuss the justification of political violence even within democracies. I define 'violence' and indicate how its evaluative force sometimes has conceptually distorting effects. Though acts of violence are at least prima facie wrong, circumstances can arise where, even in democracies, some of them are morally justified. To establish this, three paradigm cases of non-revolutionary political violence are examined. The question is then discussed whether revolutionary violence is ever justified as a means of establishing or promoting human freedom and happiness. I state the conditions which must be satisfied for such violence to be justified and argue that sometimes these conditions have been satisfied. Finally I argue that discussions of violence are frequently confused by ideological mystification and attempt to go some way towards revealing the sources of that mystification.

Die rächende Hand des Terroristen kann die Desorganisation und Demoralisation des Absolutismus hie und da beschleunigen. Den Absolutismus stürzen und die Freiheit verwirklichen kann – mit dem Terror oder ohne den Terror – nur der Massenarm der revolutionären Arbeiterklasse ...

Rosa Luxemburg, 1905

I

I shall say more about the justification of violence than about its meaning. As a reading of the literature should drive home, there are indeed puzzles about its meaning and about the meaning of related terms such as force and coercion.[1] About this I shall say something which is hopefully reasonable but still tolerably superficial. But I shall not dwell on these matters for to do so would, I believe, be a distraction deflecting our attention from what

I take to be the central issue about violence, namely a hard-nosed consideration of when, if ever, violence is justified. We, without conceptual analysis, understand the concept 'violence' well enough to come to grips with that question.

I shall also be concerned exclusively with political violence and the violence closely associated with it and I shall place my discussion about the justification of violence in the context of arguing about a socialist revolution and about counter-revolutionary activity against socialism. I do this both because of its intrinsic interest and because in such a live context general questions about how and under what circumstances violence might be justified become clearer.

I am tolerably confident that in some deep way many will disagree with what I am going to say. Indeed, some may even think that I am being partisan. I shall face that issue directly at the end of this essay when I discuss the role ideology plays here. What I want initially to plead is that when you come across things that you are inclined to disagree with, and perhaps will not even want to hear, you try not to dismiss these considerations from your minds immediately, but ask yourselves these two quite distinct questions: first, if I have got the facts roughly right, shouldn't I draw the moral conclusions I in fact do draw? And then ask yourselves, as well, popular opinion to the contrary notwithstanding, have I not got the facts roughly right? The first question is perhaps easier to answer, for it can be answered by reflecting carefully on how my arguments hang together and on your own considered moral responses. I believe that the second question can hardly be answered in the course of a day or a week but only after prolonged study. Much of this study will be historical, sociological, and economic. The understanding we need here requires more than moral sensitivity, an understanding of the functions of moral concepts and what it is to take the moral point of view. I do not mean by such a remark arrogantly to insinuate a superior 'know it all' posture. We all, and I feel this acutely myself, suffer from a kind of professional deformation here. But I do assert that to resolve with any firmness the fundamental moral questions I raise we need something of this knowledge. I do not say that meta-ethical expertise counts for nothing here, but I do think that it does not carry us very far in such contexts.[2] A philosopher complacent about his society and ignorant of such work will not, even if he exercises clearly the standard philosophical expertise, help us very much when we wrestle with such questions.[3]

II

Mass-media talk of the role of terrorism and violence generally in human affairs tends to be emotional talk with a high level of ideological distortion. I shall try to clear the air here and establish that we cannot, unless we can

make the case for pacifism, categorically rule out in all circumstances its justifiable use even in what are, formally and procedurally speaking, democracies.
However, we must keep in mind that defending the thesis that sometimes
the employment of violence is justified is not at all the same as defending
terrorism, for terrorism is a particular tactic in the employment of violence
to achieve political ends. Moreover, socialist revolutionaries, as we shall see,
have not generally regarded it as a good tactic. Yet, as Rosa Luxemburg – who
wrote sanely and perceptively on this subject – realized, terrorism is a minor
tactical weapon for revolutionary socialists, which *sometimes* may rightly be
employed to achieve the humane ends of socialism but typically is counter-
productive and often very harmful to a revolutionary movement. When and
where it should be employed is a tactical question which must be decided –
though not without some general guidelines (rules of thumb) – on a case-
by-case basis. Soberly it should be viewed like the choice of weapons in a
war. It cannot reasonably be ruled out as something to which only morally
insane beasts or fanatical madmen would resort. In the cruel and oppressive
world in which we find ourselves, it, as various other forms of violence, can
find morally justifiable employments, though, typically, but not always, its
use is a sign of weakness and desperation in a revolutionary movement and
thus, in most contexts, but not all, it is to be rejected at least on prudential
grounds.

It should hardly be necessary to add that a humane person, who understands what it is to take the moral point of view, will deplore violence, but –
unless he thinks that pacifism can be successfully defended – he will recognize that *sometimes* the use of violence is a *necessary* means to a morally
worthwhile end and that moral persons, while hating violence in itself,
must, under these circumstances, steel themselves to its employment. Such
morally committed human beings will, of course, differ as to when those
occasions will occur and will often differ over what constitutes a morally
worthwhile end.

I shall *assume* here that pacifism is not a rationally defensible moral position and that the achievement of a truly socialist society, consisting in a
genuine workers' democracy with full workers' control of the means of production and the conditions of their lives, is a desirable state of affairs, a
morally worthwhile end to achieve.[4] These assumptions are, of course, chal-
lengeable but on one occasion we cannot argue about everything. Given
these assumptions, I shall first, after some preliminary clarifications, attempt
to show under what conditions violence, even in a democracy, is justified,
and then I shall, with the minor adjustments necessary, apply this analysis
specifically to the problem of terrorism. I shall return in the latter sections
to what I take to be a series of plausible objections to my account and I shall
end by a discussion of what I take to be the central ideological mystifications
that bedevil our talk of violence.

III

Beginning at the beginning let us contrast 'violence', 'force', and 'coercion'. The OED characterizes them as follows:

1. 'Violence':   The exercise of physical force so as to inflict injury on or damage to persons or property. (However, the OED to the contrary notwithstanding, violence can also take psychological forms as when someone so tortures one mentally as to drive one mad.)
2. 'Force':   To exert physical or psychological power or coercion upon one to act in some determinate way.
3. 'Coercion':   Government by force; the employment of force to suppress political disaffection.

It is often said that it is important to distinguish between force and violence. And it is indeed true that 'violence' and 'force' are often not substitutable terms. They have different referents and a different sense. The OED to the contrary notwithstanding, violence is not just physical or psychological force (direct or indirect), but is, given its ordinary use, *by definition* illegal or unjustified force and indeed it is taken in many but not all contexts to be the unauthorized or the illegitimate use of force to effect decisions against the will of others. When 'violence' is so used, violence becomes immoral by definition. I think our language tricks us here and inclines us to view the world in an ideologically distorted manner. We should recognize that 'violence' generally has a negative emotive force. Indeed, it often functions normatively. To use it with respect to an action is to give to understand – as in 'acts of violence' or 'a violent era' – that the acts or periods in question are being disparaged or disapproved of. In the following sample utterances, we have standard employments of 'violence' and if 'force' were substituted for 'violence' in these utterances, there would be a change both in the emotive force and in the meaning of the utterances in question. To see that this is so, test out the substitution on (a), (b) and (c) below.

(a) Bend every effort to prevent violence.
(b) Do not allow well-considered goals to be obliterated by the passion of irrationality and violence.
(c) There have been acts of violence against the administration.

Where 'force' is substituted for 'violence' in the above sample sentences there is a change in emotive force and a change in meaning. Moreover, with such substitutions, (a), (b) and (c) would become to a certain extent conceptually problematic; that is to say, they would be rather indeterminate in meaning; with such substitutions the above utterances will become deviant utterances. Native speakers would balk at them, and in many contexts be in some perplexity about what was being said.

In a similar vein, consider the fact that 'legal coercion' is quite unproblematic while 'legal violence' is not, though where the law was being used in a certain very oppressive and unfairly discriminatory way, we could come quite naturally to speak in that way. Coercion, like force, is something which is in a whole range of standard circumstances morally justified, but the very meaning of 'violence' – 'something which extremists do' – is such that there is a strong presumption that an act of violence is wrong. At least it is, like breaking a promise or lying, something which, everything else being equal, ought not to be done. And while there are contexts in which 'violence' is used in a commendatory way, it is not the case that we – except in rather unusual circumstances – employ 'violence' in morally neutral descriptions.

Let us come at our distinction between 'force' and 'violence' in a somewhat different way. Anarchists apart, everyone agrees that in certain circumstances a state has not only *de facto* authority (essentially power) but also *de jure* (legitimate) authority to coerce one's behaviour, to force one to comply with its laws. That is to say, states not only have a commanding position by virtue of their power and their ability to mould social opinion to get people within their territories to accept their authoritative claims – their laws, demands, and regulations – but they have – it is also generally believed – the *right* to command and to be obeyed. The claim to have a right to command and to be obeyed is the claim to have legitimate authority.

Where (if ever) a state uses *legitimate* authority and forces one to act in the ways prescribed by that authority, this use of force is plainly not violence. And the citizens of that state, committed to its fundamental principles, have a prima facie obligation to obey the laws of that state. I say 'prima facie obligation', for no citizen has an absolute obligation to obey any law.[5] There may arise circumstances about particular laws or about the application of certain laws in certain circumstances in which obeying them would violate one's conscience or in which in some other way it would be plainly a grave mistake to obey the law. In such circumstances one's prima facie obligation – which is an *ever-present* but still *conditional* obligation – is overridden by more stringent moral considerations. But one, at least in most circumstances, does have a prima facie obligation to obey the laws of the state if that state has established its *legitimate* as well as its *de facto* authority.

A very central question in political philosophy – a question which I shall not try to answer here – is when, if ever, does a state have legitimate authority over us? *Assuming* that anarchism is mistaken (an assumption which should not be easily made), and assuming, as well, that in certain favoured circumstances a state has, generally speaking, *legitimate* authority over us, the question then becomes when, under what circumstances and with what limitations, does it have the right to exercise such authority? That is to say, when does it have the *right* to force our compliance and when has it exceeded its legitimate authority?

When it has exceeded its legitimate authority and still exercises force on people, then, where that force causes or threatens grave harm, the force is a form of violence. Thus, there is a legitimate point in speaking, as Marcuse does, of 'institutionalized violence' to characterize the use of state force in such circumstances. And here this violence, though it uses the coercive arm of the state, is also something to be disparaged and to be called 'illegitimate'. However, it is reasonable to maintain, as John Rawls and Marshall Cohen have, that as citizens of a constitutional democracy, we have a duty to support constitutional arrangements on which others in our society have relied 'so long as it is reasonable to believe that these arrangements are intended to implement, and are capable of implementing, the principles of freedom and justice'.[6] But when the state takes measures which repress the principles of freedom and social justice it is engaging in institutional violence and we have no obligation to follow such dictates, though prudence may require that we accept for the time being at least certain of its arrangements.

Our inspection of the very connotation of the term 'violence' indicates that 'acts of violence' are acts which are usually taken by the people who *so label them* as not only illegal acts but also as morally unjustified acts; but it does not follow that under *all circumstances* 'acts of violence' – even under that description – are unjustified. Surely they are prima facie unjustified, for to inflict harm or injury upon persons or their property is always something which needs a careful rational justification or else it is plainly wrong. For to be injured or harmed is plainly to have something done to one which is bad. However, what is prima facie wrong need not be something which is wrong everything considered. We need to consider the circumstances in which such acts would not be acts which are acts which are, everything considered, wrong.

There are two diverse types of circumstances in which questions concerning the justification of violence need discussing. We need to discuss (1) revolutionary violence – the violence thought necessary to overthrow the state and to bring into being a new and better or at least a putatively better social order – and (2) violence within a state when revolution is not an end at least in the foreseeable future, but violence is only being used as a key instrument of social change within a social system which as a whole is accepted as legitimate or at least as established and with a *de facto* authority. It is often argued that in the latter type of circumstance, particularly when the authority of the state is taken to be legitimate, a resort to violence is never justified, when the state in question is a democracy.

Let us first try to ascertain whether this is so. Consider first a situation in which a democratic state is engaging in institutionalized violence. Suppose, for example, there is heightened trouble in the Black community. It takes the form of increased rioting in the Black ghettoes, and suppose further that it is not adequately contained within the ghettoes, but that sporadic rioting, not involving killing but some destruction of property, breaks out into White middle-class America. Suppose further that there are renewed, ever more vigorous cries for 'law and order' until finally a jittery, reactionary but still (in the conventional sense) 'democratically elected' government begins systematically to invade the Black ghettoes and haul off Blacks in large numbers to concentration camps (more mildly 'detention centres') for long periods of incarceration ('preventative detention') without attempting to distinguish the guilty from the innocent. Would not Black people and their allies plainly be justified in resorting to violence to resist being so detained in such circumstances if: (a) they had good reason to believe that their violent resistance might be effective, and (b) they had good reason to believe that their counter-violence would not cause more injury and suffering all round than would simple submission or non-violent resistance to the violence directed against them by the state?

It might be replied that even in such appalling circumstances the Blacks should non-violently resist and fight back only through the courts, through demonstrations, through civil disobedience and the like. They should not meet this institutionalized violence with violence. Perhaps initially they should do something like that, but if the counter-violence continues and the camps begin to fill up without the above non-violent efforts producing any effective countervailing forces then the employment of violence against these repressive forces is morally justified if the conditions described at the end of the previous paragraph obtain.

In such circumstances there would be nothing unfair or unjust about violently resisting such detention. Violence and not just force has been instituted against the Blacks – the state having exceeded its legitimate authority – and the Blacks are not behaving unfairly or immorally in resisting an abuse of governmental authority – democracy or no democracy. In deliberation about whether to counter the institutional violence directed against them, the Blacks and their allies should make tough and careful utilitarian calculations, as difficult as they are to make. They need, to utilize such calculations, to try to ascertain as accurately as they can, both their chances of effectively resisting and the comparative amounts of suffering involved for them and for others from resistance as distinct from submission or passive resistance. If in resisting police seizure some police are likely to be injured or even killed, and if this means massive retaliations in the form of the police gunning down large groups of Blacks, and if the concentration camps are not modelled on Auschwitz, but on American or Canadian war-time camps for Japanese North Americans, it would seem to be better to submit and to live to fight another day. However, if instead the likelihood was that even in submitting, extensive brutalization and indeed death for many, if not all, would be their lot, then violent resistance against such a 'final solution' is in order if that is the most effective way to lessen the chance of seizure. Indeed, that is a move of desperation, but then the situation is itself a desperate one. What people faced with such morally obscene government behaviour should actually do is plainly something that cannot be rationally resolved by conceptual analysis. What we need to do here is to go carefully case by case. A clear understanding of what in each situation are the empirical facts is of central importance here. But what is evident – to put it minimally – is that there is no principled reason in such circumstances why even in a democracy counter-violence in response to institutionalized violence cannot be justified. (To say 'If such basic liberties are being so denied we no longer have a democracy' is to make 'democracy' very much an honorific term, for there still under such circumstances could be majority rule and some constitutional legalistic claims that liberties, in such an emergency, given the clear and present danger, were not being unjustly restricted. I shall return to this problem in my next section.)

Let us turn to a somewhat more complicated situation. Suppose a democratic superpower is waging a genocidal war of imperialist aggression against a small underdeveloped nation. Suppose this superpower has invaded them without even declaring war; suppose further it pursues a scorched earth policy destroying the land with repeated herbicidal doses, destroys the livestock, pollutes the rivers (killing the fish), and then napalms the people of this country, civilian and military alike. Suppose within the borders of the superpower repeated protests and civil disobedience have no effect on the policies of this superpower. It goes right on rolling along with its genocide and imperialist aggression. Suppose, further, in such a situation some conscientious and aroused citizens – but still non-revolutionary citizens – of this superpower turn to acts of violence aimed in some small measure at disrupting and thus weakening this institutionalized violence. Specifically, suppose they burn down draft offices and officers' training offices and thereby in some small way hamper the power's war effort. It does not at all seem evident to me (to put it conservatively) that they have done what in such circumstance they ought not to do, provided that the circumstances are as I have described them and that the effects of their actions do hold some reasonable promise of hampering the war effort. (Even if their actions were mainly symbolic and in reality did little to slow down the violent juggernaut, they might still reasonably be thought to be admirable provided they had a clear moral intent and did not in effect enhance the power of the juggernaut.)

Clearly there is nothing unprincipled about the resort to such violence in such a circumstance. Again the centrally relevant considerations would be for the most part, but not necessarily decisively or exclusively, utilitarian ones. We would need in the particular circumstances to weigh carefully what would be the probable consequences of resorting to such violence. If, on the one hand, only more suffering all round would result, then resort to such violence is wrong; if, on the other hand, such acts of violence are likely to lessen the sum total of human suffering and not put an unfair burden on some already cruelly exploited people, then the violence is justified.[7]

The agonizing and frightening thing is that in many situations it is exceedingly difficult even to make an educated guess concerning the probable consequences of such actions.[8] But this is not always the case, and again it is evident that there is no principled reason why a committed democrat in a state with a democratically elected government might not be justified in certain circumstances in engaging in violence even though no violence had been directed against him or his fellow citizens.

Let me now turn to a less extreme situation as my third and last example. Suppose a small, impoverished, ill-educated ethnic minority in some democratic society has its members treated as second-class citizens. They are grossly discriminated against in educational opportunities and over jobs; they are segregated in specific and undesirable parts of the country; they are not allowed to marry people from other ethnic groups or to mix socially with these other groups. Their living conditions are such that their very life expectancy is considerably lower than that of other citizens in that democracy. For years they have pleaded and argued their case but to no avail; moreover, working through the courts has always been a dead-end, and their desperate and despairing turn to non-violent civil disobedience has been tolerated – as the powerful and arrogant can tolerate it – but still utterly ignored. It isn't that such demonstrations have been met with violence; they have simply been non-violently contained and then effectively ignored. And finally suppose that this small, weak, desperately impoverished minority has no effective way of emigrating; they cannot in reality exercise the choice of 'Love it or leave it'. In such a circumstance is it at all evident that they should not act violently in an attempt to attain what are in effect their human rights?

It is again evident that there is no principled reason why it should not be true that certain acts of violence on their part are justified. The strongest reasons for their not so acting are the prudential ones that since they are so weak and their oppressors are so indifferent to their welfare and dignity, it makes it the case that the chance of their gaining anything by violent action is rather minimal. But again the considerations here are pragmatic and utilitarian. If there were good reason to think that their human rights might be secured and to think that human welfare – a justly distributed human happiness, the satisfaction of needs and the avoidance of suffering – would be enhanced by their acts of violence, then they would be justified in so acting. (Perhaps they would be justified in so acting just to secure their human rights, but, if the latter condition obtained as well, it would be even more evident that their actions were justified.)

From what we have done so far, we can draw the following conclusions. Though violence is something which is *prima facie* to be avoided, there are no adequate grounds for believing that a conscientious citizen committed to democracy and living in a democratic society must always, no matter what the situation in that society, commit him- or herself to non-violent methods.

IV

There are several quite perfectly natural objections to make at this juncture.

1. It might be expected that where there actually are such situations as those characterized in my examples we would not be living in a democracy, but either in a tyranny or, as in the last example, in something approximating a tyranny or at least an unbenevolent despotism. However, if we take anything like a descriptive view of democracy, and if we consider all the forms of democracy that C. B. Macpherson describes in *The Real World of Democracy*, or even the varieties he counts under 'liberal democracy', it is not so evident that societies with the features I characterized would not count as 'democracies'. Democracies in bad shape no doubt, but still democracies.[9]

'Democracy' like 'science' is frequently an honorific label, and where it is, we will be inclined to say – at the same time showing that we are in effect utilizing a *persuasive* definition of 'democracy' – that such societies surely would not be *real* democracies. But here democracies which are not 'real democracies' are still democracies. We are saying in effect, in utilizing such a manner of speaking, that those democracies, which we refuse to call 'real democracies', lack certain features that we regard as very precious and as crucial in a democracy. But 'democracy' is also a descriptive, open-textured term with a range of different applications. And within the range of such standard applications societies with features such as I have described would be properly called 'democracies'. Finally, it is a mute point whether or not some industrial democracies of the recent past or the present actually have at least most of these features.

2. It is also natural to object that while I may have shown that it *could* be the case – if certain conditions were to obtain and certain consequences to follow – that, even in a democracy, violence would be justified, still, *as a matter of fact, the consequences* of acting violently in such situations would not be such as to justify violence of any sort. That is to say, it is *conceivable* that such violence would be justified but in reality it never is justified.

To this it needs in turn to be replied, that once this much is admitted, there can no longer be any general *principled* moral objection to all acts of violence in a democracy. Rather, if the above claim about violence in fact never being justified is true, it only establishes the very weak conclusion that, even in those situations in which one would be tempted to resort to violence, *in fact* it so turns out that violence would be counter-productive. But the facts – plain empirical facts – could well have turned out to be otherwise. And indeed in our complex changing world it might have turned out to be otherwise. There is no deep moral impediment to such violence. What we should or should not do rests on our very fallible estimates of the probable results of various alternative courses of action.

It is surely the case that if violence becomes a frequent thing, something threatened or engaged in routinely, it would have the terrible consequence of undermining human liberty and even a minimal kind of security. In a genuinely democratic community (if there are any such yet), resort to violence can only be justified in extreme situations and can never be justified as something we should do as a matter of course. It may be the case that violence is as American as cherry pie and as pervasive in America as racism, but this is hardly something to make even more extreme by the casual use of violence. Such a resort to violence would, among other things, clearly be counter-productive.

However, in arguing that violence – including acts of terror – may sometimes be justified, it would not be reasonable to take the position Sidney Hook arbitrarily sets up as a strawman and then proceeds – predictably enough – to demolish, namely that 'violence and the threat of violence are always effective in preparing the minds of men for change'.[10] That is indeed not a reasonable position, but it does not at all follow from this, as Hook gives to understand, that it is never the case in democracies, and for democrats, that violence is justified. It does not even – as Hook suggests – follow from his above argument, nor is it in any other way justified by his argument, that resort to violence in a democracy is always or almost always counter-productive. Pointing out, as Hook does, that there have been many instances in which significant social changes have been gained without violence, the threat of violence, or even the fear of violence, is (by contrast) to make a relevant comment, but it does little to establish that in a democracy violence is never, or even hardly ever, justified, either prudentially or morally. That would be like trying to establish that one was never justified in taking radiation treatment as a cure for cancer by pointing out that people have been cured of cancer by less drastic methods of treatment. That would only be a good argument if there were good reasons to believe that the kind of cancers that people have are all of a type. If Hook could show that there were significant similarities between the types of cases where significant social changes occurred within a reasonable length of time without resort to violence or the threat of violence and my above cases and the many other at least putatively justified cases that could be mentioned where violence occurred, then his argument would be a strong one. But he has done nothing of the kind. What Hook needs to do is to show us that in situations – such as the ones I described – where violence appears at least to be required or appears at least to be the best alternative (the lesser evil), appearances are deceiving and in reality its employment is always very likely to be counter-productive.

We need not be hypothetical in our cases here. Among the bourgeois democracies Sweden is one of the most stable arid probably the most thoroughly liberal and progressive; yet in 1931 a key bit of labour violence was critical in its progressive political evolution. There was an extended strike in portions of Sweden's lumber industry when workers were actually threatened with a wage cut. Finally, some factory owners brought in strike breakers. In a factory at Aladen, where this strike-breaking was going on, the workers attacked the strike breakers in the factory and drove them out. No guns or weapons were used. The factory owners brought in more strike breakers and persuaded the government to send troops to protect them. The workers then marched peacefully to the factory where the troops were on guard. The troops opened fire on the demonstrating workers. Many innocent people were killed and this triggered a general strike across Sweden and provoked widespread indignation against the business-dominated conservative government. The conservative government fell and Sweden's social democracy began.

Perhaps such a progressive achievement would have come about anyway without the violence but it is not at all evident that it would have, and very likely it would have been slower. Here violence furthered human welfare and social justice generally, though I do not think that we should go so far as to claim it was indispensable to its achievement. But it did crack a reactionary government supporting rigid class divisions. Hook tells us that violence breeds violence and starts an endless cycle of violence. But here in a crucial case nothing like this obtained and freedom, as Hook also alleges, was not imperilled but was extended and enhanced, and orderly and democratic procedures remained fully exemplified in Swedish life.

Chronic and pervasive violence is, of course, destructive of social stability and the fabric of confidence and trust essential for civilized society. But it is at least reasonable to believe that this is not the result of the kind of in-the-extreme-case-utilization of violence of the committed democrat in an imperfectly democratic society. The above example of violence in Sweden serves to support my point.

If, by contrast, things had so deteriorated that reasonable, properly informed people found it necessary or even strongly tempting to engage repeatedly in violence, the society in question would have already so badly crumbled – so rent its social fabric – that talk of protecting social stability and orderly procedure would in effect come to a recommendation to support a rotten regime. Violence is not something that sane men will lightly engage in, particularly when it is directed against the government. Things must be in a very bad way indeed for reasonable people seriously to consider such acts. They must grow out of a desperation about the quality of life in such a society. Social tranquillity and stability have already fled. In a situation which has grown so repressive it is utterly mistaken to argue, as Hook does, that we must resist violence in order to promote stability and social harmony. It is more likely in such a chaotic and repressive situation that only after the social order has been transformed by a social revolution building on violence, will social stability and a civilized life be part of that society. If the fight to radically transform the power structures in place is a protracted one, social tranquillity and an absence of all repressiveness will not be quick in happening or easy to maintain. But the processes have been set in motion and the aim remains to attain a non-repressive society.

V

I shall now turn to a discussion of the justifiability and use of violence to attain a revolutionary transformation of society. The central question I want to ask is the question posed in Herbert Marcuse's essay, 'Ethics and Revolution'.[11] The question is this: 'Is the revolutionary use of violence justifiable as a means for establishing or promoting human freedom and happiness?' The answer I shall give – and it is also the answer Marcuse gives – is that under certain circumstances it is justified.

To discuss this question coherently, we need first to make tolerably clear what we are talking about when we speak of 'revolution'. In speaking of revolution we are speaking of 'the overthrow of a legally established government and constitution by a social class or movement with the aim of altering the social as well as the political structure'.[12] Moreover, we are talking of a 'left revolution' and not a 'right revolution', where the revolutionary aim is to enhance the sum total of human freedom and happiness. (I think in this context it is well to remind ourselves of a point made by Marcuse in 'Liberation from the Affluent Society', namely, that 'without an objectively justifiable goal of a better, a freer human existence, all liberation must remain meaningless'.[13] If there are no objectively justifiable moral principles, all talk of progress, social evolution, justifiable revolution and justifiable revolutionary violence becomes senseless.)

It is also worth stressing again these general points. Reasonable and humane human beings will be against violence generally, but this does not mean that in some circumstances they will not agree that violence is justified. However, to be justifiable the violence must be publicly defendable. That is to say, it must be such that in appropriate contexts the person advocating or defending the violence in question would be prepared to publicly advocate it and accept that, if it is indeed justified, it must be so justifiable to rational persons committed to humane and universalistic moral ends. (The appropriate circumstances are surely not those in which the state has, in effect, set its police and legal forces to trap and destroy the advocate.)

We should also remember that violence, like rationality, is something that admits of degree, and again of kind. It is, for example, extremely important to distinguish between violence against property and violence against persons. The sacking of an ROTC office is one thing; the shooting of an ROTC officer is another. And it is surely evident that violence of any considerable magnitude – particularly when it is against persons – is not justified as a purely symbolic protest against injustice. (This is even more evident when the persons in question are innocent.) There must be some grounds for believing this protest will have an appropriate beneficial effect. It is – concentration-camp-type circumstances apart – both immoral and irrational to engage in violence when all is in vain, for this merely compounds the dreadful burden of suffering. Bernard Gert is surely right in saying that 'neither purity of heart nor willingness to sacrifice oneself justifies violence, and it is even clearer that attempts to ease one's 'conscience do not do so'.[14] Rather, for violence, revolutionary or otherwise, to be justified, it must be reasonably evident that the evil being prevented by the violence is significantly greater than the evil caused. That is to say, on the plausible assumption that we want life to continue, and continue in some optimal way, we need adequate reasons for believing that, everything considered, the violence will prevent more death, pain, misery, servitude, and degradation than it causes. Though sometimes, when much violence is involved on either side and we have no way of tallying up the consequences, we will have to act rather blindly on what we expect and hope will be, everything considered, the most humane course. In defending engaging in revolutionary violence, reasonable and humane persons will require, for the situation in question, specific good reasons for believing that in that situation more evil will be prevented by violence than by refraining from such violent revolutionary acts. As Marcuse stresses, a revolutionary movement, in advocating the use of violence, must 'be able to give rational grounds for its chances to grasp real possibilities of human freedom and happiness and it must be able to demonstrate the adequacy of its means for obtaining this end'.[15] If there are equally adequate alternative non-violent means, it must use them. Surely the American Marxist, Daniel De Leon, was plainly right in declaring that if it were possible, a peaceful and constitutional victory for socialism, provided it was still the same kind of socialism, is preferable to a victory achieved through violence. Whether this is at all achievable, is another matter. The experience of the Allende experiment can hardly make us sanguine. But it is a commonplace that, everything else being equal, non-violence is preferable to violence. However, it should also be a commonplace that 'everything else may not be equal'. Indeed typically it is not. It is rather improbable, given the stakes between the contending classes, that there is any very considerable likelihood of a non-violent transition to socialism. For socialists to build a political strategy around that possibility would be Utopian. The ruling class is not likely to relinquish its privileges and control of society without a fight.

Marcuse remarks that traditionally the end of government 'is not only the greatest possible freedom, but also the greatest possible happiness of man, that is to say, a life without fear and misery, and a life in peace'.[16] Whether or not this is, as Marcuse thinks, 'a basic concept of political philosophy', is less important than the fact that, classical or not, it is of critical importance. In asking whether the revolutionary use of violence is a justifiable means for establishing or promoting human freedom and happiness, we must, Marcuse points out, ask ourselves the difficult question whether there are 'rational criteria for determining the possibilities of human freedom and happiness available to a society in a specific historical situation'.[17] Can we ever establish in any historical situation that revolutionary violence would further human freedom and happiness more adequately than any of the other available alternatives?[18] We must ask ourselves, given the technical and material progress at a particular time, what is the likelihood that the future society, as envisioned by the revolutionaries, will come into being, sustain itself in a form which is distinct from the already existing society, and utilize the technical and material advances available or reasonably possible in such a way as to substantially increase human freedom and happiness. We must make rough historical calculations here. We must (1) consider 'sacrifices exacted from the living generation on behalf of the established society', (2) 'the number of victims made in defense of this society in war and peace, in the struggle for existence, individual and national', (3) consider the resources of the time – material and intellectual – which can be deployed for satisfying vital human needs and desires, (4) consider whether the revolutionary 'plan or program shows adequate promise of being able to substantially reduce the sacrifices and the number of victims'.[19]

If we turn, with such considerations in mind, to the great revolutions of the modern period, namely the English and French revolutions, and if we keep in mind how impossible it would have been for modern conditions to have come into existence without those revolutions, it is evident that 'in spite of the terrible sacrifices exacted by them' these revolutions greatly enlarged the range of human freedom and happiness. As Marcuse well puts it:

> Historically, the objective tendency of the great revolutions of the modern period was the enlargement of the social range of freedom and the enlargement of the satisfaction of needs. No matter how much the social interpretations of the English and French Revolutions may differ, they seem to agree in that a redistribution of the social wealth took place, so that previously less privileged or underprivileged classes were the beneficiaries of this change, economically and/or politically. In spite of subsequent periods of reaction and restoration, the result and objective function of these revolutions was the establishment of more liberal governments, a gradual democratization of society, and technical progress.[20]

Moreover, as Marcuse continues

> these revolutions attained progress in the sense defined, namely, a demonstrable enlargement of the range of human freedom; they thus established, in spite of the terrible sacrifices exacted by them, an ethical right over and above all political justification.[21]

In sum, when it is the case – as sometimes it has been the case with revolutions – that, everything considered, the sum total of human misery and injustice has been lessened by a violent revolution more than it could have been in any other achievable way, then that revolution and at least some (though very unlikely all) of its violence was justified, if not, not.[22]

VI

In this context, we should view terrorism as a tactical weapon, which may or may not be employed, in achieving a socialist revolution. 'Terrorism' and 'terrorist', we should not forget, are highly emotive terms. Burke referred to terrorists as hell-hounds and the word 'terrorist' is often, when used in ideological dispute, simply a term of abuse. Partially emotively neutralizing the terms, we shall, as Marxists generally do, confine the notion of a terrorist to someone who attempts to further political ends by means of coercive intimidation. We shall view terrorism as a systematic policy designed to achieve such ends in such a manner. On that OED definition of 'terrorism' and 'terrorist', the American government and its minions in Indo-China, Nicaragua, and Chile were, and in Chile still are, prime examples of terrorist organizations because this is exactly what they did. (Recall that in Chile some ten thousand to twenty-five thousand people have been killed by the Junta. There were, even as late as 1974, six thousand political prisoners some of whom have been brutally tortured. Slums were bombed during the counter-revolution and even potential socialist leaders are still being hunted and rounded up in the remote villages.) But terrorism has typically – revealingly enough – been talked about in reference to Left revolutionaries such as the Jacobins during the French Revolution, certain extreme revolutionary groups in Russia during the late nineteenth century and the Red Brigades in contemporary Italy.[23] I shall view terrorism here in the context of socialist revolutionary activity and not consider it in the theoretically less interesting but humanly more distressing (to put it mildly) context of the truly massive terror and violence of conservative counter-revolutionary activity, (Argentina, Indonesia, and South Africa are good current examples of what I am talking about.) I want, rather, to get clear about the place of terrorism in a socialist revolution.

It is rarely the case, in such a context, that terrorist acts of assassination – as distinct from the massive acts of terroristic repression utilized by brutalitarian governments – can make any serious difference to the achievement of a revolutionary class consciousness and finally the achievement of a socialist society. Rather – as happened after the terrorist assassination of Tsar Alexander II in 1881 – reaction sets in even more fiercely. In the abortive Russian revolution in 1905 terrorists took an active part. But they were hardly a major instrument of it; rather, they were, in Rosa Luxemburg's apt phrase, merely some shooting flames in a very large fire. Their presence neither made nor broke the revolution. By contrast, the terrorist acts of the Milan Anarchists in March of 1921, after the disillusioning failure of the general strike, are perhaps characteristic of the futility of many terrorist actions – actions which typically result from desperation and weakness. They bombed a theatre, killing twenty-one people and injuring many more without achieving anything in the way of revolutionary or even progressive ends. Rather, this act alienated many workers from the anarchists and provided Mussolini's Fascists with still a further excuse to take action against the Left.[24]

Like all acts of violence in a political context, terrorist acts, if they are to be justified at all, are to be justified by their political effects and their moral consequences. They are justified (a) when they are politically effective weapons in the revolutionary struggle, and (b) when, everything considered, we have sound reasons for believing that, by the use of that type of violence, there will be less injustice, suffering, and degradation in the world than if violence were not used or some other form of violence was used. Surely, viewed in that light, terrorist acts are usually not justified, though in principle they could be and in some circumstances perhaps are, e.g. in the Algerian revolution against France, in the South Vietnamese resistance to American invasion and occupation, and in the revolutionary struggles of a few years ago in Mozambique and Angola. They are perhaps justified today in the struggles in Southern Africa. At the very least, these are the type of circumstances in which such questions become very real indeed.

However, even here we must be careful to keep distinct, on the one hand, individual or small group acts of terror to provoke revolutionary action or to fight back against a vicious oppressor – the paradigm terrorist actions – and, on the other, terrorism as a military tactic in an on-going war of liberation. For any army, vastly inferior in military hardware but with widespread popular support, terrorism in conjunction with more conventional military tactics, might very well be an effective tactic to drive out an oppressor. It is in this context that we should view such acts in South Vietnam during the American occupation and in Algeria. Where we have a less extensive struggle it may still very well be justified. But the terrorist tactics of the F.L.Q., the Weathermen, or (probably) the Irish Provisionals are something else again. They seem in the grossest pragmatic terms to have been counter-productive. We have the horror and the evil of the killings without the liberating revolutionary effect – an effect which would be, morally speaking, justified, where all human interests and other viable alternatives are considered, if the likelihood would be of preventing on balance far more human suffering and oppression in the future. (In these last cases it is very unlikely.)

Generalizing more extensively, but making a similar point, the Marxist historian Eric Hobsbawm writes:

> The epidemic of Anarchist assassinations and bomb-throwings in the 1880's and 1890's, for instance, was politically more irrelevant than the big-game hunting of the period. In all likelihood, the last ten years' political killings and shootings in the U.S.A. have not substantially changed the course of American politics; and they include the two Kennedys, Martin Luther King, Malcolm X, the Nazi George Lincoln Rockwell and Governor Wallace. I don't claim that political assassination cannot possibly make a difference, only that the list of 20th century acts of this kind, which is by

now extremely long and varied, suggests that the odds against its doing so are almost astronomical. And if we take the case of the 250 or so aircraft hijackings of recent years, what these have achieved is at most some financial extortion and the liberation of political prisoners. As a form of activity, bracking belongs to the gossip column of revolutionary history, like 'expropriation', as it's called – that is to say, political bank robbery. So far as I am aware, the only movements which have systematically used hijacking for political purposes are sections of the Palestine guerrillas; and it doesn't seem to have helped them significantly.[25]

The best case to be made for the effective use of terrorist tactics – apart from their use in an on-going war of liberation where there are actually opposed forces in the field – was in their rather extensive use in the latter part of the nineteenth century against Tsarist autocracy, though even there, as we have already noted, the case, at least in the early phases, is not very good. The Tsar had absolute power and was very much of a father-figure in Russia. Russian Absolutism was vicious in the extreme and some of the Tsar's ministers and police chiefs were particularly vicious. It was against this autocratic brutalitarianism that the Russian revolutionary anarchists directed their terror. (It should be noted here in passing that not all anarchists are terrorists.) One could see the point in assassinating the Tsar or his hangmen, but nonetheless even under such circumstances such terrorist activity did little to hasten the fall of Russian Absolutism. The relevant criteria for judging terrorist activity are its consequences – consequences in achieving the lessening of suffering, degradation, injustice, and in achieving liberty and a decent life for oppressed people. By these criteria even these Russian terrorist acts, directed against such a brutal and oppressive regime, may not have been justified.

There is no doubt, with many people at least, that there occurs a sense of moral satisfaction – a sense of justice having been done – when some thoroughly tyrannical brute has been gunned down by revolutionary terrorists or money for the poor has been extracted from the ruling class through political kidnappings, but again, as Rosa Luxemburg coolly recognized, this sense of moral satisfaction has been harmful to the cause of a socialist revolution. It tends to lull people into inaction through a sense of satisfaction that justice has been done. People are very likely to be deceived by such actions into believing that something effective is being done. In finding some hope in such terroristic activity, people are less likely to come to see the absolute necessity *(absolute Notwendigkeit)*, in making a socialist revolution, for building up a mass proletarian base of class-conscious and committed workers.

We must be careful here not to overstate – as Hobsbawm is on the verge of doing – the case against revolutionary terrorism. Writing in 1905 and speaking of Russian terrorism, Rosa Luxemburg very judiciously observed that, while terrorism could not by itself bring an end to Russian Absolutism, it did not at all follow that therefore it was a morally pointless and pragmatically unjustified activity. Luxemburg contended that in Russia the attaining of bourgeois liberties was an essential stage on the way to a *Volksrevolution*. And in turn it is crucial to recognize that without such a mass movement, emerging after the revolutionary activities initiated by the terrorists, the downfall of Russian autocracy would not have occurred. But even after such a mass movement was in place, this does not mean, in such a situation in Russia, that terrorist acts were always, or even typically, senseless or useless – that they could not have been a causal factor in bringing about the downfall of the Tsar's oppressive regime. Terrorism can serve the rather minor role, once mass revolutionary activity has started, of helping the proletariat to fight back in their on-going struggle with their oppressors and, in such a situation, it can also be used appropriately as a tactic to force such a brutal Absolutism into making concessions to the proletariat. It is one way, and a way which sometimes may be effective, in which the proletariat can fight back in their day-to-day struggles with their oppressors. Here terrorism is a weapon in the struggle to meet attempts to suppress 'the revolution with blood and iron'.[26] However, as Rosa Luxemburg goes on to say, as soon as Absolutism recognizes the ineffectiveness of such a use of force and, no matter how vacillatingly and indecisively, enters the road of constitutional concessions to the proletariat, then, just to that degree, terroristic tactics will lose their effectiveness and their rationale. Indeed, when considerable concessions are made, its role will be altogether finished and a second phase of the revolution will have begun.[27]

In sum, while Rosa Luxemburg recognizes that 'the avenging [*rächende*] hand of the terrorists can hasten the disorganization and demoralization of Absolutism', it remains the case that 'to bring about the downfall of Absolutism and to realize liberty – with or without terror – can only be accomplished by the mass arm of the revolutionary working class'.[28]

It seems to me that here she has perceptively seen the proper role and function of terrorism. In an on-going revolutionary struggle, where workers are already struggling against an overt and brutal oppressor, who will not make significant concessions or give them any significant parliamentary rights, it can in certain specific circumstances be a useful and morally justified tactic. We can see this exemplified – as I have already noted – in Algeria and South Vietnam, and it *may* very well be the road to take in Chile for some years to come. But once significant democratic concessions have been wrung from the ruling class, it is not only a useless tactic, indeed, in such a circumstance, it is positively harmful to the cause of a socialist revolution, though it should also be recognized, as my three hypothetical examples evidenced, that where these democratic guarantees are being seriously overridden, situations can arise where a violent response on the part of the exploited and oppressed is justified.[29]

VII

I recognize something which I have tried to confront at some length else-where, namely that arguments of the type I have been giving will with many people cut against the grain.[30] They will feel that somehow such calculative considerations conceptualize the whole problem in a radically mistaken way. They will say that we simply cannot – from a moral point of view – make such calculations when the lives of human beings are at stake.

My short answer is that we can and must. We, not wishing to play God, sometimes must choose between evils, and in such a circumstance a ratio-nal, responsible, and humane person, who does not have a certain kind of distinctive religious belief, must choose the lesser evil. This does not commit me to utilitarianism, for such an account is also compatible with a Rossian pluralism, the conception of justice as fairness powerfully articulated by John Rawls, and even with a Kantian conception of morality. (We should remem-ber that Kant did not say that we must never treat human beings as means, but rather that we must never treat them as means *only*.) Sane men capable of making considered judgments in reflective equilibrium will realize that judg-ments about the appropriateness of the use of revolutionary violence are *universalizable* (generalizable) and they, without being moral fanatics, will be prepared to reverse roles, though of course a member (particularly an active member) of the ruling class, placed as he is in society and with the interests he has, is in certain very important respects one kind of person and a proletar-ian is another. Their social consciousness and their self-images will typically not be the same. (This, of course, is not to say that one is a 'better person' than the other, but that their positions in society are such that they will tend to see the world differently, live differently, relate to people differently and have, in certain important respects, different values.)

The thing to keep vividly and firmly before one's mind is this: if anything is evil, suffering, degradation, and injustice are evil and proletarians and the poor generally are very deeply inflicted with these evils. Even their life expectancies, as Ted Honderich has vividly brought to our attention, are by no means the same. Even there, in such a vital part of their lives, the working class and even more so the thoroughly impoverished, get the short end of the stick.[31] At least some of these evils are avoidable evils, indeed some we already know how to avoid and some of these latter flow from the continuation of an imperialistic and repressive capitalist system. If the use of revolutionary violence in the service of socialism were to lessen this suffering, degradation, and injustice more than would any other viable alternative, then it is justified, if not, not.

The thrust of my argument has been to claim that, in the past, revolution-ary violence has been so justified and that in the future it may very well be justified again even in what are formally democracies. Terrorism, by contrast, has a much more uncertainly justifiable use. There are extreme cases – as with a leader such as Hitler or Amin – where a terrorist assassination of that leader is very likely not only a good political tactic but, from a socialist and humanitarian point of view, morally desirable as well. More significantly and more interestingly, terrorist tactics may very well be justified in the liberation struggles in Chile, Guatemala, and Uruguay. Morally concerned rational human beings must go case by case. However, in the bourgeois democracies where concessions have been made to the working class and certain vital civil liberties exist, it is not a justifiable tactic, but is rather a tactic which will harm the cause of revolutionary socialism.

VIII

I want now to say something about the current compulsive concern with violence. I shall argue that there is a considerable amount of ideological mystification at work here. The use of force and coercion is pervasive in all extant non-primitive societies and often violence will go with it. When the harm or injury that goes with this violence is involuntarily suffered the violence most certainly requires justification. My essential point has been that sometimes it is justified and sometimes it is not, and that this includes violence used as a political weapon to start turning an unjust, repressive social order into a decent social order which will provide the conditions for the free creative development of every individual, an order of social life where people will be able to sustain their self-respect and develop their potentialities. I have argued that there are sometimes ways of ascertaining, though typically with a not inconsiderable degree of fallibility, when this violence is justified and when it is not. However, there are many very morally difficult situations in which, even after careful reflection, we do not know what to say but must act on our rather subjective impressions. This is, of course, morally very worrisome, for terrible consequences may very well flow from our actions or indeed from our refraining from acting. Being in this trying circumstance does not, as many have thought, justify rejecting a resort to revolutionary violence in such situations, though it does not warrant it either. Those who think that the morally responsible thing must, in such a circumstance, consist in not taking a revolutionary turn must also face the fact, if they would be non-evasive, that not so striking against the repressive and destructive established power has its costs too. Since we cannot in such a circumstance reliably count the costs, tell, or tell with any confidence, where the greater evil lies, the idea that we must *not* meet that force with force is also without justification.[32] As Sartre and Camus recognized and dramatized, in such a circumstance we are, whatever we do, in a tormenting moral dilemma. We just have to act on those convictions we continue to have, after we have non-evasively reflected and taken the matter to heart. There is an unavoidable measure of subjectivity here. But this is so whichever way we go. It is not just a problem for the socialist revolutionary. Finally, in such a circumstance, we must just make a decision of principle.

Given that this is the reality of the situation, it is an ideological mystification to take the usual conservative and liberal dodge and conclude that because of this element of uncertainty and subjectivity we must reject the use of violence in such situations. And it is another bit of ideological mystification to regard this as a distinctive issue of principle raised by 'the violence of the Left'. What we have here instead is a particular application of a common moral problem, i.e. sometimes it is hard to calculate or otherwise ascertain the consequences of morally significant acts, and sometimes tragic moral dilemmas arise where, even when we are being thorough and conscientious, we do not know what to do. But that doesn't mean that we are always in such a situation and it would take some considerable showing to establish that we are always in such a situation with respect to revolutionary violence.

The point about ideological mystification should be made more broadly. Class societies are unavoidably coercive and the capitalist system with its authoritarian control and structuring of labour is necessarily coercive. Most people must work to live and in its most essential aspects the Capitalist owners with their managers (who are also often owners) determine who shall work, how they shall work, what they shall make and the like. There is coercion here and, in struggling against that coercion, violence can result. What is as plain as can be – particularly when we look at things in global terms – is that there is coercion and violence all around us and that it deeply affects our lives. This violence is characteristically done against the will of those to whom it is done. Most of us are not masochists, boxers, or hockey players. In varying degrees – indeed in importantly varying degrees – and, depending on what our position in society is, in more or less direct forms, harm, injury, and the violation of our autonomy are our lot. It is a pervasive fact of our cultural lives, though – showing how important the degree is – it has a far greater reality for a commodity production worker, a secretary or a dish washer, than for a doctor, a university professor or a lawyer.

The real issue about violence is the issue about the conditions under which people are entitled to use coercion on each other or on the government, and the conditions in which the government is justified in using it on people. Repeatedly to raise and remain preoccupied with the issue of violence as a separate issue neatly deflects concern with the coercive and repressive nature of our present society. Indeed it tends to conceal that fact and thus, like all properly functioning ideology, distorts our understanding of social reality and gives us a false perspective on our very human condition in such societies. Attention is directed to the fact that some political violence, particularly certain acts of terrorism, are at best misguided and at worst senseless bits of brutality. This becomes the focal point of attention and, because this is so, our attention is turned away from the manifold and pervasive ways in which the capitalist order with its essential control of state power coerces, stunts, and generally harms the lives of countless individuals. People provocatively talk about violence. The mass media exploit it and sometimes, as recently in West Germany, grow hysterical about it, while that repression and destruction of human potential which is endemic to the capitalist social order is lost sight of. It is not even usually noticed that the acts of violence focused on are often desperate acts of counterforce against this repressive order. The ideological suggestion is that the actions of radicals are different in kind from that of the state and that the real problem is to end or contain their violence when in reality the real problem is to transform the repressive order that creates it. ('Real', in both of its above occurrences, tips us off to the fact that persuasive definitions are at work here. But, as Stevenson stressed, persuasive definitions are not always arbitrary and pointless.)

IX

I want now essentially to recapitulate and, in recapitulation, to clarify and extend certain points I have made, and also to consider and perhaps go some way towards meeting, certain objections to the general thrust of my argument.

I attempted a defence of the justifiability of the use of revolutionary violence under certain conditions even within what, formally speaking, is a democracy. I did not, of course, intend it to have the character of an in-house party tract. I do not, of course, want to assume a *parti pris* posture and I do not think that I have; though self-deception here is by no means impossible. My empirical claims, like all empirical claims, are open to intersubjective assessment, and my normative claims and arguments are open to the quite general rational assessment that all justifiable normative claims can be given. (Here I am assuming the falsity of a certain kind of non-cognitivism.)[33] In those important ways my contentions are not partisan, though they are 'partisan' in what I would take to be the perfectly harmless way that they argue for a distinctive normative ethical point of view and a certain conception of society. Only if it is correct to believe, as some have (Ryle, for example), that philosophy must always be normatively neutral, will it be the case that, simply in setting to argue in the way I have, I will *eo ipso* fall from philosophical grace into partisanship, where that notion connotes (as it does in ordinary usage) bias and irrational, or at least non-rational, commitment. I have argued elsewhere against such a neutralist conception of philosophy and it is a conception which, rightly or wrongly, is no longer widely held, though its unacknowledged influence still lingers on in actual philosophical practice.[34] I have assumed its falsity here. But my claim is only in a damaging sense partisan if such severe neutralist restrictions on what constitutes proper philosophical activity are justified. Its acceptance does not require an act of faith and if one, for example, thinks socialism is not a morally justifiable form of social organization, one could still in a hypothetical form ask if socialism were a rationally and morally superior form of social organization in the way I claim, whether violence, under the circumstances elucidated by me, would be justifiable to achieve this order. I argued that there are circumstances in which it would be. This is a perfectly general argument which can be assessed in the same general way that arguments for mercy killing, abortion, and the rightness of always doing what God wills can be argued for; at no point in my argument is there the need for any non-rational commitment to a certain ideological point of view. Moreover, my arguments can be generalized. If some kind of rightist authoritarianism or bourgeois liberalism could be known or reasonably believed to be the most morally and humanly appropriate choice among the various forms of life, then we could ask questions, in the same general way as I did, about the justifiability of using violence (including terrorist tactics) for achieving or – which is the more likely situation with such forms of life – sustaining such a social order. Where the contrast is between moral and non-moral and not between moral and immoral, I agree that the rightist position, is a moral one.

There are immoral moral codes or doctrines, e.g. the Roman Catholic teaching on abortion and South African doctrine on race. There is nothing in my account which commits me to what I have elsewhere argued is false, namely the claim that all morality is class morality or that there are no general moral conclusions.[35]

I agree with those who contend that there is such a thing as institutionalized violence and who further contend that in societies such as ours, particularly when we consider our relation to the rest of the world, it is pervasive and pernicious. (We have Marcuse to thank for driving this point home.) Assuming that, I tried to show concerning such matters, that even if such talk involved some minor adjustments in the connotation of 'violence' it is still quite in order.

I did not commit myself concerning the claim that any of the *de facto* states have *de jure* legitimate authority.[36] My claim is only that *if* there is a legitimate state or social order – morally legitimate and not just legally so – the force used by it will in certain circumstances not be violence but a legitimate use of force. (Here, again, I do not take legitimacy to be simply a legal concept.) If there is no such thing as a legitimate social order then, of course, there can be no genuine distinction between force and violence and the concept of violence, as Wolff consistently argues, becomes an utterly ideological one.[37] I did assume that there could be such a thing as legitimate authority and indeed that in a socialist order, such as I characterized, there would be rules and regulations expressive of that authority. This is all, of course, arguable as the disputes turning around Wolff's *Defense of Anarchism* attest.[38] One cannot argue everything at once and if legitimate authority is a Holmesless Watson, my distinction between force and violence would indeed collapse and my argument about the justifiability of violence would have in certain respects – but only in certain respects – to be recast. But I see no good grounds for taking legitimate authority to be such a Holmesless Watson.

My concern with the justifiability (or lack thereof) of terrorism in particular and political acts of violence more generally, fastened neither on the agent's nor the sufferer's point of view, though role reversal and universalizability was assumed. It turned rather on what could be justified from a morally concerned but dispassionate general point of view, i.e. what a rational moral agent with a sense of justice would be prepared to commit himself to in a position of reflective equilibrium.[39] In trying to consider general social policies from such a point of view, would the use of violence, including acts of terror, ever be justified and if so under what circumstances would they be justified? Any justification here would have to meet the test of an acceptance by rational moral agents where they would be prepared to accept a role reversal between a sufferer and a revolutionary who does something which involves violence. For the act to be morally justified the moral agent would have to be prepared to acknowledge that, if he were the sufferer instead of the revolutionary and could still sustain impartial reasoning in such a circumstance, he would still be prepared to acknowledge that the act was justified. A moral agent, that is, must also recognize that, for the revolutionary act to be morally justified, if he were the sufferer, he must in a cool moment be prepared to acknowledge the rightness of the revolutionaries' action, though this does not at all mean or imply that he or she must *want* this to happen to him – that he or she must want to be victimized. That most people, understandably enough, rationalize here is irrelevant. In asking justificatory questions we need to know what would be accepted by rational moral agents – agents with a sense of justice – in a position of reflective equilibrium; that is, in a position where they could not be rationalizing. My argument was that from that vantage-point – the vantage-point of the moral point of view – there are conditions under which acts of revolutionary violence and sometimes perhaps even terrorist acts are justifiable.

I agree – and indeed would stress – that there are circumstances involving the use of revolutionary violence which are genuinely tragic. However, in reflecting on the justifiability of violence, we cannot avoid, if we would do it responsibly, reflecting on the underlying cause or ideal in the name of which some people will be victimized. Victimizing people is always at least *prima facie* wrong; indeed that may appear to a non-philosopher, unfamiliar with the use of 'prima facie' in philosophical argumentation, to be a crass understatement, for such acts are indeed terribly wrong. In most circumstances they are vile, totally without justification or excuse. Because of this, I argued that such actions, even in these very special circumstances, require very strong justification indeed, and this involves considering very carefully the underlying cause or ideal involved and the chances of its attainment. In that respect there is no sensible examination of the justifiability of violence in the abstract. Here the insights of Sartre and Merleau-Ponty are essential.[40]

Sometimes there is, morally speaking, no avoiding these terrible evils and we must just choose, with all the agony this brings, what we honestly take to be the lesser evil.

If the 'end of ideology' theorists are near to the mark, there are grounds for suspicion of such causes and ideals. Indeed there are grounds for being suspicious of any over-all social orientation, of anything that looks like a world-view. If that account is accepted, then arguments attempting to justify revolutionary violence will seem radically mistaken and in some circumstances even dangerously irresponsible. But this very end-of-ideology stance is itself very problematic and could very well be irresponsibly conservative. Georg Lukàcs's powerful arguments to establish that such end-of-ideology arguments are being used here ideologically to reinforce an idea of the bourgeois order as 'the only rational point of view' should not be forgotten.[41]

What we need to recognize, as Alasdair MacIntyre has well argued, is that such an end-of-ideology stance fits hand in glove with the world-view of the secular liberal – a world-view that is usually not even acknowledged or recognized by its participants to be a world-view.[42] In such a view of the world, as MacIntyre points out, 'there are only individual lives and history has no meaning'; instead secular liberals see themselves as people in various circumstances with rival and competing preferences and alternative and conflicting valuations. We are, on such a world-view, finally just faced with arbitrary choices between alternative evaluations. Good and evil, for such secular liberals, 'have to be weighed on a scale the balance of which is in the end arbitrary'.

To our western bourgeois societies such a view of the world is so pervasive and has such a hold that it is hardly seen by most people in such countries as a world-view to which there are alternatives, but is typically taken simply as what it is to be reasonable and realistic. When this claim is baldly stated like that, there is typically the reluctant admission that, after all, there are alternatives. But they are not thought of as reasonable competitors for our allegiance. The operative assumption is that they are total ideologies and that our own non-ideological liberal outlook is inescapable for the reasonable, informed man. Where this way of thinking has such a hold, any argument attempting to justify revolutionary violence is easily dismissed as 'dangerously Utopian' and/or irrational without ever getting its day in court.[43] One important aspect of MacIntyre's critique of 'the end of ideology ideology' is to show that to be such a secular liberal is not just to take what is incontestably 'the point of view of reason', but is to take a contestable point of view which is only one point of view among quite different contestable alternatives. Moreover, what is also not generally recognized – though again MacIntyre's account has done something to bring this to consciousness – is that this liberal point of view is itself ideological and a pacifying ideology at that.

I have assumed, as over against the secular liberal, another of those not uncontentious alternatives (to use MacIntyre's apt phrase). For a deeper and more fundamental justification of what I have argued, such a case for such an alternative view of the world would need to be made out. I do not believe that it is unreasonable to think that such justification is possible. I cannot undertake this here, even if it were in my power to do so, but must remain content, for the nonce, with the reminder that the principled philosophical rejection of all such general normative arguments also rests on a not uncontentious view of the world, e.g. the world-view of secular liberalism with its end-of-ideology myth.

I do not, however, want to end on such a sceptical sounding methodological note. I want rather to close by first remarking again, though this time from a different perspective, on how frequently talk of terrorism, particularly in right-wing and liberal circles, is ideological mystification, often, wittingly or unwittingly, politically inspired. I then want to return to some fundamental moral issues that remain, I believe, tolerably clear in spite of the methodological difficulties I have discussed above.

When conservative political theorists such as Sidney Hook play down the notion of institutional violence, stress the importance of the distinction between force and violence – the government, of course, using legitimate force and Left revolutionaries engaging in violence – and lament the way violence in our society 'undermines the democratic process', they are in effect arousing the emotions of many people in such a way that their thinking is deflected from raising questions about who really is justified in using coercion in a society, given that on all sides there actually exists violence.[44] In the work of such conservative theorists, the manifold forms of violence of the capitalist order, with the state as one of its instruments, gets neatly concealed or re-described as a legitimate use of force – begging all the central issues about what is and is not legitimate and how this is established. Counter-force against institutional violence is simply ruled out as a morally defensible move by linguistic legerdemain and the central *practical normative problem* concerning violence becomes, as it is for Hare, how to *prevent* it, and deep problems about justification here get trivialized, as Searle has trivialized them, by diversionary talk about 'dramatic terrorism' or 'theatrical terrorism'.[45] We all know that violence is an evil not lightly to be engaged in, but we all also know, or at least ought to know, that violence is extremely pervasive and is inflicted by many different sources. What we need to know is when, if ever, it is justified. Are we to applaud – to go back for a moment to our recent history – Kissinger-inspired terror in Chile while condemning its use by the National Liberation Front? Or should we make the reverse judgment? Or should we cry a plague on both houses and reject all claims to the justified use of violence to attain social ends or protect political commitments? And if we do that, is that not in effect to acquiesce in the acceptance of a repressive *status quo* with its massive and diverse forms of institutional violence? (When we consider this last question it is crucial to consider not only the bourgeois democracies but the whole world and particularly the relation of these democracies to the rest of the world.)

In this essay I have come down definitely on one side of this issue concerning the justification of the use of violence. Starting with the moral truism – though I take it to be a truism which is true – that, other things being equal, non-violent means are preferable tools of social change to violent ones, I argued that there are certain determinate circumstances, even in what at least formally speaking are democracies, where the use of such violent means for humane social ends is justified. This argument seems to me rather straight-forward. It seems to me that what is not generally seen and thus not faced is the not inconsiderable possibility that 'the problem of violence' (including problems of terrorism) raises no distinctive moral problems of *principle*. What needs to be examined is the possibility that making it appear that there are such problems of principle is the work of ideological apology. It is important to defuse this problem and to consider whether those who do think there is some great issue of principle are either confused or are being wilfully mystificatory. What much of the popular and semi-popular talk about violence does is to avert attention from the pervasive coerciveness of society and to insinuate falsely that the, in some cases, violent actions of revolutionaries and radicals are different in *kind* from those of the government and are, simply because they are the kinds of acts they are, unprincipled and morally unacceptable. This has the effect of distracting attention from any actual consideration of the merits of the revolutionary socialists' or radicals' cause and their actions to support that cause. Again we have ideological mystification that needs to be unmasked.

Escaping such ideological mystifications, we should not let the complexities I previously discussed, in remarking on MacIntyre's views, obscure the following moral *cum* factual point. If one travels through Latin America (for example) and is even a tolerably careful observer and one supplements one's own observation with the reading of (say) Sven Lindqvist's perceptive and in-depth factual account of conditions there, and reads as well the interpretative writings of Salvador Allende and Carlos Marighela, the conclusion is unavoidable that the level of violent oppression of masses of people in Latin America is such as to make – as Marighela would put it – a commitment to revolution to achieve socialism the moral duty of a humane and informed human being, where there is some reasonable chance of its success.[46] This is a strong claim, but I think a study of the facts about Latin America, together with an understanding of the kind of socialist goals and society Allende (for example) was trying to implement by peaceful and constitutional means, makes such a conclusion inescapable. I agree with MacIntyre that there are complex and unresolved issues about assessing world-views, that it is often quite impossible to weigh complexes of good and evil in terms of some uncontestable criterion, and that often we have to make what at least appear to be arbitrary choices. But, as Falk makes us see *vis-à-vis* Sartre, *often* is not *always*.[47] There are cases where the suffering and degradation is so extensive and the interests causing and sustaining that suffering so inconsequential morally speaking, and certain alternatives so palpably morally superior, that there is no deep moral or conceptual problem of principle about what to do.[48] Such is the case about social revolution in Latin America, Africa, and in parts of Asia as well. Neither ideological mystification, concern for the inadequacies of straight utilitarian consequentialism, nor philosophical sophistication should obscure this from us. Conceptual sophistication is, of course, important but we must beware of the cultivation of a kind of 'oversophistication' which keeps us from acknowledging what is morally speaking evident. We must avoid a cultivated incapacity to see what is there plainly before us.[49]

Notes

1. See here Jerome A. Shaffer (Ed.), *Violence*, David McKay Inc., New York 1971; Hannah Arendt, *On Violence*, Harcourt, Brace & World Inc., New York 1969; John Harris, 'The Marxist Conception of Violence', *Philosophy and Public Affairs*, Vol. 3, No. 2 (Winter 1974), pp. 192–220; Robert Paul Wolff, 'On Violence', *Journal of Philosophy*, Vol. LXVI (Oct. 1969), pp. 601–16; and J. M. Cameron, 'The Ethics of Violence', *New York Review of Books*. Vol. 15, No. 1 (2 July 1970), pp. 24–32.
2. I think something of the right mix here occurs in Ted Honderich, *Three Essays on Political Violence*, Basil Blackwell, Oxford 1976; and his 'Four Conclusions About Violence of the Left', *Canadian Journal of Philosophy*, Vol. IX, No. 2 (June 1979), pp. 211–46.
3. Roy Edgley, like Honderich, has a fine sense of the proper balance here. The complacency I mentioned above is revealed in the responses of some, but not all, of his commentators. See Roy Edgley, 'Reason and Violence: A Fragment of the Ideology of Liberal Intellectuals', in Stephan Körner (Ed.), *Practical Reason*, Basil Blackwell, Oxford 1974, pp. 113–35. See the remarks of his commentators pp. 135–69 and Edgley's reply, pp. 169–88 in the same volume.
4. Tom Regan has convincingly argued both that pacifism cannot readily, if at all, be refuted on conceptual (logical) grounds alone and that pacifism is not a very compelling or plausible moral doctrine. Tom Regan, 'A Defense of Pacifism', *Canadian Journal of Philosophy*, Vol. II, No. 1 (Sept. 1972). I have attempted to argue directly for socialism in my 'A Defense of Radicalism', *Question 7* (Jan. 1974). For a summarizing and synthesizing contemporary argument for socialism see Michael P. Lerner, *The New Socialist Revolution*, Dell Publishing Co., New York 1973.
5. Richard Wasserstrom, 'The Obligation to Obey the Law', *U.C.L.A. Law Review*, Vol. X (1963), pp. 788–90 and Marshall Cohen, 'Civil Disobedience', *The Great ideas Today*, 1971; *Encyclopedia Britannica*, Chicago 1971, pp. 239–78. In his *In Defense of Political Philosophy*, Harper & Row, New York 1972, Jeffrey H. Reiman, in the context of developing a devastating critique of Robert Paul Wolff's 'philosophical anarchism', convincingly develops this traditional notion that a citizen has no more than a prima facie obligation to obey the law. Wolff, I should add, has responded to Reiman in the 2nd ed. of his *In Defense of Anarchism*, Harper & Row, New York 1976. Reiman, in turn, has responded to Wolff in his 'Anarchism and

Nominalism: Wolff's Latest Obituary for Political Philosophy', *Ethics*, Vol. 89, No. 1 (Oct. 1978), pp. 95–110.

6. Marshall Cohen, 'Civil Disobedience in a Constitutional Democracy', *The Massachusetts Review*, Vol. 10, No. 2 (Spring 1969), p. 218.

7. The relevant sense of 'unfair' here and its role in ethical theory is approximately captured by John Rawls in his 'Justice as Fairness', *The Philosophical Review*, Vol. LXVII (1958) and in his *A Theory of Justice*, Harvard University Press, Cambridge, Mass. 1971. I do not mean to suggest by this that I am committed to his *difference* principle. I only mean that Rawls captures approximately what we are talking about here.

8. Ted Honderich brings this out convincingly in his 'Four Conclusions about Violence of the Left', op. cit.

9. On Ted Honderich's rather stronger, but still reasonable, criteria for democracies, these democracies in bad shape might not count as democracies. But then some states that are conventionally taken as paradigm democracies would not count as democracies. See Ted Honderich, *Three Essays on Political Violence*, op. cit., Ch. 3.

10. Sidney Hook, 'The Ideology of Violence', *Encounter*, Vol. XXXIV, No. 4 (April 1970), p. 34, italics mine. This article is reprinted in his *Revolution, Reform and Social Justice*, Basil Blackwell, Oxford 1976.

11. Herbert Marcuse, 'Ethics and Revolution', in Richard T. DeGeorge (Ed.), *Ethics and Society*, Doubleday & Co., New York 1966, pp. 133–47.

12. Ibid., p. 134. See also my 'The Choice Between Reform and Revolution', *Inquiry*, Vol. 14 (1971), No. 3. A revised and expanded version occurs in Virginia Held *et al.* (Eds.), *Philosophy and Political Action*, Oxford University Press, New York 1972.

13. Herbert Marcuse, 'Liberation from the Affluent Society', in David Cooper (Ed.), *The Dialectics of Liberation*, Penguin Books Inc., Harmondsworth, Middlesex 1968, p. 175.

14. Bernard Gert, 'Justifying Violence', *The Journal of Philosophy*, Vol. LXVI, No. 19 (2 Oct. 1969), p. 627.

15. Herbert Marcuse, 'Ethics and Revolution', op. cit., p. 135.

16. Ibid., p. 134. It should be remarked that here Marcuse makes a rather pardonable overstatement, for it is at least arguable that some kinds of fear give a certain spice and zest to life and thus might be desirable. What Marcuse has in mind is the persistent and massive kind of fear that goes with gross economic insecurity, powerlessness, and political repression.

17. Ibid., p. 135.

18. Ted Honderich in the latter part of his 'Four Conclusions about Violence of the Left' (op. cit.) makes us aware how difficult it often would be to determine this.

19. Herbert Marcuse, 'Ethics and Revolution', op. cit., p. 145.

20. Ibid., p. 143.

21. Ibid., pp. 143–4. It is not clear whether Marcuse recognizes that it is not enough to justify a revolution to establish that it produced desirable results; we must also show that without the revolution the desirable results would not have occurred as rapidly and with (everything considered) as little suffering and degradation. What I think he should be claiming is that when we examine the French and English revolutions that is just what we should conclude. In referring to the English revolution, I am referring to a series of revolutionary happenings that went on in the seventeenth century.

22. In the horrors of an extended civil war which might be linked with a revolution, it is very likely that on all sides there will develop indiscriminate and pointless

terror. We need, in our historical calculations, to take account of these possibilities, but this does not at all give to understand that we are justifying them. We can accept their likelihood while condemning such acts and recognizing, as Marcuse does, that 'there are forms of violence and suppression which no revolutionary situation can justify because they negate the very end for which the revolution is a means. Such are arbitrary violence, cruelty, and indiscriminate terror' (ibid., p. 141). I have developed my arguments about revolution in a more extended way in my 'On the Choice Between Reform and Revolution', op. cit., pp. 17–51, my 'On the Ethics of Revolution', *Radical Philosophy*, Vol. 6 (Winter 1973), and my 'On Justifying Revolution', *Philosophy and Phenomenological Research*, Vol. XXXVII, No. 4 (June 1977).

23. Hans Magnus Enzcasberger, *Raids and Reconstructions*, Pluto Press, London 1978, pp. 136–9; and Thomas Sheehan, 'Italy – the Theory and Practice of Terror', *The New York Review of Books*, Vol. XXVI, No. 13 (16 Aug. 1979), pp. 20–31.
24. George Woodcock, *Anarchism*, Penguin Books, Harmondsworth, Middlesex 1962, pp. 333–4.
25. Eric Hobsbawm, 'An Appraisal of Terrorism', *Canadian Dimension*, Vol. 9, No. 1 (Oct. 1972), pp. 11–12.
26. Rosa Luxemburg, *Gessammelte Werke, Band I 1893 bis 1905, Swelter Halbband*, Dietz Verlag, Berlin 1972, p. 521.
27. Ibid., p. 521.
28. Ibid., pp. 521–2. In this context the balanced discussion of the activities of the Symbionese Liberation Army by the editors *of Ramparts* shows, much in the manner of Rosa Luxemburg, political good sense. See 'Terrorism and the Left', *Ramparts*, Vol. 12, No. 10 (May 1974), pp, 21–27.
29. Luxemburg's arguments should make it evident that the terrorist activities in present-day Western Germany and Italy are very questionable indeed. The moral motivations of those terrorists *may* be exemplary but their theory leaves much to be desired.
30. See my 'On Terrorism and Political Assassination', in Harold Zellner (Ed.), *Political Assassination*, Schenkman Publishing Co., New York 1974, Sects, III and IV.
31. See here his two essays previously cited.
32. Ted Honderich, 'Four Conclusions about Violence of the Left', op. cit.
33. I have argued for what I assume here, in my 'On Looking Back at the Emotive Theory', *Methodos*, Vol. XIV (1962); and in my 'The Problems of Ethics', *Encyclopedia of Philosophy*, Paul Edwards (Ed.), Vol. III, Crowell-Collier, New York 1967.
34. See my 'For Impurity in Philosophy', *University of Toronto Quarterly*, Vol. XLIII, No. 2 (Jan. 1974); my 'Philosophy and Ideology: Programmatic Remarks for a Radical Philosophy', *Radical Philosophers' News-journal*. No. 3 (Aug. 1974); and my 'On Philosophic Method', *International Philosophical Quarterly*, Vol. XVI, No. 3 (Sept. 1976), pp. 349–68.
35. See my 'Moral-Truth', in Nicholas Rescher (Ed.), *Studies in Moral Philosophy*, Basil Blackwell, Oxford 1968; my 'Class Conflict, Marxism and The Good Reasons Approach', *Social Praxis*, Vol. II (1974), No. 2; and my *Reason and Practice*, Harper & Row, New York 1971, Ch. 26.
36. I articulate and indicate the importance of that distinction in my 'Norms and Politics', *The Philosophical Forum*, Vol. XIX (1970). Robert Paul Wolff has done much to articulate the importance of drawing that distinction and to express it clearly and show some of its implications. See his introduction to his *Political Man and Social Man*, Random House, New York 1966, pp. 3–16. See also Robert Paul

Wolff, 'On Violence', *Journal of Philosophy*, Vol. LXVI (Oct. 1969), pp. 601–6 and his *In Defense of Anarchism*, op. cit., Ch. 1. One could accept much of this without accepting his 'philosophical anarchism'.

37. Robert Paul Wolff, 'On Violence', op. cit. See the response by Bernard Gert in the same issue and see also Robert L. Holmes, 'The Concept of Physical Violence in Moral and Political Affairs', *Social Theory and Practice*, Vol. 2, No. 4 (Fall 1973).

38. Robert Paul Wolff, *In Defense of Anarchism*, Harper & Row, New York 1970 and (among others) Jeffrey H. Reiman, *In Defense of Political Philosophy*, Harper & Row, New York 1972; Tom L. Beauchamp and Ken Witkowski, 'A Critique of Pure Anarchism', *Canadian Journal of Philosophy*, Vol. II, No. 4 (June 1973); Rex Martin, 'Two Models for Justifying Political Authority', *Ethics*, Vol. 86, No. 1 (Oct. 1975); and the references in Note 5.

39. This conception is articulated in John Rawls, *A Theory of Justice*, op. cit., Ch. 1, and in his 'The Independence of Moral Theory', *Proceedings and Addresses of the American Philosophical Association*, Vol. XLVIII, 1974–75, pp. 5–22.

40. I have discussed this in my 'On the Ethics of Revolution', *Radical Philosophy*, Vol. 6 (1973); my 'On Terrorism and Political Assassination', in Harold Zellner (Ed.), *Assassination*, Schocken Books, New York 1974; and in my 'Remarks on Violence and Paying the Penalty', *Proceedings of the Center for Philosophical Exchange* (Summer 1970).

41. Georg Lukàcs, *History and Class Consciousness*, trans. by Rodney Livingstone, MIT Press, Cambridge, Mass. 1971 (German original 1922).

42. Alasdair MacIntyre, 'On the Limits of the Use of Force in Modern Warfare' at the Newark Conference on Morality and International Violence, 24 April 1974; and in his *Against the Self-images of the Age*, Gerald Duckworth, London 1971.

43. Anthony Arblaster and Steven Lukes have perceptively captured and exposed the ideological and apologetic use of 'Utopian' in their masterful introduction to their anthology, *The Good Society*, Methuen, London 1971. The use of the term 'perfectibilist' by Professor John Passmore has a similar negative emotive force. (See his *The Perfectibility of Man*, Gerald Duckworth, London 1971 and the article cited below.) Such linguistic manoeuvring, whatever its intent, in reality functions as conservative apologetics against the Left. It insinuates through the emotive force of words what has not been established by argument. This comes out clearly in John Passmore's 'Second Thoughts on a Paradise Lost', *Encounter*, Vol. XLIII, No. 2 (Aug. 1974), pp. 46–48. Social revolutionaries are, Professor Passmore tells us, men committed to taking 'the perfectibilist way'; that is to say, unlike sensible reformers (realistic men with a sense of reality), the dissatisfaction of revolutionaries is not just with this or that social defect, or this or that social system, but 'with the human condition as such'; with 'its responsibilities, its uncertainties, its insecurity, its troubles' (p. 48). Anyone familiar with the work and activities of Marx, Engels, Lenin, Luxemburg or Trotsky – classical paradigmatic revolutionaries – will not recognize Passmore's characterization of social revolutionaries. They did not seek to escape from such uncertainties or tell men there would be a heaven on earth in which they could escape human ills and uncertainties; they did not even condemn capitalism in all historic circumstances, for they clearly recognized that under certain circumstances it was progressive. They did, however, analyse and criticize a certain social system and argue that in certain historical circumstances it was an inhuman social system that should and indeed would be replaced by a more humane form of society. But this is not to say that human beings will become perfect and all human ills will come to an end, though it is to say that

things can become better than they are now and have been in the past. But such a modest belief in progress, though it may be mistaken, in no way justifies seeing these revolutionaries as apocalyptic figures inveighing against *the human condition* as such. Indeed the very conception of the human condition is not one of their conceptual categories, for they see human beings in historical terms as being deeply influenced by different historical conditions. We may be able to speak of what is distinctively human but this distinctive humanness needs always to be understood in terms which are partially historical. (See here Gajo Petrovic, *Marx in the Mid-Twentieth Century*, Doubleday & Co., New York 1967. See also his article on alienation in the *Encyclopedia of Philosophy*.)

44. I am much indebted to Professor Richard Schmitt for certain aspects of the argument I make here and in the next two paragraphs.

45. R. M. Hare, 'On Terrorism' at the Newark Conference on Morality and International Violence, 24 April 1974. John Searle's remarks were made in comments at the conference. Roy Edgley nicely captures the embedded conservatism in Hare's thinking about these matters in his response to Hare in Stephan Körner (Ed.), *Practical Reason*. Basil Blackwell, Oxford 1974, pp. 185–8.

46. Sven Linqvist, *The Shadow: Latin America Faces the Seventies*, Penguin Books, Baltimore, Maryland 1972; Salvador Allende, *Chile's Road to Socialism*, Penguin Books, Baltimore, Maryland 1973; and Carlos Marighela, *For the Liberation of Brazil*, Penguin Books, Baltimore, Maryland 1971.

47. W. D. Falk, 'Moral Perplexity', *Ethics*, Vol. 66 (1956), pp. 123–31.

48. See here Allen W. Wood, 'The Marxian Critique of Justice', *Philosophy and Public Affairs*, Vol. 1, No. 3 (Spring 1972), pp. 275–82; and my 'Class Conflict, Marxism and the Good Reasons Approach', *Social Praxis*, Vol. II, No. 2 (1974).

49. See here Noam Chomsky, *Language and Responsibility*, The Harvester Press, Sussex 1979, Ch. 1; and Noam Chomsky, *American Power and the New Mandarins*, Penguin Books, Harmondsworth, Middlesex 1969, pp. 10–12. I would like to thank Jack MacIntosh for his helpful comments on an earlier version of this essay.

COMMENTARY ON NIELSEN

Kai Nielsen, who is best known for his work on socialist ethics and philosophy of religion,[1] looks at three key issues regarding the use of violence that have been at the heart of socialist concerns throughout the twentieth century: Can violence be justified within democracies? Can revolutionary violence be justified? Can terrorism ever be justified?

The answer to all three questions is a qualified 'yes'. Nielsen starts with a useful discussion of the concept of violence; he reminds us that the evaluative force of this concept sometimes has conceptually distorting effects, therefore he wants to resist the strong presumption that an act of violence is always wrong, being immoral by definition. Instead, Nielsen suggests that acts of violence are only *prima facie* unjustified: 'what is prima facie wrong need not be something which is wrong everything considered'.

In an effort to consider circumstances when an act of violence can be justified, Nielsen contemplates the situation in which a democratic state is engaging in institutionalized violence, or when a democratic superpower is waging a genocidal war of imperialist aggression against a small underdeveloped nation, or finally when a small, impoverished, ill-educated ethnic minority in some democratic society has its members grossly discriminated against, segregated and overall treated as second-class citizens. In those cases, Nielsen believes that the recourse to (some) form of violence can be justified.

What is interesting about Nielsen's position is that, notwithstanding his strong socialist sympathies, his considerations for justifying violence are 'pragmatic and utilitarian', based on one's ability to weigh carefully what would be the probable consequences of resorting to violence: 'if, on the one hand, only more suffering all round would result, then resort to such violence is wrong; if, on the other hand, such acts of violence are likely to lessen the sum total of human suffering and not put an unfair burden on some already cruelly exploited people, then the violence is justified.'[2]

Regarding the use of violence to attain a revolutionary transformation of society, Nielsen appeals not only to consequentialist reasoning, whereby the evil being prevented by the violence is significantly greater than the evil caused, but also to the ideal of public justification: 'to be justified the violence must be publicly defendable', by which he means that the violence must be 'justifiable to rational persons committed to humane and universalistic moral ends'.

To the extent that violence can be justified, Nielsen argues that terrorism is not an exception, at least in theory. He reminds us that terrorist acts, viewed as tactical weapons, are extremely difficult to justify – but only because terrorist acts are usually not politically effective weapons, indeed terrorism tends to exacerbate rather than alleviate injustice, suffering and degradation. Nevertheless, in principle terrorist acts could be justified.[3] Nielsen's examples of justified terrorism include the Algerian revolution against France; South

Vietnamese resistance to American invasion and occupation; revolutionary struggles in Mozambique, Angola and Southern Africa.

Notes and further reading

1. See his *Why Be Moral?* New York: Prometheus 1989; *Globalization and Justice*, New York: Prometheus 2003; *Atheism and Philosophy*, New York: Prometheus, 2005. On Nielsen's impact on contemporary philosophy, see M. Seymour and M. Fritsch (eds), *Reason and Emancipation: Essays on the Philosophy of Kai Nielsen*, New York: Prometheus, 2007.
2. On Nielsen's utilitarianism, see his 'Traditional Morality and Utilitarianism', *Ethics*, Vol. 82, 1872: 113–24.
3. For a similar view on terrorism, see Alison M. Jaggar, 'What is Terrorism, Why Is it Wrong, and Could it Ever be Morally Permissible?', *Journal of Social Philosophy*, Vol. 36, Issue 2, 2005.

12
The Idea of Violence

C. A. J. Coady

ABSTRACT   *Violence is a central idea for political theory but there is very little agreement about how it should be understood. This paper examines some fashionable approaches to the concept and argues against 'wide' definitions, particularly those of the 'structuralist' variety of which that offered by the sociologist, Johan Galtung, is taken as typical. A critique is also given of 'legitimist' definitions which incorporate some strong notion of illegitimacy into the very meaning of violence. Structuralist definitions are much favoured by the political left whereas legitimist accounts are more common on the right but these connections, though psychologically understandable, are not logically tight. Both structuralist and legitimist analyses are criticised on conceptual and practical grounds and a defence of a more restricted definition is presented. The paper concludes with some remarks about the point of having a concept of violence of the type delineated.*

Hannah Arendt once complained that the careless use in political theory of such key terms as 'power', 'strength', 'force', 'authority' and 'violence' indicated not only a deplorable deafness to linguistic meanings but a kind of blindness to significant political realities. The blame for this she traced to the obsession with reducing public affairs to 'the business of dominion'.[1] I share her belief that conceptual carelessness or misunderstanding about such ideas as violence has political importance and I suspect that she may be right in her diagnosis of what lies behind a good deal of such confusion. My present concern, however, is rather different from that specifically addressed by Arendt although the two are related. Nowadays, it is not so much that theorists are, as she objected, indifferent to distinctions between the key terms listed but that they offer explicit definitions of the term 'violence' which exhibit both the deafness to linguistic patterns and, more significantly, the blindness to political and moral realities of which she complained. In what follows, I shall try to support this claim by examining several fashionable definitions of violence with an eye both to their conceptual adequacy and their moral and social implications. I shall also suggest an alternative definition to the ones criticised, urge its advantages over them, and defend it against certain difficulties.

Of course, as Arendt herself was well aware, any such definitions have to cope with the untidiness, indeterminacy and variety of purpose involved in natural languages and ordinary speech contexts. Hence any definition proposed by a theorist will involve some degree of sharpening and legislation with a consequent recognition of borderline cases and the dismissal or downgrading of certain kinds of existing usage. Social and political concepts of any importance have, however, the additional interest and complexity that they may and often do embody diverse moral and political outlooks or visions and so a theorist's definitions of such terms will reflect, and often be part of, a programme for advancing certain enterprises at once both theoretical and practical. Sometimes, understanding is best served by defining a concept such as justice in very abstract and relatively neutral terms which allow competing theories and outlooks pertaining to the subject matter thus indicated to be compared and criticised. Here it has proved useful to deploy a (relatively unanalysed) contrast of concept and conception as Rawls does in his work on justice and as Dworkin recommends in the case of law.[2] Nonetheless, the literature on violence mostly proceeds in terms of definitions that aim to capture a conceptual territory believed to be at least implicit in ordinary discourse and so I shall frame my discussion in terms of definition but with the background social and political issues very much in mind. Were the concept-conception strategy applicable to the present topic it would, I believe, require only a re-arrangement of what I want to say and not a revision of it.

The definition of violence provides a nice illustration of the complex interplay between concept and commitment. There are roughly three types of definition to be found in the philosophical, political and sociological literature on violence. We might label these 'wide', 'restricted' and 'legitimate'.[3] Wide definitions, of which the most influential is that of 'structural violence', tend to serve the interests of the political left by including within the extension of the term 'violence' a great range of social injustices and inequalities. This not only allows reformers to say that they are working to eliminate violence when they oppose, say, a government measure to redistribute income in favour of the already rich, but allows revolutionaries to offer, in justification of their resort to violence, even where it is terrorist, the claim that they are merely meeting violence with violence. Their own direct physical violence is presented as no more than a response to and defence against the institutional or quiet violence of their society.[4] An instance of such a wide definition is Newton Garver's: 'The institutional form of quiet violence operates when people are deprived of choices in a systematic way by the very manner in which transactions normally take place'.[5] But if wide definitions are naturally more congenial to the left we must not ignore the possibility of their use by the right, since it is possible for the right to see social structures as deforming in, for instance, exposing people to moral danger or leaving them too free or not economically free enough and so on.

Restricted definitions are typically those which concentrate upon positive interpersonal acts of force usually involving the infliction of physical injury. There is something to be said for this being the normal or ordinary understanding of 'violence', not only because it has the authority of dictionaries, most notably the Oxford English Dictionary, but because the proponents of the wide definitions usually take it that they are offering an extension of just such a normal or usual idea.[6] It has been argued by some that this definition has natural affinities with a reformist liberal political outlook[7] and it may be so, though I think myself that it is the most politically neutral of the definitional types (which may just show how 'liberal' it is and I am). In any case it is the type of definition in support of which I shall later argue.

The third type of definition ('legitimist') arises naturally in the context of conservative or right wing liberal political thought for it incorporates a reference to an illegal or illegitimate use of force. I think it probable that this style of definition has much more currency in the United States than elsewhere, but the usage it corresponds to does exist in other communities too. Sidney Hook is operating in this tradition when he defines violence as 'the illegal employment of methods of physical coercion for personal or group ends',[8] and Herbert Marcuse is commenting upon the usage when he says, 'Thanks to a kind of political linguistics, we never use the word violence to describe the actions of the police, we never use the word violence to describe the actions of the Special Forces in Vietnam. But the word is readily applied to the actions of students who defend themselves from the police, burn cars or chop down trees'.[9] One can see the advantages of this outlook for the defenders of established orders, but once more the connection, though natural, is not inevitable. Robert Paul Wolff, for one, has accepted this sort of definition in order to argue a kind of left-wing case by purporting to show that the concept of violence is incoherent.[10] I shall consider Wolff's view in detail as a representative legitimist definition, even though he gives it an untypical twist, but first I want to begin with a wide definition. The one I shall consider is that given by the Norwegian philosopher-sociologist Johan Galtung in his paper, 'Violence, peace and peace research'.[11]

Galtung claims in this article and elsewhere that there are various types of violence and that it is important to have a very broad concept of violence in order to accommodate them all. He distinguishes, for instance, between physical and psychological violence, giving as cases of the latter, lies, brainwashing, indoctrination and threats, but, more interestingly, he locates both of these within the category of personal violence which he then contrasts with structural violence. By so doing he generates a perspective from which one can see two types of peace. On the one hand there is negative peace which is the absence of direct or personal violence (roughly what a restricted definition determines as violence) and, on the other, positive peace which is the absence of indirect or structural violence (cf. p. 183). Structural violence is also referred to as social injustice and positive peace as social justice. At this point Galtung's definition of violence should be cited, a definition which is meant to support the possibility of the two types of violence mentioned. What he says is: 'Violence is present when human beings are being influenced so that their actual somatic and mental realizations are below their potential realizations' (p. 168). Galtung confesses to some unease about this definition as soon as he formulates it, saying that it 'may lead to more problems than it solves', but this avowal seems to have no more than ritual significance since no such problems are raised in the course of the article. Galtung is, however, aware that he has framed what he calls 'an extended concept of violence', and feels obliged to try to justify the extension as 'a logical extension'. By talking of his definition as extending the concept of violence Galtung seems to be acknowledging what is, indeed, surely the case, that in its usual use the term violence covers only what he calls personal violence, whereas he wants to hold that violence also exists where social arrangements and institutions have the effect of producing substandard 'somatic and mental realisations'. Indeed, if we were to invoke the authority of the OED we might conclude that even personal violence is too extended since that authority gives a 'restricted' definition of violence in purely physical terms as follows:

The exercise of physical force so as to inflict injury on or damage to persons or property; action or conduct characterised by this.

I shall discuss this definition later since it faces certain difficulties and requires some clarification. First we should notice, that, on this definition, there can be various metaphorical or otherwise extended uses of 'violence', 'violent', 'violently' and suchlike words which relate in more or less direct ways to episodes of the infliction of damage by physical force, e.g. 'Sir John Kerr did violence to the Australian Constitution' or 'Dennis waved his arms about violently' or 'The violent motions of the machine surprised him'. It seems plausible to treat the use of the noun 'violence' in the utterance about Sir John Kerr as an attempt to dramatise the awfulness of the governor-general's behaviour with respect to the Constitution, but the adjectival and adverbial uses are more interesting in being less metaphorical. Neither Dennis nor the machine was engaged in violence yet their movements are intelligibly described as violent because of affinities between the way their limbs and parts behaved and the way in which genuine violence manifests itself. In this respect, the employment of 'Violent' and 'violently' in such contexts is like that of such expressions as 'furious' and 'furiously' since we do not suppose that the team which rows furiously is actually in a fury.

Once this is understood we should be under no temptation to think that such usages somehow license the sort of extension that Galtung is promoting. (John Harris seems to think something of the kind but we will look more closely at his view later.) Certainly it would normally be very queer to say that violence is present when (and because) a society legislates for more tax concessions for big business, or refuses to remove unjust legislation such as the denial of voting rights to certain minority groups. It seems, however, to be no less bizarre to characterise such enactments as violent in anything like the way that Dennis and the machine can be so characterised.

We should pause to eliminate some sources of possible confusion. When people speak of structural or institutional violence they often run together three things which should be kept separate. First there is what Galtung is principally concerned with, namely, the way in which people are injured and harmed by unjust social arrangements which could be otherwise even though no violence in the restricted (or 'personal') sense is being done to them. Secondly, there is the phenomenon of ordinary person-to-person violence with pronounced social or structural causes (e.g. police harassment of racial minorities, race riots, or prison brutality, to name just a few plausible candidates). Thirdly, there is the widespread readiness to resort to socially licensed violence which is implicit in much of social life. Galtung puts this into the category of 'latent violence', but appears to treat it as a type of violence (cf. p. 172), which seems wrong for the perfectly general reason that tendencies and dispositions should not be confused with their displays. There are, of course, plenty of displays of the State's capacity for violence, both domestically and externally, and the role of (restricted) violence in civil life is both easy to ignore and almost equally easy to exaggerate. It is easy to ignore partly because when one has a comfortable position in society it is hardly ever personally encountered (in peacetime) and partly because second-hand knowledge of the facts tends to be clouded by euphemism. The presumed legitimacy of State violence can also create the feeling that it is a quite different activity from unauthorised violence and so lead to the legitimist idea that it is not violence at all. The point about State violence is easy to exaggerate from a different direction, especially if the distinctions made above are neglected. Some thinkers and activists speak as if nothing but violence goes on in such a State as Britain or Australia and as if political obedience rests entirely upon the fear of violent treatment by the authorities. If we are thinking of violence in some restricted sense and we do not confuse it with the capacity for violence then both of these claims are absurd. And even if we allow reference to the State's capacity for violence in discussing the roots of political obedience, then it is surely implausible to hold that most people accept political authority because they fear the State's capacity for violence against them. More plausible is Thomas Hobbes' view that the State's power to use violence ('the right of the sword') enters into most people's thinking about obedience primarily through the reassuring thought that it provides a sanction against someone else's violent behaviour. As Hobbes argued, most people in an ordered, half-decent society get such benefits from civil life as will make it clearly in their interest to accept civil authority most of the time, but this is conditional upon those who don't have such an interest (or who don't think that they have such an interest) being intimidated into conformity and upon the majority being so intimidated on those occasions (necessarily rare, so Hobbes may have believed) when conformity does not *seem* to be in their interests. There is some plausibility in this sort of picture of the role of violence in securing political obedience, but it is more complex than the picture often presented in popular polemics.

If Galtung is not merely concerned to draw attention to the social causes of much personal violence nor the amount of latent personal violence involved in normal social life, what good reason does he have for extending the concept of violence in the way he does?

First, let us look briefly at the formulation of his definition, which has some rather curious features. It seems to follow from it that a young child is engaged in violence if its expression of its needs and desires is such that it makes its mother and/or father very tired, even if it is not in any ordinary sense 'a violent child' or even engaged in violent actions. Furthermore, I will be engaged in violence if, at your request, I give you a sleeping pill that will reduce your actual somatic and mental realisations well below their potential, at least for some hours. Certainly some emendation is called for, and it may be possible to produce a version of the definition that will meet these difficulties (the changing of 'influenced' to 'influenced against their will' might do the job, but at the cost of making it impossible to act violently towards someone at their request, and that doesn't *seem* to be impossible, just unusual). I shall not delay on this, however, because I want rather to assess Galtung's reason for seeking to extend the concept of violence in the way he does. His statement of the justification of his definition is as follows:

> However, it will soon be clear why we are rejecting the narrow concept of violence – according to which violence is *somatic* incapacitation, or deprivation of health, alone (with killing as the extreme form), at the hands of an *actor* who *intends* this to be the consequence. If this were all violence is about, and peace is seen as its negation, then too little is rejected when peace is held up as an ideal. Highly unacceptable social orders would still be compatible with peace. Hence an *extended concept of violence is indispensable* but the concept should be a logical extension, not merely a list of undesirables. (p. 168)

So, for Galtung, the significance of his definition of violence lies in the fact that if violence is undesirable and peace desirable, then if we draw a very wide bow in defining violence we will find that the ideal of peace will commit us to quite a lot. Now it seems to me that this justification of the value of his definition is either muddled or mischievous (and just possibly both). If the suggestion is that peace cannot be a *worthy* social ideal or goal of action unless it is the total ideal, then the suggestion is surely absurd. A multiplicity of compatible but non-inclusive ideals seems as worthy of man's pursuit as a single comprehensive goal and, furthermore, it seems a more honest way to characterise social realities. Galtung finds it somehow shocking that highly unacceptable social orders would still be compatible with peace, but only the total ideal assumption makes this even surprising. It is surely just an example of the twin facts that since social realities are complex, social ideals and ills do not form an undifferentiated whole (at least not in the perceptions of most men and women) and that social causation is such that some ideals are achievable in relative independence of others. Prosperity, freedom, peace and equality, for instance, are different ideals requiring different characterisations and justifications and although it could be hoped that they are compatible in the sense that there is no absurdity in supposing that a society could exhibit a high degree of realisation of all four, yet concrete circumstances may well demand a trade-off amongst them – the toleration, for instance, of a lesser degree of freedom in order to achieve peace or a less general prosperity in the interests of greater equality.

On the other hand, it may be that Galtung does not mean to say that a narrower definition of violence would provide us with a notion of peace that was not sufficiently worth pursuing, but rather that since people are against violence (narrowly construed) and for peace (narrowly construed), then their energies can be harnessed practically on a wide front against all sorts of social injustice if they come to think of peace as encompassing the whole of social justice. There are some indications in the text that this is what Galtung means and that he is not averse to achieving this goal through the promotion of what he sees himself to be confused thinking.

> The use of the term 'peace' may in itself be peace-productive, producing a common basis, a feeling of communality in purpose that may pave the ground for deeper ties later on. The use of more precise terms drawn from the vocabulary of one conflict group, and excluded from the vocabulary of the opponent group, may in itself cause dissent and lead to manifest conflict precisely because the term is so clearly understood. By projecting an image of harmony of interests the term 'peace' may also help bring about such a harmony. It provides opponents with a one-word language in which to express values of concern and togetherness because peace is on anybody's agenda. (p. 167)

Nonetheless it is not clear how seriously this is intended. The passage occurs before the attempt at definition and it may not be charitable to take it as an indication of the true significance of Galtung's definitional strategy. If it were so taken, then it should be remarked that not only does the strategy have much the same moral status as propaganda, but it shares the disadvantages of propaganda in that it is likely in the long term to defeat the ends, good or ill, it is designed to serve. The deliberate promotion of muddle or unclarity is liable to be detected and when detected resented, because it is seen for what it is, namely, an exercise in manipulation. One is reminded of some of the Communist Party's operations with United Front (and other 'front') organisations of the 1940s and '50s, and of the subsequent damage done to numerous radical causes by the disillusionment of those who had been manipulated.

Let us suppose, however, that Galtung's strategy is not as dubious as this and let us rather interpret him as seeking to call attention to genuine similarities between personal and structural violence in the hope that once they are seen then people who are concerned to oppose the violence of, for example, war will also work to oppose the structural violence of (as it may be) inequitable tax scales, income inequities, private schools, inadequate health services and so on. (I am deliberately not using such instances of social injustice as racism which usually involve the use of 'restricted' violence, and so can lead to some confusion, as noted earlier.) To this I think there are three replies.

(a) The similarities between personal violence and structural violence seem to be far too few and too general to offset the striking differences between them. The basic similarity which Galtung's definition enshrines in a somewhat cumbersome way is that violence and social injustice both involve the production of some sort of hurt or injury broadly construed but the type of harm and the conditions of its production are terribly different.

In recent English writings on moral and political philosophy a good deal of ingenious and often impressive effort has been expended on arguments which might seem to make the similarities more convincing and the differences less striking. Most of the effort has gone into an attack upon what Jonathan Glover has called the acts/omissions doctrine and writers like Glover, Singer, Bennett, Harris and Honderich (most of them utilitarians of one sort or another) have drawn various, though related, conclusions from their critique.[12] Insofar as the discussion has served to stress the way in which various failures to act may be morally significant, it seems to me to have been of great importance. But the critique has more ambitious, if, at times, confusingly presented, intentions. So it sometimes seems that the project is to show that there is no real conceptual distinction between acts and omissions, at other times that there is a distinction but that it is never of moral significance, at other times again that there is a distinction which is sometimes morally significant but not in the special circumstances of interest to the moral theorist (e.g. euthanasia or abortion). This is not the place to explore this important issue further, but it is worth noting that while Honderich concludes that the positive acts of the violent are in the relevant respects quite unlike the omissions of the non-violent (e.g. their failure to aid third world countries) even though such omissions are seriously culpable, Harris claims that such omissions or, as he prefers, negative actions *are* acts of violence.[13] Some of his arguments for this conclusion are similar to Galtung's but others involve an attempt to undermine the 'restricted definition' by appeal to counter-examples. The latter I will consider when I look more carefully at attempts to provide a restricted definition, but the former can be briefly considered here.

Harris is not only interested in extending the notion of violence; more generally, he does not want to include any reference to the *manner* in which harm or injury is done, other than its being done knowingly. His definition goes as follows:

> An act of violence occurs when injury or suffering is inflicted upon a person or persons by an agent who knows (or ought reasonably to have known), that his actions would result in the harm in question.[14]

He asserts that the questions that interest about violence would be trivial if they were only concerned with injuries brought about in a certain manner. Our concern with such questions is motivated by the desire to solve 'the problem of violence', that is, 'to minimise its use or even remove it entirely from human affairs' and in the restricted sense of the term we might do this 'and yet leave intact all the features of the problem of violence which make a solution desirable. Death, injury and suffering might be just as common as before, only the characteristic complex of actions by which they are inflicted would have changed'.[15] And he adds that we are not so much interested in the particular methods men use to inflict injury, suffering or death, but in the fact that they cause each other such harms. As his definition indicates, Harris' primary concern, unlike Galtung's, is with personal violence, although he wants to make a dramatic extension of that category. If certain kinds of omission can count as violence then the way to structural violence is at least clearer since the damage done to people by the structures and institutions of their society can be seen as sustained by personal failures to act. Moreover a successful extension of the term 'violence' to cover omissions might make the further move to violence without individual agents more palatable.

Clearly a good deal here turns upon how we determine the question of negative actions, but even if we allow that failure to give money to Oxfam (a favoured example in the literature) with the foreseeable consequence that someone in India dies is causing some person to die, it still does not follow that we do or must have the same interest in both kinds of deed. In fact, it is quite clear that most people are interested in and exercised about the one to a much greater degree than, and in a different way from, their concern about the other. Whether this differentiation is morally praise-worthy or defensible is another question, but the fact that they do so differentiate is indisputable. So Harris' claim that we are not really interested in the manner in which damage is caused is, as a factual claim, simply mistaken. Furthermore, such generalised differentiation is surely plausibly explained by the striking dissimilarities between what is done on the one hand in stabbing a beggar to death and, on the other hand, in ignoring his plea for assistance. These dissimilarities extend usually both to the manner of acting and to the way in which the outcome ensues. I say 'usually', because although cases can be constructed in which death is immediately consequent upon our refusal of aid, the more common cases involve our negative action being, at most, merely a partial cause of death and injury and hence it is usually left open that, for instance, someone else will aid the beggar.[16] This, I suspect, is one reason why most people are more impressed by, and worried about, restricted violence than about other ways in which human beings contribute to harming one another.

A related, and important, point is that our positive actions to cause injury are standardly intentional under some relevant description (such as killing, stabbing or battering) whereas our omitting to do something which would have prevented injury or suffering may or may not be intentional with reference to that upshot even if we are fully aware that failure to act will probably have just such consequences. This will not show that the act/omission distinction *always* makes a moral difference; quite the contrary, for there will be cases where someone may omit to do something precisely because his failure to act will contribute to bringing about injury and he may even choose the negative rather than positive action in order that the victim suffer more. Imagine a malevolent nurse who stands to gain a lot from the death of a detested patient and who decides to provide a more painful death by omitting to give a vital medicine rather than simply hitting him over the head. Here, the course of intentional omission seems to be more reprehensible than the positive action. Nonetheless, the difference between the ways in which positive and negative actions are generally related to the category of the intentional does show that there is a moral significance to the distinction. Just what significance, will depend upon the role that one's moral outlook gives to intentional action. I do not claim that morality is only concerned with intentional action – the category of negligence shows that this cannot be so – but it does appear that intentional action is of distinctive importance. It is true that utilitarian moral theory either makes light of the idea or tries to stretch it so as to make all foreseen consequences of one's act intentional thus obliterating this difference between the homicidal nurse and the chap who spends all his money on his family rather than giving some of it to Oxfam whose workers will, he believes, use it to save lives. It is, I think, fairly clear that any such conceptual manoeuvre is a departure from ordinary thinking about intention and I am not sympathetic to the reasons usually offered for so departing but further discussion of this issue would take us into a debate about the best structure for an adequate moral theory and hence too far afield. My aim here is only to show that there is much more to the widespread interest in sharply distinguishing positive acts of violence from harmful failures to act than such theorists as Harris allow. I conclude then that the objection from dissimilarity still stands.

(b) Furthermore, even certain similarities that do exist are not all that they appear. Both the existence of social injustice (i.e. 'structural violence') and restricted violence within, or between, communities are matters for moral concern but the way in which each relates to morality seems to be different. It is hard to be confident about this if only because of the obscurity of the expression 'social justice' and the different moral understandings that are implicit in its use by different people but, on the whole, the allegation that some procedure or activity is unjust is a more decisive moral condemnation than the criticism that it is violent. It seems clear that, quite apart from the debate about just wars, some acts of domestic violence may be morally legitimate, for example, the violent restraint or hindrance of someone who is violently attacking someone else. By contrast, the idea that social injustice may be morally legitimate is more surprising. All but fairly extreme pacifists would agree that we could be morally justified in using violence to defend ourselves against violent attack but there is no ready parallel to this idea in the case of social injustice. There could indeed be a reason for restricting the liberty or wealth of a class of citizens or for otherwise injuring them but such a reason would normally preclude us from describing the restriction or injury as unjust. It is not that one social injustice has been rightly used to defeat another but rather that the good reason for using some measure which rectifies a social injustice renders that measure socially just or, at least, not unjust. This is, I think, how it would be natural to describe most justified acts of social reform, even cases of positive discrimination which are usually defended as embodiments of social justice rather than violations of it. Some may prefer to say that while this is generally so, nonetheless social injustice is sometimes morally justifiable (just as restricted violence is) because, being only one ideal amongst others, it can be overridden by some other value like maximising happiness or, more plausibly, the needs of social order. So someone might admit that slavery offends against social justice but argue that it may justifiably continue or be freshly imposed because the economy or the intellectual culture would collapse without it. Suppose such a claim were accepted as true and overriding. Would we best describe the situation by saying that slavery here is unjust but morally acceptable or by saying that slavery here is unjust and hence immoral but it is nonetheless required or necessary here to be immoral? These are difficult issues (reminiscent of some of those addressed by Machiavelli), but I think that if we allow such an overriding (as I should, in fact, be loathe to do), it is best described in the second fashion and if so, there is still no parallel with the case of restricted violence. The first form of description will, however, preserve the similarity and so suit the theorist of structural or other wide violence. The preservation is, however, purchased at a price which I suspect few such theorists would be willing to pay because it involves the admission that social injustice – usually their primary social evil – can sometimes be *morally* acceptable.

(c) Perhaps more important than either of these points is the fact that the wide definition of violence and peace is likely to have undesirable practical consequences. As remarked earlier, the realities of social causation are such that some ideals are achievable in relative or even total independence of others, and it is very plausible to suppose that such goals as the reduction of the level of armed conflict between or within nations or even its total elimination between them may be achievable independently of the achievement or even the significant advance of social justice within one or more such nations. Furthermore, as a corollary, it may well be that quite different techniques, strategies and remedies are required to deal with the social disorder of (restricted) violence than are needed to deal with such issues as wage injustice, educational inequalities and entrenched privilege. The use of the wide definition seems likely to encourage the cosy but ultimately stultifying belief that there is one problem, the problem of (wide) violence, and hence it must be solved as a whole with one set of techniques.

An analogy with slavery may be instructive. It would be possible to produce a Galtung-style typology of slavery which has as its sub-divisions physical slavery and structural slavery, indeed the notion of a 'wage-slave' is perhaps a contribution to this sort of enterprise. Yet not only is physical slavery, for the most part, very different from structural slavery, but it is palpably eliminable independently of eliminating structural slavery since, in much of the world, it *has* been eliminated whilst structural slavery remains. Furthermore, some of the methods used to eliminate physical slavery may not be appropriate to the elimination of structural slavery (e.g. the use of the British Fleet).

It is worth saying something under this heading about Harris' claim mentioned earlier that one might deal with the problem of violence narrowly conceived and indeed eliminate all such violence from the face of the earth, and yet find that 'Death, injury and suffering might be just as common as before, only the characteristic complex of actions by which they are inflicted would have changed'.[17] We should not here be seduced by the philosopher's typical and understandable concern for fantastic possibilities because *here* such a possibility will surely fail to be instructive, and the fact equally surely is that this suggested possibility is merely fantastic. Suppose, what is hard enough, that we have vastly reduced wars, revolutions, assassinations, riots, military coups, police and criminal violence, is it really conceivable that, other things being equal, the lot of mankind *could* remain unimproved with respect to death, injury and suffering?[18] One can answer 'No' to this question even while believing that violence may sometimes be morally permissible and while deploring other ways in which human suffering occurs. This is because the most telling justification for violence is as a defence against other violence and because even justified violence is regrettable. In our world and any empirically similar world, a vast reduction in the level of (restricted) violence would surely mean the elimination of a great deal of what serves to bring premature death and extensive misery. Think of the parallel with slavery. No doubt many awful indignities must remain after slavery is abolished, and the act of abolition may itself create new disabilities for the former slaves but, in most imaginable circumstances, it is hard to believe that their lot is not an improved one. It seems to me that the matter is even clearer in the case of violence.

In so far then as wide definitions like Galtung's are open to the criticisms made above, their underpinnings are theoretically unsound and the practical consequences of adopting them are likely to be at the very least, disappointing.[19]

I come now to a rather different attempt at defining violence, one belonging to the 'legitimist' category and offered by Robert Wolff in his paper 'On violence'.[20] We shall not here be able to engage with all of Wolff's manoeuvres in this swashbuckling piece of polemic but we should note that his strategy is to use a legitimist definition of violence in order to show that the concepts of violence and non-violence are 'inherently confused' because they rest fundamentally upon the idea of legitimate authority which is itself incoherent. He thus feels entitled to dismiss as meaningless (except for its role as 'ideological rhetoric' aimed at helping certain political interests) all debates and discussions about the morality of violence and about the respective merits of violent and non-violent political tactics (cf. p. 602). Some of what I have to say bears upon these startling conclusions but I shall not comment upon his basic argument against the notion of legitimate political authority except to record my conviction that it is unsuccessful.

Wolff defines violence as meaning 'the illegitimate or unauthorised use of force to effect decisions against the will or desire of others' (p. 606). Like one interpretation of Galtung's definition, this has the consequence that one could never be violent to another if he sought to be injured but this is surely wrong, for a bank-robber's accomplice may want the robber to beat him up in order to throw the police off the scent. It also, more significantly perhaps, makes a normative political element part of the meaning of the term, violence. Wolff does allow what he calls a descriptive sense of the word too but this is not, as might be suspected, a restricted sense since it still contains a reference to political authority but this time merely *de facto* instead of legitimate. A *de facto* authority is one 'generally accepted' as legitimate in the territory. He goes on to say, 'Descriptively speaking, the attack on Hitler's life during the second World War was an act of violence, but one might perfectly well deny that it was violent in the strict sense, on the grounds that Hitler's regime was illegitimate. On similar grounds, it is frequently said that police behaviour toward workers or ghetto dwellers or demonstrators is violent, even when it is clearly within the law for the authority issuing the law is illegitimate' (p. 606).

The strange consequences of Wolff's position are here strikingly illustrated. It is tempting to think that anyone who believes that the deliberate blowing up of the conference room in the attempt to kill Hitler and thereby successfully killing and wounding others is *not* a violent act needs sympathy. Independently of any question of legitimacy, this is, on the face of it, the sort of act which should be a test of a definition of violence. If the definition doesn't determine it as an act of violence, then it is a defective definition. The question of whether the act was illegitimate or unauthorised is simply irrelevant. It may be replied that such a reaction merely shows the strength of my own commitment to a restricted understanding of the term violence but, on the contrary, it is surely rather an indication of how remote Wolff's usage is from linguistic realities, and of how difficult it is to discuss serious political issues clearly with such a definitional apparatus.

As Wolff develops his discussion this becomes even more striking. He says, for instance, *a propos* the student demonstrations at Columbia University in 1968 that it is 'totally wrong' to say such things as 'In the Columbia case violence was justified' even though, as he believes, the whole affair seems to have been a quite prudent and restrained use of force. Wolff believes this to be so partly because of his definition of violence since the sentence comes close to 'In the Columbia case the illegitimate use of force to effect decisions against the will or desire of others was legitimate'. (Actually he does not object to the sentence in quite such direct terms but argues that it implies the doctrine of legitimate government or legitimate authority, and since this is an absurdity so is the sentence itself.) Yet if there is any absurdity here it surely resides in the implications of Wolff's definition since on a more restrictive definition of violence which makes no reference to legitimate authority, etc. we can ask reasonably clear moral and political questions about the students' use of violence and hence decide the quite separate question of whether or not it was justified. Some of the issues thus raised will be similar to, if not identical with, those Wolff wants to treat in a more roundabout and, I think, contrived way by employing the much looser terminology of force.

Wolff seems at times to recognise this and in discussing what he calls 'the doctrine of non-violence' he says that if violence is understood (non-strictly) as the use of force to interfere with somebody in a direct physical way or to injure him physically then the doctrine of non-violence is 'merely a subjective queasiness having no moral rationale'. He cites the case of a sit-in at a lunch-counter which not only deprives the proprietor of profits, but may ruin him if persisted in. Wolff says that he has been done

> a much greater injury than would be accomplished by a mere beating in a dark alley. He may deserve to be ruined, of course, but, if so, then he probably also deserves to be beaten. A penchant for such indirect coercion as a boycott or a sit-in is morally questionable, for it merely leaves the dirty work to the bank that forecloses on the mortgage or the policeman who carries out the eviction (p. 610).

Stirring stuff, but not, I believe, a contribution to the debate about the respective merits of violent and non-violent forms of political action or protest. This is not the place to engage in that debate but plainly it raises serious issues which are simply obscured by Wolff's treatment. Just to take the example of the sit-in: the normal defence of such an action would not be in terms of an intention to ruin the proprietor and bring him to destitution, but to bring sharply to his attention and the attention of apathetic or hostile citizens, *within* the framework of laws and conventions about the law which you all to some extent share, your beliefs that his operations have severely harmed others and are likely to bring inconvenience and financial discomfort upon him unless he mends his ways. There are numerous considerations that may be advanced to support a preference for this way of proceeding over beating him up or maiming or killing him. It may plausibly be argued that it is tactically better from the point of view of public reaction, that it has better social consequences, that violence is essentially prone to get out of hand and that the victim suffers much less. When Wolff says, 'He may deserve to be ruined, of course, but, if so, then he probably also deserves to be beaten', he is engaging in no more than schoolboy bravado. Even if ruin were the object of the exercise it is far from obvious that this is worse or on a par with the effects of beating, e.g. possible permanent physical and psychological damage, if not death. One may very well have good reason for putting someone out of business without thereby being justified in mutilating or killing him.

On the assumption that no more needs to be said about Wolff's detailed argumentation, I want to conclude my consideration of legitimist definitions by raising a final objection to their procedures which is, I think, a very serious one. What will such definitions allow us to say about that pre-eminent use of violence, warfare? In the case of Wolff's definition, for instance, the absurd consequence is immediately generated that if there are two sovereign states, both of which have politically legitimate governments, then they may not be engaged in violence, even though they are bombarding each other with nuclear rockets. This will happen if both legitimate governments legally authorise the particular resort to war. This is surely not an uncommon or fantastic case. Wolff would be saved from this absurdity only by his belief that there is no such thing as political legitimacy, but others, such as Hook and Honderich who propose legitimist definitions have no such escape route. Honderich, it is true, explicitly excludes warfare from the scope of his discussion but purports nonetheless to be discussing political violence. The restriction of political violence to internal or domestic political contexts is, I think, astonishing and the case of warfare rightly raises difficulties for his definition which includes reference to 'a use of force prohibited by law'. His full definition of political violence is: – 'a considerable or destroying use of force against persons or things, a use of force prohibited by law and directed to a change in the politics, personnel or system of government, and hence to changes in society'.[21] As we can see from this definition the problem posed by the example of warfare strikes at the roots of the legitimist outlook. For Honderich, even the *illegal* internal use of severe force by police, security organisations or even non-governmental agencies is not political violence if it is aimed at preserving the status quo! Given Honderich's generally radical stance, this is not only a curious outcome but it exhibits starkly the tendency of legitimist theories to present the use of violence as posing a moral problem only for those who think of deploying force *against* the established or legitimate government. Yet surely even the legal employment of 'destroying force' raises issues about the role and nature of political violence. Comparisons between states, for instance, can rightly raise questions about the moral standing of greater or less recourse to violence, and degrees of readiness to have such recourse, in the legitimate administrations of the different polities. Such questions are not only real but they are clearly related to the questions faced by those who contemplate the use of violence against legal authority either that of their own state or of another.

Let me turn all too briefly now to a clarification and defence of a restricted definition of violence. In a sense, most of the paper has been a defence of such a definition, for it has sought to show the inadequacies of its competitors, but I think that a little more is required at least by way of clarification of possible misunderstandings.

I cited earlier the OED definition and I want to endorse something like it, but first we must distinguish violence from *force* and from *coercion*. A good deal of confusion in the literature is generated by the failure to make these distinctions. A few examples will make clear the need to distinguish. Take the examples of what Ronald Miller has called 'gentle removal'[22] – the courteous use of force to remove unresisting but unco-operative demonstrators from a building (admittedly rare but possible) or the gentle but firm restraining of someone who wants to rush into a blazing building to rescue relatives or even, a slightly different kind of case, the use of force by a surgeon in operating to remove a piece of shrapnel from a man's leg in order to save his life. For coercion, we need only consider that threats are coercive and they need not even be threats to do violence (e.g. a threat to tell someone's wife of his disreputable behaviour). Various classical non-violent tactics of resistance and demonstration are coercive, e.g. the blocking off of a road on which officials usually proceed by having large numbers of demonstrators lie down on the roadway. Violence is, of course, one way of coercing, but only one.

Ideally at this point I should provide definitions of force and coercion, but limitations of space will have to be my excuse for dodging that difficult task here.[23] Instead I want to turn to the OED definition mentioned earlier and raise some questions about it. It defines violence as: 'The exercise of physical force so as to inflict injury on or damage to persons or property; action or conduct characterised by this'.

The first problem with this is that it rules out the possibility of psychological violence and there is at least a case for including it. I suspect that whether we want to allow for a non-metaphorical use of the term violence in the psychological cases will depend upon whether we can realistically view some of these cases as involving the application of force. It is useful here to think of the notion of overpowering which seems as if it must figure as an element in the analysis of force. Now if we consider a case in which someone skilfully works upon another's emotions and fears with a combination of words and deeds short of physical force, but with intentionally overpowering effects, then we may well feel that this is close enough to the physical model to be a case of violence. Newton Garver gives an interesting and profoundly sad example of the Arizona parents who decided to punish their daughter's act of adultery in an unusual way. The girl, Linda Ault, owned a dog, Beauty, of which she was very fond. According to a newspaper report,

> ... the Aults and Linda took the dog into the desert near their home. They had the girl dig a shallow grave. Then Mrs Ault grasped the dog between her hands, and Mr Ault gave his daughter a .22 caliber pistol and told her to shoot the dog.
> Instead the girl put the pistol to her right temple and shot herself.[24]

Clearly a dreadful act, and perhaps deserving of the name of violence, but if we do so treat it this will not be because of the reasons given by Garver (which are to do with deprivation of autonomy and lead pretty quickly to a version of structural violence). There is a tendency in the literature to slide from psychological violence to structural violence, but this seems to embody a confusion since it rests on the tendency to think of psychological violence as *impalpable* and then to feel that its admission endorses the even more impalpable structural violence. However, the examples which make the category of psychological violence plausible are all very palpable indeed. In Garver's example, for instance, what strikes one is the sheer immediacy and specificity of the pressure which is brought to bear upon the unfortunate girl with such overwhelming effects. Even if she had not shot herself we would feel that she had still been the victim of severe and damaging force. The surrounding circumstances of the outrage are tinged with physical violence for not only was she ordered to kill with a gun but one imagines that force was used to get her to dig the grave and even to get her to the place of punishment (though we are given no details of this). Consequently, to describe the case as one of quiet violence and hence a half-way house to structural violence is unconvincing.

A further category concerns those cases of great damage which do not seem to involve force though they do involve physical means. Poisoning is often given as an example, and Harris gives as well the case of the Belfast children who tie a cheese-wire between two lamp-posts across a street at a height of about six feet. As one of the kids says, 'There's always a soldier standing on the back of the jeep; even with the search lights he can't see the wire in the dark. It's just at the right height to catch his throat'.[25] Harris concludes from such examples that we can have an *act of violence* in the absence of a *violent act*. But for most of his examples we can surely appeal to the 'accordion effect' beloved of philosophers of action. The planned and fully intended results of stretching the wire are properly describable as what the children did, as their act. Their violent act was not merely stretching gently a wire across a road but ripping a man's throat open. This resort is certainly available where the incorporated consequences are intended by the agent and Harris' cases are all of this kind. Two of his examples, however, seem to raise problems for the restricted definition, even acknowledging the accordion effect. They both focus upon the interpretation of the term 'force' in the definition rather than upon the idea of a positive act. One example is a stabbing to death with a stiletto gently slid between the ribs. (Harris somewhat painfully jokes that this is 'the thin edge of the wedge'.) A second example (or class of examples) concerns poisoning or gassing. I have not produced a definition of force but my instinct is to treat the stiletto case as a use of force especially when the immediate, overpoweringly forceful effects upon the victim's body are taken into account (and the killer's intention certainly encompasses them). As to poisons, if we take a case of slow poisoning (i.e. slow-acting and requiring repeated dosing) where the destructive effects are gradual and cumulative, easily mimicking a slowly-acting sickness, I suspect that we should not call the poisoning a violent act – it's one that could be ordered or done by the proverbially fastidious criminal who abhors violence. By contrast, the use of poison gas in war, or the like swiftly-acting poison, would be much more like dealing a blow, and fairly clearly a violent act.

The concept of force needs more attention but I shall assume that this can be successfully negotiated and that the poisoning cases can either be dealt with in the way suggested or else treated as territory which is uncomfortably borderline between violence and non-violence. It is also relevant to certain cases of poisoning that a background of violence will colour our attitudes to a particular case. Consider, for instance, a siege or a blockade which may not be violent in as much as troops or ships are just patrolling and waiting for starvation or despair to produce surrender. Nonetheless the waiting part of the siege is usually a sort of interlude in a violent campaign and the siege itself essentially involves the declared intention to use very considerable violence against anyone who attempts to leave the besieged area. Most sieges in fact produce a great deal of actual violence. Against such a background it would be natural to describe even a siege in which no shooting or killing occurred as an exercise in violence.

Finally, we might ask: what is the point in having a concept of violence of this kind? Without an answer to this question the criticism of alternative definitions is incomplete. An answer must begin by noting certain very general facts about our condition. Life is hazardous in many different ways and we may be harmed by natural disasters and accidents or by disease or the indifference and lack of consideration of our fellows or by social arrangements which are to our disadvantage. We can sometimes take steps to guard against all of these – we can avoid certain areas, move from certain communities, cultivate friends and so on. But in addition to all the hazards mentioned there is another which many people fear very greatly, namely, the forceful intrusion into their lives of those who are intent upon inflicting harm and injury upon their person. It is not surprising that this should be so and that a distinctive way of speaking should arise to mark the reality to which we react in this way.

Nor is it surprising that a particular type of concern should exist for this kind of intrusion into our lives. In the first place we know that human malevolence is liable to be effective and difficult to avoid just because it is directed by intelligence; in the second place the unjustified employment of violence damages the character and worth of the user in distinctive ways or so many people believe – hence the point of expressions such as 'bully', 'sadist', or 'thug'; thirdly, the principal way of avoiding such malevolent intrusion is to resort to violence oneself or to have agents do it for you and this in turn is dangerous both in the short or the long term as is so vividly dramatised in Hobbes' picture of a State of Nature;[26] fourthly, it is arguable that even the justified resort to violence has damaging effects upon those who employ it even where they remain physically unharmed – this argument marks one area in which pacifist contentions are commonly produced but even non-pacifists can acknowledge the appeal of some such arguments; fifthly, and relatedly, there is the fact that violence, particularly large-scale violence is hard to control and its consequences are hard to predict. The third, fourth and fifth reasons make it plausible that resort to violence even when morally justifiable should commonly be regarded as a matter for regret. More generally, all those considerations bear upon debates about the comparability of violent and non-violent tactics, about the advantages of societies with a low level of officially sanctioned violence, and the appeal as a social ideal of, what Galtung would call, negative peace.

It must of course be conceded that this ideal does not have equal weight with all who consider it. Although anyone can recognise the distinctive facts that underpin the concept of violence I have been defending, not everyone will have the same reactions to them. There will be variations in both personal and cultural terms here even amongst men and communities who are in no obvious way corrupt or wicked. There are individuals who are much more sensitive to and worried about violence than others, just as there are whole groups, such as warrior castes, for whom violence is, to some degree, an accepted and even welcome part of their lives. Such groups may be less enthusiastic than others about projects to limit the scope of violence within and between communities and an argument with them would involve exploring further the value of peace in comparison with other values as well as conducting a debate about certain empirical issues. Such a debate must await another occasion; I hope I have done something here to prepare the ground for it.[27]

Correspondence: C. A. J. Coady, Department of Philosophy, University of Melbourne, Parkville, Victoria 3052, Australia.

Notes

1. Hannah Arendt, *On Violence*, London, 1970, pp. 43–4.
2. John Rawls, *A Theory of Justice*, Oxford, 1972, pp. 5–6. Ronald Dworkin, *Taking Rights Seriously*, Duckworth (new impression) 1978, pp. 134–6, p. 266 and also in lectures in Oxford in 1982. I have some reservations about Dworkin's use of the concept/conception distinction but this is not the place to discuss them nor even to argue a case for believing (as I do) that the distinction is likely to have less fruitful application in the case of violence than in that of justice or law.
3. There is a discussion of those types under the labels 'expansive', 'observational' and 'narrow' in K. W. Grundy & M. A. Weinstein, *The Ideologies of Violence*, Columbus, Ohio, 1974. Cf. pp. 8–13. Their discussion is useful, but not entirely convincing.
4. It is not just that they can accuse their critics of like behaviour and, crying 'tu quoque', expose their inconsistency. This is the interpretation Ted Honderich places upon this sort of use of the notion of structural violence (see Ted Honderich, *Violence For Equality – inquiries in political philosophy*, Penguin, 1980, pp. 96–100) but Honderich fails to observe that revolutionaries can try to justify their own violence as a form of defence against structural violence.
5. Newton Garver, 'What violence is', *The Nation*, 209, (24 June 1968), p. 822. This is reprinted in James Rachels and Frank A. Tillman (Ed.), *Philosophical Issues – a contemporary introduction*, New York, 1972, pp. 223–8. The quoted passage is on p. 228 and future references in the text to Garver will be cited from Rachels & Tillman.
6. Cf. N. Garver, op. cit., p. 224 and J. Galtung, 'Violence, peace and peace research' in *The Journal of Peace Research*, Vol. 6, 1969, p. 168 and 173. Page references from this paper will henceforth be bracketed in the text immediately after a quotation.
7. Cf. K. W. Grundy & M. A. Weinstein, op. cit., pp. 10–11, where they also see it as involved in revolutionary attitudes to totalitarian regimes.
8. Quoted in Grundy & Weinstein, op. cit., p. 12.
9. *New York Times Magazine*, 27 October 1968, p. 90.
10. Robert Paul Wolff, 'On violence', *Journal of Philosophy*, Vol. 66, 1969.
11. Galtung, op. cit.
12. See Jonathan Glover, *Causing Deaths and Saving Lives*, Harmondsworth, 1977; Peter Singer, *Practical Ethics*, Cambridge, 1979; John Harris, *Violence and Responsibility*, London, 1980; Ted Honderich, *Violence for Equality*, Harmondsworth, 1980.
13. Honderich, op. cit., pp. 96–9 and 152–4; Harris, op. cit., Chapter 2.
14. Harris, op. cit., p. 19.
15. Harris, op. cit., p. 18.
16. The dissimilarities with respect to the ways in which outcomes are tied to positive acts and to failures to act do not obtain universally since there may be circumstances in which a positive act takes a long time to realise its outcome and allows for some high prospect of failure, but I do not think that this sort of case can yield a model for the normal case of action and hence it does not vitiate a contrast drawn in terms of that case.
17. Harris, op. cit., p. 18.
18. Actually Harris has some special views about poisoning and other 'non-forceful' positive acts of killing which are germane to his position here but which I shall consider later.
19. I do not mean to deny the value of metaphorical or extended employments of the term violence in appropriate contexts. Heinrich Boll's novel, *The Lost Honour*

of Katherina Blum, for instance, is subtitled, 'How violence develops and where it can be lead' and it makes impressive play with the devastating effects of media smears and distortions upon the personality of an innocent woman caught up in a police investigation. Katherina's actual violence (she eventually murders the journalist principally responsible for the destruction of her reputation) is made to seem an almost natural, healthy reaction against the unscrupulous power of the popular press which has shattered her private world in ways analogous to a series of blows. There may well be a case for treating some of the episodes in the narrative as psychological violence, a category about which I shall have more to say later, but much of the novel's success lies in its symbolic and metaphorical deployment of the idea of violence and the ironic parallels between the effects of violence and the impact of journalistic irresponsibility and sensation-seeking.

20. Robert Paul Wolff, 'On violence' *Journal of Philosophy*, Vol. LXVI, 1969. Subsequent page references to this article will be bracketed in the text.
21. Honderich, op. cit., p. 154. Honderich's general definition of violence makes reference neither to law nor political change but only to a use of force etc. 'that offends against a norm' (p. 153). He could thus admit a category of illegal State violence and presumably even such legal State violence as could be construed as offending against a norm (whatever that might mean). Yet the facts remain that, (i) he shows no interest in working with the broader notion of violence, (ii) gives no idea of what sort of norms he has in mind, and (iii) is, in any case, committed to seeing these exercises of violence as non-political whatever their rationale.
22. R. Miller in *Violence* Ed. J. A. Shaffer, New York, 1971, p. 27.
23. Cf. Miller op. cit.
24. Garver, op. cit, pp. 225–6.
25. Harris, op. cit., p. 16.
26. The mention of Hobbes should remind us that one traditional way of viewing the legitimacy of the State is to see it as the safest form of the agency defence against the dangers of violence. Here too we may locate some of the point behind legitimist definitions of violence because the authorised violence of the State is seen as so contrasting with the violence against which it offers protection as not to deserve the name violence at all. Nonetheless, violence it is and even where authorised there remain moral questions about its employment.
27. Versions of this paper were read at philosophy colloquia in Oxford and London in 1983, when I was a Visiting Fellow at Corpus Christi College, Oxford, and partic- ularly benefitted from comments by Alan Ryan, G. A. Cohen and C. C. W. Taylor. It originally appeared in *Philosophical Papers*, Vol. XIV (1), May 1985.

COMMENTARY ON COADY

C. A. J. Coady belongs to that rare breed of philosophers who has made a lasting impact on different areas of philosophy, from epistemology[1] to moral philosophy.[2] He has recently published yet another seminal work, this time on political violence: *Morality and Political Violence*.[3]

In this article, which originally appeared in *Philosophical Papers*, Vol. XIV (1), May 1985, Coady takes issues with two standard ways of understanding the idea of violence, respectively, the 'wide' or 'structuralist' definition, and the 'legitimist' definition'.

By wide or structuralist definitions, Coady has in mind Johan Galtung's 'structural violence', and Newton Garver's 'institutional violence'. As Coady explains, these types of definition 'tend to serve the interests of the political left by including with the extension of the term "violence" a great range of social injustices and inequalities'. Alternatively, legitimist definitions of violence incorporate a reference to an illegal or illegitimate use of force; this is of course the definition of violence endorsed by Robert Paul Wolff.

In the first two-thirds of the article, Coady presents a clear, detailed and disparaging critical analysis of both Galtung's and Wolff's argument. Regarding Galtung's wide definition, Coady argues that contrary to what advocates of structural violence seem to believe, there are important and striking differences between personal and structural violence, of a conceptual and moral nature. Furthermore, Coady argues that the wide definition of violence, and the related definition of peace championed by Galtung, is likely to have undesirable practical consequences.

Moving on to Wolff's legitimist definition, Coady argues that issues of legitimacy are either irrelevant to the definition of violence, or, alternatively, this definition may lead to nonsensical conclusions. For example, Coady argues that according to the legitimist definition, warfare is not an act of violence: 'the absurd consequence is immediately generated that if there are two sovereign states, both of which have politically legitimate governments, then they may not be engaged in violence, even though they are bombarding each other with nuclear rockets.'

But Coady does not limit his analysis to simply exposing the weaknesses of the two types of definitions mentioned above. He also argues in favour of a 'restricted' definition, which invokes the authority of the Oxford English Dictionary: 'The exercise of physical force so as to inflict injury on or damage to persons or property; action or conduct characterised by this.' Coady is quick to alert us to the limits of this definition, for example the fact that it rules out the possibility of psychological violence, or the possibility of damage being done without the use of force. Coady acknowledges that the concept of force needs more attention, nevertheless he still believes that a restricted definition is preferable to a wide or legitimist definition.

Notes and further reading

1. His book *Testimony: A Philosophical Study* Oxford: Clarendon Press, 1994, is a modern classic of contemporary epistemology. See also J. Lackey and E. Sosa (eds), *The Epistemology of Testimony*, Oxford: Clarendon Press, 2006.
2. C. A. J. Coady (ed.), *What's Wrong with Moralism?*, Oxford: Blackwell, 2006.
3. C. A. J. Coady, *Morality and Political Violence*, Cambridge: Cambridge University Press, 2008.

13
Violence and the Perspective of Morality
Robert L. Holmes

> I object to violence because, when it appears to do good, the good is only temporary; the evil it does is permanent.
> — M. K. Gandhi

'The characteristic feature of all ethics,' Simone de Beauvoir once wrote, 'is to consider human life as a game that can be won or lost and to teach man the means of winning.'[1] The point, we may suppose, is that without ethics there is no purpose to life, no winning or losing, no reason to live one way rather than another. This, we may suppose further, is true even for those with a religious commitment, for even religion bears upon conduct only to the extent that it at least implies an ethics.

De Beauvoir was speaking here of individual human life, of course. But much the same might be said of the collective life of humankind. And one need be no more than a casual observer of the course of events in the nuclear age to appreciate the fact that humankind may not win the game of life. Without a change in the direction of civilization it may not even have a future.

Can ethics 'teach' us a way of winning this game? Not in any ordinary sense. It imparts no simple prescriptions that will miraculously achieve that end, and such prescriptions as are offered in philosophical and religious thought often contain divergent counsel. The means must be worked out by people themselves, drawing upon their own resources and wisdom. But without ethics it is unlikely they will succeed.

There are many possible ethics, among them the ethics of power, love, freedom, profit, work, and honor, each comprising a system of rules and principles for the guidance of conduct or, alternatively, presenting models – religious, historical, political, or even literary – of how to live and what sorts of considerations to regard as final in giving direction to one's life. Each, to extend de Beauvoir's metaphor a bit, represents a different way of playing the game of life. And each counts different things as winning. Ethics becomes embodied in various ways of life when people so shape their lives by its values as to give a certain bent to the very character and design of their convictions, which in turn gives a unique quality to their engagement with the world and those around them. This can come about in different ways: sometimes from unexpected, momentous events, as with Paul on the road to Damascus; sometimes from deliberate choice. For most people it comes about through the gradual and almost imperceptible assimilation of a life pattern from family, friends, and society.

The fundamental question of ethics, therefore – indeed of human existence, if we may dramatize it a bit – is how should I live? or what sort of person should I be? And it is a question to which we all give an answer, if only tacitly, in the decisions and commitments we make in the course of living. This is as true of the scientist as of the theologian, of the militarist as of the pacifist. Short of rejecting life itself, all that is open to us is whether to bring reflection to bear upon the answering of the question or simply to allow ourselves to be swept along by whatever currents come our way.

I

The ethical question in this sense is not, however, the fundamental moral question. Indeed, one way of answering the ethical question is by opting for the moral life. Morality is a perspective or way of viewing life – a game of life, if you like – that one may adopt or reject along with the others. And it too comprises values and standards that one may or may not choose to honor. But while it may embrace the values implicit in many of the above ethics, it cannot be reduced to any of them. It involves a commitment to assess when relevant any other point of view from its perspective and to override the other's claims if they conflict with its own. And its claims, unlike those of most of the others, are binding irrespective of whether one adopts its point of view. As Kant saw, one cannot release himself from moral obligations merely by disavowing an interest in the ends that actions discharging those obligations promote. Being amoral does not preclude one's also being immoral.

Is there anything that compels us to view the world in a moral light? Or, more specifically for our purposes, to approach the problem of war from a moral perspective? There is not. This should be acknowledged at the outset. One *can* view the world in amoral terms if he chooses. One can so intellectualize behavior that, in those terms, it is no longer susceptible of moral assessment. And one can compartmentalize moral concerns in such a way that whole domains of behavior are exempt from that assessment. Socrates made this clear as he awaited the hemlock in Plato's *Phaedo*. Why was he sitting there when he had been given a chance to escape? One could have answered this by describing his bodily movements, the contraction of his muscles, the changing positions of his bones and tendons, and so on. But to do so would have left out the fact that it was a *moral decision* that was central to his being there, a rational act. No description of bodily movements alone adds up to the performance of an action. It must include the notions of intention, deliberateness, and self-directedness, as well as at least implied reference to the values that are part of the makeup of the character of the person in question. And no purely scientific explanation does this, either, however microscopic in detail. We could describe Lincoln's assassination quite correctly as the rearrangement of one set of molecules (those making up Lincoln's brain) by another set (those making up the bullet fired by Booth). But the event becomes invested with moral significance only when it is seen as the killing of a person as the result of a deliberate action by another person. Human beings, by some scientific accounts are just byproducts of chance combinations of chemicals millions of years ago and can be described painstakingly in those terms exclusively. But to do so is not to describe persons as moral agents and as fitting subjects for moral praise or blame.

Only if we choose to do so can we view the world as a moral world, suffused with value and raising questions of good and bad. And only then do the doings of human beings constitute conduct subject to standards of right and wrong. To view the world in this light does not commit us to any particular values or standards. It does not tell us precisely of what morality consists. It does not provide us with a moral theory. But it provides the perspective in which moral questions can arise and in which moral theory can make sense.

I stress this because it is from a moral perspective that we shall approach the problem of war. I shall not take seriously moral nihilism or even skepticism; not because there are not interesting and challenging arguments to be confronted from each of those directions but because to deal with them adequately would take me afield from my main concerns. I shall take seriously, however, attempts to show that morality does not extend to the sphere of international relations, and to war in particular. For this represents one way of trying to compartmentalize moral concerns and to suspend them in one major area of human activity. Not that one *cannot* do this. It is done all the time. One finds it in academic studies of war and international relations. And one suspects it is the accepted mode of treatment of these matters by governments. Just as there are ways of describing individual behavior that render it impervious to moral assessment, so there are ways of describing the behavior of nations that do the same. Political realism, as we shall see in the next two chapters, does precisely this. But one need not do this. And I shall argue that if one allows the relevance of morality to individual human conduct, it cannot consistently be denied to the conduct of states. For the moment, however, I want to say more about the moral perspective from which I shall be proceeding.

Morality's concern, I say, is with conduct, specifically with its rightness or wrongness. But rightness and wrongness have no meaning in the abstract.

They are significant only in the context of purposive human activities. And these activities vary greatly. There are right and wrong ways to swing a golf club, bake a cake, fly an airplane, or launch a military attack, determined by the aims, goals, or purposes of these undertakings or of those of which they are a part. But there are not only right and wrong ways of performing specific operations like these (in which right and wrong have very nearly the force of 'effective' or 'ineffective'), there are also right and wrong ways of treating persons, whatever the activities in which one is engaged. These are determined by the moral point of view, whose function, at the minimum, is to minimize suffering and unhappiness.

Sometimes what is required of us from one point of view, or from the standpoint of some ethical system of the sort enumerated above, conflicts with what is required from another. This happens, for example, when self-interest or prudence conflicts with a legal obligation, as may happen when one receives a draft call during wartime or when that same legal obligation conflicts with a felt moral obligation to oppose an immoral war. All of us feel the pull of varied and sometimes conflicting obligations as we shift from one role to another in our daily lives. But it is only the moral obligations among these that can properly claim highest priority for anyone purporting to lead the moral life. That life involves recognizing that the demands of morality not only supercede personal desires and interests, including self-interest, when and if they conflict, but also override other obligations as well. Thus, violence that is militarily justified (say, by the principles of sound strategy) may or may not be legally justified from the standpoint of international law; and what is militarily and legally justified may or may not be morally justified. There is no reason to believe that correct assessments from these and other points of view will always coincide, and when they do not, precedence must be given to one over the others if one is to act rationally at all.

If right and wrong presuppose criteria from some perspective or point of view, what criteria distinguish morality? Western moral philosophy answers this in different ways. But the answers center about different ways of assessing the relevance of *consequences* and *value*. Those who affirm the paramountcy of consequences in the making of moral judgments usually stress that what is important is the value produced by those consequences, either in itself or relative to the disvalue that is realized. They typically assert that acts are right if and only if they realize as great a balance of value over disvalue as any alternative action, and obligatory if they realize a greater balance. Those who deny the paramountcy of consequences hold either that the value actually produced by actions is irrelevant, as Kant believed, or, more often, that it is relevant but not decisive, and that other kinds of considerations, such as whether one is violating a moral rule, acting unjustly, or infringing moral rights, must also be considered.

When dealing with substantive moral problems, philosophers typically stake out a position among those described above and then try to show

how, within it, one or another stand on the issue in question (whether it be abortion, capital punishment, euthanasia, or whatever) is justified. I shall not do this. In the absence of some a priori apparatus by which to certify some moral standards over others, I believe we must start at the other end, so to speak, and decide first where we stand on particular issues and only then look to see to what that commits us in the way of a more general theory. That is, I believe that one cannot convincingly do moral philosophy of a normative sort by first stating the whole array of theories, selecting one, and then proceeding to defend it against every objection of which one can think. One must first try to understand what is right in particular cases, or at least particular types of cases, and only then look to see to what sort of theory this commits one. It is this that I propose to do with the question of the morality of war.

I shall, however, proceed from a minimal basis of what may be called moral personalism, by which I mean the conviction that any plausible moral theory must have at its center a concern for the lives and well-being of persons. If we do not value persons, including ourselves, there can be no point to valuing other things – not property, possessions, national boundaries, the flag, or anything else. I shall take this to mean at the least, so far as conduct is concerned, that we should minimize avoidable harm to ourselves and others (including, I should add, animals, who, though they are not moral agents, are capable of experiencing pleasure and pain and hence deserve moral consideration).

This gives the barest rudiments of a moral position. But it suffices to establish the importance of violence to the moral assessment of human affairs. For violence is the paradigmatic way of mistreating persons. It involves harming or killing them and destroying things they value. As H. L. A. Hart has said, it is rules that 'restrict the use of violence in killing or inflicting bodily harm' that are the most important. 'If there were not these rules,' he asks, 'what point could there be for beings such as ourselves in having rules of *any* other kind?'[2]

II

There has always been violence, of course, and it might seem that there is little reason to give it anymore than usual attention today. But with modern technology it has metamorphosed into new and frightening forms, some of which we scarcely comprehend and most of which we are incapable of controlling with any justifiable confidence. Nuclear weapons, radiation, and biological agents cannot render a man any more dead than the broadsword or the crossbow, but they have added a new dimension of horror to warfare. And they have done so at just the time that mechanization and bureaucracy have desensitized us to that horror. As Konrad Lorenz put it:

> The man who presses the releasing button [of modern remote control weapons] is so completely screened against seeing, hearing, or otherwise

emotionally realizing the consequences of his action, that he can commit it with impunity.... Only thus can it be explained that perfectly good-natured men, who would not even smack a naughty child, proved to be perfectly able to release rockets or to lay carpets of incendiary bombs on sleeping cities, thereby committing hundreds and thousands of children to a horrible death in the flames. The fact that it is good, normal men who did this, is as eerie as any fiendish atrocity of war.[3]

The heroic spectacle of brave men contending on a darkling plain has given way to the prosaic impersonality of modern industrial society, in which the efforts of millions of ordinary persons – from taxpayers and defense workers to comfortably isolated functionaries in air-conditioned missile silos – conspire to promote and sustain a system for which everyone, and yet no one, is directly responsible. A multitude of loyalties are so arrayed as to generate a potential evil far greater than the goods they severally constitute.

Moreover, the problem of violence once seemed of manageable size. Wars could be waged full tilt, so to speak, with all of the zest and enthusiasm that dangerous adventures inspire; but when they were over the world went on pretty much as before – scarred and shaken sometimes, but always with hope of a better future, or at least of some kind of future. Now all of that has changed. The nuclear age has done more than just enlarge our capacity for violence; it has transformed the whole context in which our thinking about it must take place. Whereas previously violence could be used rationally in the service of human aims, at least in the sense of providing a means to certain clearly attainable ends (whether or not these in turn were rational), its character today threatens the very conditions essential to the attainment of *any* ends, good or bad.

This is a problem of our own making. Whereas our greatest struggles were once against the forces of nature, today they are against forces of our own creation. These include not only the brilliant means devised specifically for the purpose of destroying our fellow men but also the complex socioeconomic and political systems designed to better human life but whose operation redounds in countless ways to the advantage of a few, the despair of many, and the ultimate impoverishment of all. However else we characterize them, they represent ways of doing violence to the world and its inhabitants.

Contributing to the problem is the root assumption of most social and political thinking, which is that without the constraint of coercive institutions our fellow men (always others, never ourselves) would immediately fall upon one another, plundering, murdering, and raping at will; that only the threat of force restrains them, and hence that the agencies and institutions making good that threat must be maintained at all costs. This assumption provides the basis for our fear of anarchy and the belief that anything less than a firm response to disorder will be interpreted as weakness. And weakness, it is thought in turn, can only whet men's appetites to push the limits of restraint ever farther back, until the very fabric of civilization disintegrates and we are all cast into that cauldron of unrestrained violence that Hobbes calls the state of nature, in which life is 'nasty, brutish, and short.'

Such thinking places a premium upon the use of violence. To the extent the Hobbesian state of nature is feared, its avoidance is sought by reliance upon the very behavior deemed most dreadful in it. If harm is what each most wants to avoid, then what better way to avoid it than to threaten it in return – if not personally, as in the state of nature, then collectively, through the state? It is thus that there grow up laws, police, and prisons by which to carry out that threat domestically and armies by which to do it internationally. Violence has in fact become a fixture of contemporary civilization. The production and maintenance of means for its use have become a major commitment of most societies, sustained by the economy, government, and educational system. Beneath the overlay of courtesies and formalities that ease our daily interaction lies a readiness to use it not only against other peoples but, through the agencies of police and government, against one another as well. If only a few of us ever wield the nightsticks or carry the rifles, we are the mainstay of those who do.

This fact of the pervasiveness of violence has been noted by Sergio Cotta, who contends that violence has come to dominate our times. Modern communication has brought about what he calls a perception of the 'spatial diffusion' of violence; it is perceived as omnipresent. It dominates the news (and, we might add, film and television) to such an extent that 'violence appears as the norm rather that the exception. Only excessively brutal violence becomes exceptional.'[4] Relatedly, he contends, the rush and immediacy of news, pervaded by reports of violence, gives a perception of a concentration of violence in time as well. And there has, he says, also been an extension of the field of violence. Whereas previously not all harmful or unjust acts were characterized as violence, today violence is perceived to pervade activities and institutions to the point where '[s]cience, instruction, and knowledge in general are considered subtle and hidden forms of violence against the one who must learn, regardless of the use that may be made of them.'[5]

Cotta sees two attitudes predominating here. One views today's violence as differing little from that of the past; the other sees it as entirely new in meaning and historical significance. Politically the *Realpolitiker* represents the first point of view, the revolutionary the second. But neither of these, he thinks, adequately reflects the nature of the current dominating influence of violence. What is genuinely new, he contends, is our perception of violence and our *exaltation* of it.

> In fact, if we have violence in *everything* and *everywhere*, we have one, and only one choice: either to suffer it with resignation (in which case violence appears to be the supreme law of life, man's destiny) or to try to eliminate it. But if we choose the second, we become prisoners of an

all-encompassing premise: in order to eliminate violence it is necessary to make use of it, since there is no other means for antiviolent action. Such action, therefore, will not renounce the *materiality* of violence, but will reverse its direction: something destructive will be rendered constructive in the hope that through this reversal it will be neutralized and will disappear.[6]

Cotta here puts his finger on the most persuasive of the justifications for the use of violence: that it is necessary to prevent violence. The worse one considers violence to be, the readier one is to use it in return, to the point where, if the violence threatened is unlimited, one's response will be unlimited. Carried to its logical conclusion, this provides the rationale for the balance of terror in the nuclear age.

If I am correct about the assumption underlying most social and political thinking, and if Cotta is even approximately correct about the contemporary exhaltation of violence, we can see the power of the forces impelling us to rely upon it. There is no simple way to defuse them and for that reason no simple solution to the problem of war. The overriding moral issue is to confront that 'all-encompassing premise,' as Cotta calls it, to the effect that the only way to eliminate violence is to use it; and confront it, for our purposes, by asking whether the violence of war can be morally justified. This requires looking more closely at the precise nature of violence and the moral issues its use raises.

III

It has been argued that the very concept of violence, as well as that of non-violence, is inherently confused. For this reason it has also been said that 'a number of familiar questions are also confusions to which no coherent answers could ever be given, such as: when it is permissible to resort to violence in politics; whether the black movement . . . should be nonviolent; and whether anything good in politics is ever accomplished by violence.'[7] If this should be correct, then the central questions that concern us in connection with warfare, and that have occupied just war theorists over the centuries, are likewise unanswerable, for they can be formulated only by presupposing that violence has some coherent meaning.

The advocate of this view, Robert Paul Wolff, takes violence to be '*the illegitimate or unauthorized use of force to effect decisions against the will or desire of others;*'[8] or again, '*the political use of force in ways proscribed by a legitimate government.*'[9] This he claims to be a normative account, distinguished from a parallel descriptive account in which it is understood simply as 'the use of force in ways that are proscribed or unauthorized by those who are generally accepted as the legitimate authorities.'[10] He then claims that the notion of legitimate authority is incoherent and, that being the case, that the concepts of violence and nonviolence, and the host of questions about their use, are also incoherent. This means that the issue turns upon the analysis of the concept of violence: specifically upon whether it is normative and, if so, whether it yields the alleged conclusion.[11]

People do sometimes speak as though violence were wrong by definition, which would make violence a normative concept, in the sense that to characterize something as an act of violence would suffice to settle what its moral evaluation should be. To establish that an action or policy is violent would suffice to condemn it. For this reason we sometimes hear slums, poverty, and ignorance characterized as violence, while acts of war – the paradigms of violent acts – are often referred to merely as the use of force.

But this view does not hold up well under scrutiny. To see why it does not, let us begin by distinguishing broadly the different sorts of things we mean by violence.

On the one hand, there is the violence of nature represented by hurricanes, earthquakes, windstorms, and the like. On the other hand, there is the violence done by humans, including violence against other living things (persons and animals) and that against property and inanimate things. As environmental issues become of increasing concern, there is growing awareness of what might be called violence against nature as well. As it is the effect of violence upon living things – whether or not directed specifically against them – that is of ultimate moral concern, and inasmuch as only such of that violence as is done by humans is subject to moral assessment, I shall call violence by persons against living things primary. Violence against property or inanimate things is of interest only insofar as it has some bearing upon the lives and well-being of living things.[12] For that reason I shall call it secondary.

We can better understand this by considering that there are *central*, *extended*, and *peripheral* uses of the concept. Consider the following statements:

A

Historically speaking, violence and assassination have marked almost every society created by man.[13]

Our own era is marked by the collective self-concept of a country in which violence is prevalent and in which there is a growing fear of falling prey to a violent criminal in the streets.[14]

The emergence of the U.S. as a great power has been accompanied by a growing commitment to violence as a technique for implementing policy.[15]

B

[The Liberal Church] is furthermore usually oblivious to the fact that nonviolence may be covert violence. Children do starve and old people freeze to death in the poverty of our cities.[16]

What the school determines to accomplish it does so in a constant and total atmosphere of violence. We do not mean physical violence; we mean violence in the sense of any assault upon, or violation of the personality. An examination or test is a form of violence. ... Compelled attendance in the classroom, compulsory studying in study hall, is violence.[17]

The injustices within Brazilian society constitute Violence Number One, and terrorism is Violence Number Two.[18]

C

Destruction and violence! How is the ordinary man to know that the most violent element in society is ignorance.[19]

We need only think of the cacophony of sound that does violence to our traditional image of concert music. ... Not only is the resulting composition violent in character; its method of execution is violence also.[20]

An interviewer can do violence to a reputation simply by quoting verbatim.[21]

The references to violence in group A call to mind the phenomena most often associated with violence in our common-sense thinking, and for that reason I call them central uses. Here the idea of destructive physical force is prominent. Those in group B are extended uses in that, although they refer to primary violence, it is not of an exclusively or even prominently physical sort (though the third quotation in B juxtaposes a central use, the second occurrence, with an extended use, the first occurrence). Most uses that relate closely to the concept of violation fall into this second category, as do those relating to what has come to be called psychological violence. The second quotation illustrates both. Those in category C I call peripheral uses because they are either metaphorical or highly attenuated (though the first passage contrasts a peripheral use with a central one).

In some of the passages, notably those in group B and C, violence is tacitly defined in such a way as to convey disapproval of the phenomena characterized. In fact it is probably the strong disapproval most people feel toward violence that explains why the notion is so readily extended to other modes of conduct of which they disapprove. Thus when paint was splattered on a Soviet violinist during a New York concert, a reviewer wrote that '[t]his work [Bach's *Chaconne* in D Minor] is so demanding and musically profound, that when it is well performed ... such an act of violence is akin to taking a knife to the *Mona Lisa*.'[22] Such statements conceal a condemnatory moral judgment. Given the strong negative emotive force of the word 'violence,' to apply it in this way serves to focus upon the act the full force of one's disapproval. Splattering paint upon a performer during a concert is a symbolic act and (presumably) causes no injury. But however wrong it might be, it is not an act of violence in any strict sense. Any word that has strong emotive meaning in the way in which 'violence' does (and words like 'terrorist' do) is subject to such use.

The lines dividing these categories are not sharp, of course, but they do not need to be for our purposes. I want to focus upon the central uses, specifically those that relate, as do most or perhaps all of them, to physical violence. In its strictest sense physical violence is the use of force with the intent to harm, kill or cause destruction; or at the least, the use of force that has harm, death, or destruction as a foreseeable outcome (a terrorist's bombing is an act of violence even if the intention is only to publicize a cause). This leaves it open whether a given act succeeds, since success in execution is not necessary to an act's being an act of violence (the shot may miss or the bomb fail to explode). By 'force' in this characterization I mean pronounced physical force. We can use force (such as to lift heavy objects), do things forcefully (like arguing a point of logic), or force others to do certain things (like moving their king in a game of chess), without resorting to violence. This is because the use of force in its broadest sense is the effecting of change, and this may be done violently or nonviolently. Indeed, Gandhi in his concept of Satyagraha, or Truth Force, and Martin Luther King, Jr., in his philosophy of Soul Force, expressly utilized the concept of force to designate nonviolent ways of effecting change. But physical violence cannot occur in the absence of such force, even if it does not need to be exercised directly by dint of one's own effort (sometimes it is enough to pull the trigger of a gun or depress the plunger of a detonator). So while we often use 'force' and 'violence' interchangeably, the two cannot be equated.

There is, of course, some violence in which there is neither a specific intention of the required sort nor expectable consequences of harm, destruction, or death. A deranged person flailing about in a padded cell or someone who is drugged or whose brain has been electrically stimulated may be violent but have no intention at all, much less be able to foresee any consequences of what he does. Almost anything from waging an argument to conducting an orchestra can be done violently without any intention to harm. This observation relates to the use of 'violent' to characterize the *way* something is done rather than what is done. Not all things done violently are acts of violence, nor are all acts of violence done violently.

Put another way, imagine a scale of human behavior, one end of which represents calm, controlled, self-directed behavior, the other of which represents strenuous, agitated, and sometimes uncontrolled behavior. As one ascends from the former to the latter there will be a threshold at which it begins to be appropriate to characterize what is done as done violently, whatever it is that is being done. Between that point and the extreme of agitated behavior there is a further threshold at which it begins to be appropriate to speak of the *person* in question as becoming violent – in each case without reference to purposes, intentions, or expectations. In neither case will it be appropriate, without expansion of the descriptions, to characterize

278 *Violence: A Philosophical Anthology*

the behavior as involving the commission of *acts* of violence. These uses of 'violent,' unlike those in expressions like 'act of violence,' will sometimes be central and sometimes not, depending upon whether the conduct so characterized is purposive and, if so, to what ends. Thus we can distinguish a vertical scale of degrees of turbulence in behavior and a horizontal scale of projected and expectable consequences considered with respect to whether they cause harm, destruction, or death. Both are relevant to determining the appropriateness of various uses of the concept of violence. Normally it is only those cases on the vertical scale that also have a place on the horizontal scale that fall within the range of central uses because only those are directed against persons and things.[23]

There are, however, some uses of force to cause destruction that are not acts of violence in any usual sense: the demolition of a building, the sinking of an obsolete ship by gunfire, or the use of explosives in mining operations. Destructive uses of force *as such*, in other words, do not constitute violence. The reason why they do not is because they may or may not be legitimate and which they are makes a difference to the appropriateness of calling them violence.[24] To this extent Wolff's analysis is on the track of an important feature of the concept of secondary violence. It is hard to think of any uses of physical force against objects or property that can unequivocally be called acts of violence (excluding acts so-called by virtue of being violently done) if they are not unauthorized or illegitimate.[25] But the distinction between authorized and unauthorized force does not do the same service in the case of force directed against persons. Hangings, executions by firing squad, and shootings by police are acts of violence however legal they may be.

For this reason it is important to mark off two separate dimensions, or, if you like, two different concepts of physical violence, the one relating to force used against persons or animals, the other relating to force used against objects only. Thus primary physical violence is the use of force with the intention to harm or kill (or where that will be a foreseeable consequence). Secondary physical violence is the unauthorized use of force to cause destruction. This gives conceptual acknowledgement within the range of central uses to the distinction marked earlier between primary and secondary violence.

Harm is the key notion in the concept of primary violence. Sometimes it suffices to warrant saying that when someone has been harmed he has been caused pain, suffering, anguish, and so forth. But in a stricter sense, going back as far as Plato, people have been harmed only if they have been made worse off as a result of what was done to them. This might or might not be as a result of having been caused pain. Even in the most expert and successful of treatment doctors and dentists often unavoidably cause pain and suffering; probably more so in fact than do many who use violence against others (the average mugger, for example, probably causes less pain in the world than the average surgeon). Though it is appropriate to say in these cases that my doctor or dentist *hurt* me in the course of treatment, it is not appropriate on the strength of that alone to say that he *harmed* me. Nor of course is it correct to say that doctors and dentists do their yankings, cuttings, and sawings *in order to harm*, even in the weaker sense. This suggests that the causing of pain in order to benefit (and, we might add, where it can reasonably be expected that benefit will result) is not usually thought of as the causing of harm. Even less is it thought of as violence. But *unless* deliberate infliction of pain against a person's will, or the doing of things that can reasonably be expected to cause pain, are done with a view to benefiting him, they can be said to constitute harm at least in the weaker sense. It is not enough to have had no intention to worsen a person's overall state when causing pain in order to be said not to have harmed him (forcibly abducting a person at gunpoint for terrorist purposes without actually intending to harm him in the stronger sense might meet that condition). One must have intended to better it, or at least have had a warrantable expectation that betterment would result.

Nor, it should be said, does the fact that acts of primary violence are usually performed against the will of the person affected mean that they would cease to be acts of violence if consent were involved. In this respect Cotta misleadingly characterizes both force and violence as forms of what he calls 'activity contra,' meaning that they are exercised 'without the consent of those affected.'[26] Typical cases of violence, to be sure, are nonconsensual; but contravention of the will of the person affected is not a necessary condition of violence. Shooting someone is no less an act of violence for the fact the person asked to be shot. Nor is it always an act of violence deliberately to kill another person, even where such killing clearly constitutes murder. An injection that brings about a peaceful death is not an act of physical violence (whatever the morality of such killing) because it does not involve the appropriate use of force.

Neither primary nor secondary physical violence, it should be noted, can be understood in purely behavioral terms. Acts of secondary violence require an institutional setting in which the notions of legitimacy or authorization acquire meaning.[27] They cannot be understood simply by reference to physical behavior or to the destructiveness of the force used. Acts of primary violence do not similarly presuppose an institutional setting and for that reason cannot be understood in terms of the legitimate/illegitimate distinction. But they do presuppose certain purposes or expectations pertaining to the causing of harm. It is these that distinguish them from accidental uses of destructive or deadly force. We do speak of 'observing' acts of violence of both sorts, of course, but this is because the context normally warrants assumptions about intentions, expectations, or authorizations not warranted by the observation of physical behavior alone. As we saw earlier in our discussion of the concept of morality, human behavior alone, however closely described, does not by itself add up to the performance of actions. Acts of violence of the sorts I have characterized are therefore not among the more primitive facts about the world. On a scale from primitive to complex facts (including at the latter end what have come to be called institutional facts), violence of the two sorts I have been describing would fall between the two, with secondary violence higher on the scale than primary violence.

If this is correct, and if Wolff's account aims to clarify the central uses of the concept of violence, that analysis is inadequate. For the notion of morally legitimate government plays no role in those uses. If, on the other hand, his argument is intended to elucidate only what might be called a political concept of violence, then even granting that there is such a concept, and that it is analyzable as he proposes, one could accept his argument insofar as it applies to uses of that concept and still maintain that all of the social and moral questions about justification can be asked with regard to the central (and other) uses. Either way there is no reason to believe that questions about the use and justifiability of violence and nonviolence are incoherent and cannot in principle be answered. And that is all that is necessary to justify the central place of violence in the assessment of war.

IV

We can now say that primary violence is an evaluative notion by virtue of the centrality to its analysis of the notion of harm. In its stronger sense, as we have seen, harm is what makes a person worse off. To determine that some- one has been harmed requires making an evaluative judgment. But this does not make primary violence wrong by definition, if by that we mean actu- ally or absolutely wrong. If to establish that someone has knowingly harmed someone does not suffice to show that he has acted wrongly, then showing that someone has performed an act of violence against someone does not suffice to show that either. It is important to distinguish between evaluative concepts in our judgments of the goodness or badness of things and nor- mative concepts used to judge that conduct as right, wrong, or obligatory. Violence in its central uses is of the first type. Acts of violence, as we have seen, involve the intention to harm or the expectation that it will result. Absent a theory about the nature of moral obligation and the relationship between obligation and value, there is no warrant for saying that the fact that an act is harmful by itself renders it impermissible, anymore than the fact that the act is good by itself renders it obligatory. For either of these further judgments one needs a premise connecting the notions of value and obligation or some reason to believe that there is a conceptual link between the two. No final moral assessment of acts that result in harm to oneself or others can be assumed to be dictated by the mere characterization of such acts as causing harm, and accordingly no such assessment is dictated by the notion of an act of violence. Otherwise, we should be able to show that war is wrong simply by noting that it involves performing acts of violence.

But if violence is not wrong by definition, it is nonetheless prima facie wrong, or wrong all other things being equal, just by virtue of the fact that it is prima facie wrong to harm people. Whether this connection between harm and prima facie wrongness is a necessary one, written into the very meanings of the concepts themselves (which *would* give violence a norma- tive as well as an evaluative character by entailing that acts of violence are by definition prima facie wrong), or a contingent one requiring an additional substantive premise, we need not determine; though *if* lightness and wrong- ness are definable by reference to value terms, then the concept of harm is a plausible candidate for inclusion in their analysis. Either way, if what I am maintaining is correct, then while acts of violence are not wrong by defi- nition, they are all of them prima facie wrong and in need of justification. Secondary violence, on the other hand, has a clearly normative character by virtue of its incorporation of the notion of authority or legitimacy. But it is not evaluative in the manner of primary violence. One can speak of an object's being destroyed without being committed to a value assessment of the object or its resultant state in a way that he cannot when he says of someone that he has been harmed. Moreover the notion of authorization as we have employed it does not say anything about the moral legitimacy of the form of government under which it is gained. It does not even entail the legality of all authorized uses of force within the broader context, say, of a country's constitution (local governments might authorize actions that higher courts later rule unconstitutional; but this would not alter the fact that the initial actions were genuinely authorized). Much less does it imply any actual or possible form of government under which such authorization is given is morally justified.

V

What I have been saying should not be taken to mean that all wrongdoing consists of violence. Critics of pacifism correctly point out that there are ways of harming people other than by violence. In the quotation cited earlier, Niebuhr speaks of nonviolence as sometimes being 'covert violence,' where he has in mind by violence the results of poverty, freezing, and starvation. And he pointed out elsewhere that boycotts of British cotton by Gandhi's followers in India could have deleterious effects upon the textile workers in Lancashire, England.[28]

Gandhi himself acknowledged the problem and attempted to meet it head on. A critic had written:

> Gandhi, as I understand him, proclaims the Way of Love. And yet he does not see that 'Non-co-operation is a way of violence.' Suppose the milk drivers of New York had a real and just and even terrible grievance. Sup- pose that they should strike and cut off the milk supply from the babies of New York. They might never raise a hand in violent attack on any one and yet their way would be the way of violence. Over the dead bodies

of little children they would by 'non-cooperation' win their victory. As Bertrand Russell said of the Bolsheviki, 'such suffering makes us question the means used to arrive at a desired end.' Non-cooperation means suffering in Lancashire and is an appeal in the end to violence rather than reason.[29]

In his reply Gandhi distinguished between a strike simply to protest, say, against the municipality for mismanagement of its trust and one in which the drivers were starving as a result of underpayment and had exhausted all other means of redress. In the first case, he said, their action would be a 'crime against humanity,' but in the second it would be justified. In elaborating, he said of the second case: 'Their refusal will certainly not be an act of violence though it will not be an act of love. They were not philanthropists. They were driving milk carts for the sake of their maintenance. It was no part of their duty as employees under every circumstance to supply milk to babies. There is no violence when there is no infraction of duty.'[30]

Of conceptual interest here is the fact that Gandhi implicitly defines violence in a normative way, so that an act qualifies as violence only if it constitutes a violation of duty. We have seen grounds for rejecting this as an adequate account of physical violence, but as we shall see, there is more to be said for it in connection with the notion of psychological violence. Of moral interest is the fact that Gandhi apparently does not regard consequences as decisive in appraising the moral quality of acts. The consequences – that is, the deaths of the babies – might be identical in the two hypothetical cases. Yet on this view the one act is justified and the other is not. What makes the difference for Gandhi is the circumstances of the performance of the acts. What precisely it is about the circumstances that makes the difference he does not specify. Some of what he says suggests it is the fact that in the one case, but not in the other, it is a matter of either not acting and letting one group of persons starve (namely, the milk drivers) or acting and allowing another group to starve (namely the babies), and that the drivers qua drivers have no duty to supply milk to the babies. Even so, their act, he says, would not in that case be an act of love; it is just that it would not be an act of violence either. Implied in all of this, though he does not develop the point, is the judgment that we have at least a qualified duty to regard the well-being of those who may need our help but to whom we have no fixed commitment to provide help. The more general question is whether we are principally obligated to do good for people, or simply to refrain from harming them, issues that we shall encounter in Chapter Six.

My concern for the moment is to acknowledge that there are literally non-violent ways of harming people (by which I mean merely ways that involve no physical violence) that are as bad as violent ways. This means that there is no particular virtue in nonviolent or pacifistic action per se. Intentions to cause harm, destruction, or death commonly associated with acts of violence may be equally present in nonviolent actions. It may be an awareness of this that prompts Cotta to remark:

> Its correlation with the idea of revolution and of 'new beginning' explains why violence was able to prevail so widely during these last years over the opposite ideal of nonviolence, which seemed destined to worldwide success in the wake of Gandhi. But violence succeeded even in making nonviolence its own instrument. In fact, the nonviolent techniques are now reversed from their proper sense and utilized for the tactics of a more crafty and effective struggle.[31]

The absence of physical force in nonviolence is not, then, in and of itself particularly relevant. There is, of course, the difference noted earlier between violence and nonviolence that acts of violence are by their nature prima facie wrong whereas acts of nonviolence are not. But both must be appraised in the contexts in which they are contemplated, with due regard for the character of the acts and their consequences. The mere absence of war, as Augustine perceived, does not make peace in any meaningful sense; there must be justice and tranquility as well. Likewise the mere absence of violence does not make nonviolence in any significant sense. There must be some positive features of conduct, minimally in the way of a concern or respect for others, in order for it to exemplify nonviolence as a moral position. This has been true of the philosophies of nonviolence advocated by Tolstoy, Gandhi, and King.

The harmful consequences of 'nonviolent' actions (as I shall denote acts that are nonviolent only in the sense of not involving violence) may be either purely physical, as in the case of the hypothetical milk drivers, where it is the starvation that is at issue, or mental. That is, we need to distinguish physical and mental harms and to recognize that one can be as bad as the other and that either can be caused by violent or 'nonviolent' actions.

Consider the following account by Jonathan Kozol in *Death at An Early Age:*

> Although Stephen did poorly in his school work, there was one thing he could do well. He was a fine artist. He made delightful drawings. The thing about them that was good, however, was also the thing that got him into trouble. For they were not neat and orderly and organized but entirely random and casual, messy, somewhat unpredictable, seldom according to the instructions he had been given, and – in short – real drawings. For these drawings, Stephen received considerable embarrassment at the hands of the Art Teacher. ... If Stephen began to fiddle around during a lesson, the Art Teacher generally would not notice him at first. When she did, both he and I and the children around him would prepare for trouble. For she would go at his desk with something truly like a vengeance and would shriek at him in a way that carried terror. 'Give me that. Your paints

are all muddy. You've made it a mess. ... I don't know why we waste good paper on this child.' Then: 'Garbage. Junk. He gives me garbage and junk. And garbage is one thing I will not have.' ... [S]he did not know or care anything at all about the way in which you can destroy a human being.[32]

The teacher used no physical violence. She had not even caused physical harm or injury of the sort represented by the poverty or starvation alluded to in the earlier examples. Yet she was causing harm. But it was of an emotional or psychological sort. So great may such harms be – extending in extreme cases to the devastation of a personality – that the term 'psychological violence' has come increasingly to characterize their infliction. Mental harms can be inflicted by means of physical violence, with torture probably being the best example. But they may also result from 'nonviolent' actions. And with regard to 'nonviolent' acts we may distinguish between those whose express aim is to effect harm and those in which such an outcome is merely a byproduct, perhaps unforeseen, of acts directed toward other ends. Brainwashing illustrates the former; in it a person's mental processes can be so altered that he is no longer certain of what he has done in the past and can eventually become convinced that he has done things he in fact has not done. Given enough time, almost any normal person can be broken down in this way. On the other hand, effects that, though not comparable to these, are nonetheless severely damaging, can be brought about in the course of child raising, sometimes by parents who have no intention to harm their children but who nonetheless treat them in ways that cause irreparable harm by destroying their confidence and self-esteem.

Language has a convenient resource for enabling us to distinguish these different modes of violence. It is in the idea of 'doing violence.' This notion is not as close to the surface of our common-sense thinking as is that of physical violence. But it is important to assessing the ethical questions in the use of violence. Consider the debilitating effects of prolonged and intensive brainwashing, or of ghetto schools upon young children, or of the continual humiliation and debasement of a child by parents. In none of these cases need physical violence be used. But in each case violence is done, and of a sort that may be far more injurious that most physical violence.[33]

Violence in this sense, as Newton Garver has pointed out,[34] has a closer kinship with the notion of violation than with physical force. We may violate laws, rules, orders, good manners or the spirit of an agreement; and we speak of the violation of persons in at least one type of physical violence, namely, rape. Similarly one can *do violence* to a wide range of things: language, facts, the truth, an author's intentions, the memory of a deceased, and to persons, including oneself. In each case something having value, integrity, dignity, sacredness, or generally some claim to respect is treated in a manner that is contemptuous of this claim. According to what I have called moral personalism, persons are preeminently worthy of respect and have claims upon those whose conduct may affect them to be treated in ways that do not diminish them. To deprive them of their freedom, degrade them, or destroy their confidence are all ways of doing the latter. And all are accomplishable without resort to physical violence. Indeed, most of them can be effected through the subtlest forms of personal and social interaction, inasmuch as it is in these areas that people are often the most vulnerable. The preceding example of the teacher simply illustrates the doing of violence in a relatively heavy-handed way. The insidiousness of racism, for example, consists in the fact that some of its most damaging effects are essentially unquantifiable ones, wrought upon the psyche of a whole people through prolonged oppression. The same with sexism.

This highlights the importance I have stressed of distinguishing between physical and mental (or psychological) harms. The former tend to be conspicuous and come most readily to mind when one thinks of harm. The latter are often inconspicuous and for that reason discounted or insufficiently attended to in the assessment of ways of treating people.

Philosophers have, however, at various times showed an awareness of such harms and occasionally even provided the rudiments of a theory for understanding them. Plato, for example, holds that to harm a person is to make him less perfect, where this means disrupting the inner harmony of the soul that enables one to function effectively as a rational being. He may even have thought, as his mentor Socrates did, that this is the only way to harm a person and that what we are calling physical harms cannot really harm a virtuous person and might (in the form of punishment) even benefit one who is not virtuous. We shall see in Chapter Four how rather similar thinking is developed by Augustine in the context of Christianity. Other philosophers like Kant, Dewey, and the existentialists, by stressing freedom and the value of the person, explicitly or implicitly direct attention to the fact that one can be harmed in other than physical ways. Marx does the same in characterizing the forms of alienation under capitalism that he believes dehumanize and ultimately reduce men to the level of animals. While it is not possible to sum up this mode of violence in anything like a neat formula or definition, we may say that to do violence to persons in any of these ways is to diminish them as persons.

I shall speak of the use of physical or psychological violence against persons as the doing of violence to them. And the doing of violence in these ways I take to be prima facie wrong – that is, wrong all other things being equal or in the absence of countervailing moral considerations. Many things are wrong other things being equal, of course, but nonetheless right in practice. There is not even invariably a presumption that what is *prima facie* wrong is also wrong on balance because often acts that in some respects are prima facie wrong are in other respects prima facie right.[35] But there is, I believe, a presumption of wrongness about the doing of violence to people. In fact,

286 Violence: A Philosophical Anthology

the infliction of the sorts of harms it represents is a paradigm of how not to treat people.

This, however, is not the central claim I want to advance. I want to defend only the weaker claim that it is presumptively wrong to do violence to *innocent* persons. One must start somewhere in morals as well as science, mathematics, or any other mode of inquiry with something for which further justification is not asked, at least for purposes of that inquiry. I propose to do that with this claim. For there is probably no stronger presumption is morals. It is not one that tips the scales in the assessment of war one way or the other. Both militarists and pacifists can equally accept it; in fact, as we shall see in Chapter Five, something approximating it is the mainstay of most conceptions of what constitutes justice in the conduct of war. It does not even tip the scales within morality between advocates of one type of moral theory as opposed to another. Those who view morality as purely a matter of consequences can accept it as well as those who think morality is mainly a matter of rights or of largely nonconsequentialist considerations. It tips the scales only, as I have indicated, between those who are willing to view the world in a moral light and those who are not. Morality as experienced, and not necessarily as treated in the abstract, presents some things to us as right and others as wrong, some as right or wrong all other things being equal, and some as carrying presumptions of varying strengths as to their rightness or wrongness. The doing of violence to innocent persons – the use of violence against them, physical or psychological, killing or harming them, or inflicting mental or physical injury – is, I propose, in this sense presumptively wrong. This does not mean that doing these things is never justified; whether that is so must be determined by examining the various kinds of circumstances in which one might propose to do them. It is just that the burden rests upon anyone who proposes to do these things to innocent persons to produce the justification. I take this to be the starting point for dealing with the moral problems of violence and war.

If what I have been saying is correct, it means that we cannot adequately understand violence apart from at least tacit reference to moral and evaluative questions. This does not mean, I stress, that violence is wrong by definition; that would be too easy a way with many complex moral problems. But it does mean that one omits relevant considerations if he tries to assess violence apart from any considerations of moral factors.

VI

Because war by its nature is institutionalized violence, it, too, cannot be fully assessed independently of moral considerations. And these considerations extend to the consequences of both physical and psychological violence. For war inflicts both.

While it is the physical violence that is usually stressed, war's consequences also include the incalculable grief and anguish of those who lose loved ones, and whose lives are sometimes permanently diminished as a result of those losses, as well as harms done to those combatants who survive only to go through the rest of their lives emotionally and psychologically impaired. These never appear in statistics about war. Yet they are among its highest costs. Lives shattered by alcoholism, drug abuse, or suicide as a result of wartime experiences – as, notably, have been those of many veterans of the Vietnam War – are casualties of war as surely as those shattered on the battlefield. Those who suffer such harms have been done violence whether or not they have suffered physical wounds.

Their sufferings are the same, of course, whether they voluntarily offered themselves up for the business of war or not. But, morally, they are particularly tragic when they are the result of their having been compelled to fight. And more often than not they have been compelled. For most nations rely upon conscription to supply their war machines – almost universally, once a war is underway, and often in peacetime as well. And conscription represents one of the severest infringements of individual liberty the state has devised. To be forced to yield up one's very person to a government, to be told what to do, what to wear, what to eat, and when to come and go is servitude. And to be compelled to do these things is involuntary servitude – about as clear a case, short of slavery, as there is. But, it is not merely the servitude that is significant; it is the use to which conscripts are put. For among the things they are told to do is when to kill other human beings, whether or not they approve of, or even understand, the policies by which they are so ordered and whether or not they have had any say in the determination of those policies (or the choice of those who determine them). Even convicted felons are not made to engage in compulsory killing. Yet the civilized nations of the world demand it of their sons.

The young are impressionable and frequently malleable. For this reason a disproportionate share of the burden of war falls upon them. In the American experience alone, tens of thousands of fifteen- and sixteen-year-olds fought in the Civil War, and the average age of the U.S. combat soldier in Vietnam was nineteen. Many of the Vietnamese fighting with the Vietcong were even younger. And in more recent wars children in their early teens, and sometimes younger, have fought in Afghanistan on the side of the mujahideen, in Nicaragua on the side of the contras, and in the Middle East on the side of Iran. Both boys and girls – between two and three thousand of them – fought in the Ugandan civil war. The Peace Union in Finland estimated in 1983 that children were serving in the military in at least twenty nations.[36]

Many of these are more or less volunteers, often with irregular armies or guerrilla forces. But whether their participation is compelled or not, the psychological effects upon them, as they learn at an early age that the way to resolve conflicts is through killing, must be reckoned among the imperceptible consequences of war, a continuing invisible tax upon societies that exploit their young in these ways.

This does not mean that military training is all bad, by any means. Some youths, and many adults as well, respond to the structure and discipline it provides. Others find that having basic decisions made for them postpones the time when they must assume full responsibility for their lives, something for which they may be unready at the time. And still others, particularly among the poor and disadvantaged, find military life preferable to unemployment. But the fact remains that its primary function is to train them to kill (or to support those who do). And this requires overcoming their natural revulsion to killing and suspending in their minds the connection between some of the highest principles society tries to instill in them, such as respect for persons and the value of human life, and what they are asked to do for the state. They must learn to compartmentalize their moral concerns, to exclude whole populations from the constraints against killing. They must become divided persons.

The techniques for effecting this have been refined, and the armies of the world specialize in them. As a study by the American Friends Service Committee characterized it, 'Depreciation of self-esteem, reduction to a state of relatively helpless suggestibility, and then rescue by identification with military superiors, and reliance on early training in the acceptance of arbitrary authority are all parts of a carefully engineered process in basic military training.'[37] And these techniques are remarkably effective. Young males the world over – in whom readiness to use violence is easily associated with masculinity – become trained killers by the hundreds of thousands when told to by their governments. And there is not that much difference among them. J. Bronowski reflected upon this in connection with Mussolini's blackshirts and Hilter's storm troopers during World War II. 'I did not know the young men in Italy' he writes, 'but I knew them in Germany; I was at school with them there. Nothing in my mind to this day marks them off from the young men with whom I was at school in the same years in England.... If you want to recruit for an army of destruction, the material is there, in every classroom.'[38]

It was precisely this transformation of human beings into instruments of violence that Simone Weil saw as the deeper function of war itself. In her penetrating study, *The Iliad: A Poem of Force*, she wrote:

> ... [T]he conquering soldier is like a scourge of nature. Possessed by war, he, like the slave, becomes a thing. ... Such is the nature of force. Its power of converting a man into a thing is a double one, and in its application double-edged. To the same degree, though in different fashions, those who use it and those who endure it are turned to stone.... battles are fought and decided by men ... who have undergone a transformation, who have dropped either to the level of inert matter, which is pure passivity, or to

the level of blind force, which is pure momentum. Herein lies the secret of war, a secret revealed by the *Iliad* in its similes, which liken the warriors either to fire, flood, wind, wild beasts, or God knows what blind causes of disaster, or else to frightened animals, trees, water, sand, to anything in nature that is set into motion by the violence of external forces. ... The art of war is simply the art of producing such transformations, and its equipment, its processes, even the casualties it inflicts on the enemy, are only means directed toward this end – its true object is the warrior's soul.[39]

Effective armies require virtually unquestioning obedience. And that is secured at the cost of turning rational persons into instruments of violence for use by others. Often it is at the cost of turning young people into instruments of violence for the use of adults. They become, as Weil points out, like things, or forces of nature, precisely the opposite of what is required for considerate and humane social life in community with others. That as many of them as do are able to readjust to civilian life without lasting emotional scars attests to the resilience of human beings, as well as to the effort of governments to mask the reality of what war is all about. Medals, parades, honors, and speeches are all part of the process. They glorify the enterprise of war and help to focus attention upon patriotism and the willingness to sacrifice for others and away from the true nature of what they are asked to do in fighting, which is to kill and be killed by others who have been transformed by a similar process by their societies.

    All of these considerations, I suggest, from those pertaining to the nature of morality, to those showing morality's link with the very concept of violence, establish that, however many other perspectives there may be from which it can be viewed, and for whatever purposes it may be so viewed, war cannot be fully assessed apart from the point of view of morality. And people cannot presume to have given it any but the flimsiest of justifications if they fail to examine it in a moral light. This does not of itself indicate one way or the other what the moral assessment of war should be. Just war theorists who believe that war is sometimes morally permissible can accept this conclusion as readily as pacifists. It means only that one must be prepared to examine war seriously from a moral standpoint if one proposes to engage in it.

    For all of this, there are nonetheless those who would challenge this conclusion. They are prepared to accord morality full respect in their personal lives, in the sense of being basically fair, trustworthy, truthful, and nonviolent in their relations to others, but they condone lying, deception, violence, and destruction in international relations, particularly in warfare. They contend that at the international level morality is either irrelevant or at most of limited relevance. Here, they say, duplicity and violence are the norm and one has no choice but to play by the rules. Appeals to morality, on this view, should therefore be foregone in the interests of clear thinking, objectivity, and effective action – qualities precluded by what they allege to be the emotionalism and subjectivism of morality. Such is the counsel of political realism. It is to the examination of this outlook as it has been found in twentieth-century American thought that I want to turn next.

Notes

1. *The Ethics of Ambiguity* (New York: Citadel Press, 1962), p. 23.
2. H. L. A. Hart, *The Concept of Law* (Oxford: Oxford University Press, 1963), p. 190.
3. *On Aggression* (Harcourt, Brace & World, 1963), pp. 242–3.
4. *Why Violence? A Philosophical Interpretation* (Gainesville: University of Florida Press, 1985), p. 9.
5. Ibid., p. 13.
6. Ibid., p. 16.
7. Robert Paul Wolff, 'On Violence,' *Journal of Philosophy* 66 (Oct. 1969): 602; reprinted as 'Violence and the Law' in R. P. Wolff, *The Rule of Law* (New York: Simon and Schuster, 1971), pp. 54–72. Page references are to the former.
8. Ibid., p. 606.
9. Ibid., p. 610. He also recognizes other interpretations. One is of violence as 'uses of force that involve bodily interference or the direct infliction of physical injury' (p. 606). But he thinks that this definition 'usually serves the ideological purpose of ruling out, as immoral or politically illegitimate, the only instrument of power that is available to certain social classes.' He also acknowledges a possible definition of violence as the unjustified use of force (p. 608). Wolff's account should be distinguished from claims *about* legitimate violence, such as those put forth by E. Friedenberg. Friedenberg says that 'our belief that *legitimated* violence is morally acceptable is very deeply rooted, and stems, I believe, from our opportunism – for this is ever the land of opportunity where failure, not murder, is the unforgiveable sin.' See 'Legitimate Violence,' *The Nation*, June 24, 1968, p. 822. Friedenberg also holds that 'if by violence one means injurious attacks on persons or destruction of valuable inanimate objects … then nearly all the violence in the world is done by legitimate authority … yet their actions are not deemed to be violence.' See 'The Side Effects of the Legal Process,' in Wolff, *The Rule of Law*, p. 43. By this account there are legitimate authorities, and what they do is not deemed violence but is so in fact.
10. Wolff, 'On Violence,' p. 606.
11. Both sides on the issue of whether 'violence' is a normative term are found in the literature. Bernard Gert gives an expressly normative analysis of an act of violence in terms of the intentional violation of certain moral rules in 'Justifying Violence,' *Journal of Philosophy* 66 (Oct. 1969): 616–28. Charner Perry builds both evaluative and normative elements into his account, characterizing violence as 'in its nature, evil, a violation of rights, an offense against society.' See 'Violence – Visible and Invisible,' *Ethics* 81 (Oct. 1970): 9. Francis C. Wade distinguishes between descriptive and normative senses and similarly takes the notion of a violation of rights to be central to the latter in 'On Violence,' *Journal of Philosophy* 68 (June 1971): 369–77. Newton Garver introduces a normative element in terms of the violation of personality in 'What Violence Is,' *The Nation*, June 24, 1968,

pp. 819–22, reprinted in expanded form in A. K. Bierman and James A. Gould, eds., *Philosophy for a New Generation*, 2d ed. (New York: MacMillan Company, 1970), pp. 256–66. Gandhi likewise tacitly defines violence normatively when he says that 'there is no violence when there is no infraction of duty.' See M. K. Gandhi, *Non-Violent Resistance* (New York: Schocken Books, 1961), pp. 167–8. A normative account similar to Wolff's is given by R. Hartogs and E. Artzt, eds., *Violence: Causes and Solutions* (New York: Dell, 1970), p. 14, who say that 'violence may be defined as an extreme form of aggression making illegitimate or unjustified use of force.' And in his *On Understanding Violence Philosophically* (New York: Harper and Row, 1970), p. 19, Glen Gray interprets force in terms of legitimate authority and violence in terms of the absence of such authority. On the other hand, R. B. Miller and R. Audi both characterize violence in such a way that it is not wrong by definition. See their 'Violence, Force, and Coercion' and 'On the Meaning and Justification of Violence' in J. Shaffer, ed., *Violence* (New York: David McKay, 1971). For a good critique of Wolff's argument, see P. Flanagan, 'Wolff on Violence,' *Australasian Journal of Philosophy* 50, no. 3 (Dec. 1972): 271–8.

12. Not that it may not sometimes be as, or more, important than primary violence. One can, as Gandhi noted, sometimes do a person more harm by destroying his property than by physical violence against his person (*Non-Violent Resistance*, p. 371). But when this is the case, it is still the effect of violence upon persons that invests it with moral significance.

13. Harrison E. Salisbury, 'Introduction' to *Assassination and Political Violence, A Report to the National Commission on the Causes and Prevention of Violence*, J. F. Kirkham, S. G. Levy, W. J. Crotty (New York: Bantam Books, 1970), p. xxi.

14. S. Endleman, ed., *Violence in the Streets* (Chicago: Quadrangle Books, 1968), p. 9.

15. Ibid., p. 20.

16. Reinhold Niebuhr, *Love and Justice: Selections from the Shorter Writings of Reinhold Niebuhr*, ed. D. B. Robertson (Cleveland: World Publishing Company, 1967), p. 257.

17. C. A. Reich, *The Greening of America* (New York: Bantam Books, 1971), p. 148.

18. Brazilian priest, Dom Helder, quoted by J. A. Page in 'The Little Priest Who stood Up to Brazil's Generals,' *New York Times Magazine*, May 23, 1971.

19. Emma Goldman, 'Anarchism: What It Really Stands For,' in *Nonviolence in America: A Documentary History*, ed. S. Lynd (Indianapolis: Bobbs-Merrill, 1966), p. 121.

20. R. G. Francis, 'Kapow ! !: An Argument and a Forecast,' in Endleman, ed., *Violence in the Streets*, p. 152.

21. W. J. Weatherby, 'Talking of Violence,' in Endleman, ed., *Violence in the Streets*, p. 85.

22. Peter G. Davis, *New York Times*, Nov. 9, 1976.

23. Although the behavior of deranged persons is often properly characterized as physical violence, I am confining my attention to purposive conduct of the sort usually signified by expressions like 'act of violence.'

24. On this issue see R. Audi, 'On the Meaning and Justification of Violence,' pp. 57–8, and R. B. Miller, 'Violence, Force, and Coercion,' pp. 17–20, in Shaffer; ed., *Violence*.

25. Speaking here of domestic violence. International violence is a more difficult case, partly because so much of it is primary violence, partly because even straightforward property destruction resulting from acts of war is always unauthorized by the nation suffering the destruction and authorized by the nation inflicting

it. Thus there is no mutually acceptable frame of reference from which the question of authorization can be settled. There is, of course, the overarching point of view of international law; but it conspicuously fails to duplicate effectively the function of domestic law. Even where war has been duly declared and the targets are 'legitimate' military targets, the fact that authorization from the nation suffering destruction is absent seems to suffice to render these acts of violence.

26. Cotta, *Why Violence?* p. 60.
27. For a discussion of some theories of violence that expressly relate it to social settings, see H. Bienen, *Violence and Social Change* (Chicago: University of Chicago Press, 1968), pp. 68–9.
28. Reinhold Niebuhr, *Moral Man and Immoral Society* (New York: Charles Scribner's Sons, 1932), p. 241.
29. Gandhi, *Non Violent Resistance,* p. 166.
30. Ibid., pp. 167–8.
31. Cotta, *Why Violence?* pp. 17–18.
32. Jonathan Kozol, *Death At An Early Age* (New York: Bantam Books, 1968), pp. 2–4.
33. Violence was seen in the Old Testament to be bound up in pride (Psalms 73:6), wealth (Micah 6:12), and in leading others astray (Proverbs 16:29). And the Stoic Marcus Aurelius catalogued a variety of ways in which a man might 'do violence' to himself, from becoming vexed to being insincere and threatening harm to others. See *Meditations,* (Pleasant Valley, Pa.: Gateway, 1956), p. 18. Eastern philosophies often expressly distinguish mental from physical harms and associate violence with both. The second Yama, or restraint, of Yoga ethics requires that 'if we adhere to the principle of nonviolence we shall have to give up falsehood, because if we are not truthful and thus deceive others we shall cause them mental injury.' See I. C. Sharma, *Ethical Philosophies of India* (Lincoln, Neb.: Johnsen Publishing Company, 1965), p. 209. Gandhi clearly intends the same when he says that 'under violence I include corruption, falsehood, hypocrisy, deceit and the like' *(Non-Violent Resistance,* p. 294). Tolstoy makes much of this aspect of violence, even though he does not always distinguish it carefully from physical violence. See, for example, his *A Confession: The Gospel in Brief and What I Believe* (New York: Oxford University Press, 1961), pp. 321 and 351.
34. Garver, 'What Violence Is,' pp. 819–822. Garver's is one of the more influential analyses of violence, and his essay contains a good discussion of the notion of psychological violence. For a critique of his discussion and an argument against analyzing violence other than by reference to physical force, see Joseph Betz, 'Violence: Garver's Definition and a Deweyan Correction,' *Ethics* 87, no. 4 (July 1977): 339–51. See also Robert Audi, 'On the Meaning and Justification of Violence,' in Shaffer, ed., *Violence,* and William Robert Miller, *Nonviolence: A Christian Interpretation* (New York: Association Press, 1964), chap. 1. Gandhi is interpreted by Erik H. Erikson as grounding his opposition to nonphysical harms in the injunction never to violate another person's essence in his *Gandhi's Truth: On the Orgins of Militant Nonviolence* (New York: Norton & Company, 1969), p. 412.
35. Following W. D. Ross's explication in *The Right and the Good* (Oxford: Oxford University Press, 1930), chap. 2.
36. For further data and a good discussion of the issue of children and warfare, see Sara Terry, 'When Children See Life through a Gun Barrel,' *The Christian Science Monitor,* July 7, 1987, part of a series on the exploitation of children entitled 'Children in Darkness: The Exploitation of Innocence.'

37. *The Draft?* A Report Prepared for the Peace Education Division of the American Friends Service Committee (New York: Hill and Wang, 1968), p. 13.
38. J. Bronowski, *The Face of Violence* (New York: The World Publishing Company, 1968), pp. 47–8.
39. Simone Weil, *The Iliad, or The Poem of Force*, trans. Mary McCarthy (Wallingford, Pa.: Pendle Hill, 1956), pp. 25–6.

COMMENTARY ON HOLMES

In 1989 Robert L. Holmes published a very important book on the ethics of war, *On War and Morality*.[1] Although war is the principal focus of this work, the piece reprinted in this anthology, which is taken from his book, deals with the broader question of morality and violence in general, two areas where Holmes has made a lasting contribution.[2]

Holmes's interest in violence is specifically moral, although his approach is different from what philosophers typically do when confronted with practical issues. Thus, instead of relying on some *a priori* apparatus, whereby a fully worked out ethical position is already in place before the issue in question is introduced, Holmes's approach is bottom-up, where the starting point is a particular issue, from which a more general theory is discovered by a process of induction. The only moral assumption Holmes makes is what he calls 'moral personalism', the belief that 'any plausible moral theory must have at its centre a concern for the lives and well-being of persons'.

Holmes rejects the view that violence is wrong by definition, suggesting instead that violence is only *prima facie* wrong, or wrong all other things being equal, and therefore in need of justification. He goes on to distinguish between three uses of the concept of violence: central (based on the idea of destructive physical force), extended (based on the idea of violation) and peripheral (based on metaphorical or highly attenuated uses of the term). Regarding the central use, he says that in its strictest sense physical violence is the use of force with the intent to harm, kill or cause destruction. He also makes a further distinction between primary physical violence (force used against persons or animals) and secondary physical violence (force used against objects). Harm is the key notion in the concept of primary violence, although Holmes is aware that we also need to distinguish between physical and mental harms, that 'one can be as bad as the other and that either can be caused by violent or 'nonviolent' actions'.

Returning to the minimal moral assumption of moral personalism, Holmes argues that to do violence to persons is to diminish them as persons. More specifically, Holmes wants to defend the claim that it is presumptively wrong to do violence to *innocent* persons: 'the doing of violence to innocent persons – the use of violence against them, physical or psychological, killing or harming them, or inflicting mental or physical injury – is, I propose, in this sense presumptively wrong [...]. I take this to be the starting point for dealing with the moral problems of violence and war.'

Notes and further reading

1. Robert L. Holmes, *On War and Morality*, Princeton, NJ: Princeton University Press, 1989.
2. See Robert L. Holmes, 'Violence and Nonviolence', in Jerome A. Shaffer (ed.), *Violence*, New York: David McKay, 1971; 'The Concept of Physical Violence in Moral and Political Affairs', *Social Theory and Practice*, Vol. 2, No. 4, Fall 1973; *Basic Moral Philosophy*, 4th edn, California: Wadsworth, 2006.

14
Violence and Power

Robert F. Litke

Violence is intriguing. It is universally condemned yet to be found everywhere. Most of us are both fascinated and horrified by it. It is a fundamental ingredient in how we entertain ourselves (children's stories, world literature, the movie industry) and an essential feature of many of our social institutions. In most parts of the world it is notoriously common in family life, religious affairs, and political history. I hope to throw some light on this phenomenon by examining some of the connections between violence and power.

I

The first issue to be discussed is the meaning of 'violence'. Etymologically, 'violence' means 'to carry force towards' something. Now there are endless ways in which force is carried towards something or someone. Indeed, virtually every human action could be described in such a way. The concept will be useful only if it can be defined more narrowly.

I will begin with a brief review of some attempts to do so. The first two entries in the unabridged edition of *The Random House Dictionary of the English Language* bring to light three distinct elements: (1) the idea of intensity (as in a storm); (2) the idea of injury (as in death by accident); (3) the idea of *physical* force. It is noteworthy that this dictionary does not commit itself to the view that the injury must always result from physical force for 'violence' to be the appropriate word. The sixth entry allows for injuries through distortion of meaning and fact (as in 'the translation did violence to the original'). These elements provide the ingredients for different philosophical views of what violence is.

For example, Robert Audi makes use of the first two elements and proposes that violence is a vigorous attack or abuse of persons in physical or psychological ways.[1] He supports his proposal by showing that we can carry force against people in a variety of physically *and* psychologically devastating ways. More common in the philosophical literature, however, are narrower views of violence requiring all three elements: violence is causing injury through the use of vigorous physical force.[2] And sometimes it is proposed that a fourth element should be required, namely, that the injury be intended or foreseen.[3]

A rather different set of philosophical views emerges if one is willing, as Garver and Holmes suggest, to *extend* the meaning of violence by focusing on the idea of violating persons.[4] Since persons can be gravely violated in both physical and psychological ways, initially these views look like Audi's account. However, violations of persons may be a matter of subtle rather than vigorously abusive treatment so the cases will be somewhat different from those captured by Audi's definition. This stems from the fact that construing violence as essentially a matter of violating a person requires a substantial shift in one's perspective. Rather than thinking about violence by focusing on *the nature of the force being carried and on the agent who is doing so*, one is now focused on the effects of such force *on the recipient of it*. Roughly, it requires a shift of attention from the perpetrator to the victim of violence.

It is not my intention to take up the matter of which is the best definition. The challenge is to define 'violence' narrowly enough for it to be useful. But what counts as useful will depend very much on what one wishes to do with the concept. And a general discussion of that is not the purpose of this article. I offer the above outline of possibilities for two reasons. First I hope to have shown that the matter of what we want to mean by 'violence' is neither straightforward nor trivial. Our linguistic intuitions are rich enough to support a variety of ways of construing the meaning of 'violence'. And given that there are various purposes which we may wish the concept to serve, fruitful discussion of the meaning of 'violence' will likely continue for some time. The second reason for the above outline is to make explicit how my exploration of the relationship between violence and power connects with the literature. In brief, my investigation takes place within the kind of perspective offered by Garver's account of violence as the violation of persons. Such a perspective puts one in a good position to appreciate how the exercise of power and the experience of violence are related to each other. I will now outline his position.

Garver suggests that we focus on violence not as a matter of physical force but rather as the violation of a person. He illustrates how persons can be violated either with respect to their bodies (physical violence) or with respect to their ability to make their own decisions (psychological violence) and he shows that each kind of violence has both personal and institutionalized forms. Here are some obvious examples arranged according to his schemes: In real life things are seldom so simply categorized. Rape is not only an attack on someone's body but usually has devastating effects on a person's ability to make appropriate decisions concerning their subsequent sexual life. And in both terrorism and war one is as much preoccupied with coercing the decisions of one's adversary as with successfully executing a physical attack.

What is essential to all Garver's cases is that they can be shown to be the violation of at least one of two basic human rights:

	Physical	Psychological
Personal	muggings rape murder	paternalism personal threats character assassination
Institutional	riots terrorism war	slavery racism sexism

1. the right to determine what one's body does and what is done to one's body;

2. the right to make one's own decisions and to deal with the consequences of one's acts.[5] I do not wish to take issue with Garver's account. There may be other ways of violating people in fundamental respects, and it may be difficult in certain cases to determine whether one's impact on another's body or decision-making processes constitutes a violation of them. But Garver's account is valuable as it stands. It gives a useful way of viewing a vast range of very diverse and often spectacular human behaviour, a way which enables us to see through the diversity and spectacle to certain essential features.

Garver roots his account of violence in a specific moral practice, namely, the evaluation of behaviour in terms of fundamental human rights. We can get an even greater resolution of the diversity if we focus on the question of what is common to these two basic kinds of violence.

Much of who we are depends upon our ability to act in concert with each other. This is true of our physical survival. Few of us could live for more than a few days, and none of us would have matured into adults, without the ongoing support of various forms of interaction. This interdependence is also true of our cultural life. Our language, our knowledge, our art, all of our social structures, and even much of our sense of self are a function of our capacity for interaction. I think it is fair to say that most of what we value in life is creatively woven out of our capacity for complex, diverse, sustained, and systematic interactions.

However, our ability *to interact* with each other is obviously dependent upon our (logically) prior capacity as individuals *to act*. And at the core of our ability to act are the two kinds of power upon which Garver's account turns: bodily capacities and decision-making abilities. Without these the various matrices of interaction from which we benefit cannot arise. Clearly the effects of enhancing or diminishing someone's power to interact in such ways would ramify throughout the life of the individual and the culture. Consequently it is crucial that these powers be singled out for special protection.

This we do with the concept of violence. We use the term to censure the fact that some or all of a person's power to act, and interact, in bodily and decision-making ways has been diminished or destroyed by someone else. That is the heart of violence: the disempowerment of persons. The genius of violence is that it disempowers in such fundamental ways that its effects cascade out in many directions and for a long time to come. With violence we can diminish human prospects systematically in every conceivable direction. The pity of violence is that with it we weaken the very thread out of which we weave the fabric of who we are, as individuals, communities and cultures. It is a puzzle to me, therefore, that we so often choose to harm each other in such fundamental and far-reaching ways, ways which in the end can only be self-destructive. I believe that a consideration of power, especially Thomas Hobbes' account of it, can help us to understand why humans are so often prepared to defeat themselves by violating each other.

II

In its most general sense 'power' simply means the ability to act. For example, this is the first entry under 'power' in the unabridged edition of *The Random House Dictionary of the English Language*. Also, this is approximately how Hobbes first defines power in the *Leviathan:* he suggests that power is simply the ability to satisfy one's desires.[6] Because there are endless ways of acting there must be innumerable kinds of power. So unspecific is this initial sense of power that we seldom have occasion to use it. What occurs more frequently is a second sense of power which requires that we have some specific capacities in mind, for example, 'power of speech'. I was approaching this notion of power when I suggested in the previous section of this article that violence can be considered as the disempowerment of persons with respect to two general kinds of abilities, namely, bodily capacities and decision-making abilities. I will discuss this type of power further in the last section of the article when I consider how to avoid violence. I shall refer to these two senses as 'power(1)' and 'power(2)'.

It is to a third sense of power that we must look if we are to understand the widespread occurrence of violence, namely power as domination, i.e. power as the ability to control or command – 'power(3)'. Not only does this merit a separate entry in the dictionary but it has become the standard notion of power in the political context over the last three centuries. C.B. Macpherson summarizes this piece of our western intellectual history in a convenient way:

Most of the literature of modern political science, from its beginnings with Machiavelli and Hobbes to its twentieth-century empirical exponents, has to do with power, understood broadly as men's ability to get what they want by controlling others. Hobbes put it succinctly in 1640.... The reduction of power to power over others had become even more explicit by the nineteenth century. The high point was reached in the propositions James Mill announced in 1820.... When we move on to the twentieth-century empirical political theorists we find the same assumption that the only significant power in any political view is one man's or one group's power over others.[7]

A representative example of twentieth-century thinking is the work of H. J. Morgenthau, the father of political realism. In the opening pages of *The Politics of Nations* we find the following statement:

Power may comprise anything that establishes and maintains the control of man over man. Thus power covers all social relationships which serve that end, from physical violence to the most subtle psychological ties by which one mind controls another. Power covers the domination of man by man, both when it is disciplined by moral ends and controlled by constitutional safeguards as in Western democracies, and when it is that untamed and barbaric force which finds its laws in nothing but its own strength and its sole justification in its aggrandizement.[8]

Such power is taken to be the central fact of political life. And the working assumption of political realists is that political activity at every level is a variation on our universal and endless struggle to dominate and not be dominated. I do not intend to argue with such assumptions. I think this reading of political history is a valuable one. Thus I wish to concede that power as domination is likely to remain a central fact of our foreseeable social and political life. What is striking about Morgenthau's formulation of power as domination is that it puts him on the threshold of taking the position that political activity is inevitably violent (in Garver's sense of violence). But then we face a paradox: a fundamental purpose of political activity is that it should enhance our ability to interact with each other so as to improve our lives; but violence (as I have construed it) clearly diminishes this ability. The challenge therefore, is to discover forms of political activity which avoid or at least diminish the likelihood of self-defeat by violence. This was Hobbes' problem in the *Leviathan*. He has given us the classic account of why dominating power is inevitable in human affairs and of how it defeats us. I will now give a brief outline of his brilliant account.[9]

The first point is that unmet desires continuously arise within us. This is so for three primary reasons. In the first place, many desires are recurring, such as the desire for food or sex. Secondly, there is no imaginable limit to the kinds of things which humans can desire. Today's novelties are tomorrow's necessities, as new novelties emerge on the horizon of our desire. Thirdly, some desires are in principle insatiable. I am thinking of our desire for such things as loyalty, fidelity and security. As long as we want such things, we want what we cannot presently be assured of having, namely, that the future will unfold in a certain kind of way. Hobbes' general conclusion is that as long as we are alive, we are never satisfied in any final and lasting way. He put it this way: 'there is no such thing as perpetual Tranquility of mind, while we live here; because Life itself is but Motion, and can never be without Desire'.[10]

The second point is this: because there is no end to our desires there is no limit to our need for the means with which to satisfy them. In other words, our unlimited desires generate in us an insatiable desire for power(l). Hobbes makes this second point explicit in chapter 11 of the *Leviathan:* 'I put for a general inclination of all mankind, a perpetual and restless desire of Power after power, that ceaseth only in Death'.[11] Only when desires stop does our need for power(1) come to an end.

The third point is that in the context of competition which naturally arises in any society our unlimited desire for power(1) inevitably generates in us a desire to dominate – power(3). According to Hobbes' account, the substance of our power lies in our bodily and mental capacities, and in what further powers we acquire by these in the way of riches, reputation, friends etc.[12] These are the means by which we can control our situation, now and in the future, so as to obtain the satisfaction of our desires. However, the efficacy of our ability to satisfy our desires – power(1) – is determined not merely by the substance but also according to the degree to which our control of the situation (so that it serves our ends) can override the control which others have (so that it serves their ends). Hobbes understood that our desires may conflict with those of others. Power(1), in such cases, is the ability to prevail. In other words, power(1) must include the ability to dominate – power(3). Otherwise it is no power at all. It follows, therefore, that our unlimited need for power(1) generates in us an insatiable desire for power(3), under conditions of actual or possible competition.

A point which is corollary to this, which is thoroughly Hobbesian even if Hobbes did not make it explicit is this: domination is zero-sum; my gain in the ability to override your control in the situation created by our competing desires is your loss in the ability to override my control of the situation. Thus we are likely to compete not only at the level of our initial desires but also at a second level, namely at the level of our desire to be dominant. And as we have recently discovered in the case of nuclear arms-racing between the superpowers, when two parties compete with each other for dominance, their need for power(3) must escalate if they are to avoid defeat. This is an independent source of the insatiability of our need for power(3).

The fourth point, which is a conjecture of mine arising out of my detailed exegesis of Hobbes position,[13] is that the pursuit and exercise of dominating power tends to blind us to the self-defeating characteristics which sometimes are associated with domination. Our actions always have collateral effects. In Hobbes' case, the case of social interaction, our dominating behaviour will have consequences for the satisfaction of our desires, consequences for those we are dominating, and consequences for the larger social context in which our activity is taking place. The second-level desire to dominate will tend to focus us on our ability to control others in order to satisfy our relevant first-level desires. But precisely this focus will tend to exclude from our purview both the immediate and long-term effects we are having on those we are dominating and the immediate and long-term effects we are having on the larger context in which the activity is taking place. It is safe to assume that we are having such collateral effects on others and on the context but they will be considered relevant only to the extent that they are perceived as having a bearing on our current dominating capabilities. We tend to disregard everything else. And it often turns out that these unseen collateral effects have devastating consequences for our future prospects for satisfying our desires.

This is precisely Hobbes' concern in the *Leviathan*. He understood that too narrow a focus on being able to do what one wants and on being able to dominate others when they would prevent one from doing what one wants would lead to the general breakdown of civil society, the condition he calls war:

> Competition of Riches, Honour, Command, or other power, enclineth to Contention, Enmity, and War. Because the way of one Competitor, to the attaining of his desire, is to kill, subdue, supplant, or repel the other.[14]

And with the loss of society we lose access to most of the benefits of civilized life; according to Hobbes these include agriculture, transportation, the construction industries, knowledge, the arts and literature.[15] Paradoxically, we lose the capacity to satisfy the bulk of our desires because we are too narrowly focused on satisfying them, to the exclusion of attending to the collateral effects we are having on the larger social context. Surely Hobbes is right. A society can contain only limited amounts of adversarial activity. Like a symphony concert it must be woven together continuously by the co-operative activity of its members. If they are always at odds with each other in all the relevant ways there can be no music – the society must tear apart. Hobbes' argument in the *Leviathan* is that we can prevent such a disaster only if we can devise adequate means for the preservation of the larger social patterns which make civilized life and the pursuit of one's desires possible. He also argued that we must institute a civil authority to do this on our behalf because we cannot trust individuals bent on their own satisfaction to *see* what is required. Indeed, his argument is that we are so unreliable in this regard that we must have a sovereign authority autocratically dictate to us what the rules of social co-ordination shall be.[16]

Whether or not my conjecture is correct and whatever one's view of Hobbes' low estimate of our ability to create and maintain crucial social patterns, his final point stands. There is a natural and inevitable development of power from the innocuous ability to satisfy simple desires – power(1) – to a competitive drive to dominate each other – power(3) – and this latter type of power-seeking is a socially destructive force which we must control if we are to avoid the irony and frustration of completely defeating ourselves in the course of trying to satisfy our desires. What remains to be seen is the connection between violence and domination.

From a strictly conceptual point of view, domination power(3) is neutral with respect to violence (in Garver's sense). Its focus is on the control of others, not on whether the effects of such control constitutes a violation of them. But it is evident from the passages I have quoted that both Hobbes and Morgenthau quite naturally assume that in the field of practical human affairs domination will tend to be violent. And there is no mystery in this, for one very effective way of controlling people is to disempower them through the use of physical force or psychological manipulation. We can note, therefore that domination is not necessarily violent but that, as a matter of fact, it often is.

Hobbes is particularly interesting in this regard. Not only does he conceive of the problem in essentially violent terms – the competitive drive for domination will bring about the complete destruction of society into a war of every man against every man – but his proposed solution is also inherently violent. His prescription for the prevention of civil war is the installation of a sovereign authority which has absolute dominating power in two respects: the power to dictate to people how they shall interact with each other[17] and the power to ensure that people will do so through the threat of death.[18] Hobbes specifically argues that we cannot trust people to have the social intelligence to co-ordinate themselves with each other or to have adequate motivation to avoid the social chaos which the drive to domination would otherwise precipitate.[19] His solution, therefore, is to set up a regime of psychological violence (in Garver's sense) in which a central authority takes all the responsibility for deciding how members of the society shall interact and why they shall do so. But this can only weaken the thread out of which the remaining social order is woven. The best we can achieve in this way is a well-regulated group of psychologically truncated individuals, all of whom should understand that they are incapable of organizing their social/political lives so as to improve their lot. The worst is a badly regulated group of truncated individuals, badly regulated because no central authority can competently deal with more than a fraction of the enormous complexities of any human social order. Is this not the lesson which authoritarian regimes are constantly relearning?

I take Hobbes' *Leviathan,* both in its conception of the problem and in its proposed solution, to be a paradigm illustration of why and how humans defeat themselves by violating each other.

I am convinced by Hobbes' account that we cannot avoid the pursuit and exercise of dominating power in political and social domains. I also understand that domination tends to be violent and that its focus on control tends to obscure from our vision precisely its violent collateral effects. But since I do not relish the idea of the human race forever engaging in destructive self-defeat I insist on wondering whether there are ways of preventing domination from becoming violent and therefore self-defeating.

III

Hobbes was surely right in his belief that dominating power must be restrained if we are to avoid being carried into self-defeat through violence. As we have seen, however, he was mistaken in thinking that this could be done simply by putting into the hands of a political authority sufficient dominating power to dominate all political subjects. What he apparently did not understand was that dominating power *itself* must be restrained and that this must be done by means of other *kinds* of power. My conjecture is that to be effective as sources of restraint, these other kinds of power must have an impact on our lives at the level of social interaction (as does domination) and that our desire for such powers must be as natural, inevitable and pressing as our desire for domination. It is my view that such powers could serve as a counterbalance to our insatiable and competitive drive to dominate each other. They would be the substance of what I think of as a General Theory of Restraints, an important part of any general account of society.

I am not now in a position to offer such a theory. I am confident, however, that such a theory would give central place to the two kinds of power I shall discuss briefly: concertive power and developmental power. Each of these powers can serve as a natural restraint on dominating power.

In her intriguing book *On Violence*, Hannah Arendt offers the following:

> *Power* corresponds to the human ability not just to act but to act in concert. Power is never the property of an individual; it belongs to a group and remains in existence only so long as the group keeps together. . . . What makes a man a political being is his faculty of action; it enables him to get together with his peers, to act in concert, and to reach out for goals and enterprises that would never enter his mind, let alone his heart, had he not been given this gift – to embark on something new.[20]

We do not have to contend with Arendt's surprising claim that individuals do not have power. We can agree with what she needs to claim, namely, that groups of individuals can have types of power and desires and goals which individuals would not enjoy on their own. I shall refer to the particular kind of power she is bringing to our attention as *concertive power*.

As indicated in the first section of this article, this ability is of inestimable worth to us. Not only our physical survival but most of what we value in life is dependent upon our ability to act in concert with each other. Without our capacity for complex, diverse, sustained and systematic interactions the entire range of social/cultural institutions and arrangements which make civilized life possible would not arise, i.e. such things as natural languages and other notational systems, the various ways we have of gathering and communicating knowledge (e.g. the academic disciplines, folk systems of knowledge and various crafts and practices), all the art forms being practised around the world, and the vast spectrum of economic, political and social arrangements by means of which we organize ourselves. It seems that this entire range of cultural phenomena is spun out of our ability to co-ordinate ourselves with each other systematically by adhering to complex self-imposed limits on our behaviour.[21] Moreover, it seems that we are able to learn creatively how to do this in an apparently endless variety of ways. Who would want to claim that new ways of organizing ourselves aesthetically, politically, agriculturally, scientifically etc. will no longer be found, that we have exhausted all possibilities already?

As noted above, a fundamental purpose of political activity is to enhance our ability to interact with each other so as to improve our lives. Clearly the various modes of interactivity just mentioned do this. They enrich us by amplifying our ability to satisfy our desires, power(1), through concerted activity. It is just as clear that diminishing each other's ability to participate in such forms of interactivity impoverishes us all, sometimes in violent ways.

Whether or not diminishing someone's ability to participate in the relevant modes of interactivity would count as a case of violence (in Garver's sense) would depend upon the impact of this on the life of the individual. Let us consider both sexism and racism. To be violent, racist or sexist behaviour must have consequences of a certain depth and intensity. For example, barring someone from joining a private athletic club or a debating society (because of race or gender) may be unjust but it would probably not be violent. However, making someone believe that they lack the intelligence to learn basic skills for living (because of race or gender) and thereby making them dependent on others in relevant ways would count as an infringement on their right to make their own decisions (psychological violence) and it may, under certain conditions, also count as an infringement on their right to determine what is done to their body (physical violence).

The quality of life for individuals, for communities and for the culture at large can only decline as our capacity for interactivity declines. We see, therefore, that it is in general *undesirable* for us to dominate others in ways which gratuitously diminish our future prospects for such interactions. My general recommendation, therefore, is that our natural and reasonable desire to dominate each other should be counter-balanced by an equally natural and reasonable desire to not diminish (but perhaps enhance) each other's capacity for interactivity. Dominating power must be restrained by considerations of concertive power, if we are to avoid setting the stage for our self-defeat. Now I shall turn to developmental power.

It is evident that the creation and maintenance of these various forms of concerted activity presuppose substantial imaginative, perceptual, emotional, intellectual, and bodily capacities on our part. And even though such capacities may fully emerge only under conditions of social interactivity they remain as attributes of individuals; they are, in fact, paradigm examples of power(2). I think of these capacities as constituting the physical and psychological substrate of the various modes of interactivity mentioned above. Consequently, if we wish to enjoy the benefits of such interactivity, namely, the benefits of civilized life, we must protect this substrate.

I take C.B. Macpherson to be focusing on precisely this type of issue with his concept of *developmental power:* people's ability to use and develop their essentially human capacities.[22] He concedes that one could consider various human attributes in the course of such an investigation and he takes for granted that the final list may vary with one's theoretical interests. His purpose is to develop a theory of democracy; his suggestion is that 'developmental power' might therefore embrace the following capacities:

> the capacity for rational understanding, for moral judgment and action, for aesthetic creation or contemplation, for the emotional activities of friendship and love, and, sometimes, for religious experience, ... the capacity for wonder or curiosity, ... the capacity for controlled physical/mental/aesthetic activity, as expressed for instance in making music and in playing games of skill.[23]

The primary function of his notion of developmental power is that it focuses us on *impediments* to the use of and development of essential human capacities, impediments which social theory should help us to anticipate and forestall. For the case at hand, where the issue is the matter of how to prevent domination from involving us in self-defeat, I would want the concept of developmental power to embrace all those human capacities (both physical and psychological) which are essential for one's participation in the various modes of interactivity mentioned above. This would obviously include much of what appears in Macpherson's list. We can see immediately, without going into details, that it is *undesirable* for us to dominate each other in ways which gratuitously incapacitate each other in such essential ways. For if I dominate you in such a way as to make it impossible for you to interact with me in the future (by destroying substrate capacities), I thereby lose access to all those benefits which could arise from future cases of interactivity, some of which could be further cases of my dominating you.

It is worth noting that this is exactly what makes violence (in Garver's sense) such a tempting alternative in certain situations. The promise is that if I can disempower you at the level of bodily and decision-making capacities I will have an effect on you which will, as I have said, cascade out in many directions and for a long time to come. The promise is that I can effectively deal with the situation *once and for all.* Surely this is the charm of homicide and the lure of terror, as problem-solving choices. My conclusion about violence is not that we should never commit it but that it often turns out to be a very, very expensive way of responding to human problems. Quite often the disbenefits eclipse the benefits.

My second general recommendation therefore is this: our natural and reasonable desire to dominate each other should be counterbalanced by an equally natural and reasonable desire to not diminish (but perhaps enhance) each other's developmental power. Dominating power must be restrained by considerations of developmental power if we are to avoid the embarrassment and frustration of self-defeat.

IV

I will conclude by summarizing my findings on how violence and power are connected with each other.

To dominate means to control others, to have power over them. That is its essential nature; that is why we sometimes need it. Sometimes we obtain such power by disempowering others. Whether or not such disempowerment will be experienced as violent or will be considered to be improper in some other way will depend on three things: the type of power involved, one's concept of violence and one's criteria of propriety. In this article I have argued the following: it is undesirable gratuitously to disempower others with respect to their concertive power and their developmental power. I have noted that some cases of such disempowerment will count as violent in Garver's sense of violence. However, it has been my intention to allow for the possibility that when all things are considered it may be desirable in certain cases to disempower people in precisely such ways. I have wanted to argue only that it is *prima facie* imprudent for us to do so. I have done this because of my abiding conviction that much of the violence in the world stems from thoughtlessness, lack of awareness, human error – things of that sort, rather than from evil intent. That is why I have discussed things in terms of prudence, rather than from the point of view of morality. I believe that we would avoid much violence and self-defeat if we were to counter-balance our natural desire to dominate with two other equally natural desires, namely, the desire to develop and express essential human capacities and the desire to act in concert with each other.

Notes

1. R. Audi, 'On the Meaning and Justification of Violence'. J. A. Shaffer, (ed.), *Violence*. New York: David McKay, 1971, pp. 45–99.
2. J. Betz, 'Violence: Garver's Definition and a Deweyan Correction'. *Ethics* Vol. 87, No. 4, July, 1977; C. A. J. Coady. 'The Idea of Violence'. *Journal of Applied Philosophy* Vol. 3, No. 1, 1986.

3. R. B. Miller, 'Violence, Force and Coercion'. In Shaffer, *op. cit.*, pp. 9–44; see also R. Holmes, *On War and Morality.* Princeton, N.J.: Princeton University Press, 1989, ch. 1.

4. Newton Garver, 'What Violence Is'. *The Nation,* No. 209, 24 June, 1968, pp. 817–22. Reprinted in Rachels and Tillman, (eds.), *Philosophical Issues.* New York: Harper & Row, 1972. Holmes embraces both the narrow view requiring physical force and the extended view based on violating persons (ch. 1).

5. Garver, p. 224.

6. Thomas Hobbes, *Leviathan,* C.B. Macpherson (ed.), New York: Penguin Books, 1980, p. 150.

7. C. B. Macpherson, *Democratic Theory.* Oxford: Oxford University Press, 1975, pp. 42–5.

8. H. J. Morgenthau, *Politics Among Nations.* New York: Alfred A. Knopf, 1973, p. 9.

9. I have discussed Hobbes' account of domination in two other papers: 'Democracy as a Solution to the Problem of Domination'. *Contemporary Philosophy,* Vol. XIII. No 9, 1991, pp. 5–8; 'Hobbes' Solution to the Problem of Power'. Forthcoming in R. Werner and D. Cady (eds.), *Just War, Nonviolence and Nuclear Deterrence* (Longwood Academic).

10. Hobbes, *op. cit* pp. 129–30.

11. *Ibid.*, p. 161

12. *Ibid.*, p. 150.

13. See note 9.

14. Hobbes, *op. cit.*, p. 161.

15. *Ibid.*, p. 186.

16. *Ibid.*, pp. 252, 258.

17. *Ibid.*, p. 228.

18. *Ibid.*, p. 478.

19. See the articles mentioned in note 9.

20. Hannah Arendt, *On Violence.* New York: Harcourt, Brace & World, Inc., 1970, pp. 44–82.

21. Although he did not emphasize the matter in the *Leviathan,* and even though he did not conceive of it as a particular kind of power. Hobbes did recognize the importance of what I am referring to as concertive power: he enshrines his belief in our natural sociability in the Fifth Law of Nature when he speaks of 'mutual accommodation'. Hobbes, *op. cit.*, pp. 209–10.

22. Macpherson, p. 42.

23. Macpherson, pp. 53–4.

COMMENTARY ON LITKE

Robert F. Litke, who is the co-editor of an important compilation of essays on collective violence,[1] investigates the connections between violence and power. What is particularly interesting about Litke's analysis is that instead of discussing those connections from the point of view of morality, he does so in terms of prudence. That is to say, the question is not whether it is morally right or wrong to indulge in acts of violence, but whether it is in my interest to do so.

Following a brief review of the literature on the meaning of violence, Litke adopts Garver's definition, which suggests that we focus on violence not as a matter of physical force, but rather as the violation of a person. In particular, Garver highlights two kinds of powers that define the person: bodily capacities and decision-making abilities. Litke argues that violence occurs precisely when these powers are being diminished or destroyed by someone else: 'that is the heart of violence: the disempowerment of persons'.

To be precise, Litke suggests that we can think of power in three different ways: the ability to satisfy one's desires (power 1); bodily capacities and decision-making abilities (power 2); the ability to control or command (power 3). It is this third sense of power, namely power as dominion, which explains the widespread occurrence of violence.[2]

By basing his analysis on a detailed reading of Hobbes's political theory, Litke argues that power as domination is a socially destructive force, since domination tends to be a violent, zero-sum game: 'there is a natural and inevitable development of power from the innocuous ability to satisfy simple desires – power(1) – to a competitive drive to dominate each other – power(3).'

Litke adds an original twist to this long-established analysis of violence by suggesting that, on grounds of prudence, it is imperative that dominating power itself must be restrained, and that this must be done by two other kinds of power: concertive power and developmental power.

The idea of concertive power is taken from Hannah Arendt's famous claim that power corresponds to the human ability to act in concert.[3] Litke argues that it is in our interest not to diminish each other's capacity for inter-activity, since 'not only our physical survival but most of what we value in life is dependent upon our ability to act in concert with each other'. Furthermore, concertive power is a precondition to what Litke calls developmental power, or people's ability to use and develop their essentially human capacities. It is in our interest to find ways for these two powers to counter-balance our natural desire to dominate.

Notes and further reading

1. See Robert Litke and Deane Curtin (eds), *Institutional Violence*, Amsterdam: Rodopi, 1999.

2. On the concept of power in general, see P. Morriss, *Power: A Philosophical Analysis*, Manchester: Manchester University Press, 2002; K. Dowding, *Power*, Minnesota: University of Minnesota Press, 1996.
3. Hannah Arendt, *On Violence*, New York: Harcourt, Brace & World, 1969, pp. 44–82.

15
The Different Categories of Violence

Jamil Salmi

Most people think of violence in a narrow context, equating it with images of war, murders or riots. But violence comes in many more forms. The range of phenomena that could be included under this label is quite extensive. If one accepts the notion that any act that threatens a person's physical or psychological integrity is a form of violence, then one needs to consider that occurrences as diverse as racism, pollution or poverty can be symptoms of violent situations.

The existence of different categories and forms of violence calls for a rigorous classification, free of the biases and shortcomings discussed earlier. An impartial and thorough analytical presentation of the different categories of violence must respect two criteria, namely *objectivity* and *exhaustivity*.

The need for *objectivity* implies a value-free definition, independent of the cultural perceptions and political slogans of a given regime, or of the codification of a given legal system. In particular, it is imperative to reject any ideological preconceptions that may be likely to introduce elements of bias into the analysis, whether they be the individualistic prejudices typical of the capitalist approach or the collectivist prejudices commonly found in communist countries. In the former case, emphasis is put on the civil rights of man taken as an isolated individual (what Marx referred to as the 'so-called rights of egocentric man'), while the existence and implications of the social relationships woven by people living in organised society are ignored. In the latter case, more importance is granted to respecting the socio-economic rights of the members of a community, but the protection of civil rights and political freedom is neglected. Instead of endorsing the moral vision of a particular society or group of people, or relying on the opinion of political leaders, judges or neighbours, the viewpoint of the victims should be the guiding principle in considering any objective classification of human rights violations.

The quest for an *exhaustive* classification cannot be satisfied without a systematic definition embodying all the various forms of violence that can be inflicted upon a human being. For this purpose, the typology proposed must take into account all the theoretically conceivable categories (logical exhaustivity) as well as the various forms that can be encountered in reality (empirical exhaustivity). Violence will therefore be considered throughout this book as any avoidable action that constitutes a violation of a human right, in its widest meaning, or which prevents the fulfilment of a basic human need. This definition relies on the principle that, for each fundamental human need, there should be a corresponding human right entitled to legal protection. It is meant to include accidental outbreaks of violence as well as patterns of structural violence inherent in the daily operation of an institution (for example, sexual discrimination at work) or a whole society (for example, apartheid in South Africa). It deals equally with all categories of violence regardless of the number or nature of the people or the entities responsible for the violence, be it an individual, a group of people, an institution, the state, or society at large.

Four main analytical categories can be put forward to satisfy the two criteria discussed above.[1] These are direct violence, indirect violence, repressive violence, and alienating violence.

Direct violence

Direct violence refers to acts of deliberate violence resulting in a direct attack on a person's physical or psychological integrity. This category includes all forms of homicide (genocide, war crimes, massacres of civilians, murders) as well as all types of coercive or brutal actions involving physical or psychological suffering (forced removal of populations, kidnapping, torture, rape, maltreatment). Such behaviour corresponds in all instances to illegal acts running counter to the most basic of all human rights, the right to life.

Indirect violence

Indirect violence is a category intended to cover harmful, sometimes even deadly situations or actions which, though due to human intervention, do not necessarily involve a direct relationship between the victims and the institution, person or people responsible for their plight. Two sub-categories of this type of violence need to be distinguished: violence by omission and mediated violence.

Violence by omission is defined by drawing an analogy with the legal notion of non-assistance to persons in danger. In the same way as legislators have deemed it mandatory to penalise, at the individual level, the passive behaviour of any citizen who refuses or neglects to help a victim of an accident or aggression in need of urgent care, it is essential to introduce at the social or collective level the notion of 'criminal failure to intervene' whenever human lives are threatened by phenomena whose harmful effects are technically avoidable or controllable by society. For example, some people have condemned the US government for failing to intervene directly to prevent, or at least hinder, the genocide of six million Jews during the Second World War, given that the State Department had received information about Hitler's Final Solution as early as August 1942. Only in January 1944, after reading the conclusions of a secret memorandum entitled 'Acquiescence of This Government in the Murder of the Jews', did President Roosevelt order his government to take steps to rescue the victims of Nazi extermination plans.[2]

The hunger issue may also serve as an illustration of this particular form of indirect violence. Each time human beings starve or are undernourished, not because of an absolute lack of food after a natural disaster but simply because food is not available for social or political reasons (insufficient income, unequal regional distribution of food supplies, inadequate delivery channels, policy of export promotion regardless of the degree of satisfaction of local needs), it is legitimate to consider these people as the victims of a form of social violence for which readily identifiable people or institutions are responsible (for example, an agro-industrial multinational corporation or a state marketing board). Such phenomena can sometimes reach levels of boundless cruelty. In 1944–5, for example, the French occupation forces in Indo-China contributed to the deaths of two million Vietnamese by starvation by denying them access to rice stocks after the crop had failed;[3] more recently, during the Biafra war, the Nigerian federal government deliberately starved the secessionist Ibo population. Besides such extreme cases, one finds, in some areas of the planet, less extreme but no less dramatic situations of starvation reflecting patterns of very unequal land distribution. As Pierre Spitz suggests, hunger is the 'silent violence' of modern times.[4] According to official UN statistics, 10,000 human beings die of starvation every day and the total number of people suffering from chronic malnutrition reaches the mindboggling figure of 500 million, among whom are 150 million children under the age of five.[5]

Insofar as it is not solely a biological or physiological phenomenon, illness is another example of violence by omission. As Ivan Illich points out, 'the analysis of mortality trends indicates that the general environment [the notion includes living conditions] is the first determinant of the global state of health of the population'.[6] Within a country, it is common to observe that people's vulnerability to diseases varies considerably according to regional, social or ethnic factors. In particular, living conditions (urban versus rural areas, quality of housing, food availability and consumption patterns, access to drinking water), purchasing power (access to private medicine and type of health insurance) and political power (chances of influencing how much public money is apportioned to the health sector) play a key role.

These two examples of hunger and illness allow us to understand why Mark Twain called poverty 'the greatest terror'. From this perspective, the underprivileged peasants who leave the rural areas of Africa and Asia for the slums of rapidly expanding Third World cities could be described as 'poverty refugees'. Generally speaking, groups in society with less protection than others in terms of satisfying their basic needs, that is, those denied access to medical facilities, to the means of preventing accidents, or to assistance in cases of natural catastrophes such as hurricanes or earthquakes, are the victims of indirect violence on society's part.

Contrary to violence by omission, which happens in a passive way, *mediated violence* is the result of deliberate human interventions in the natural or social environment whose consequences to other human beings are felt in an indirect way. The potential harmful effects are not immediate, but come from mediating factors. Thus, the people or institutions responsible for this type of violence and their victims are not in direct relationship.

All forms of ecocide, meaning acts of destruction, disturbance or damage against our natural environment, belong to this category of violence inasmuch as they may induce death, suffering or mutilation in man. For instance, Agent Orange, the defoliant widely used by the US army during the Vietnam War and by the Soviet army in Afghanistan, which was primarily intended to destroy crops in enemy territory, has turned out to have caused genetic malformations among newly born babies in the areas concerned and cancer among US and Soviet war veterans. Further examples of mediated violence include atomic bomb tests, industrial pollution or the sale of products that pose a danger to their users. For instance, several studies document the common practice among US and European multinationals of selling a wide range of toxic products to Third World countries that are banned in their home countries because they can induce cancer, genetic malformations or miscarriages. Such products include pesticides such as DDT, drugs such as Depo Provera (used for contraception), textiles such as baby clothes manufactured with carcinogenic Tris fibres, or food products containing carcinogenic cyclamate.[7]

As a general rule, any modification of the social and economic environment likely to bring about a substantial deterioration of living and health conditions falls under this category of indirect violence. Colonial and post-colonial agricultural policies in many African, Asian and Latin American countries may be examined in this context. The progressive replacement of traditional food crops with cash crops for export has often resulted in a marked decrease in food availability among rural communities.[8] Famines occurring after this type of evolution are therefore not natural phenomena due to unfavourable climatic or geographical circumstances, or rapid population growth, but the logical outcome of a specific economic strategy. As Bertolt Brecht once put it, 'famines do not just happen; they are organised by the grain business'. Finally, among the various forms of mediated violence, one should also include any situation in which a population becomes poorer or witnesses a deterioration in its living conditions as a result of being unfairly dispossessed of its natural resources.

Two remarks are called for before concluding this presentation of the main forms of indirect violence. First, there is a large degree of complementarity between violence by omission and mediated violence. Whereas the first category is generally characteristic of a stable state of affairs, mediated violence is more often associated with a dynamic perspective corresponding to the causal link between a modification of the environment and the appearance of harmful effects. Manifestations of mediated violence can very often explain the origin of violence by omission, as in the ease of the hunger issue.

Second, the people or institutions responsible for indirect violence are not always considered guilty of a criminal offence by the law or by society. Their harmful interventions or practices may be undertaken in strict respect for the law or may assume very peaceful aspects. For instance, if certain forms of pollution are not banned by the legislation of a given country, the polluting firm or individual cannot be regarded as a criminal from a purely legal viewpoint. But the legal or illegal nature of an act of pollution does not diminish the reality of the offence if it can be objectively demonstrated that this act has dangerous consequences for other human beings. Even when indirect violence is due solely to indifference or neglect in a situation of latent danger, the social obligation of those who are actually responsible remains. Many of the victims of the October 1986 earthquake in El Salvador would not have died if, after the 1965 earthquake, dangerous high-rise buildings like the Ruben-Dario skyscraper, which had been identified as unsafe, had been demolished as the experts had recommended.[9] In Mexico too, thousands of lives could have been saved if stricter building standards had been enforced. Experts also hold that the Armero catastrophe in Colombia (1985) would not have killed as many people as it did had the Nevada del Ruiz volcano been carefully observed and the population evacuated in time.[10]

Repressive violence

Repressive violence corresponds to the deprivation of basic rights other than the right to survival and protection from injury. This category therefore includes human rights violations which, though not directly or indirectly endangering the lives of the people concerned, nevertheless constitute important infringements on the freedom, dignity or equality of rights to which human beings are entitled. Repressive violence relates to three groups of fundamental rights: civil rights, political rights and social rights. The main civil rights are freedom of thought and religion, freedom of movement, privacy, equality before the law and the right to a fair trial. Political rights refer to the degree to which citizens can participate democratically in the political life of their region or country (right to vote, holding of elections, freedom to meet and to form associations or parties, freedom of speech and opinion, and freedom of the press). With respect to social rights, one of the most usual forms of repressive violence is that which prevents people from creating or belonging to a trade union, or from going on strike.

Alienating violence

Alienating violence refers to the deprivation of a person's higher rights, such as the right to emotional, cultural or intellectual growth. The need to define and include this category of human rights in the present classification stems from the recognition that it is important to a person's well-being that certain non-material human needs be fulfilled. Satisfaction at work, the opportunity to engage in creative activities, a young child's need for affection, the feeling of social belonging or cultural identity are some examples of such rights which can also be violated, whether deliberately or not.

One of the most serious forms of alienating violence is what can be defined as 'ethnocide', that is, policies or actions that significantly alter the prevailing material or social conditions under which the cultural identity of a group of people, or whole community, is guaranteed. This can happen in many different ways. The restrictions may be cultural, such as when children are taught in an official language other than their mother tongue (as in most African countries), or when the educational curriculum systematically depreciates or ignores the pupils' cultural background (as with Native Americans in the US and Kurds in Turkey, Iraq and Iran), or when the official history books deliberately overlook events that are important to a particular cultural group (for example, the Armenian genocide denied by the Turkish authorities, or the Japanese version of the conquest of Manchuria), or when cultural groups are denied the right to express freely their identity (for example, Bulgarians of Turkish origin forced to adapt their names to 'pure' Bulgarian).

Economic or social measures may also have a negative impact if a significant change in the material living conditions of a group poses a serious threat to its specific form of culture. The forced sedentarisation of nomad populations in Iran under the Shah, or the forced integration into modern life of so-called 'primitive' tribes (Indians in the Amazon Basin or Aboriginals in Australia) are typical of such phenomena.

As an analytical tool, the notion of alienating violence is useful. Not only can it deal with extreme situations of ethnocide or cultural oppression, but it can also be used to explain the more ordinary aspects of daily life, such as the inhuman nature of work in certain industrial settings (routine tasks, coercive hierarchical relationships) or the marginalisation of old people denied a social role in overcrowded, anonymous old people's homes.

The various rights discussed under the two categories of repressive and alienating violence may be violated either by groups of people, the state itself, or society as a whole. Racism, for instance, which is an injury to human dignity and often leads to violations of the right to equal treatment before the law, may result from individual or group prejudice in a nation that officially condemns racism (Arabs and black Africans in France, Turks in Germany, West Indians in the United Kingdom and blacks in the US), but it can also be the product of a deliberate discriminatory policy against certain religious, cultural or ethnic groups. Sometimes, such state policies are not officially acknowledged, as with anti-Semitism in the USSR or Poland;[11] sometimes the prejudice is blatant, as it was in the southern states of the US until 1954, in Rhodesia until it became Zimbabwe in 1979 and even now in South Africa, Repressive and alienating violence may therefore be manifested either as harmful social behaviour or as legal stipulations running counter to the full enjoyment of a human being's basic rights.

It is worth emphasising that a given historical event does not necessarily correspond to only one category of violence, but that it may involve several forms at the same time. For example, an account of the African slave trade between the 15th and 19th centuries would encompass all four main categories of violence: the direct violence of the manhunt on the West African coasts and of slavery in the US; the indirect violence of the slaves' living conditions during the transatlantic journey and on the US plantations; the repressive violence insofar as slavery was, by definition, the absolute negation of any human right; and, finally, the alienating violence of completely uprooting the slaves from their home villages, country and continent and forcibly plunging them into a totally alien geographical, cultural and social universe.

On the basis of this methodological discussion, it is important to bear in mind the complexity of violence as a social phenomenon and the need to go beyond common ideological biases, cultural prejudices and legal codifications to be able to analyse its multiple dimensions.

Typology of Different Categories and Forms of Violence

Direct Violence
Deliberate injury to the integrity of human life

- homicide
  genocide
  massacre
  murder

- brutal acts
  torture
  rape
  maltreatment ⟶

– restrictions or physical constraints
  forced removal of population
  kidnapping
  taking of hostages
  imprisonment
  forced labour

Indirect Violence
Indirect violations of the right to survival

– violence by omission (non-assistance to human beings in danger; non-satisfaction of vital material needs)
  lack of protection against social violence (hunger, disease, poverty)
  lack of protection against accidents
  lack of protection against natural violence (hurricanes, earthquakes)

– mediated violence (dangerous modifications of the natural and social environment)

Repressive Violence
Deprivation of fundamental rights

– social rights
  trade unionism
  social equality
  participation in social and economic life
  protection of material individual and collective property

– civil rights (protection from the state)
– political rights (democratic participation in political life)

Alienating Violence
Deprivation of higher rights

– alienating living conditions (at work, home, school)
– social ostracism (hostility against certain members and groups of society: for example, women, old people, gay people, immigrants, ethnic groups, carriers of the Aids virus)
– ethnocide

Notes

1. The approach proposed here owes much to the typology developed by Johan Galtung in his chapter on 'The Specific Contribution of Peace Research Typologies', in *Violence and its Causes* (Paris, Unesco, 1981). The main difference lies in the definition of 'structural violence'. While Galtung includes under this concept all three categories of indirect, repressive and alienating violence, it seems appropriate, for the purpose of this book's classification, to apply the accidental/structural dichotomy to all forms and types of violence.
2. A. Morse, *While Six Million Died*, New York, Ace Publishing Corporation, 1967.
3. See H. Zinn, p. 461.
4. P. Spitz, 'Silent Violence: Famine and Inequalities', *International Review of Social Sciences*, vol. XXX, no. 4, 1978.
5. FAO, 'World Food and Agriculture Situation 1987–1988', collection 'FAO Agriculture', no. 21, Rome, 1989.
6. I. Illich, *Némésis médicale*, Paris, Le Seuil, 1975, p. 24.
7. K. Ahmed, W. Morehouse and R. Shaikh, 'Forbidden Products', *Development Forum*, January 1982.
8. S. George, *How the Other Half Dies of Hunger*, London, Penguin, 1976.
9. See the article entitled 'El Salvador: après le séisme du 10 Octobre. Le secteur privé est chargé par le gouvernement de gérer l'aide internationale', *Le Monde*, 16 October 1986.
10. C. Vanhecke, 'Armero ne devait pas être détruite', *Le Monde*, 30 November 1985.
11. On Poland, see for instance L. Trepper, *Le Grand Jeu*, Paris, Albin Michel, 1975. On the Soviet Union, see M. Heller and A. Nekrich, *Utopia in Power: The History of the Soviet Union from 1917 to the Present*, Summit Books, 1986; Y. Gilbes, *The Black Years of Soviet Jewry*, London, Little, Brown and Company, 1971; H. Carrère d'Encausse, *L'Empire éclaté*, Paris, Flammarion, 1978; A.M. Rosenthal, *L'Antisémitisme en Russie*, Paris, PUF, 1982.

COMMENTARY ON SALMI

Jamil Salmi is an economist with the World Bank. His most recent research has been on issues of tertiary education.[1] In this chapter, taken from his book *Violence and Democratic Society: New Approaches to Human Rights*,[2] Salmi starts from a broad definition of violence, grounded on the notion that any act that threatens a person's physical or psychological integrity is a form of violence. As one might anticipate, there are clear echoes of Galtung's structural violence in Salmi's own definition: 'violence will therefore be considered throughout this book as any avoidable action that constitutes a violation of a human right, in its widest meaning, or which prevents the fulfilment of a basic human need'.

An aspect of Salmi's analysis worth noting is that he takes the viewpoint of the victim as the guiding principle in considering any objective classification of violence. Starting from this perspective, Salmi goes on to discuss four main analytical categories of violence: direct, indirect, representative and alienating.

Direct violence is the least controversial of the four categories, as it refers to acts of deliberate violence resulting in a direct attack on a person's physical or psychological integrity. Indirect violence is a more polemical category, as it refers to harmful actions which do not necessarily involve a direct relationship between the victims and the institution, person or people responsible for their plight. There are two subcategories of indirect violence: violence by omission and mediated violence. Indirect violence by omission happens in a passive way, whenever someone refuses or neglects to help victims in need. Salmi gives the example of hunger: 'each time human beings starve or are undernourished, not because of an absolute lack of food after a natural disaster but simply because food is not available for social or political reasons [...] it is legitimate to consider these people as the victims of a form of social violence.' Indirect mediated violence is the result of deliberate intervention in the natural or social environment whose consequences to other human beings are not immediate, but come from mediating factors, such as ecocide, including the military use of Agent Orange.

Repressive violence is the deprivation of basic rights other than the right to survival and protection from injury, including civil, political and social rights. Repressive violence constitutes infringements on the freedom, dignity or equality of rights to which human beings are entitled. Finally, alienating violence refers to the deprivation of a person's right to emotional, cultural or intellectual growth, such as by means of racism, social ostracism or ethnocide.

Salmi also reminds us that these four categories of violence are not mutually exclusive, since it is possible for a given historical event to involve several or even all forms of violence at the same time, as in the case of the African slave trade between the fifteenth and nineteenth centuries.

Notes and further reading

1. See, for example, J. Salmi, A. Rodriguez and C. Dahlman, *Knowledge and Innovation for Competitiveness in Brazil*, World Bank Publications, 2008.
2. J. Salmi, *Violence and Democratic Society*, London: Zed Books, 1993.

16
Poverty and Violence

Steven Lee

The question whether poverty is a cause of violence is a question for a sociologist, but the question whether violence is the cause of poverty is a philosopher's question. The latter question would normally be understood conceptually, while the former would be understood empirically. The question whether violence is the cause of poverty, understood conceptually, assumes that we have a grasp of the kinds of acts that bring about poverty and that the issue is whether or not it is appropriate to classify such acts, when they do cause poverty, as acts of violence. This is the question I take up: Are acts causing poverty properly labeled as acts of violence? Is poverty the result of violence? This is sometimes imprecisely cast as the question whether poverty *is* violence, but, strictly speaking, poverty itself is no more violence than the broken nose caused by an assault is violence. Both poverty and a broken nose, however, may be caused by acts of violence.

Violence is a topic that was examined by analytic philosophers during the first great wave of 'applied philosophy' in the late 1960s and early 1970s.[1] It is appropriate, as we observe the anniversaries of some of the violent political events of that era, again to consider philosophically the issue of violence. Certainly, the often violent political turmoil of that time was one of the principal factors bringing about the 'applied turn' in philosophy, which continues to this day. It is, then, not surprising that some of the early essays in applied philosophy were on the subject of violence. The most visible violence of the sixties was anti-institutional, a response to the institutionalized economic and social injustices of the status quo, and one of the concerns of those essays was the normative question whether a violent response to such injustice is justified. But a related conceptual question taken up in the essays is the extent to which institutional injustices could themselves be considered forms of violence. The conceptual question is prior to the normative question not only because we cannot know whether or not violence is justified until we know what we are talking about, but also because, if institutional injustices are forms of violence, this would be relevant to determining whether a violent response on the part of those who are being treated unjustly is justifiable, as, under common moral notions, the violence of aggression can sometimes justify the violence of defense. My concern is the conceptual question rather than the normative one, and I will focus on the particular institutional injustices resulting in poverty, asking whether those injustices can be regarded as a form of violence.

Before beginning, however, there is an important objection that must be addressed. Is not the question whether poverty is caused by violence merely verbal, hence a trivial matter? Is not the dispute over this question simply part of a rhetorical battle between defenders of the status quo and their critics over the moral high ground involved in the use of the pejorative 'violence'? On the contrary, it is not a matter merely of how we choose to use the term. This is a question about which argument is appropriate. The issue is subject to argument in two different ways. First, there are considerations about ordinary usage, and second, there are pragmatic considerations concerning the value or disvalue of proposals for linguistic legislation. Arguments of both sorts arise in regard to the question whether it is appropriate to regard the human causes of poverty as acts of violence. Thus, the answer to the question is not merely stipulative. There are good reasons for or against positions one can take on it. It is these reasons I will examine.

In the first section I discuss some necessary preliminaries. In the second section I begin to consider the question by critically examining the soundness of a strong presumptive argument, based on considerations of ordinary usage, that acts causing poverty should not be regarded as acts of violence. Finally, in the third section, I consider whether there are positive reasons of a pragmatic sort to support the extension of the term 'violence' to cover acts causing poverty.

1

The first preliminary concerns the definition of 'poverty.' I understand 'poverty' in a more limited sense than is usual, but in a sense which is consistent with that used by those who claim that poverty is a result of violence. Poverty, as I will use the term, is an institutional injustice causing or tending to cause significant harm. Only when one's being poor is a harmful injustice is one in poverty, in my sense. Thus, my thesis is that someone's being poor, when this is a harmful injustice, is the result of violence.

Given my sense of 'poverty,' there are three conditions which must be satisfied in order that someone who is poor be in poverty. The first two conditions indicate that the privation is an injustice, and the third indicates that it involves significant harm. The first condition is that one not be poor voluntarily. If one has voluntarily made or kept oneself poor, as when one takes a vow of poverty for religious reasons, then one's being poor, in virtue of its being voluntary, is not an injustice. The question of when one's being poor is voluntary would be a matter of contention. Some may argue that most if not all of those who are poor in a market economy are poor voluntarily. But I will assume that this is not the case, that many or most of those who are poor in a market economy are not poor voluntarily, and hence satisfy the first condition for being in poverty.

The second condition for poverty is that one must be poor in a society where others have significant wealth. If others in the society do not have significant wealth, the resources are not available to alleviate the poor person's lack of resources, in which case, one's being poor cannot count as an injustice. This condition needs to be clarified in two respects. By 'significant wealth' I mean enough wealth to allow the wealthy substantially to reduce the poorness of the poor. The wealthy would lack significant wealth, first, if their wealth were so meager, in relative terms, that it would, if redistributed, not substantially improve the condition of the poor, or, second, if the society already satisfied Rawls's difference principle, in which case redistributing resources from the wealthy to the poor would lead to less for the poor in absolute terms.[2] The second clarification concerns the size of the society in which the significant wealth may reside. I am inclined to endorse the view that, given the extent of global economic interdependence, the relevant sense of 'society' should be the whole world rather than individual nations or smaller social groupings.[3]

The third condition for a poor person's being in poverty is that the person must be so lacking in resources that significant harm to him or her results or tends to result from that lack. In other words, my notion of poverty entails that the resources of a person in poverty fall below some level necessary for a minimally decent life (or for the satisfaction of basic needs), where that level is defined in terms of the resources needed to avoid significant harm. Because this level is at least partly independent of what standard of living others in the society enjoy, my notion of poverty is at least partly nonrelative. The notions of basic needs and minimally decent life, and the notion of significant harm in terms of which I would define them, are, of course, notoriously vague. I will try to make them somewhat more precise by stipulating that someone is significantly harmed by lack of resources when that lack results in objective, dysfunctional physical or mental conditions such as malnutrition, serious medical or psychological problems, or a shortened lifespan. This third condition is independent of the first two (though consistent with them), because there can be injustices of economic distribution which do not result in their victims' falling below a minimally decent standard of living. Thus I am not claiming that all injustice is the result of violence.

Thus, violence and poverty have in common that they cause or tend to cause harm. It is important to consider, in the case of poverty, how the harm is caused. Poverty is created and maintained when individuals are denied the resources they need for a minimally decent life. This denial is often accomplished through individual acts of omission, whether deliberate or not. The beggar remains hungry or homeless because a number of passers-by do not place money in his or her cup. The third-world child remains malnourished because a number of well-off first-worlders do not contribute to OXFAM or UNICEF. There are, in addition, collective, especially governmental, omissions involved: the failure of the social welfare system to house the beggar and the failure of first-world governments to provide sufficient developmental aid to keep the child from malnutrition. But there are also institutional structures of distribution, consisting of laws, social rules, economic relationships, and the like, which keep the beggar and the child (or the child's parents) from having the opportunities to provide resources for themselves through social and economic participation. Were these structures different, there would be no need for aid or charity to keep the beggar and the child from poverty. These institutional structures are the main sources of poverty, and it is the acts through which they are maintained that are the main causes of poverty. Most of these acts are acts of commission rather than omission. But, whether the acts causing poverty are omissive or commissive, individual or collective, there are in most cases human agents responsible for the acts, as there are in the simple case of violence where one individual assaults another. The complexity of the causes of poverty and the fact that they involve omissions as well as commissions serve as no bar to viewing them as acts of violence.[4]

Once it is appreciated that the primary sources of poverty are the institutional structures determining distribution, it becomes clear that there is one noncontroversial sense in which poverty is caused by violence. This is due to the role of the threat of force in maintaining these structures. Because people are not in poverty voluntarily, and thus have a strong inclination to act in ways violative of the rules of these structures to secure for themselves a larger distribution of resources (as when the hungry steal food), the threat of force is necessary to maintain these structures and enforce their rules. But the threat of force is effective in enforcing the rules only if it is credible, and its credibility depends on those against whom the rules are enforced believing that those making the threats are disposed to carry them out. The principal basis of this belief is their awareness that the threats have been carried out in the past, and threats are often carried out through acts of violence. In this indirect way, poverty is caused by acts of violence. While this line of thought does provide a positive answer to the question whether poverty is caused by violence, I want to investigate in the remainder of the paper whether there is a more direct sense in which poverty is caused by violence. So, I shall understand the question to be whether poverty causes violence in a sense in addition to the one discussed in this paragraph.

2

The philosophers who have written on the topic would disagree on the question whether acts causing poverty are acts of violence. Robert Audi argues that it is a conceptual confusion to regard 'discrimination and exclusion,' and he would presumably include poverty as well, as forms of violence, in so far as they are 'peacefully maintained.'[5] In a similar vein, Ronald Miller argues that neglecting someone in need, which is a cause of poverty, cannot count as violence, because 'neglecting cannot be done with great force.'[6] On the other hand, Robert Holmes speaks of 'the debilitating effects...of ghetto schools upon young children' as a form of violence, even though involving no 'physical violence.'[7] Presumably, Holmes would include poverty as resulting from violence as well, because poverty has the same kinds of debilitating effects as have the ghetto schools to which he refers. Likewise, John Harris defends what he refers to as the Marxist view that 'deaths caused by the indifference and neglect of society or its rulers must be seen as being as much a part of human violence as the violent acts of revolutionaries.'[8] Since poverty is the main way through which such deaths occur, poverty, on this view, would clearly be the result of violence.

What is the source of this disagreement? Consider a proposed definition of violence. According to Ted Honderich, an act of violence 'is a use of considerable or destroying force against people or things, a use of force which offends against a norm.'[9] This definition suggests three features characteristic of violence. An act of violence (1) involves a vigorous application of force; (2) results or tends to result in serious harm or injury; and (3) involves the violation of a rule. The disagreement seems to be over whether (1) is a necessary condition of violence: those who deny that the cause of poverty is violence regard (1) as a necessary condition, while those who assert that the cause of poverty is violence do not. Audi and Miller argue that discrimination and neglect, and presumably poverty, cannot be the result of violence because, being peacefully maintained, they do not involve the application of vigorous force. This implies that they regard the application of vigorous force as a necessary condition for violence. On the other hand, Newton Garver suggests that (1) is not a necessary condition when he argues: 'Violence in human affairs is much more closely connected with the idea of violation than with the idea of force. What is fundamental about violence is that a person is violated.'[10]

The question whether the cause of poverty is violence is, then, dependent on whether or not the application of vigorous force is a necessary condition of violence. All agree that an act of violence causes or tends to cause harm to persons.[11] But there is disagreement on whether it must be an act of vigorous force. How is this matter to be decided? Those who believe that vigorous force is a necessary condition of violence usually appeal to ordinary usage, and with considerable plausibility. Paradigm cases of violence do involve the application of vigorous force, as, for example, in a physical assault. It is, I think, fair to say that the ordinary usage of 'violence' does indeed entail that an act of violence involves the application of vigorous force, and thus that an appeal to ordinary usage establishes at least a presumption against the claim that the cause of poverty is violence.[12] In the remainder of this section,

I present an argument meant to rebut this presumption. I attempt, to show that the application of vigorous force need not be regarded as a necessary feature of an act of violence, and hence that it is wrong to reject the claim that the cause of poverty is violence on the grounds that the harms resulting from poverty are not brought about through the application of vigorous force. I argue that vigorous force need not be a necessary feature of violence by suggesting how vigorous force plausibly, but mistakenly, has come to be regarded as a necessary feature.

My argument focuses on the role that rule-violation plays in our labeling acts as acts of violence. Condition (3) derived from Honderich's definition is that violence involves the violation of a rule, suggesting that the violation of a rule is a necessary feature of an act of violence. Inclusion of this condition would yield a definition of violence of the sort that C.A.J. Coady refers to as 'legitimist,' that is, a definition which 'incorporates a reference to an illegal or illegitimate use of force.'[13] Coady objects to such a definition, in part because it would, for example, preclude our referring to repressive police activities, such as the clubbing of peaceful demonstrators, as acts of violence, so long as no legal rules were violated. Such police activities clearly should count as acts of violence, and so much the worse for any definition that would not allow this. Coady's objection, in fact, represents one half of a dilemma which arises concerning the definition of violence. Either it is or it is not a necessary condition of an act of violence that it violates a rule; if it is, then repressive police activities do not count as violence; if it is not, then acts such as the surgeon's removal of the gangrenous leg count as violence. But this dilemma, and Coady's objection to a legitimist definition of violence, arise only on a very narrow understanding of rules. In addition to positive rules, existing social and legal rules, there are what I will call ideal rules; critical (rather than conventional) moral rules, including social and legal rules as they would be in a just society.[14] Police repression is not normally a violation of positive rules, but it is a violation of ideal rules. Thus, a definition of violence under which rule violation is a necessary condition can accommodate our clear intuitions that the police clubbing of peaceful demonstrators is an act of violence.

Here is one way the distinction between positive and ideal rules plays a role in what we label as violence. Consider first the role of positive rules, and, as an example, hockey. Hockey inevitably involves a great deal of rough physical contact between players and such contact is expected. At the same time, certain forms of physical contact are not allowed and are indeed penalized. Say I interact with my opponent in a way which results in his receiving a concussion. If my interaction were a normal bodycheck, resulting in his falling and hitting his head on the ice, my action would not, despite the vigorous force applied and the harm done, normally be called an act of violence. But if the interaction involved my braining him with my stick, one would naturally call this an act of violence. The reason is that the first form of vigorous force is allowed by the rules, and so is a legitimate use of force, while the second is not. In the second case my action breaks a rule of hockey, in particular, the rule against highsticking, while in the former case my action, a simple case of bodychecking, does not. In other words, violence is restricted to illegitimate force, legitimacy being defined by the relevant rules. Legitimate force, even when resulting in serious harm, is not regarded as violence. This follows from the claim that a necessary feature of violence is that it involve the breaking of a rule.

The same pattern occurs in the social and political realm, except that there there is a rule-based asymmetry between the 'teams.' Legal rules allow government officials, especially the police, to apply force in defense of the social order, but citizens are, in general, not allowed to use force. But, as in sports, the rules define limits in the use of force beyond which those permitted to use force are not allowed to go. Corresponding to the distinction between bodychecking and highsticking, there is a distinction between acceptable and excessive police force, the latter being regarded as illegitimate, as a form of 'police brutality' or violence. Police activity within the rules, however, is not generally regarded as violence.

Now consider the role of ideal rules. One can criticize the game of hockey or the activity of the police as a whole by criticizing the sets of positive rules which underlie or constitute the practices. It is always possible to criticize a set of rules and the practice constituted by those rules in terms of an idea of a better set of rules, a set of ideal rules, and the better practice those rules would constitute. Radical critique, a redrawing of the bounds of legitimacy, is always an option. In the hockey case, one need not be bound to respect the distinction as drawn by the game rules between acts that are violent and acts that are not violent. One can treat both bodychecking and highsticking as violent by categorizing the whole game as violent. One can, thus, condemn the whole practice of hockey in favor of some other (often unspecified) sports activity whose rules would not allow the sort of vigorous force and resulting harm allowed in hockey. In the political case, one is free to reject the rule-imposed distinction between legitimate and illegitimate police force by rejecting the social order the police activities maintain, treating their activity as illegitimate, as a form of repression.[15] This is normally done in the name of a proposed social order constituted by a different set of social and legal rules.

The general point is that the difference between positive and ideal rules affects what gets labeled as violence. What is not regarded as violence from the perspective of positive rules may be regarded as violence from the perspective of ideal rules. Now I want to consider a different way in which the difference between the two kinds of rules may affect what gets labeled violence. In this case, I will forsake the sports analogy and focus exclusively on the political realm.

One of the main functions of legal and social rules (whether positive or ideal) is to create and maintain social order, in the sense of providing individuals with some level of personal security from attack or aggression by other members of society. The harm of social disorder is individual aggression, and this is what the rules seek to avoid. Because the harm to individuals when legal and social rules are disobeyed and social order breaks down is the result of attack or aggression, it generally involves the application of vigorous force, as in the paradigm case of individual assault. Thus, due to this concomitance between harm resulting from rule violations and the application of vigorous force, such harms tend to be viewed as always involving the application of vigorous force. As a result, from the perspective that regards the function of social and legal rules as maintaining social order, the personal harm that results from rule violation also results from the application of vigorous force, and it is not surprising that all three features would be seen as necessary conditions for violence.

But the distinction between positive and ideal rules is based on the assumption that social order is not the only important good that rules can achieve. Two systems of legal and social rules may achieve the same degree of social orderliness, but not be equally valuable. There is the distinction between good and bad, just and unjust social order. An ideal set of rules would achieve not simply order, but good order. The radical critique of an existing social order is based on an appeal to the injustice of that order, that is, to the harms done through that social order, rather than the harms of individual aggression done through the violation of that order. Many if not most of the harms of social order do not involve the application of vigorous force. The basis of a radical critique is that, while the existing social order, and the positive social and legal rules which constitute it, may serve to keep individual citizens from aggressing against each other, they also serve to maintain an unjust distribution of power and wealth in society. In a society which has poverty, the maintenance of the poverty involves no positive rule violation, since it is an injustice of the status quo, and is normally maintained without the direct application of vigorous force. But poverty does involve ideal rule violation.

It is the radical critique of a social order which calls to our attention the harms of that social order, the injustice they involve, and our individual and collective responsibility for them. But my point is that the radical critique does more than this. In pointing out the harms of social order, harms other than those of social disorder, it breaks the contingent link between personal harm resulting from rule violations and the application of vigorous force. The harms of social order are ideal rule violations, as opposed to positive rule violations of the harms of social disorder. Thus, the connection between personal harm resulting from rule violations and the application of vigorous force is an artifact of attending exclusively to the harms of social disorder and the value of an existing set of positive social and legal rules in avoiding those harms. When the causes of those harms are labeled acts of violence, it is natural that the application of vigorous force would come to be seen as one of the necessary conditions for the label. In other words, the application of vigorous force as a condition for violence may be seen as derivative from the principal feature of violence, which is personal harm caused by rule violations, in the context of a focus on exclusively positive rules. Once we go beyond this context and the contingent link between the three features is broken, the presumption that violence must involve the application of vigorous force is no longer secure. This demonstration of how vigorous force could plausibly but mistakenly have come to be seen as a necessary feature of violence should thus count as a rebuttal of that presumption.

3

This rebuttal of the presumption that violence necessarily involves vigorous force, however successful it may be, cannot by itself establish the conclusion that it is appropriate to label the causes of poverty as violence. While the rebuttal may remove a primary reason against extending the term in this way, it does not provide any reasons for extending it. Are there reasons of a pragmatic sort for extending the term? Critics of extension have argued that there are pragmatic reasons against it. Audi argues, for example, that to extend the term 'violence' in this way 'would increase the risk of ambiguity and equivocation' and substitute 'a vague general term of disapproval for one which ... describes the specific grievance needing attention.'[16] In a similar vein, Thomas Platt argues that a risk of extending the term is that we may 'obscure significant distinctions, thus managing to confuse ourselves as well as others and increase the likelihood of falling into fallacious lines of reasoning.'[17] Coady argues that extending the term 'is likely to have undesirable practical consequences,' because it would encourage the view that 'one set of techniques' would be sufficient to solve all of the problems encompassed by the term, when 'it may well be that different techniques, strategies and remedies are required.'[18]

In contrast, the pragmatic argument for extension may be cast in terms of the moral continuity between the harms of social disorder and the harms of social order. In terms of moral seriousness or importance, these harms are on an equal footing. Only the blindness of an unreflective defense of the status quo would lead one to fail to appreciate this. The term 'violence' is a very important term of moral evaluation, specifically, of moral condemnation, so to fail to extend it to the harms of social order would be to fail to recognize their moral seriousness, their moral continuity with the harms of social disorder. To make clear that each kind of harm is equally worthy of moral condemnation, we should extend over both of them our vocabulary of serious moral condemnation, which includes prominently the term 'violence.' This point can be made by considering an act of violence as a violation, as suggested in the earlier quotation from Garver.[19] An act of physical assault is certainly a violation of the victim's humanity, and for this reason it is called an act of violence and is subject to serious moral condemnation. But to keep someone in poverty, with all of the harms that that involves, harms which seriously compromise that person's potential for a decent life, is also a violation of his or her humanity. To refuse the term 'violence' to such harm, restricting the term to acts against a positive rule, is to risk mistaking the violation of a person's humanity for the violation of a positive rule. In fact, those who morally condemn violence while restricting its scope in this way may be guilty of just this equivocation on 'violation.'

The critics are correct that broadening the term's extension would, in one sense, decrease its discriminatory power. But the linguistic function of a term should be to allow us not only to distinguish things which are relevantly different, but also to group together or comprehend things that are relevantly similar. So, the question here is what are the appropriate criteria of relevance. Is it the similarities or the dissimilarities between (a) an act of physical assault and (b) an act causing poverty that are more relevant in deciding how the term 'violence' should be used. Because of the strong moral condemnatory force of 'violence,' the most important criterion of relevance must be a moral one, and in this respect the similarities take precedence over the dissimilarities. In the case of both (a) and (b), serious harm has been unjustly caused to a human being. The two have this in common morally. Where they differ, of course, is in whether or not vigorous force is used, which is not a factor in itself of great moral relevance. Thus the principle of comprehending similar phenomena takes precedence in this case over the principle of distinguishing differing phenomena, and 'violence' should be extended. To put the point a different way, extending the term entails a loss of discriminatory power from the perspective of a set of positive rules, but a gain in comprehensive power from the perspective of a set of ideal rules. Because of the moral force of 'violence,' it is the ideal-rule perspective that is the determining one. Both the outlaw and the maintainer of an unjust status quo are capable of great moral wrongs, and we should not let this point be obscured by reserving the strongest condemnatory language for only one of them.[20]

There is an important analogy to this proposed extension of the term 'violence' in the way in which we extend the term 'justice.' The basis for extending the term 'violence' from the harms of social disorder to the harms of social order is similar to that for extending the term 'injustice' from the unfair application of existing rules (formal injustice) to the unfairness of the rules themselves (substantive injustice). In both cases, these strong terms of moral condemnation should not be bound in their application to an unreflective acceptance of existing rules. In the case of injustice, one should recognize, through a critique of existing rules, that unfairness can result from the scrupulous application of those rules, as it can from an incorrect application of them. 'Injustice' should be applicable to both forms of unfairness. Likewise, in the case of violence, a critique of existing rules can reveal that the social order under those rules may be as much a violation of a person as social disorder can be. So, 'violence' should be applicable to both forms of violation. It is no more appropriate to limit the term 'violence' to acts of vigorous force than it is to limit the term 'injustice' to violations of existing rules. The conclusion is that a society does violence to those of its members who are in poverty, as some of its members do violence to others through physical assault.

Despite the reasonableness of this argument, however, the linguistic legislation it proposes is radical. Referring to the causing of poverty as 'violence' strongly flies in the face of the way people normally use the term, and there seems little prospect that the recommended change will be adopted. The causing of poverty ought to be referred to as violence, but it is doubtful that it will come to be. The argument, however, is still of value, because the important thing is not that language use change, but that the world change in the direction of greater social justice. The argument that there is a moral continuity between the harms of social disorder and the harms of social order may play a part over time in leading to a lessening of the latter, as positive rules become less at odds with ideal rules. As poverty decreases, there will be fewer and fewer instances beyond the ordinary extension of 'violence' to which, according to my argument, the term ought to refer. In the just society, the ordinary use of the term would be vindicated.[21]

Notes

1. See, for example: the essays by Robert Holmes, Bernard Harrison, Robert Audi, and Ronald Miller in Jerome Shaffer (ed.), *Violence* (New York: David McKay, 1971); Robert Paul Wolff, 'On Violence,' *Journal of Philosophy* 66 (1969): 601–16; John Harris, 'The Marxist Conception of Violence,' *Philosophy and Public Affairs* 3 (1974): 192–220; Newton Garver, 'What Violence Is,' *The Nation* 206, no. 26 (June 24, 1968): 819–22; Hannah Arendt, *On Violence* (New York: Harcourt, Brace, and World, 1969); and Ted Honderich, *Political Violence* (Ithaca: Cornell University Press, 1976). A more recent essay of importance is C. A. J. Coady, 'The Idea of Violence,' *Journal of Applied Philosophy* 3 (1986): 3–19.
2. John Rawls, *A Theory of Justice* (Cambridge, Mass.: Harvard University Press, 1971), pp. 76–80.
3. For a discussion of the relation between matters of distributive justice and the economic interdependence of nations, see Charles Beitz, *Political Theory and International Relations* (Princeton: Princeton University Press, 1979), pp. 143–54.
4. Coady would argue that acts causing poverty are not acts of violence, in part because acts causing poverty differ too much from paradigm acts of violence in that acts causing poverty involve omissions rather than commissions ('The Idea of Violence,' pp. 8–10). But, if I am right that poverty is brought about by commissions as well as omissions, his point has much less force than it would otherwise have.
5. Audi, 'On the Meaning and Justification of Violence,' in Shaffer, *Violence,* p. 66.
6. Miller, 'Violence, Force and Coercion,' in Shaffer, *Violence,* p. 20.
7. Holmes, 'Violence and Nonviolence,' in Shaffer, *Violence,* p. 110.
8. Harris, 'The Marxist Conception of Violence,' p. 192.

9. Honderich, *Political Violence*, p. 98.
10. Garver, 'What Violence Is,' p. 819.
11. Although we also speak of acts of violence where the direct harmful effect is visited upon a nonhuman animal or to an inanimate object, or even where there is no harmful effect at all, the senses of the term involved in these usages are not central and I will not be concerned with them.
12. Not everyone would agree. John Harris argues that ordinary usage does not entail that vigorous force is a necessary condition of an act of violence, pointing out, for example, that a war in which everyone was killed by radiation would not be regarded as any less violent ('The Marxist Conception of Violence,' p. 216).
13. Coady, 'The Idea of Violence,' p. 4.
14. Wolff raises this distinction in the context of his discussion of violence, presenting it in terms of the contrast between *de facto* and *de jure* authority ('On Violence,' p. 606).
15. Recall that critics referred to the activities of the Chicago police during the 1968 Democratic National Convention as a 'police riot.'
16. Audi, 'On the Meaning and Justification of Violence,' pp. 66–7.
17. Thomas Platt, 'The Concept of Violence as Descriptive and Polemic,' *International Social Science Journal* 44 (1992): 185–91.
18. Coady, 'The Idea of Violence,' pp. 11–12.
19. Garver, 'What Violence Is,' p. 819. See also Holmes, 'Violence and Nonviolence,' pp. 110–13.
20. As Woody Guthrie pointed out, some rob you with a six-gun and some rob you with a fountain pen.
21. An earlier version of this paper was presented at the 1993 convention of Concerned Philosophers for Peace, and I would like to thank those who commented on my presentation for their helpful suggestions and criticisms. I would like especially to thank for their comments Stephen Nathanson, Alison Jaggar, and an anonymous reviewer of this manuscript.

COMMENTARY ON LEE

Steven Lee, who has published extensively on the ethics of war,[1] in this piece explores the relationship between the concepts of poverty and violence.[2] While there is a great deal of empirical research on the issue of whether poverty is a cause of violence, Lee is more interested in the conceptual question whether violence is the cause of poverty: 'This is the question I take up: Are acts causing poverty properly labelled as acts of violence? Is poverty the result of violence?' A related conceptual question is the extent to which institutional injustices could themselves be considered forms of violence.

Lee defines poverty in a more limited sense than is usual, namely as an institutional injustice causing or tending to cause significant harm. Thus, for someone who is poor to be in poverty, three conditions must be satisfied: that one must not be poor voluntarily; that one must be poor in a society where others have significant wealth; that one must be so lacking in resources that significant harm results from that lack, since the resources of a person in poverty fall below some level necessary for a minimally decent life.

Lee suggests that poverty is created and maintained when people are denied the resources needed to avoid significant harm. What is particularly interesting about Lee's analysis is the idea that 'this denial is often accomplished through individual acts of omission, whether deliberate or not'. In other words, just like John Harris's account of violence as Negative Actions, Lee argues that in order to see the causes of violence, we need to look at deliberate and non-deliberate acts of omissions. And echoing Newton Garver, Lee suggests that the primary sources of poverty are the institutional structures determining the distribution of resources.

Lee accepts the view that rule violation is a necessary condition of a definition of violence, but he elaborates on this by suggesting that there are two different types of rules: positive rules (existing social and legal rules) and ideal rules (moral rules, including social and legal rules as they would be in a just society). The distinction between positive and ideal rules is crucial in order to accommodate our intuition that police repression is an act of violence, even if the police are operating within legal rules. Furthermore, distinguishing between positive and ideal rules enables us to see poverty for what it is, as a consequence of violence, since poverty involves ideal rule violation: 'The general point is that the difference between positive and ideal rules affects what gets labelled as violence. What is not regarded as violence from the perspective of positive rules may be regarded as violence from the perspective of ideal rules.'

Finally, Lee defends the claim that it is appropriate to extend the term violence to cover issues relating to poverty. Contrary to those who argue against such conceptual expansions, since this raises the risk of ambiguity, equivocation, and ultimately of obscuring significant distinctions, Lee invites us to consider the moral continuity between the harms of social disorder and the harms of social order. From a moral point of view, there is no difference between the outlaw and the maintainer of an unjust status quo, therefore it is imperative that we use the strongest condemnatory language in both cases: 'The term "violence" is a very important term of moral evaluation, specifically, of moral condemnation, so to fail to extend it to the harms of social order would be to fail to recognize their moral seriousness, their moral continuity with the harms of social disorder.'[3]

Notes and further reading

1. See his *Morality, Prudence, and Nuclear Weapons*, Cambridge: Cambridge University Press, 1993; *The Nuclear Predicament: Nuclear Weapons in the Twenty-First Century*, 3rd edn, co-author, Englewood Cliffs, NJ: Prentice Hall, 2000; *Nuclear Weapons and the Future of Humanity*, co-editor, Totowa, NJ: Rowman & Allanheld, 1986.
2. See also S. Lee, 'Is Poverty Violence?', in D. Curtin and R. Litke (eds), *Institutional Violence*, Amsterdam: Rodopi, 1999.
3. For a similar view, see C. Perry, 'Violence – Visible and Invisible', *Ethics*, Vol. 81, No. 1, 1970. For a critique of this line of argument, see also T. Platt, 'The Concept of Violence as Descriptive and Polemical', *International Social Science Journal*, Vol. 44, No. 2, 1992.

17
Outliving Oneself

Susan J. Brison

I died in Auschwitz, but no one knows it.

— Charlotte Delbo[1]

Survivors of trauma frequently remark that they are not the same people they were before they were traumatized. As a survivor of the Nazi death camps observes, 'One can be alive after Sobibor without having survived Sobibor.'[2] Jonathan Shay, a therapist who works with Vietnam veterans, has often heard his patients say, 'I died in Vietnam.'[3] Migael Scherer expresses a loss commonly experienced by rape survivors when she writes, 'I will always miss myself as I was.'[4] What are we to make of these cryptic comments?[5] How can one miss oneself? How can one die in Vietnam or fail to survive a death camp and still live to tell one's story? How does a life-threatening event come to be experienced as self-annihilating? And what self is it who remembers having had this experience?

How one answers these questions depends on, among other things, how one defines 'trauma' and 'the self.' In this chapter, I discuss the nature of trauma, show how it affects the self, construed in several ultimately interconnected ways, and then use this analysis to elaborate and support a feminist account of the relational self.[6] On this view the self is both autonomous and socially dependent, vulnerable enough to be undone by violence and yet resilient enough to be reconstructed with the help of empathic others.

My methodology differs from that used in traditional philosophizing about the self, and yields distinctly different results. Philosophers writing about the self have, at least since Locke, puzzled over such questions as whether persons can survive the loss or exchange of their minds, brains, consciousness, memories, characters, and/or bodies.[7] In recent years, increasingly gruesome and high-tech thought experiments involving fusion, fission, freezing, dissolution, reconstitution, and/or teletransportation of an individual have been devised to test our intuitions about who, if anyone, survives which permutations.[8] Given philosophers' preoccupation with personal identity in extreme, life-threatening, and possibly self-annihilating situations, it is odd that they have neglected to consider the accounts of actual trauma victims who report that they are not the same people they were prior to their traumatic transformations.[9] This oversight may result from the fact that imaginary scenarios, however far-fetched, are at least *conceivable*, whereas the experiences of rape victims, Holocaust survivors, and war veterans are, for most of us, unthinkable. In addition, philosophers are trained to divert their gaze from the messy real world to the neater, more controllable, and more comprehensible realm of pure thought.

As I discussed in the previous chapter, however, feminist theorists writing in the areas of ethics and social, political, and legal philosophy have recently argued for the necessity of focusing on the actual experiences of real people and have made use of first- and third-person narratives in their attempts to do this.[10] Feminist theorists have also stressed the importance of taking context into account, recognizing that we all reason from a 'positioned perspective' and that some of us, with 'multiple consciousness,' reason from a variety of sometimes incompatible perspectives.[11] In addition, feminist theorists have adopted interdisciplinary approaches to subjects, such as personal identity, previously thought to be the exclusive domain of one discipline. I use these feminist methodologies here, incorporating survivor testimonies, situating philosophical questions of the self in the context of actual individuals' lives, acknowledging my own perspective as a survivor, and drawing on the clinical literature on trauma.

Trauma and the undoing of the self

There is a much clearer professional consensus among psychologists about what counts as a traumatic event than there is among philosophers concerning the nature of the self.[12] A traumatic event is one in which a person feels utterly helpless in the face of a force that is perceived to be life-threatening.[13] The immediate psychological responses to such trauma include terror, loss of control, and intense fear of annihilation. Long-term effects include the physiological responses of hypervigilance, heightened startle response, sleep disorders, and the more psychological, yet still involuntary, responses of depression, inability to concentrate, lack of interest in activities that used to give life meaning, and a sense of a foreshortened future. A commonly accepted explanation of these symptoms of post-traumatic stress disorder (PTSD) is that, in trauma, the ordinarily adaptive human responses to danger that prepare the body to fight or flee are of no avail. 'When neither resistance nor escape is possible,' Judith Herman explains, 'the human system of self-defense becomes overwhelmed and disorganized. Each component of the ordinary response to danger, having lost its utility, tends to persist in an altered and exaggerated state long after the actual danger is over' (Herman 1992, 34). When the trauma is of human origin and is intentionally inflicted, the kind I discuss in this book, it not only shatters one's

338 *Violence: A Philosophical Anthology*

fundamental assumptions about the world and one's safety in it, but it also severs the sustaining connection between the self and the rest of human-ity. Victims of human-inflicted trauma are reduced to mere objects by their tormenters: their subjectivity is rendered useless and viewed as worthless. As Herman observes, 'The traumatic event thus destroys the belief that one can *be oneself* in relation to others' (Herman 1992, 53). Without this belief, I argue, one can no longer *be oneself even* to oneself, since the self exists fundamentally in relation to others.

How one defines 'self' depends in part on what explanatory work one wants the concept of a self to do. Philosophers have invoked this concept in various areas of the discipline in order to account for a wide range of phenomena. The self is, in metaphysics, whatever it is whose persistence accounts for personal identity over time. One metaphysical view of the self holds that it is bodily continuity that accounts for personal identity and the other, that it is continuity of memory, character traits, or other psychological characteristics that makes someone the same person over time. There is also the view, held by poststructuralists, that the self is a narrative, which, properly construed, is a version of the view that psychological continuity constitutes personal identity.[14] In ethics the self is viewed as the locus of autonomous agency and responsibility and, hence, is the subject of praise or blame. Most traditional accounts of the self, from Descartes' to contemporary theorists', have been individualistic, based on the assumption that one can individuate selves and determine the criteria for their identity over time independent of the social context in which they are situated. In contrast, feminist accounts of the self have focused on the ways in which the self is formed in relation to others and sustained in a social context. On these accounts, persons are, in Annette Baier's words, 'second persons,' that is, 'essentially successors, heirs to other persons who formed and cared for them.'[15] In addition, the self is viewed as related to and constructed by others in an ongoing way, not only because others continue to shape and define us throughout our lifetimes, but also because our own sense of self is couched in descriptions whose meanings are social phenomena (Scheman 1983).

In what follows, I argue that the study of trauma reveals that the accounts of the embodied self, the self as narrative, and the autonomous self are com-patible and complementary, focusing on different aspects of the self. I also argue that the study of trauma provides additional support for the view that each of these aspects of the self is fundamentally relational.

The embodied self

Although we recognize other persons most readily by their perceptible, that is, bodily, attributes, philosophers have been loath to identify the self with a body for a host of reasons.[16] A dead body cannot be said to be anyone's self, nor can a living, but permanently comatose, one. We do not typically use a bodily criterion of identity to determine who we ourselves are, and most of us, when imagining Locke's prince, whose soul 'enters and informs' the body of a cobbler, would suppose the resulting person to be the prince (Locke 1974, 216). Some philosophers[17] have been concerned to show that the self can survive the death of the body, but perhaps the primary reason philosophers have not identified the self with the body is an ancient bias against our physical nature.[18] Plato praised philosophers for 'despising the body and avoiding it,' and urged that '[i]f we are ever to have pure knowledge of anything, we must get rid of the body and contemplate things by themselves with the soul by itself.'[19] This rejection of the body has been most apparent in the disparaging of the female body, which has been presented as the antithesis to reason. Although, as Sara Ruddick notes, '[t]here is nothing intrinsically masculine about mind and objectivity or anything feminine about passion and physicality, ... philosophers have tended to associate, explicitly or metaphorically, passion, affection, and the body with femininity and the mind with masculinity' (1989, 194). How some bodies came to be viewed as 'more bodily' than others is a puzzle that Ruddick answers by arguing that the lack of intellectual control over menstruation, pregnancy, labor, and nursing set such female bodily functions against reason, which was viewed as detached, controlled, and impersonal – that is, masculine.

Even Simone de Beauvoir, while arguing that 'one is not born, but rather becomes, a woman' (1953, 301), views childbirth and nursing as completely passive, and thus dehumanizing, processes, which keep women mired in immanence. She suggests that 'it is not in giving life but in risking life that man is raised above the animal; that is why superiority has been accorded in humanity not to the sex that brings forth but to that which kills' (1953, 72). Although Beauvoir rejects the conclusion that this sex difference justifies male dominance, she nonetheless accepts the premise reducing childbirth to a purely 'animal' function.[20]

Beauvoir was the first female philosopher I read and, as a teenager, I shared her disdain for (socially) compulsory marriage and maternity for women in this society. I still share her concerns about constraints on women's reproductive freedom, but I reject her view of pregnancy and motherhood as necessarily passive and tedious processes, even when voluntary. The work of Ruddick and other feminists who have been redefining motherhood has led me to see the liberatory potential in *chosen* maternity, childbirth, and childrearing. Reading Ruddick's *Maternal Thinking* in 1989, I recognized the ways in which my philosophical training had exacerbated my preexisting tendency to value the cerebral over the corporeal. In pursuing the life of the mind, I had accepted unthinkingly (because unconsciously) its incompatibility with the life of the (gestating and birthing) female body. My reading of Ruddick happened to coincide with a visit to a gynecologist who told me that I might have difficulty conceiving and that if I even suspected I would want to have a child someday I should start trying now. My philosophical bias against maternity, combined with a personal (and political) reaction against what I perceived as pressure to have a baby (as in the words of one academic woman's mother who said, 'I'd rather be a grandmother than the mother of a Ph.D.') suddenly gave way to the startling realization that I might *want* to experience the particular kind of embodiment and connection pregnancy and motherhood provide, and that these things were not incompatible with being a philosopher. After years of considering my body little more than an unruly nuisance, I found myself wanting to yield up control over it, to learn what it had to teach me, to experience the abandon of labor and childbirth, what Margaret Walker has called 'the willing or grateful surrender of "I" to flesh.'[21]

Plato praised those 'who long to beget spiritually, not physically, the progeny which it is the nature of the soul to create and bring to birth. If you ask what that progeny is, it is wisdom and virtue in general.... Everyone would prefer children such as these to children after the flesh' (quoted in Ruddick 1989, 192–193). It occurred to me that this preference was not, after all, universal, and that, in any case, one did not have to choose between pursuing wisdom and virtue, on the one hand, and having children, on the other. My husband (who never felt as compelled to make such a choice) and I started trying to conceive, or, rather, as a friend put it more aptly, stopped trying not to. It was just six months later, however, that I was jumped from behind, beaten, raped, strangled, and left for dead in a ravine. The pleasures of embodiment were suddenly replaced by the pain and terror to which being embodied makes one prey.

I was no longer the same person I had been before the assault, and one of the ways in which I seemed changed was that I had a different relationship with my body. My body was now perceived as an enemy, having betrayed my newfound trust and interest in it, and as a site of increased vulnerability. But rejecting the body and returning to the life of the mind was not an option, since body and mind had become nearly indistinguishable. My mental state (typically, depression) felt physiological, like lead in my veins, while my physical state (frequently, incapacitation by fear and anxiety) was the incarnation of a cognitive and emotional paralysis resulting from shattered assumptions about my safety in the world. The symptoms of PTSD gave the lie to a latent dualism that still informs society's most prevalent attitude to trauma, namely, that victims should buck up, put the past behind them, and get on with their lives. My hypervigilance, heightened startle response, insomnia, and other PTSD symptoms were no more psychological, if that is taken to mean under my conscious control, than were my heartrate and blood pressure.[22]

The intermingling of mind and body is also apparent in traumatic memories that remain in the body, in each of the senses, in the heart that races and skin that crawls whenever something resurrects the only slightly buried terror. As Jonathan Shay writes in his study of combat trauma, 'Traumatic memory is not narrative. Rather, it is experience that reoccurs, either as full sensory replay of traumatic events in dreams or flashbacks, with all things seen, heard, smelled, and felt intact, or as disconnected fragments. These fragments may be inexplicable rage, terror, uncontrollable crying, or disconnected body states and sensations' (1994, 172). The main change in the modality as well as in the content of the most salient traumatic memories is that they are more tied to the body than memories are typically considered to be.

Sensory flashbacks are not, of course, merely a clinical phenomenon, nor are they peculiar to trauma. Proust describes the pleasantly vivid flashbacks brought on by the leisurely savoring of a tea-soaked madeleine (1981, 1:48–49).[23] Trauma, however, changes the nature and frequency of sensory, emotional, and physiological flashbacks. They are reminiscent of the traumatic event itself, as Shay writes, in that '[o]nce experiencing is under way, the survivor lacks authority to stop it or put it away. The helplessness associated with the original experience is replayed in the apparent helplessness to end or modify the reexperience once it has begun' (1994, 174). Traumatic flashbacks immobilize the body by rendering the will as useless as it is in a nightmare in which one desperately tries to flee, but remains frozen.

The bodily nature of traumatic memory complicates a standard philosophical quandary concerning which of two criteria of identity – continuous body or continuous memories – should be used to determine personal identity over time. Locke's bodily transfer puzzle in which we are asked to decide who survives 'should the soul of a prince ... enter and inform the body of a cobbler' (1974, 116) no longer presents us with an either/or choice, depending on which criterion we invoke. If memories are lodged in the body, the Lockean distinction between the memory criterion and that of bodily identity no longer applies.[24]

The study of trauma also replaces the traditional philosophical puzzle about whether the soul can survive the death of the body with the question of whether the self can reconstitute itself after obliteration at the hands of another, after what Cathy Winkler has labeled 'social murder' (1991). Winkler describes the way in which, during a rape, the victim is defined out of existence by the attitudes and actions of the rapist, which incapacitate the victim's self. 'Without our abilities to think and feel as we choose ... our existence becomes like a body on life support,' Winkler writes. 'During an attack, victims have confronted social death, and grappled with it to save themselves' (1991, 14). The victim's inability to be – and to assert – her self in the context of a rape constitutes at least a temporary social death, one from which a self can be resurrected only with great difficulty and with the help of others.

In the aftermath of trauma, not only is the victim's bodily awareness changed,[25] but she may also attempt to change her body itself in an effort to enhance her control over it. Eating disorders are a common reaction to sexual abuse, as is dressing in ways that disguise one's body. After my own assault, I wished I could add eyes in the back of my head, but I settled for cutting my hair so short that, when viewed from behind, I might be mistaken for a man.

The study of trauma does not lead to the conclusion that the self can be identified with the body, but it does show how the body and one's perception of it are nonetheless essential components of the self. It also reveals the ways in which one's ability to feel at home in the world is as much a physical as an epistemological accomplishment. Jean Améry writes, of the person who is tortured, that from the moment of the first blow he loses 'trust in the world,' which includes 'the irrational and logically unjustifiable belief in absolute causality perhaps, or the likewise blind belief in the validity of the inductive inference.' More important, according to Améry, is the loss of the certainty that other persons 'will respect my physical, and with it also my metaphysical, being. The boundaries of my body are also the boundaries of my self. My skin surface shields me against the external world. If I am to have trust, I must feel on it only what I *want* to feel. At the first blow, however, this trust in the world breaks down' (1995, 126). Améry goes on to compare torture to rape, an apt comparison, not only because both objectify and traumatize the victim, but also because the pain they inflict reduces the victim to flesh, to the purely physical. This reduction has a particularly anguished quality for female victims of sexual violence who are already viewed as more tied to nature than men and are sometimes treated as mere flesh.[26] It is as if the tormentor says with his blows, 'You are nothing but a body, a mere object for my will – here, I'll prove it!'

Those who endure long periods of repeated torture often find ways of dissociating themselves from their bodies, that part of themselves which undergoes the torture. As the research of Herman (1992) and Terr (1994) has shown, child victims of sexual and other physical abuse often utilize this defense against annihilation of the self, and, in extreme cases, even develop multiple personalities that enable one or more 'selves' to emerge unscathed from the abuse. Some adult victims of rape report a kind of splitting from their bodies during the assault, as well as a separation from their former selves in the aftermath of the rape.

Charlotte Delbo writes of her return from Auschwitz:

life was returned to me
and I am here in front of life
as though facing a dress
I cannot wear.
   (1995, 240)

A number of Holocaust survivors, whose former selves were virtually annihilated in the death camps, gave themselves new names after the war, Jean Améry (formerly Hans Maier) and Paul Celan (formerly Paul Antschel) being among the most well-known. In a startling reappropriation of the name (literally) imposed on him during his incarceration at Auschwitz, one survivor retained and published under the name 'Ka-Tzetnik 135633,' meaning 'concentration camp inmate number 135633.'[27] Others were forced to assume new names and national and religious identities (or, rather, the appearance of them) in order to avoid capture, and probable death, during the war. The dislocations suffered by what Rosi Braidotti has called 'nomadic subjects' (1994) can be agonizing even when the migrations are voluntary or, as in the case of Eva Hoffman (1989), whose family moved from Poland to Canada when she was 13, involuntary, but unmarked by violence. Given how traumatic such relocations can be, it is almost unimaginable how people can survive self-disintegrating torture and then manage to rebuild themselves in a new country, a new culture, and a new language. Nermina Zildzo, a recent refugee from the war in Bosnia, describes her new life in America, in which she struggles to become someone who can be herself in English, as that of 'a cadaver,' which is to say, not a life at all.[28]

Some who survived the Holocaust, such as Delbo, have written about a distinct self that emerged in the camps and then, in some sense, stayed there after the liberation. 'Auschwitz is so deeply etched in my memory that I cannot forget one moment of it. – So you are living with Auschwitz? – No. I live next to it,' Delbo writes (1985, 2). 'No doubt, I am very fortunate in not recognizing myself in the self that was in Auschwitz. To return from there was so improbable that it seems to me 1 was never there at all. . . . I live within a twofold being. The Auschwitz double doesn't bother me, doesn't interfere with my life. As though it weren't I at all. Without this split I would not have been able to revive' (1985, 3).

What can we conclude from these clinical studies and personal narratives of trauma concerning the relationship of one's self to one's body? Does trauma make one feel more or less tied to one's body? That may depend on one's ability to dissociate. Since I, like most victims of one-time traumatic events, did not dissociate during the assault, I felt (and continue to feel) more tied to my body than before, or, at any rate, more vulnerable to self-annihilation because of it.[29] Those who survived ongoing trauma by dissociating from their bodies may feel that an essential part of themselves was untouched by the trauma, but even they experience, in the aftermath, the physical intrusions of visceral traumatic memories.

These various responses to trauma – dissociation from one's body, separation from the self one was either before or during the trauma – have in common the attempt to distance one's (real) self from the bodily self that is being degraded, and whose survival demands that one do, or at any rate be subjected to, degrading things. But such an attempt is never wholly successful and the survivor's bodily sense of self is permanently altered by an encounter with death that leaves one feeling 'marked' for life. The intense awareness of embodiment experienced by trauma survivors is not 'the willing or grateful surrender of "I" to flesh' described by Walker, but more akin to the pain of Kafka's 'harrow,' cutting the condemned man's 'sentence' deeper and deeper into his body until it destroys him.[30]

The self as narrative

Locke famously identified the self with a set of continuous memories, a kind of ongoing narrative of one's past that is extended with each new experience (1974). The study of trauma presents a fatal challenge to this view, since memory is so drastically disrupted by traumatic events, unless one is prepared to accept the conclusion that survivors of such events are distinct from their former selves. The literature on trauma does seem to support the view, advocated by Derek Parfit (1986), that the unitary self is an illusion and that we are all composed of a series of successive selves.[31] But how does one remake a self from the scattered shards of disrupted memory? Delbo writes of memories being stripped away from the inmates of the death camps, and of the incomprehensibly difficult task of getting them back after the war: 'The survivor must undertake to regain his memory, regain what he possessed before: his knowledge, his experience, his childhood memories, his manual dexterity and his intellectual faculties, sensitivity, the capacity to dream, imagine, laugh' (1995, 255).

This passage illustrates a major obstacle to the trauma survivor's reconstructing a self in the sense of a remembered and ongoing narrative about oneself. Not only are one's memories of an earlier life lost, along with the ability to envision a future, but one's basic cognitive and emotional capacities are gone, or radically altered, as well. This epistemological crisis leaves the survivor with virtually no bearings to navigate by. As Améry writes, 'Whoever has succumbed to torture can no longer feel at home in the world' (1995, 136). Shattered assumptions about the world and one's safety in it can, to some extent, eventually be pieced back together, but this is a slow and painful process. Although the survivor recognizes, at some level, that these regained assumptions are illusory, she learns that they are necessary illusions, as unshakable, ultimately, as cognitively impenetrable perceptual illusions.[32]

In addition, though, trauma can obliterate one's former emotional repertoire, leaving only a kind of counterfactual, propositional knowledge of emotions. When alerted to the rumors that the camp in which he was incarcerated would be evacuated the next day, Primo Levi felt no emotion, just as for many months he had 'no longer felt any pain, joy or fear' except in a conditional manner: 'if I still had my former sensitivity, I thought, this would be an extremely moving moment' (1993, 152–153). The inability to feel one's former emotions, even in the aftermath of trauma, leaves the survivor not only numbed, but also without the motivation to carry out the task of constructing an ongoing narrative.

Some have suggested that an additional reason why trauma survivors are frequently unable to construct narratives to make sense of themselves and to convey what they experienced is that, as Levi writes, 'our language lacks words to express this offense, the demolition of a man' (1985, 9). It is debatable, however, whether that is the case, or whether the problem is simply others' refusal to hear survivors' stories, which makes it difficult for survivors to tell them even to themselves. As Paul Fussell observes, in his account of World War I:

> One of the cruxes of war ... is the collision
> between events and the language available – or
> thought appropriate – to describe them. ...
> Logically, there is no reason why the English
> language could not perfectly well render the
> actuality of ... warfare: it is rich in terms like
> *blood, terror, agony, madness, shit, cruelty, murder,*
> *sell-out* and *hoax*, as well as phrases like *legs blown*
> *off, intestines gushing out over his hands, screaming*
> *all night, bleeding to death from the rectum*, and the
> like. ... The problem was less one of "language"
> than of gentility and optimism. ... What listener
> wants to be torn and shaken when he doesn't have
> to be? We have made *unspeakable* mean
> indescribable: it really means *nasty*. (1975, 169–70)

In order to construct self-narratives we need not only the words with which to tell our stories, but also an audience able and willing to hear us and to understand our words as we intend them. This aspect of remaking a self in the aftermath of trauma highlights the dependency of the self on others and helps to explain why it is so difficult for survivors to recover when others are unwilling to listen to what they endured.

Survivors attempting to construct narratives out of their traumatic memories also encounter the obstacle of despair, of the seeming futility of using language to change the world and the pointlessness of doing anything else. Commenting on the inability of language to convey the horror of what he witnessed in the Warsaw ghetto, Abraham Lewin writes:

> Perhaps because the disaster is so great there is
> nothing to be gained by expressing in words
> everything that we feel. Only if we were capable of
> tearing out by the force of our pent-up anguish the
> greatest of all mountains, a Mount Everest, and with
> all our hatred and strength hurling it down on the
> heads of the German murderers of our young and

old – this would be the only fitting reaction on our
part. Words are beyond us now. Our hearts are
empty and made of stone.
(May 25, 1942; quoted in Langer 1995a, 3)

As Langer comments, it is not 'the poverty of language' Lewin rebukes in this
passage, but, rather, its uselessness 'as a weapon against the current enemy
bent on destroying him and his fellow victims' (1995a, 3). Lewin was writing this during the war, however, and one might think that this explanation
would not apply to those constructing narratives out of memory from a position of relative safety and power after the war. Granted, bearing witness makes
more sense, and even comes to seem imperative, once one is able to be heard
by those willing to help. It can be difficult, though, for survivors to realize
when this occurs, and to tell their stories when it does, due to the obliteration
of their sense of time. Primo Levi describes the disappearance of the future
in the minds of the prisoners in Auschwitz:

Memory is a curious instrument: ever since I have been in the camp,
two lines written by a friend of mine a long time ago have been running
through my mind:
'... Until one day
there will be no more sense in saying: tomorrow.'
It is like that here. Do you know how one says 'never' in camp slang?
'*Morgen früh*', tomorrow morning (1993, 133).

According to John Rawls, the possession of a 'rational plan of life' (1971,
561) is essential to personhood, or, at any rate, to moral personhood. Diana
Meyers argues that this ability to envisage, pursue, and carry out one's rational plan of life is a prerequisite for self-respect (1986). But the ability to form a
plan of life is lost when one loses a sense of one's temporal being, as happened
to Levi and the other prisoners in Auschwitz: 'We had not only forgotten our
country and our culture, but also our family, our past, the future we had imagined for ourselves, because, like animals, we were confined to the present
moment' (1989, 75). Thinking of his former life, Levi noted, 'Today the only
thing left of the life of those days is what one needs to suffer hunger and cold;
I am not even alive enough to know how to kill myself' (1989, 143–144).

The disappearance of the past and the foreshortening of the future are
common symptoms among those who have survived long-lasting trauma of
various kinds. As Jonathan Shay observes in his study of combat trauma in
Vietnam War veterans, 'The destruction of time is an inner survival skill.
These words, written about concentration camp prisoners, apply equally to
soldiers in prolonged combat:

Thinking of the future stirs up such intense yearning
and hope that ... it [is] unbearable; they quickly

learn that these emotions ... will make them
desperate.... The future is reduced to a matter of
hours or days. Alterations in time sense begin with
the obliteration of the future but eventually progress
to obliteration of the past.... Thus prisoners are
eventually reduced to living in an endless present.
(Shay 1994, 176, quoting Herman 1992, 89)

The shrinking of time to the immediate present is also experienced in the
aftermath of trauma, at least until the traumatic episode is integrated into the
survivor's life narrative. 'My former life?' Delbo wrote after being returned
to Paris from the death camps. 'Had I had a former life? My life afterwards?
Was I alive to have an afterwards, to know what afterwards meant? I was
floating in a present devoid of reality' (1995, 237). The unreality of Delbo's
experience resulted not only from the absence of a past and future, but also
from the lack of connection with others who could understand what she had
survived. Much of her writing about what she endured in the camps took
the form of imagined conversations with others in her convoy (Delbo 1995,
233–354). Recreating this community of survivors who could bear witness
to one another and know that they would be heard may have been a crucial
part of Delbo's recovery.

By constructing and telling a narrative of the trauma endured, and with
the help of understanding listeners, the survivor begins not only to integrate
the traumatic episode into a life with a before and an after, but also to gain
control over the occurrence of intrusive memories. When I was hospitalized
after my assault I experienced moments of reprieve from vivid and terrifying
flashbacks when giving my account of what had happened – to the police,
doctors, a psychiatrist, a lawyer, and a prosecutor. Although others apolo-
gized for putting me through what seemed to them a retraumatizing ordeal,
I responded that it was, even at that early stage, therapeutic to bear witness
in the presence of others who heard and believed what I told them. Two and
a half years later, when my assailant was brought to trial, I found it healing
to give my testimony in public and to have it confirmed by the police, the
prosecutor, my lawyer, and, ultimately, the jury, who found my assailant
guilty of rape and attempted murder.[33]

How might we account for this process of 'mastering the trauma' through
repeated telling of one's story? The residue of trauma is a kind of body memory, as Roberta Culbertson notes, 'full of fleeting images, the percussion of
blows, sounds, and movements of the body – disconnected, cacophonous,
the cells suffused with the active power of adrenalin, or coated with the
anesthetizing numbness of noradrenalin' (1995, 174). Whereas traumatic
memories (especially perceptual and emotional flashbacks) feel as though
they are passively endured, narratives are the result of certain obvious choices
(e.g., how much to tell to whom, in what order, etc.). This is not to say that

the narrator is not subject to the constraints of memory or that the story will ring true however it is told. And the telling itself may be out of control, compulsively repeated. But one can control certain aspects of the narrative and that control, repeatedly exercised, leads to greater control over the memories themselves, making them less intrusive and giving them the kind of meaning that enables them to be integrated into the rest of life.

Not only present listeners, but also one's cultural heritage, can determine to a large extent the way in which an event is remembered and retold, and may even lead one to respond as though one remembered what one did not in fact experience.[34] Yael Tamir, an Israeli philosopher, told me a story illustrating cultural memory, in which she and her husband, neither of whom had been victims or had family members who had been victims of the Holocaust, literally jumped at the sound of a German voice shouting instructions at a train station in Switzerland. The experience triggered such vivid 'memories' of the deportation that they grabbed their suitcases and fled the station. Marianne Hirsch (1992–93) discusses the phenomenon of 'postmemory' in children of Holocaust survivors and Tom Segev writes of the ways in which the Holocaust continues to shape Israeli identity: 'Just as the Holocaust imposed a posthumous collective identity on its six million victims, so too it formed the collective identity of this new country – not just for the survivors who came after the war but for all Israelis, then and now' (1993, 11). The influence of cultural memory on all of us is additional evidence of the deeply relational nature of the narrative self.

The relational nature of the self is also revealed by a further obstacle confronting trauma survivors attempting to reconstruct coherent narratives: the difficulty of regaining one's voice, one's subjectivity, after one has been reduced to silence, to the status of an object, or, worse, made into someone else's speech, an instrument of another's agency. Those entering Nazi concentration camps had the speech of their captors literally inscribed on their bodies. As Levi describes it, the message conveyed by the prisoners' tattoos was 'You no longer have a name; this is your new name.' It was 'a non-verbal message, so that the innocent would feel his sentence written on his flesh' (1989, 119).[35]

One of the most chilling stories of a victim's body being used as another's speech is found in the biblical story of the traveling Levite, a story that also reveals the extent of our cultural complicity in the refusal to see trauma from the victim's perspective. The Levite's host had been approached at his home by members of a hostile tribe who asked him to hand over the Levite, so that they could rape him. This the host refused to do: instead, he offered to the angry crowd the Levite's wife, who was then, with the clear complicity of the Levite, shoved out the door. The Levite's wife (who is unnamed in the Bible, but is given the name 'Beth' by Mieke Bal in her account of this story) was gang-raped all night, and when the Levite found her body in the morning (whether she was alive or dead is not clarified in the text) he put her on a donkey, took her home, and cut up her body into twelve pieces, which were then sent as messages to the tribes of Israel.[36]

This biblical story is a striking example of a woman's body used as men's language. (Other instances include rape as the humiliation of the man whose 'property' is stolen or as a nation's sign of victory in war, as well as some forms of pornography.) Reflecting on this story reveals some parallels between the dismemberment and dispersal of Beth and the shattered self and fractured speech of the survivor of trauma. Piecing together a dismembered self seems to require a process of remembering in which speech and affect converge. This working through, or remastering of, the traumatic memory involves going from being the medium of someone else's (the torturer's) speech to being the subject of one's own. The results of the process of working through reveal the performative role of speech acts in recovering from trauma: *saying* something about a traumatic memory *does* something to it. As Shay notes in the case of Vietnam veterans, 'Severe trauma explodes the cohesion of consciousness. When a survivor creates fully realized narrative that brings together the shattered knowledge of what happened, the emotions that were aroused by the meanings of the events, and the bodily sensations that the physical events created, the survivor pieces back together the fragmentation of consciousness that trauma has caused' (1994, 188). But one cannot recover in isolation, since '[n]arrative heals personality changes only if the survivor finds or creates a trustworthy community of listeners for it' (1994, 188). As Levi observes, 'Part of our existence lies in the feelings of those near to us. This is why the experience of someone who has lived for days during which man was merely a thing in the eyes of man is non-human' (1993, 172). Fortunately, just as one can be reduced to an object through torture, one can become a human subject again through telling one's narrative to caring others who are able to listen.

Intense psychological pressures make it difficult, however, for others to listen to trauma narratives. Cultural repression of traumatic memories (in the United States about slavery, in Germany and Poland and elsewhere about the Holocaust) comes not only from an absence of empathy with victims, but also out of an active fear of empathizing with those whose terrifying fate forces us to acknowledge that we are not in control of our own. I recently felt my own need to distance myself from a survivor's trauma when I read the story of Ruth Elias, who was three months pregnant when she arrived in Auschwitz in December 1943. After she gave birth, Josef Mengele decided to experiment on her son to see how long a newborn could live without food. 'In the beginning, the baby was crying all the time,' Elias recalled. 'Then only whimpering.' After a week, a Jewish doctor took pity on her and gave her some morphine with which she euthanized her child. 'It didn't take long before the child stopped breathing.... I didn't want to live anymore.'[37] How she managed (how she manages) to continue living is incomprehensible to me. I realize, though, that I manage to bear the knowledge of such an atrocity by denying that such a thing could ever happen to a child of mine. I can (now) live with the (vivid) possibility that I might be murdered. But I cannot live with even the possibility that this kind of torture could be inflicted on my child. So I employ the usual defenses: it couldn't happen here/now/to me/and so on.

As a society, we live with the unbearable by pressuring those who have been traumatized to forget and by rejecting the testimonies of those who are forced by fate to remember. As individuals and as cultures, we impose arbitrary term limits on memory and on recovery from trauma: a century, say, for slavery, fifty years, perhaps, for the Holocaust, a decade or two for Vietnam, several months for mass rape or serial murder. Even a public memorialization can be a forgetting, a way of saying to survivors what someone said after I published my first article on sexual violence: 'Now you can put this behind you.' But attempting to limit traumatic memories does not make them go away; the signs and symptoms of trauma remain, caused by a source more virulent for being driven underground.

In *The Book of Laughter and Forgetting*, Milan Kundera writes that 'The struggle against power is the struggle of memory against forgetting.'[38] Whether the power is a fascist state or an internalized trauma, surviving the present requires the courage to confront the past, reexamine it, retell it, and thereby remaster its traumatic aspects. As Eva Hoffman, who returns repeatedly in her memoir to a past in which she was 'lost in translation' after moving from Poland to Canada, explains, 'Those who don't understand the past may be condemned to repeat it, but those who never repeat it are condemned not to understand it' (1989, 278).

And so we repeat our stories, and we listen to others'. What Hoffman writes of her conversations with Miriam, her closest North American friend, could also describe the remaking of a survivor's self in relation to empathic others: 'To a large extent, we're the keepers of each other's stories, and the shape of these stories has unfolded in part from our interwoven accounts. Human beings don't only search for meanings, they are themselves units of meaning; but we can mean something only within the fabric of larger significations' (1989, 279). Trauma, however, unravels whatever meaning we've found and woven ourselves into, and so listening to survivors' stories is, as Lawrence Langer describes reading and writing about the Holocaust, 'an experience in *un*learning; both parties are forced into the Dantean gesture of abandoning all safe props as they enter and, without benefit of Virgil, make their uneasy way through its vague domain' (1995b, 6–7). It is easy to understand why one would not willingly enter such a realm, but survivors' testimonies must be heard, if individual and cultural recovery is to be possible.

To recover from trauma, according to psychoanalyst Dori Laub, a survivor needs to construct a narrative and tell it to an empathic listener, in order to reexternalize the event. 'Bearing witness to a trauma is, in fact, a process that includes the listener' (1992, 70). And to the extent that bearing witness reestablishes the survivor's identity, the empathic other is essential to the continuation of a self. Laub writes of Chaim Guri's film, *The Eighty-First Blow*, which 'portrays the image of a man who narrates the story of his sufferings in the camps only to hear his audience say: "All this cannot be true, it could not have happened. You must have made it up." This denial by the listener inflicts, according to the film, the ultimately fateful blow, beyond the eighty blows that man, in Jewish tradition, can sustain and survive' (1992, 68).

The autonomous self

The view of the self most central to ethics, as well as to social, political, and legal philosophy (at least in the analytic tradition), is one that holds that the self is the locus of autonomous agency, that which freely makes choices and wills actions. This is a self that is considered responsible for its decisions and actions and is an appropriate subject of praise or blame. It is the transformation of the self as autonomous agent that is perhaps most apparent in survivors of trauma. First, the autonomy-undermining symptoms of PTSD reconfigure the survivor's will, rendering involuntary many responses that were once under voluntary control. Intrusive memories are triggered by things reminiscent of the traumatic event and carry a strong, sometimes overwhelming, emotional charge. Not only is one's response to items that would startle anyone heightened, but one has an involuntary startle response to things that formerly provoked no reaction or a subtler, still voluntary one. The loss of control evidenced by these and other PTSD symptoms alters who one is, not only in that it limits what one can do (and can refrain from doing), but also in that it changes what one *wants* to do.

A trauma survivor suffers a loss of control not only over herself, but also over her environment, and this, in turn, can lead to a constriction of the boundaries of her will. If a rape victim is unable to walk outside without the fear of being assaulted again, she quickly loses the desire to go for a walk. If one's self, or one's *true* self, is considered to be identical with one's will, then a survivor cannot be considered to be the same as her pre-trauma self, since what she is able to will post-trauma is so drastically altered. Some reactions that once were under the will's command become involuntary and some desires that once were motivating can no longer be felt, let alone acted upon.

Such loss of control over oneself can explain, to a large extent, what a survivor means in saying, 'I am no longer myself.' The trauma survivor identifies with her former self not only because that self was more familiar and less damaged, but also because it was more predictable. The fact that, as has been recently discovered, certain drugs, such as Prozac, give PTSD sufferers greater self-control, by making them better able to choose their reactions to things and the timing of their responses, accounts for the common response to such drugs: 'they make me more myself' (Kramer 1993). It may also be that after taking Prozac such a person is better able to endorse, or identify with, her new self.[39]

In order to recover, a trauma survivor needs to be able to control herself, control her environment (within reasonable limits), and be reconnected with humanity. Whether the latter two achievements occur depends, to a large extent, on other people. Living with the memory of trauma is living with a kind of disability, and whether one is able to function with a disability depends largely on how one's social and physical environments are set up (Minow 1990). A trauma survivor makes accommodations, figuring out how to live with her limits, but she also realizes that at least some externally imposed limits can be changed. In the year after my assault, when I was terrified to walk alone, I was able to go to talks and other events on campus by having a friend walk with me. I became able to use the locker room in the gym after getting the university to put a lock on a door that led to a dark, isolated passageway, and I was able to park my car at night after lobbying the university to put a light in the parking lot.

These ways of enhancing my autonomy in the aftermath of my assault reinforced my view of autonomy as fundamentally dependent on others. Not only is autonomy compatible with socialization and with caring for and being cared for by others (Meyers 1987, 1989, 1992), but the right sort of interactions with others can be seen to be essential to autonomy. In 'Jurisprudence and Gender,' Robin West (1988) discusses the tension within feminist theory between, on the one hand, the desire for connection and fear of alienation (in cultural feminism)[40] and, on the other hand, the desire for autonomy and fear of invasion (in radical or 'dominance' feminism)[41] Once one acknowledges the relational nature of autonomy, however, this apparent tension can be resolved by noting that the main reason all of us, especially women, have to fear violent intrusions by others is that they severely impair our ability to be connected to humanity in ways we value. It is this loss of connection that trauma survivors mourn, a loss that in turn imperils autonomous selfhood. In order to reestablish that connection in the aftermath of trauma, one must first feel able to protect oneself against invasion. The autonomous self and the relational self are thus shown to be interdependent, even constitutive of one another.

Virginia Held defends a relational account of autonomy in which autonomy does not consist of putting walls around oneself or one's property (as in Isaiah Berlin's phrase for autonomy, 'the inner citadel'),[42] but instead, of forming essential relationships with others. Held cites Jennifer Nedelsky, who suggests that 'the most promising model, symbol, or metaphor for autonomy is not property, but childrearing. There we have encapsulated the emergence of autonomy through relationship with others.... Interdependence [is] a constant component of autonomy' (Nedelsky 1989, 11).

Trauma survivors are dependent on empathic others who are willing to listen to their narratives. Given that the language in which such narratives are conveyed and are understood is itself a social phenomenon, this aspect of recovery from trauma also underscores the extent to which autonomy is a fundamentally relational notion.[43]

Primo Levi recalls a dream in which he is telling his sister and others about the camp and they are completely indifferent, acting as though he is not there. Many others in the camp had this dream. 'Why does it happen?' he asks. 'Why is the pain of every day translated so constantly into our dreams, in the ever-repeated scene of the unlistened-to story?' (1993, 60). Why is it so horrifying for survivors to be unheard? There is a scene in the film *La Famiglia* (Ettore Scola, 1987) in which a little boy's uncle pretends not to see him, a game that quickly turns from a bit of fun into a kind of torture when the man persists long beyond the boy's tolerance for invisibility. For the child, not to be seen is not to exist, to be annihilated. Not to be heard means that the self the survivor has become does not exist for these others. Since the earlier self died, the surviving self needs to be known and acknowledged in order to exist.

This illuminates a connection among the views of the self as narrative, as embodied, and as autonomous. It is not sufficient for mastering the trauma to construct a narrative of it: one must (physically, publicly) say or write (or paint or film) the narrative and others must see or hear it in order for one's survival as an autonomous self to be complete. This reveals the extent to which the self is created and sustained by others and, thus, is able to be destroyed by them. The boundaries of the will are limited, or enlarged, not only by the stories others tell, but also by the extent of their ability and willingness to listen to ours.

In the traditional philosophical literature on personal identity, one is considered to be the same person over time if one can (now) identify with that person in the past or future. One typically identifies with a person in the past if one can remember having that person's experiences and one identifies with a person in the future if one cares in a unique way about that person's future experiences. An interesting result of group therapy with trauma survivors is that they come to have greater compassion for their earlier selves by empathizing with others who experienced similar traumas. They stop blaming themselves by realizing that others who acted or reacted similarly are not blameworthy. Rape survivors, who typically have difficulty getting angry with their assailants, find that in group therapy they are able to get angry on their own behalf by first getting angry on behalf of others (Koss and Harvey 1991).

That survivors gain the ability to reconnect with their former selves by empathizing with others who have experienced similar traumas reveals the extent to which we exist only in connection with others. It also suggests that healing from trauma takes place by a kind of splitting off of the traumatized self which one then is able to empathize with, just as one empathizes with others.[44] The loss of a trauma survivor's former self is typically described by analogy to the loss of a beloved other. And yet, in grieving for another, one often says, 'It's as though a part of myself has died.' It is not clear whether this circular comparison is a case of language failing us or, on the contrary, its revealing a deep truth about selfhood and connectedness. By finding (some aspects of) one's lost self in another person, one can manage (to a greater or lesser degree) to reconnect with it and to reintegrate one's various selves into a coherent personality.

The fundamentally relational character of the self is also highlighted by the dependence of survivors on others' attitudes toward them in the aftermath of trauma. Victims of rape and other forms of torture often report drastically altered senses of self-worth, resulting from their degrading treatment. That even one person – one's assailant – treated one as worthless can, at least temporarily, undo an entire lifetime of self-esteem (see Roberts 1989, 91). This effect is magnified by prolonged exposure to degradation, in a social and historical context in which the group to which one belongs is despised. Survivors of trauma recover to a greater or lesser extent depending on others' responses to them after the trauma. These aspects of trauma and recovery reveal the deeply social nature of one's sense of self and underscore the limits of the individual's capacity to control her own self-definition.

But what can others do to help a survivor recover from trauma, apart from listening empathically? Kenneth Seeskin argues, in discussing an appropriate response to the Holocaust, that we who did not experience it cannot hope to understand it and yet to remain silent in the aftermath of it would be immoral. And so, he suggests, we should move beyond theory, beyond an attempt to understand it, to a practice of resistance. As Emil Fackenheim writes, 'The truth is that to grasp the Holocaust whole-of-horror is not to comprehend or transcend it, but rather *to say no to it, or resist* it.'[45] The 'no' of resistance is not the 'no' of denial. It is the 'no' of acknowledgment of what happened and refusal to let it happen again.

Remaking oneself

A child gave me a flower
one morning
a flower picked
for me
he kissed the flower
before giving it to me....
There is no wound that will not heal
I told myself that day
and still repeat it from time to time
but not enough to believe it.

— Charlotte Delbo (1995, 241)

What is the goal of the survivor? Ultimately, it is not to transcend the trauma, not to solve the dilemmas of survival, but simply to endure. This can be hard enough, when the only way to regain control over one's life seems to be to end it. A few months after my assault, I drove by myself for several hours to visit a friend. Although driving felt like a much safer mode of transportation than walking, I worried throughout the journey, not only about the trajectory of every oncoming vehicle, but also about my car breaking down, leaving me at the mercy of potentially murderous passers-by. I wished I'd had a gun so that I could shoot myself rather than be forced to live through another assault.[46] Later in my recovery, as depression gave way to rage, such suicidal thoughts were quickly quelled by a stubborn refusal to finish my assailant's job for him. I also learned, after martial arts training, that I was capable, morally as well as physically, of killing in self-defense – an option that made the possibility of another life-threatening attack one I could live with. Some rape survivors have remarked on the sense of moral loss they experienced when they realized that they could kill their assailants (and even wanted to!) but I think that this thought can be seen as a salutary character change in those whom society does not encourage to value their own lives enough.[47] And, far from jeopardizing their connections with a community, this newfound ability to defend themselves, and to consider themselves worth fighting for, enables rape survivors to move among others, free of debilitating fears. It gave me the courage to bring a child into the world, in spite of the realization that doing so would, far from making me immortal, make me twice as mortal, by doubling my chances of having my life destroyed by a speeding truck.[48]

But many trauma survivors who endured much worse than I did, and for much longer, found, often years later, that it was impossible to go on. It is not a moral failing to leave a world that has become morally unacceptable. I wonder how some can ask, of battered women, 'Why didn't they leave?' while saying, of those driven to suicide by the brutal and inescapable aftermath of trauma, 'Why didn't they stay?' Améry wrote, 'Whoever was tortured, stays tortured' (1995, 131) and this may explain why he, Levi, Celan, and other Holocaust survivors took their own lives decades after their (physical) torture ended, as if such an explanation were needed.

Those who have survived trauma understand well the pull of that solution to their daily Beckettian dilemma, 'I can't go on, I must go on,' for on some days the conclusion 'I'll go on' cannot be reached by faith or reason.[49] How does one go on with a shattered self, with no guarantee of recovery, believing that one will always 'stay tortured' and never 'feel at home in the world'? One hopes for a bearable future, in spite of all the inductive evidence to the contrary. After all, the loss of faith in induction following an unpredictable trauma also has a reassuring side: since inferences from the past can no longer be relied upon to predict the future, there's no more reason to think that tomorrow will bring agony than to think that it won't. So one makes a wager, in which nothing is certain and the odds change daily, and sets about

356 *Violence: A Philosophical Anthology*

willing to believe that life, for all its unfathomable horror, still holds some undiscovered pleasures.[50] And one remakes oneself by finding meaning in a life of caring for and being sustained by others. While I used to have to will myself out of bed each day, I now wake gladly to feed my son whose birth, four years after the assault, gives me reason not to have died. He is the embodiment of my life's new narrative and I am more autonomous by virtue of being so intermingled with him. Having him has also enabled me to rebuild my trust in the world around us. He is so trusting that, before he learned to walk, he would stand with outstretched arms, wobbling, until he fell, stiff-limbed, forwards, backwards, certain the universe would catch him. So far, it has, and when I tell myself it always will, the part of me that he's become believes it.

Notes

1. Delbo (1995, 267) attributes this statement to one of her fellow deportees.
2. Quoted in Langer (1995b, 14). The irony of calling the author of this quote a 'survivor' is evident, but, it seems to me, linguistically unavoidable.
3. Shay (1994, 180). Shay writes, 'When a survivor of prolonged trauma loses all sense of meaningful personal narrative, this may result in a contaminated identity. "I died in Vietnam" may express a current identity as a corpse.'
4. Scherer (1992, 179).
5. I do not mean to imply that the traumas suffered by these different groups of survivors are the same, or even commensurable. However, researchers such as Judith Herman, in *Trauma and Recovery* (1992), and Ronnie Janoff-Bulman, in *Shattered Assumptions: Towards a New Psychology of Trauma* (1992), have persuasively argued that many of those who survive life-threatening traumatic events in which they are reduced to near-complete helplessness later suffer from the symptoms of post-traumatic stress disorder. I would add that they experience a similar disintegration of the self. In this essay, I use the term 'victim' as well as the term 'survivor' to denote someone who has been victimized by, and yet survived, such a life-threatening trauma. Clearly, many civilians are more traumatized by war (and with greater injustice) than the veterans to whom I refer in this chapter. I mention the latter simply because trauma research on survivors of war has focused on veterans – U.S. veterans in particular – whose trauma symptoms our federal government is obliged to attempt to understand and treat.
6. In defending a feminist account of the relational self, I do not mean to imply that all relational accounts of the self are feminist. Some that are not (necessarily) feminist are those advocated by Hegel, Marx, and contemporary communitarians.
7. See Locke (1974, orig. pub. 1694), Noonan (1989), and Perry (1975) for treatments of personal identity by seventeenth- and eighteenth-century philosophers.
8. See Ungar (1990), Parfit (1986), Noonan (1989), Rorty (1976), and Perry (1975) for discussions of contemporary theories of personal identity.
9. While most philosophers writing about personal identity have neglected to consider *any* actual transformations of real persons, there are a few notable exceptions. Kathleen Wilkes argues that the 'bizarre, entertaining, confusing, and inconclusive thought experiments' so common in philosophical writing about personal

identity are not helpful, and, in any case, not needed, 'since there are so many actual puzzle-cases which defy the *imagination*, but which we none the less have to accept as facts' (Wilkes 1988, vii). She does not discuss trauma, however, and uses third-person scientific accounts of neurological disorders rather than first person narratives in her analysis. Although he does not discuss trauma and the self either, Thomas Nagel examines the effect of commissurotomy on the self in 'Brain Bisection and the Unity of Consciousness' (1975). Three philosophers, however, have in recent writings departed from this tradition of ignoring trauma and have analyzed alleged cases of trauma-induced dissociation and subsequent recovered memories. Ian Hacking (1995) presents a deeply skeptical treatment of the alleged splitting of the self that occurs during severe child abuse, while Naomi Scheman considers the multiple personalities constructed by severely abused children to be 'a comprehensible, perhaps even rational, response to an intolerable situation, a way of maintaining some degree of agency in the face of profoundly soul-destroying attacks on one's ability to construct a sense of self' (1993, 164). Diana T. Meyers, in 'The Family Romance' (Meyers, 1997, 440–57), mediates between these two views with an account focusing, not on whether the incest trope that 'figures' such recovered memories is historically accurate, but, rather, on whether such a figuration is useful to the alleged victims.

10. For discussions of the usefulness of such narratives, see Brison (1995a) and Brison (1995b).

11. See King (1988), Lugones (1987), and Matsuda (1989).

12. This is not (merely) because philosophers are a more disputatious lot, but rather because psychologists need at least the appearance of clarity and agreement in order to categorize illnesses, make diagnoses, carry out research, fill out insurance claim forms, and so on.

13. This paraphrases Judith Herman's description of traumatic events (1992, 33). This description and the following discussion of trauma are distilled from Herman's book as well as from Janoff-Bulman (1992) and Shay (1994).

14. While some poststructuralists hold that the self is a fiction, not all do, and this is not, in any case, implied by the view that it is a narrative. I think the clinical studies and narrative accounts of trauma discussed below show that the self is not a fiction, if that is taken to mean that it is freely constructed by some narrator. No one, not even Stephen King, would voluntarily construct a self so tormented by trauma and its aftermath.

15. Baier (1985, 84). For other discussions of the relational self, see Jaggar (1983) and Meyers (1987, 1989, 1992, 1994). Virginia Held gives an excellent survey of feminist views of the relational self in so far as they bear on moral theory (Held 1993, 57–64).

16. An exception is Bernard Williams (1970), who presents a thought experiment that prompts the intuition that in at least some cases of so-called body transfer, we would identify with the surviving individual who has our body, and not the one who has our memory and other psychological characteristics.

17. Most famously, Descartes (1984).

18. In refreshing contrast to this disciplinary bias is the philosophical writing on embodiment by Iris Young (1990).

19. Plato, *Phaedo*, IL65c–67d (quoted in Ruddick 1989, 188).

20. Two critiques of Beauvoir's position on maternity and childbirth are presented in Ruddick (1989, 192–3, 275, n. 11) and Mackenzie (1996).

21. Quoted in Ruddick (1989, 212).

22. That fear, anxiety, and so on are psychological, and hence controllable, responses to trauma is an assumption underlying the view, held by many liberals, that victims of hate speech should simply toughen their emotional hides to avoid being affected adversely by it. This view presupposes a mind-body split more thoroughgoing than that defended by Descartes (1984).
23. See also the discussion of charged memory in Proust in Glover (1988, 142–5).
24. If memories do not reside solely in the mind or in the body, but rather are a function of the way in which consciousness 'inhabits' a body, then not only Locke's thought experiment, but also Sydney Shoemaker's (Perry 1975, 119–34) and Bernard Williams' (1970) appear to be incoherent as described.
25. And, in the case of the extreme trauma endured by Holocaust survivors, their bodies themselves were drastically changed, by starvation, disease, and torture.
26. An especially striking literary illustration of this is the scene in *Studs Lonigan* in which the narrator says of the woman Weary Reilly is about to rape, 'She was his meat' (James T. Farrell, *Studs Lonigan*, Book II [New York: Vanguard, 1935], 396). I thank Blanche Gelfant for drawing my attention to this passage.
27. Ka-Tzetnik 135633 (1989). I thank Alexis Jetter for showing me the work of this author.
28. Nermina Zildzo, essay for English 2, Dartmouth College, Fall 1995.
29. See Terr (1994) for an account of different responses to one-time and ongoing traumas.
30. Kafka, Franz, 'In the Penal Colony,' in *The Penal Colony: Stories and Short Pieces*, trans. Willa and Edwin Muir (New York: Schocken, 1948), 191–227.
31. Parfit would not, however, agree with the relational account of the self I am defending here. In her comments on a draft of this chapter, Susan Dwyer wondered 'how many people who have not suffered trauma have a clear sense of what it was like to be them at some earlier point in their lives.' She guessed 'not many,' and suggested that this 'explains a number of rituals we engage in, taking photographs of significant events, keeping a diary, marking anniversaries, valuing family (i.e., people who were there, too, who can tell you about your former self).'
32. Bruno Bettelheim discusses the 'personality-disintegrating' effects of being in a German concentration camp (1979, 25). 'Being subjected to living in an extreme situation somehow contaminates permanently the old life and the old personality. This suggests that a personality which did not protect the individual against landing in an extreme situation seems so deficient to the person that he feels in need of widespread restructuring' (1979, 123–4). In spite of this conviction, trauma survivors are forced to reacquire at least some of their earlier illusions if life is to continue to be livable.
33. Of course, not many rape survivors are fortunate enough to have such an experience with the criminal justice system, given the low rates of reporting, prosecuting, and conviction of rapists. I also had the advantage of having my assailant tried in a French court, in which the adversarial system is not practiced, so I was not cross-examined by the defense lawyer. In addition, since the facts of the case were not in dispute and my assailant's only defense was an (ultimately unsuccessful) insanity plea, no one in the courtroom questioned my narrative of what happened.
34. I am not suggesting that for this reason the memories of trauma survivors are less reliable than others' memories. In the subsequent story, Yael Tamir did not have a false memory of actually having lived through the Holocaust. Rather, the cultural climate in which she was raised led her to respond instinctively to certain

things (a shouting German voice at a train station) in ways characteristic of those who had actually been deported. In any case, since all narrative memory involves reconstruction, trauma survivors' narratives are no less likely to be accurate than anyone else's. (I thank Susan Dwyer for encouraging me to make this last point more explicit.)

35. Levi writes that '[a]t a distance of forty years, my tattoo has become a part of my body,' which no longer taints his sense of self (1989, 119).
36. Judges, chapter 19, verses 26–8, which Mieke Bal mentions in Bal 1988b and discusses at length in Bal (1988a) and Bal (1991).
37. *Newsweek*, January 16, 1995, 54.
38. Milan Kundera, *The Book of Laughter and Forgetting* (New York: Knopf, 1980), 3. I thank Joan Bolker for reminding me of this quote, with which she begins her review (1995, 12) of Terr (1994). In this article Bolker also refers to 'term limits on memory' which, she says, were what the U.S. electorate really voted for in the November 1994 elections (1995, 15).
39. For an example of an endorsement account of autonomy, see Frankfurt (1988, chs. 5 and 12).
40. Two of the most prominent proponents of what West calls 'cultural feminism' (and others have called 'difference feminism') are Carol Gilligan (1982) and Sara Ruddick (1989).
41. The best-known advocate of 'radical' or 'dominance' feminism is Catharine MacKinnon (1987).
42. The militaristic nature of this image is brought out by an update of this notion mentioned to me by Diana Meyers: autonomy as 'the inner missile silo'!
43. In addition, not simply what we are able to express, but also what we are able to feel, can be seen to be a function of one's social relations. See Scheman (1983).
44. This is one of the positive aspects of a kind of multiple consciousness. Cf. Scheman (1993), Lugones (1987), Matsuda (1989), and King (1988).
45. Seeskin (1988, 120), quoting Emil Fackenheim, *To Mend the World* (New York: Schocken, 1982), 239.
46. When I later mentioned this to my therapist, she replied, reasonably enough, 'Why not shoot the assailant instead?' But for me that thought was not yet thinkable.
47. I should make a distinction here between the ability to kill in self-defense and the desire to kill as a form of revenge. While I think it is morally permissible to possess and to employ the former, acting on the latter is to be morally condemned.
48. The idea that a child makes one twice as mortal comes from Barbara Kingsolver. A character in her story 'Covered Bridges' says, 'Having a child wouldn't make you immortal. It would make you twice as mortal. It's just one more life you could possibly lose, besides your own. Two more eyes to be put out, and ten more toes to get caught under the mower.' Barbara Kingsolver, *Homeland and Other Stories* (New York: Harper & Row, 1989), 59–60.
49. Beckett (1965, 414). What Beckett actually writes is 'you must go on, I can't go on, I'll go on,' translating his original ending to *L'Innommable* (Paris: Minuit, 1953), 213: '*il faut continuer, je ne peux pas continuer, je vais continuer.*' I'm grateful to Thomas Trezise for pointing out this passage.
50. For a discussion of Pascal's wager, see Pascal (1958) and for William James' discussion of 'the will to believe,' see James (1896).

Bibliography

Améry, Jean. 1995. 'Torture.' In *Art from the Ashes: A Holocaust Anthology*, ed. Lawrence Langer. New York: Oxford University Press.

Baier, Annette. 1985. *Postures of the Mind: Essays on Mind and Morals*. Minneapolis: University of Minnesota Press.

———. 1994. *Moral Prejudices: Essays on Ethics*. Cambridge, MA: Harvard University Press.

Bal, Mieke. 1988a. *Death and Dissymetry: The Politics of Coherence in the Book of Judges*. Chicago: University of Chicago Press.

———. 1988b. *Murder and Difference: Gender, Genre, and Scholarship on Sisera's Death*. Bloomington: Indian University Press.

———. 1991. *Reading 'Rembrandt': Beyond the Word-Image Opposition*. New York: Cambridge University Press.

Bal, Mieke, Jonathan Crewe, and Leo Spitzer, eds. 1999. *Acts of Memory: Cultural Recall in the Present*. Hanover: University Press of New England.

Beauvoir, Simone de. 1953. *The Second Sex*. Trans. H. M. Parshley. New York: Vintage.

Beckett, Samuel. 1965. *Three Novels*. New York: Grove.

Bettelheim, Bruno. 1979. *Surviving and Other Essays*. New York: Knopf.

Bolkert, Joan L. 1995. 'Forgetting Ourselves.' *Readings: A Journal of Reviews and Commentary in Mental Health*, June 12–15.

Braidotti, Rosi. 1994. *Nomadic Subjects: Embodiment and Sexual Difference in Contemporary Feminist Theory*. New York: Columbia University Press.

Brison, Susan. 1993. 'Surviving Sexual Violence: A Philosophical Perspective.' *Journal of Social Philosophy* 24, no. 1: 5–22.

———. 1995a. 'The Theoretical Importance of Practice.' *Nomos* 37: 216–38.

———. 1995b. 'On the Personal as Philosophical.' *APA Newsletter* 95, no 1: 37–40.

———. 1998. 'Speech, Harm, and the Mind-Body Problem in First Amendment Jurisprudence.' *Legal Theory* 4: 39–61.

Culbertson, Roberta. 1995. 'Embodied Memory, Transcendence, and Telling: Recounting Trauma, Re-establishing the Self.' *New Literary History* 26: 169–95.

Delbo, Charlotte. 1985. *Days and Memory*. Trans. Rosette C. Lamont. Marlboro, VT: The Marlboto Press.

———. 1995. *Auschwitz and After*. Trans. Rosette C. Lamont, New Haven: Yale University Press.

Descartes, René. 1984. (orig. pub. 1641). *Meditations*. In *The Philosophical Writings of Descartes*, vol. II, trans. John Cottingham, Robert Stoothoff and Dugald Murdoch. New York: Cambridge University Press.

Felman, Shoshana, and Dori Laub, eds. 1992. Testimony: *Crises of Witnessing in Literature, Psychoanalysis, and History*. New York: Routledge.

Frankfurt, Harry. 1988. *The Importance of What We Care About*. New York: Cambridge University Press.

Fussell, Paul. 1975. *The Great War and Modern Memory*. New York: Oxford University Press.

Gilligan, Carol. 1982. *In a Different Voice*. Cambridge, MA: Harvard University Press.

Glover, Jonathan. 1988. *I: The Philosophy and Psychology of Personal Identity*. London: Allen Lane, Penguin.

Hacking, Ian. 1995. *Rewriting the Soul: Multiple Personality and the Sciences of Memory*. Princeton: Princeton University Press.

Held, Virginia. 1993. *Feminist Morality: Transforming Culture, Society, and Politics*. Chicago: University of Chicago Press.

Herman, Judith Lewis. 1992. *Trauma and Recovery.* New York: Basic.

Hirsch, Marianne. 1992–93. 'Family Pictures: *Maus,* Mourning, and Post-Memory.' *Discourse* 15, no. 2: 3–29.

——. 1997. *Family Frames: Photography, Narrative, and Postmemory.* Cambridge, MA: Harvard University Press.

Hoffman, Eva. 1989. *Lost in Translation.* New York: Dutton.

Jaggar, Alison M. 1983. *Feminist Politics and Human Nature.* Totowa, NJ: Rowman & Allanheld.

James, William. 1896. *The Will to Believe and Other Essays in Popular Philosophy.* New York: Longmans, Green.

Janoff-Bulman, Ronnie. 1979. 'Characterological versus Behavioural Self-Blame: Inquiries into Depression and Rape.' *Journal of Personality and Social Psychology* 37, no. 10: 1798–809.

——. 1992. *Shattered Assumptions: Towards a New Psychology of Trauma.* New York: The Free Press.

Ka-Tzetnik 135633. 1989. *Shivitti: A Vision.* New York: Harper & Row.

King, Deborah K. 1988. 'Multiple Jeopardy, Mutiple Consciousness: The Context of a Black Feminist Ideology.' *Signs* 14, no. 1: 42–72.

Koss, Mary P., and Mary R. Harvey. 1991. *The Rape Victim: Clinical and Community Interventions,* 2nd edn. London: Sage.

Kramer, Peter. 1993. *Listening to Prozac.* New York: Viking.

Langer, Lawrence. 1995a. *Admitting the Holocaust.* New York: Oxford University Press.

——. Ed. 1995b. *Art from the Ashes.* New York: Oxfor University Press.

Levi, Primo. 1985. *If Not Now, When?* New York: Penguin.

——. 1989. *The Drowned and the Saved.* New York: Random House.

——. 1993. *Survival in Auschwitz.* New York: Macmillan.

Locke, John. 1974. (This section on personal identity was orig. pub. 1694) *An Essay Concerning Human Understanding,* ed. A. D. Woozley, 210–20. New York: New American Library.

Lugones, Maria. 1987. 'Playfullness, 'World'-Travelling, and Loving Perception.' *Hypatia* 2, no. 2: 3–19.

Mackenzie, Catriona. 1996. 'A Certain Lack of Symmetry: de Beauvoir on Autonomous Agency and Women's Embodiment.' In *Texts in Culture: Simone de Beauvoir, 'The Second Sex,'* ed. Ruth Evans, Manchester: Manchester University Press.

Mackinnon, Catherine. 1987. *Feminism Unmodified: Discourses on Life and Law.* Cambridge, MA: Harvard University Press.

——. 1993. *Only Words.* Cambridge, MA: Harvard University Press.

Matsuda, Mari. 1989a. 'Public Response to Racist Speech: Considering the Victim's Story.' *Michigan Law Review* 87, no. 8: 2320–81.

——. 1989b. 'When the First Quaill Calls: Multiple Consciousness as Jurisprudential Method.' *Women's Rights Law Reporter* 11, no. 1: 7–10.

Meyers, Diana Tietjens. 1986. 'The Politics of Self-Respect: A Feminist Perspecive.' *Hypatia* 1, no. 1: 83–100.

——. 1987. 'The Socialised Individual and Individual Autonomy: An Intersection between Philosophy and Psychology.' In *Women and Moral Theory,* ed. Eva Feder Kittay and Diana Tietjens Meyers. Savage, MD.: Rowman & Littlefield.

——. 1989. *Self, Society, and Personal Choice.* New York: Columbia University Press.

——. 1992. 'Personal Autonomy or the Deconstructed Subject? A Reply to Hekman.' *Hypatia* 7, no. 124–32.

——. 1994. *Subjection & Subjectivity: Psychoanalytic Feminism & Moral Philosophy.* New York: Routledge.

——. Ed. 1997. *Feminist Social Thought: A Reader.* New York: Routledge.

Ninow, Martha. 1990. *Making All the Difference: Inclusion, Exclusion, and American Law.* Ithaca, NY: Cornell University Press.

——. 1993. 'Surviving Victim Talk.' *UCLA Law Review* 40.

Nagel, Thomas. 1975. Brain Bisection and the Unity of Consciousness.' In *Personal Identity*, ed. John Perry. Berkley: University of California Press.

Nedelsky, Jennifer. 1989. 'Reconceiving Autonomy: Sources, Thoughts and Possibilities.' *Yale Journal of Law and Feminism* 1, no. 7: 7–36.

Noonan, Harold. W. 1989. *Personal Identity.* New York: Routledge.

Parfit, Derek. 1986. *Reasons and Persons.* Oxford: Oxford University Press.

Pascal, Blaise. 1958. *Pensées.* Trans. W. F. Trotter. New York: Dutton.

Perry, John. 1975. Personal Identity. Berkley: University of California Press.

Proust, Marcel. 1981. *Remembrance of Things Past.* Trans. C. K. Scott Moncrieff and Terence Kilmartin. New York: Vintage.

Rawls, John. 1971. *A Theory of Justice.* Cambridge, MA: Harvard University Press.

Roberts, Cathy. 1989. *Women and Rape.* New York: New York University Press.

Rorty, Amélie Oksenberg, ed. 1976. *The Identities of Persons.* Berkley: University of California Press.

Ruddick, Sara. 1989. *Maternal Thinking: Towards a Politics of Peace.* Boston, MA: Beacon.

Scheman, Naomi. 1983. 'Individualism and the Objects of Psychology.' In *Discovering Reality: Feminist Perspectives on Epistemology, Metaphysics, Methodology, and Philosophy of Science*, ed. Sandra Harding and Merril B. Hintikka, 225–44. Boston, MA: D. Reidel.

——. 1993. 'Though This Be Method, Yet There Is Madness in It.' In *A Mind of One's Own*, ed. Louise M. Antony and Charlotte Witt. Boulder, CO: Westview.

Scherer, Migael. 1992. *Still Loved by the Sun: A Rape Survivor's Journal.* New York: Simon & Schuster.

Seeskin, Kenneth. 1988. 'Coming to Terms with Failure: A Philosophical Dilemma.' In *Writing and the Holocaust*, ed. Berel Lang. New York: Holmes & Meier.

Segev, Tom. 1993. *The Seventh Million.* Trans. Haim Watzman. New York: Hill & Wang.

Shay, Jonathan. 1994. *Achilles in Vietnam: Combat Trauma and the Undoing of Character.* New York: Atheneum.

Terr, Lenore. 1994. *Unchained Memories.* New York: HarperCollins.

Ungar, Peter. 1990. *Identity, Consciousness and Value.* New York: Oxford University Press.

West, Robin. 1988. 'Jurisprudence and Gender.' *University of Chicago Law Review* 55, no. 6: 1–72,

Wilkes, Kathleen. 1988. *Real People.* New York: Oxford University Press.

Williams, Bernard. 1970. 'The Self and the Future.' *Philosphical Review* 79, no. 2: 161–80.

Winkler, Cathy. 1991. 'Rape as Social Murder.' *Anthropology Today* 7, no. 3: 12–14.

——. 2002. *One Night: Realities of Rape.* Walnut Creek, CA: Altamira.

Young, Iris Marion. 1990. *Throwing Like a Girl and Other Essays in Feminist Philosophy and Social Theory.* Indianapolis: Indiana University Press.

COMMENTARY ON BRISON

In 1990, while on a walk along a peaceful country road in a village outside Grenoble, France, Susan Brison was grabbed from behind, pulled into the bushes, beaten, and sexually assaulted. The attacker smashed a rock into her forehead, strangled her to unconsciousness, and left her for dead. In this book, a truly original work of philosophy, Brison gives the most unsettling but enlightening account of violence from the victim's point of view. Brison's *Aftermath: Violence and the Remaking of a Self* is unique: a sophisticated philosophical exploration of trauma, and the undoing and remaking of a self in the aftermath of violence.[1]

In the third chapter of the book, reproduced here, Brison analyses the full impact of her traumatic experience of violence on what philosophers call 'the self'. Brison defines a traumatic event as 'one in which a person feels utterly helpless in the face of a force that is perceived to be life-threatening'. She goes on to explain that when a trauma is of human origin and is intentionally inflicted, the impact is devastating: 'it not only shatters one's fundamental assumptions about the world and one's safety in it, but it also severs the sustaining connections between the self and the rest of humanity.'

Of the many valuable aspects of Brison's analysis, two in particular deserve to be singled out. First, Brison's view that 'the self' exists fundamentally in relation to others. An act of violence not only defines the relationship between perpetrator and victim, but it can redefine the relationship of the victim towards themselves and the world around them. Brison explains how after her ordeal, she was no longer the same person she had been before the assault: 'one of the ways in which I seemed changed was that I had a different relationship with my body'.

Secondly, the idea that an act of violence can be said to violate, for lack of a better term, a person's physical and psychological integrity. We have already encountered the idea of violence as a violation of a person (Garver) or of integrity (Salmi and MacCallum). Brison does not use this terminology, but her language suggests the same image: how the self is vulnerable enough to be 'undone' by traumatic violence; how it can 'shatter' one's safety in the world; how it 'demolishes' one's world, and 'destroys' a perfectly good, intact, life.

There is something fundamentally tragic and yet vitally optimistic in Brison's work. Brison is able to make us understand why so many survivors of extreme violence claim to have died during their traumatic torment, and indeed why it is not surprising that so many of them took their own lives after surviving the unthinkable.[2] And yet, while mourning her pre-traumatic self, Brison reminds us that, with the help of others who are willing to listen to their narratives, a person may be able to reconstruct their conception of the 'self': 'Since the earlier self dies, the surviving self needs to be known and acknowledged in order to exist.'

Notes and further reading

1. On philosophical issues raised by violence against women, see also S. French, L. Purdy and W. Teays (eds.), *Philosophical Perspectives on Violence against Women*, Ithaca, NY: Cornell University Press, 1988.
2. See Charlotte Delbo, *Auschwitz and After*, New Haven, CT: Yale University Press, 1995; Primo Levi, *Survival in Auschwitz*, New York: Macmillan, 1993.

18
Thinking Clearly about Violence

Allan Bäck

There is a lot of rhetoric and commotion about 'violence', even in the scientific community itself. We hear daily about *violent* military conflicts, *violations* of human rights, domestic *violence, violence* in the media and in sports, and emotional and verbal *violence*. In 1972 58% of American males thought that burning a draft card or holding a sit-in is violent.[1] UNESCO commissioned twenty scientists to make a platform statement, the 'Seville Statement on Violence' (November, 1989), to condemn the notion that human beings have a biological, genetically determined basis for violence and aggression. Moreover, social scientists have been debating how to define 'violence' for practical reasons. Particularly in doing empirical research, it becomes a practical issue to have a clear definition of 'violence': is the incidence of domestic violence, of violence in school, of aggressive displays in troops of chimpanzees on the rise? How to tell, if we have no criteria for what constitutes violent or aggressive behavior? It is ironic that a large literature has arisen recently in and across various social sciences on the meaning of 'aggression' and 'violence' independently of much reference to or involvement by philosophers.[2]

It is ironic since the analysis of the conception of violence and its connections to related conceptions seems to fall squarely in the provenance of philosophy. Moreover, the current lack of philosophers becomes even more puzzling given the considerable philosophical interest on this topic during the sixties and seventies – incited by the civil rights movement and the Vietnam War.[3]

In any case, I shall proceed. I propose here to define 'violence'. In doing so, I shall distinguish 'forcefulness', 'aggression' and 'violence'. Because the current usage, both in ordinary language and in the various academic fields, is not consistent, my definitions, although descriptive, will also be somewhat stipulative and precising.

'Violence' in its original sense connotes 'force'. We speak of a strong wind as a 'violent' wind; a strong passion as a 'violent' passion. Yet someone 'violent' in this way need not be bad. Moreover, certainly the thing that is 'violent' in this sense need not be morally blameworthy nor even be a moral agent. In contrast, 'violent', in many of its current uses and connotations, does have such moral dimensions.[4] Let me then call this basic, amoral sense, of an agent using force while doing something with more force, effort, or effect than usual 'forceful'. Inanimate as well as animate objects can act 'forcefully' in this sense.

This basic conception of forcefulness agrees with the concept of force in physics. Following Feynman, Rubin Gotesky defines 'force' as that 'which is capable of producing or does produce a change in motion, in shape, in quality, or in all of these aspects.' 'Power' then will be 'the amount or degree of force in operation', and 'forcefulness' the 'extensive and radical changes within a short interval of time produced by given forces in the qualities or structures of anything'.[5] Note that forcefulness is defined by the effects upon the recipients of the force, and not by an intrinsic character of the action. A small event can produce rapid, radical change. A butterfly flapping its wings can cause a thunderstorm;[6] a twitch of a finger on a trigger or button can kill. So then an act is forceful in terms of the effects that it has – not in terms of its own rapidity, effort, quantity of force exerted etc. I also leave it open whether acts of omission can be forceful, as they can cause radical change. For instance, failing to close the floodgates can drown many; not having safety inspections can cause many to fall ill. In this way we shall not decide, by the fiat of definition, whether certain institutional policies towards workers or towards the poor are not 'violent', since they are not 'forceful'.[7]

In line with its root sense of 'approach' or 'attack', aggression is a particular conception of forcefulness where the force is directed towards a particular object.[8] Thus, we do not often speak of an 'aggressive' storm, as the storm does not pick out its targets. This selective attention on the part of the agent suggests purposive behavior and an intentional aspect. Aggression appears to be intentional forceful action. Although inanimate objects may act 'forcefully', only animate agents, human or animal, capable of goal-directed behavior, can act 'aggressively' in this sense.

Moreover, 'aggression' has the connotation of seeking to do something for the sake of the aggressor at the expense of the one being attacked. I suggest that we exclude this connotation from the definition of 'aggression' in order to avoid making every act of aggression be morally wrong by the fiat of definition. It might be that aggression is generally wrong. For an aggressive act, when successful, typically causes its recipient harm. Yet, this should require argument and may have exceptions, so many say. Moreover, social scientists generally wish to avoid making moral judgments or acknowledge a moral dimension to their subject matter.[9] (Accordingly, it is common for them to speak of 'aggression' more than of 'violence'.) In philosophy there is no need to avoid this moral dimension. However, even if all aggressive acts be bad morally, such a moral judgment ought not to follow merely in virtue of its definition. Hence, aggression should be defined in a morally neutral way.[10]

However, many social scientists are not satisfied even with this amoral definition of 'aggression'. They want also to avoid having to determine or refer to the intentions of the agent. Indeed, as many insist, how are human ethologists to know the intentions of a fish, a goose, a rat, a bonobo? Rather than guess, they tend to define 'aggression' behaviorally, without reference to the intentions or goals of the agent animal.[11]

Accordingly, many follow E.O. Wilson, who defines 'aggression' as 'a physical threat or threat of action by one individual that reduces the freedom or genetic fitness of another.'[12] This follows the major *O.E.D.* definition, 'the exercise of physical force...tending to cause bodily injury, or forcibly interfering with personal freedom'. By 'freedom', Wilson means 'freedom of movement and action [of an animal], to use its abilities and develop its capacities'. By 'genetic fitness', Wilson means 'the ability of the individual to survive and to reproduce its own kind, by contributing to the gene flow'.[13]

It would be charitable to understand Wilson's conception of 'action' broadly, so as to include not only direct acts but also at least some omissions, or failures to act. One member of a species, say, a mother, may withhold food from another, say, her young, until the young individual acts in a certain way. Now she is not acting directly. But, as the young animal depends on the parent to survive, and withholding food threatens both the freedom and the genetic fitness of the young individual, it might very well be that the mother is 'threatening' the young individual and acting aggressively through an omission instead of an action. Once again, I do not think that it should be settled, by definition, whether in fact a failure to act is an act of omission or simply the absence of an action.[14] Recall my claim that the forcefulness of the action should be measured by its effects and not by its intrinsic character.

Many have made other objections and emendments to Wilson's definition. First, some object that it would not count as aggressive failed attempts at aggression.[15] We can rectify that by talking instead of the type of action of which the act in question is an instance. The individual act would be aggressive if that type of act of which it is an instance tends to reduce, or is intended to reduce, the freedom or genetic fitness of an individual.

Others object that aggression lies on a continuum ending at completely non-violent behaviors. The difficulty lies in there being actions at all points of the continuum that are used to resolve successfully problems between members of the same species.[16] So aggression seems neither wrong nor clearly demarcated. We can handle these problems by insisting that aggressive acts be 'forceful' as defined above and by insisting also that an aggressive act is not necessarily a destructive or a morally bad act.[17] Rather, take 'aggression' to have no moral dimensions by definition.

This insistence would also allay the fears, mentioned above, of those who do not want to call the behavior of parents towards their young 'aggressive'. We can admit that this behavior is aggressive, in that the freedom of the young is indeed being restrained, often physically, by the parent. Still, it is in the young animal's best interest, in terms of surviving, to be, e.g., pulled away from a cliff or from an electrical receptacle.[18]

Although we may eliminate the notions of moral evil and destructiveness from the conception of aggression, still it does seem hopeless, despite the hope of some social scientists, to eliminate the notion of intention from it.[19] Often the element of intention sneaks in by speaking of a 'threat' or of 'the behavior of one animal towards another'. Yet 'behavior towards' and 'threat' indicate an intentional component. A clumsy animal that causes another animal to fall out of a tree would hardly be acting aggressively – although acting forcefully – even if the fallen one has lost both freedom of action and genetic fitness, by breaking a leg. We can say, again metaphorically, that a clumsy action, like a flood, can 'threaten' the life of an animal. Yet to say that one animal threatens another suggests something intentional. Reports of animal behavior commonly talk this way, of goals and motives. We may as well admit the intentionality. Again, let me repeat that I do not mean to require a deliberate, self-conscious intentionality. Rather intentionality here concerns the basic, minimal sort, in conformity with which an animal moves towards a food source or away from a threat 'intentionally'.[20]

We may then define 'aggression' as 'a forceful action, done intentionally by an agent, of a type of action that tends, or intends, to reduce both the freedom or the genetic fitness of those affected by that action'.

In short, aggression is forcefulness plus intention and injury. I define 'injury' as 'reducing the freedom or (inclusive 'or') the genetic fitness of those affected'. For, if I am injured, my present or future survival becomes less likely, and my present and future ability to act is lessened. Pain typically functions as a symptom or an indication to a sentient animal that its freedom or genetic fitness is being reduced or has a threat of being reduced.[21] Also, I assume here that the subjective feeling of pain (the *quale*) is intrinsically bad: *ceteris paribus*, pain ought not to be felt. Accordingly, I define 'harm' as 'injury or pain'.

So far, in defining 'forcefulness' and 'aggression', I have included no moral component. It is certainly possible also to define 'violence' amorally too. For, as we have noted, there is no person morally to blame for a 'violent' storm or a 'violent' sneeze. Still, we do need a sense of 'violence' that carries moral weight to address current issues and usage. Moreover, in many contexts, as noted above, 'violence' has negative connotations. For to call something 'violent' is often to give at least a *prima facie* reason why it is morally wrong.

However, being morally wrong differs from being in the moral sphere. So as not to beg any questions, it would be prudent to have two different conceptions of violence, a basic one having a component of moral responsibility and a pejorative one having that component as well as carrying the negative connotation of being wrong. After developing these definitions, we shall be in a position to see why even the former definition implies a *prima facie* moral wrong.

In contrast to aggression, I shall thus take 'violence' in the basic sense to signify a certain sort of aggression, namely an aggressive activity to which moral judgments, of being good or bad, apply. In many moral and legal theories, such judgments require, among other things, considering the conscious volitions of the moral agent(s). According to such views, if you are aware of what you are doing, will to do so, and could do otherwise, you are morally responsible for those acts.[22] You might, then, be able to do something without being morally responsible, if you did not will the act, or were not aware of what you are doing, or were in a mental state of extreme duress or emotion. At any rate, I shall suppose here that normal cases of human intentional action are subject to moral judgment and are chosen.

Accordingly, an action is violent in this basic sense when it is aggressive and is chosen. Violence, then, contains a moral component associated with choosing to engage in actions that harm another person and attempting to force that person to act as you want.[23] To get violence in the pejorative sense, we need to add the condition that the choice made is a morally wrong one. That is, the agent ought not to make that choice.[24]

We sometimes talk of 'emotional violence' or 'mental violence', where, via propaganda or emotional outbursts, you may force another to your views. Audi emphasizes this point and insists on the recognition of these types of 'violence'.[25] Robert Nozick even goes so far as to call rational philosophical arguments coercive, or 'violent' in this sense.[26] So long as it is admitted that emotional and verbal outbursts cause harm, the definitions, of 'violence' in both senses, can apply. Still, not automatically: we must provide justifications on a case-by-case basis.

To sum up, I am proposing the following:

- An act is violent in the basic sense iff (1) the attempted action is aggressive (2) the agent is morally responsible for that attempt to cause harm (pain or injury) to the patient.
- An act is violent in the pejorative sense iff (1) the attempted action is aggressive (2) the agent is morally responsible for that attempt to cause harm (pain or injury) to the patient (3) the agent ought not to will to inflict that harm, and (4) the patient should not want to suffer that harm. (I.e., the action unjustly violates the rights of the victim, where 'rights' signifies the morally ideal set of entitlements that the recipient of the action (typically a person) ought to have.)

As many moral theorists agree, a person may be generous without doing generous acts at times.[27] So too, a person may not be violent and still do violent acts. Again, a violent person may do non-violent acts. To account for this difference, I define 'a violent person' as 'a person who does violent acts regularly for their own sake', or, more precisely:

- A person is violent iff (1) she does a violent action or wills it 'for its own sake' or 'in itself' and (2) she knows what she is doing, or wanting to do. (An act is done for its own sake if the agent would want to do it even if, *ceteris paribus*, there were another way to act that causes less pain or injury to the patient or victim, and the agent would not choose that alternative. The 'wanting' here signifies a strong commitment to action, and not merely wishful thinking.)
- A person has a violent character iff she is violent regularly.

Some problems arise with what 'ought' means in these definitions. Oftentimes, we make a choice that we consider, given the alternatives available to us, to be the best one. Yet, we may not think that the action is the best one possible. In more traditional terminology, we do not chose the act without qualification, but only relative to a particular context, in a respect.[28]

What does it mean then for the person to will a violent action 'for its own sake'? The idea is that she would want to act violently even if there were some other way of reaching her goal. She would not be violent in the pejorative sense even if deliberately choosing to do a act violent in the basic sense, if, were there another way of acting so as to reach the intended result, without inflicting harm, she would not have chosen to act thus.

In this way a surgeon who orders chemotherapy for a patient while knowing full well that that patient will suffer a lot of pain can be said not to act violently in the pejorative sense. Again, take a teacher who gives a student a low grade. She knows that, most likely, she will be causing the student to feel anguish at a low grade. Yet she may intend only to be reporting to the student and others how well the student has performed.

In these two cases, it might be said that no right not to have suffered pain unjustly has been violated.[29] For the patient or the student has willingly entered into a situation where they know that pain or injury is possible. Still, if there *were* a less painful way for the surgeon or teacher to reach her goal, it would be morally wrong for her not to use it. A right not to suffer pain unjustly requires that the agent causing the harm not have another way available, of achieving the same end while causing less harm, *ceteris paribus*. Rather, the agent is justified in causing pain or injury, not merely if this were the result of helping the patient, but also if there *were* no other way currently available to her to reach her goal. The 'other way' has to be available to the agent, not to people centuries later or miles away.[30]

Thus a person is morally responsible for deliberately choosing to inflict pain. She then is committing a violent act, in the basic sense. Whether or not the act is violent in the pejorative sense may be distinguished by counterfactuals. If the agent would have chosen an available way that would not harm but still have the same benefits, then the act is not violent in the pejorative sense. If she would not have preferred otherwise, then the pain is intentional, and her action is violent in the pejorative sense. For in the latter case she wishes to inflict pain, while in the former case she does not. The third condition in the definition applies. This makes a doctor normally not violent in the pejorative sense when she causes the patient to suffer while undergoing chemotherapy. Likewise for the teacher when she causes a student to feel anguish at a low grade.[31] Yet, if there were a less painful alternative, the agent would have a *prima facie* obligation to learn about and to acquire proficiency in it. In this way, the definition leaves it open that certain institutionalized practices are violent in the pejorative sense and bad wholesale.

On account of a person doing an act violent in the basic sense having this *prima facie* obligation to seek out less painful alternatives, acts violent even in the basic sense are *prima facie* wrong. That is, all else being equal, we ought not to choose them. Yet it does not follow, despite popular rhetoric to the contrary, that a violent act is necessarily a bad act.

What then? Are all types of passive resistance, all strategies of non-violence violent in the basic sense and hence *prima facie* wrong? Yes.[32] Lest my admission be taken as a *reductio ad absurdum* – as well as a blasphemous condemnation of those like Gandhi and M. L. King Jr. – let me point out that this is the position of, e.g., Gandhi. He himself admitted that his political activity in India was not *ahimsa* (non-violence):

> I have admitted my mistake. I thought our struggle was based on non-violence, whereas it was in reality no more than passive resistance which is essentially a weapon of the weak. It leads naturally to armed resistance whenever possible.[33]

To march up to soldiers weaponless in protest, to sit in or in front of a business, and to go into a restaurant with the expectation of being thrown out do indeed limit the freedom of action of those whom you have targeted.[34] Perhaps they do indeed deserve it! Perhaps, but the case must be made, that more normal and peaceful methods of negotiation cannot succeed.

Notes

1. *Science*, Vol. 23 (June, 1972), pp. 1300–3, as cited in the *O.E.D.*
2. On recent material in the social sciences, cf. James Silverberg and J. Patrick Gray, 'Violence and Peacefulness as Behavioral Potentialities of Primates', in J. Silverberg and J. Gray (eds.), *Aggression and Peacefulness in Humans and Other Primates*, (Oxford, 1992), pp. 3ff. On the lack of recent material in philosophy, cf. Steven Lee, 'Is Poverty Violence?', in D. Curtin and R. Litke (eds.), *Institutional Violence* (Amsterdam, 1999), p. 11, n. 1.
3. Indeed, another irony lies in the lack of discussions on the conception of violence in political theory at that time. Cf. Hannah Arendt, *On Violence* (New York, 1970),

pp. 8, 40, who bewails the lack of discussion in political science on 'violence', 'strength', 'authority', 'power', 'violence'.

4. Kai Nielson, 'On Justifying Violence', *Inquiry* 24 (1981), p. 24, claims, in opposition to the *O.E.D.*, that 'violence' has a negative connotation so that when it is used it 'becomes [*prima facie?*] immoral by definition.' Robert Paul Wolff, 'On Violence', *Journal of Philosophy* 66 (1969), p. 606: 'Strictly speaking, violence is the illegitimate or unauthorized use of force to effect decisions against the will of others.'

Inter alia, the O.E.D. gives the following definitions: ' "violence" is the exercise of physical force so as to inflict damage or injury to persons or property,' and 'to force' is 'to exert physical or psychological power or coercion upon one to act in some determinate way.'

5. Rubin Gotesky, 'Social Force, Social Power, and Social Violence', in S. Stanage (ed.), *Reason and Violence* (Totowa, N.J., 1974), p. 146; he calls this 'violence'. Cf. Richard Feynman, *The Feynman Lectures on Physics*, Vol. 1 (Reading, MA, 1961), §§12.1 and 13.1. This conception amounts to what Sherman Stanage, 'Violatives: Modes and Themes of Violence', in S. Stanage (ed.), *Reason and Violence* (Totowa, N.J., 1974), p. 225, calls 'power'. Cf. Hannah Arendt, *On Violence* (New York, 1970), p. 40; R.G. Collingwood, *The New Leviathan* (Oxford, 1942), pp. 141–2.

6. The butterfly effect in chaos theory.

7. Ronald P. Miller, 'Violence, Force, and Coercion', in J. Shaffer (ed.), *Violence* (New York, 1971), pp. 31–2. Some however take forcefulness to be determined by the intrinsic character of the act, like its effort or quantity of energy, and not by its effects. E.g., Robert Audi, 'On the Meaning and Justification of Violence', in J. Shaffer (ed.), *Violence* (New York, 1971), p. 66, says that discrimination and exclusion are not violent since they are 'peacefully maintained'. Miller (p. 20), says that neglect is not violent 'since neglecting cannot be done with great force'.

8. 'Is directed towards' should be understood in the middle voice, and not (necessarily) in the passive voice. That is, I am leaving it open whether or not an act of aggression must be committed by a moral agent, I shall claim that it must be committed by an agent having intentions, in a weak sense of 'intention', according to which all animals have them.

9. Janes Silverberg and J. Patrick Gray, 'Violence and Peacefulness as Behavioral Potentialities of Primates', p. 5. Cf. G. Siann, *Accounting for Aggression* (Boston, 1985), p. 12.

10. Cf. Miller, 'Violence, Force, and Coercion', p. 23; Audi, 'On the Meaning and Justification of Violence', pp. 59, 88.

11. Cf. S. Howell and R. Willis, *Societies at Peace: Anthropological Perspectives* (London, 1989), who favor the etic over the emic.

12. E. O. Wilson, *Sociobiology* (Cambridge, MA, 1975), p. 577; cf. pp. 242–4. Also cf. Konrad Lorenz, *On Aggression* (New York, 1966), p. ix, who defines 'aggression' as 'the fighting instinct in beast and man which is directed against members of the same species.' At p. 18, however, he does use 'aggression' in describing behavior towards another species. (In a section omitted from this version of the paper, I discuss and reject weakening Wilson's definition to '...that reduces the freedom *and* genetic fitness of another'.)

13. E. O. Wilson, *Sociobiology*, p. 585.

14. Cf. Jonathan Glover, *Causing Death and Saving Lives* (Reading, England, 1977), pp. 94–7.

15. James Silverberg and J. Patrick Gray, 'Violence and Peacefulness as Behavioral Potentialities of Primates', p. 4.
16. Franz De Waal, 'Aggression as a Well-Integrated Part of Primate Social Relationships: A Critique of the SSSV', in J. Silverberg and J. Gray (eds.), *Aggression and Peacefulness in Humans and Other Primates* (Oxford, 1992), p. 39, describes violence as one of many tactics to pursue social goals, but one having high costs. So too in philosophy. Cf. Sherman Stanage, 'Violatives: Modes and Themes of Violence', in S. Stanage (ed.), *Reason and Violence* (Totowa, N.J., 1974), pp. 215–19.
17. James Silverberg and J. Patrick Gray, 'Violence and Peacefulness as Behavioral Potentialities of Primates', p. 3, likewise define 'aggression' as 'the assertiveness (or forcefulness) indicated by one actor's initiating toward some other(s) of an act that is higher on the violence scale than the previous act in a given interaction sequence.' This agrees with my account if by 'violence' they mean what I have called 'forcefulness'.
18. Still, it would be better not to restrain the young if the same benefits could be gained otherwise. Indeed, this is a common Japanese criticism of American childrearing practices! I discuss below why such practices are *prima facie* wrong.
19. For instance, Carol Lauer, 'Variability in the Patterns of Agonistic Behavior in Pre-School Children', in J. Silverberg and J. Gray (eds.), *Aggression and Peacefulness in Humans and Other Primates* (Oxford, 1992), p. 172, complains that aggression is difficult to observe because of its intentional element and because even of the difficulty to deciding when freedom is restrained. Hence, she suggests, we should use 'agonistic activity', which she defines as: 'An agonistic act is any behavior relating to conflict situations, whether assertive or submissive.' Well, first we would have to define 'conflict' which seems intentional. For example, one animal bumping into another clumsily has not started a 'conflict' although the one being bumped *might* react *as if* the bumping were a conflict. And it would react thus because *typically* such acts have been goal-directed and intentional. How then to judge what constitutes a 'conflict'? Again, via considering intent and common practice. Moreover, it does sound strange to call completely submissive behavior 'agonistic' just because it occurs in a 'conflict situation'. Cf. though E. O. Wilson, *Sociobiology* (Cambridge, MA, 1975), p. 578, who defines 'agonistic' as any activity related to fighting.
20. I.e., first-order intentionality, and not second-order intentions about intentions. Cf. Harry Frankfurt, 'Freedom of the Will and the Concept of a Person', in the *Importance of What We Care About* (Cambridge, 1988), pp. 12–19.
21. Cf. Aristotle, *Nicomachean Ethics* X.4.
22. E.g., Aristotle, *Nicomachean Ethics* III.2; Immanuel Kant, *Foundations of the Metaphysics of Morals* II, pp. 416–17.
23. Cf. Robert Simon, *Sports and Social Values* (Englewood Cliffs, 1985), p. 38: 'Typically or paradigmatically...cases of violence involve the intentional use of physical force designed to harm a person or property.'
24. This distinction amounts to what Audi calls 'doing violence to' a person, versus 'violating' a person, where only the latter is 'wrong by definition'. Robert Audi, 'Violence, Legal Sanctions, and Law Enforcement', in S. Stanage (ed.), *Reason and Violence* (Totowa, N.J., 1974), p. 32. The pejorative sense takes the violation of persons as the most important feature of 'violence', as Newton Garver, 'What Violence Is', in T. Rose (ed.), *Violence in America* (New York, 1969) (= *The Nation*, 24 June 1968, p. 819), pp. 6–7, wants: 'What is fundamental about violence is that a person is violated...violence in human affairs amounts to violating persons.'

This definition agrees also with Ted Honderich, *Political Violence* (Ithaca, 1976), p. 98: a violent act is 'a use of a considerable or destroying force against people or things, a use of force which offends against a norm.' Also cf. Harry Girvetz, 'An Anatomy of Violence', in S. Stanage (ed.), *Reason and Violence* (Totowa, N.J., 1974), p. 184, who defines 'force or violence' as 'harm perpetrated on persons or property ranging, in the case of persons, from restraining their freedom of movement to torture and death, and, in the case of property, from simple fine or damage to complete expropriation or total destruction.'

25. Robert Audi, 'Violence, Legal Sanctions, and Law Enforcement', p. 38; 'On the Meaning and Justification of Violence', pp. 52, 54.
26. Robert Nozick, *Philosophical Explanations* (Cambridge, MA, 1981), pp. 4–6. So too Andrew Norman, 'Epistemological Violence', in D. Curtin and R. Litke (eds.), *Institutional Violence* (Amsterdam, 1999), p. 252.
27. Aristotle, *Nicomachean Ethics* II.4; Kant, *Foundations of the Metaphysics of Morals* I, pp. 393–4.
28. This distinction can be made also in terms of the distinction between an antecedent versus a consequent will.
29. Judith Jarvis Thomson, 'Self-Defense', *Philosophy and Public Affairs* 20.4 (1991), pp. 294, 303.
30. Cf. Aristotle, *Nicomachean Ethics* III.3 on what is up to us.
31. It also prevents a person from having the casuist excuse of appeal to the doctrine of double effect, sc., of willing only one of the consequences when she knows full well that the other consequence will follow. Cf. Alison MacIntyre, 'Doing away with Double Effect', *Ethics* 11.2 (2001), pp. 222–5; 225, n. 12.
32. To be *violent*, such acts would also have to be *forceful* in the sense described above. Still instances that were successful would tend to be forceful, as they would have great consequences. Cf. John Lewis, *The Case Against Pacifism* (London, 1939), pp. 109–10.
33. Quoted in Thomas Merton (ed.), *Gandhi on Non-Violence* (New York, 1965), p. 75.
34. To be *violent*, such acts would also have to be *forceful* in the sense described above. Cf. John Lewis, *The Case Against Pacifism* (London, 1939), pp. 109–10.

COMMENTARY ON BÄCK

Allan Bäck is a philosopher (and martial arts teacher) who has published in a variety of areas, including the history and philosophy of logic, ancient and mediaeval philosophy, and comparative philosophy.[1] In this essay Bäck makes a compelling argument for the indispensable contribution of philosophy to our efforts to understand the nature of violence. All empirical research of violence depends on a clear definition of 'violence', and yet the literature on violence in the social sciences has developed 'independently of much reference to or involvement by philosophers'. This is regrettable, since the social sciences would avoid much unnecessary ambiguity by learning from what philosophy has to offer. Thus, Bäck's aim is not only to define 'violence', but also to distinguish this concept from two related but distinct terms: 'forcefulness' and 'aggression'.

The essays by Dewey and Coady in this anthology remind us that in its original sense 'violence' connotes 'force', and yet these two concepts should not be confused. Bäck defines 'forceful' in a strictly amoral sense, in terms of an agent using force while doing something with more force, effort or effect than usual. Furthermore, Bäck reminds us that forcefulness is defined by the effects upon the recipients of the force, and not by the intrinsic character of the action. 'Aggression' is a particular conception of forcefulness, where an agent purposefully and intentionally directs the force towards another agent or object. Thus, aggression appears to be intentional forceful action.

When social scientists use the term 'aggression', as for example in socio-biology, they want to avoid having to determine or refer to the intentions of the agents. This is a mistake, since as Bäck says, 'aggression is forcefulness plus intention and injury'.

While aggression has no moral dimension by definition, violence is aggressive activity to which moral judgments apply. In other words, an act of violence is chosen: 'Violence, then, contains a moral component associated with choosing to engage in actions that harm another person and attempting to force that person to act as you want.' What Bäck is saying here is that when doing violence, and contrary to being simply forceful or aggressive, a person is morally responsible for deliberately choosing to inflict pain.

On the basis of his analysis of violence, at the end of his essay Bäck is able to turn the tables on those who claim the moral high ground by championing the politics of non-violence. In fact, Bäck suggests that all types of passive resistance, all strategies of non-violence, are violent in the basic sense that a person has a *prima facie* obligation to seek out less painful alternatives, therefore even passive resistance becomes *prima facie* wrong.

Note and further reading

1. Allan Bäck, *Aristotle's Theory of Predication*, Leiden: Brill, 2000.

Index